I0644899

Praise for

The Illusion of Will, Self, and Time

"We are taken step by step in a stunning tour of many powerful yet still disputed ideas that were fervently argued a century ago. Congratulations to Jonathan for a book that every psychologist should read whether doubtful of current paradigms or searching for new ones but mostly, for an enriching experience that brings these age-old controversies into relation with findings in modern physics and psychology."

— Jason W. Brown, MD, Center for Cognition and Communication

The Illusion of Will, Self, and Time

SUNY series in Transpersonal and Humanistic Psychology
Richard D. Mann, editor

The Illusion of Will, Self, and Time

WILLIAM JAMES'S RELUCTANT GUIDE TO ENLIGHTENMENT

JONATHAN BRICKLIN

SUNY PRESS

Cover image of William James from the Houghton collection "Letters to William James from various correspondents and photograph album" courtesy of Harvard College Library.

Published by State University of New York Press, Albany

© 2015 State University of New York

All rights reserved

Printed in the United States of America

No part of this book may be used or reproduced in any manner whatsoever without written permission. No part of this book may be stored in a retrieval system or transmitted in any form or by any means including electronic, electrostatic, magnetic tape, mechanical, photocopying, recording, or otherwise without the prior permission in writing of the publisher.

For information, contact State University of New York Press, Albany, NY
www.sunypress.edu

Production, Ryan Morris
Marketing, Kate R. Seburyamo

Library of Congress Cataloging-in-Publication Data

Bricklin, Jonathan, [date]
The illusion of will, self, and time : William James's reluctant guide to enlightenment / Jonathan Bricklin.
pages cm. – (SUNY series in transpersonal and humanistic psychology)
Includes bibliographical references and index.
ISBN 978-1-4384-5627-0 (hc : alk. paper)—978-1-4384-5628-7 (pb : alk. paper)
ISBN 978-1-4384-5629-4 (e-book) 1. James, William, 1842–1910. 2. Psychologists—United States. 3. Philosophers—United States. 4. Transpersonal psychology. I. Title.
BF109.J28B75 2015
150.19'87—dc23

2014024577

10 9 8 7 6 5 4 3 2 1

For Sharda Rogell

All are but parts of one stupendous whole,
Whose body Nature is, and God the soul;
That, chang'd thro' all, and yet in all the same;
Great in the earth, as in th' ethereal frame;
Warms in the sun, refreshes in the breeze,
Glows in the stars, and blossoms in the trees,
Lives thro' all life, extends thro' all extent,
Spreads undivided, operates unspent;
Breathes in our soul, informs our mortal part,
As full, as perfect, in a hair as heart:
As full, as perfect, in vile Man that mourns,
As the rapt Seraph that adores and burns:
To him no high, no low, no great, no small;
He fills, he bounds, connects, and equals all.

—Alexander Pope

The great cosmic Intellect is one in all of us,—true!
Yet every man we meet requires to be humored.

—William James

CONTENTS

PREFACE

People love a sense of destiny without loving destiny itself. We love to feel we have arrived at where we were always meant to be—but only at certain points along the way. Believing, say, that something mysterious—more than chance and chemistry—was responsible for bringing us together with our beloved, we embrace the concept of fated encounters yet spurn the concept of Fate.

But at the end of their lives, two of the most celebrated thinkers of the modern age suggested that Fate itself might be part of a vaster, more diffused, order of things. "For us believing physicists, this separation between past and future has the value of mere illusion, however tenacious," wrote Einstein,[1] three weeks before he died, endorsing the most radical interpretation of the new physics he launched in 1905 with his publication of "Special Relativity."[2] "Is . . . consciousness already there waiting to be uncovered and is it a veridical revelation of reality?" asked William James a few months before *he* died in 1910, in an essay entitled "A Suggestion About Mysticism," oblivious to the space-time revolution already underway (ASAM, 1280).

Sage that he was, even "spiritual prophet" who "cut through the riddle that perplexed the ancients,"[3] Einstein's mission was not, however, to probe deeply into the psychological and spiritual questions implied by his cosmic answer. The "*demand*" of his physics, as Jacob Needleman said, "to think in new categories about the universe . . . to search for a new structure of mind, a new consciousness, based on confrontation with the fact that . . . [we] do not know what . . . [we are] in this universe of immense pattern and incomprehensible force"[4] was not a demand to be met by a physicist.[5] But this was precisely the demand met by William James.

James thought that his mystical suggestion of "consciousness already there waiting to be uncovered" would not be verified "in this generation or in the next" (*ASAM* 1280). A century after his death, as if on schedule, physicists, neuroscientists, psychologists, and parapsychologists have gathered new evidence in its support. Few, however, know what to do with this evidence, and in this, too, they follow James, who treated his mystical revelation as an unwanted child he had to acknowledge but not legally adopt.

Yet despite resisting his revelation's implication of timelessness, James had well prepared the way. Recognized today as the father of transpersonal psychology,[6] his research into "consciousness *beyond the margin*" (*ML*, 70) challenged both the commonsense boundary of subject-object duality and the brain's role as the generator of consciousness. One of the most esteemed philosophers of the last century credited him with launching "a new epoch in philosophy," by directly undermining Cartesian dualism.[7] And as an explorer of what we now call entheogenic experiences, and a founder of the American Society for Psychical Research, James fully engaged, without prejudice, evidence of "ultra-phenomenal unity," such as clairvoyant knowledge, acquired beyond the "ordinary waking use of . . . eyes and ears and wits" (*ILR*, 60; *WB*, 694). The "most urgent intellectual need," James declared, was that "science be built up again" in a form in which such phenomena "have a positive place" (ibid.). Independently of Einstein's relativity revolution, he believed that "the limits of the admitted order of things" had "broken down," and insofar as science denied such research, it lay "prostrate in the dust" (ibid.).

That James—a self-described "dry and bony *individual*, repelling fusion" (*C8*, 221)—did not inhabit this "positive place" he had helped establish; that he found his own epoch-making nondualism a form of "madness," and the dualism of "Common Sense" "the biggest stroke of genius ever made in philosophy" (*C7*, 292); that he lived his entire life believing he was an individuated self, willing consequential actions in linear time; is what makes him such a valuable guide to all the evidence that suggests otherwise. For the evidence, in both James's era and our own, is not lacking; only the capacity to receive it. As Charles Tart recently expressed this limited capacity in relation to the most baffling of all transpersonal phenomena:

> [P]recognition . . . has so much experimental evidence attesting to its reality that no reasonable person could doubt it . . . [but] at some deep level, I find the idea of precognition, where the inherently unknowable future can sometimes be known, so incomprehensible that I just never think about precognition in a serious way.[8]

This book is about finding such a way.

Obviously, we experience something that feels like will, self, and time; the experience of them is not in question. But what precisely *is* that something we feel? How does the feeling differ from our interpretation? For it is that *interpretation*, not merely the feeling itself, that forms our belief. "The 'inner world' is full of phantoms . . . the will is one of them," wrote James's contemporary Nietzsche, and he identified self, what he called will's "afterbirth," as another.[9] In the following pages we will enter this "inner world," where not only will and self, but time reside, only to discover that will, self, and time do not so much reside in an inner world, as constitute it. And the door, as Rumi came to realize, opens outward:

> I have lived on the lip of insanity
> Wanting to know reasons
> Knocking on a door. It opens
> I've been knocking from the inside![10]

ACKNOWLEDGMENTS

The seed of this book was planted on a 1989 Vipassana retreat at *Insight Meditation Society* in Barre, Massachusetts. Christopher Titmuss led that retreat, and his direct engagement with the dharma has been a sustaining inspiration. I am also deeply indebted to IMS for providing a haven for spiritual inquiry these past three decades.

The first opportunity to publicly share some of these core ideas was on *Advaita-L*, where I especially benefited from exchanges with Allan Curry and Vidyasankar Sundaresan. Sandra Martin of *Paraview* had the temerity to represent an early draft of this book more than two decades ago. Anthony Freeman and Keith Sutherland were the first to see some of it into print, and I have been immensely enriched by my ongoing collaboration with their pioneering *Journal of Consciousness Studies*. I am also grateful to Marcie Boucouvalas for adding my voice to the essential *Journal of Transpersonal Psychology*. The encouraging response to these early efforts by Benjamin Libet, Leslie Combs, Eugene Taylor, Oliver Sacks, Benny Shanon, Ramesh Balsekar, William Lyons, and Jerry Katz helped sustain my labors. And the affirmation of Richard Mann and Catherine and Julian Noyce were critical to my sense of completion.

Ralph White gave me an incomparable opportunity to engage a wide range of international transpersonal scholars and practitioners at his *New*

York Open Center, and many of their voices are reflected in these pages. I am also grateful to Sandy Levine and Walter Beebe for their part in creating and sustaining this preeminent institution for holistic studies.

For the past two decades, I have been privileged to be a part of the Tai Chi Alchemy community led by my beloved friend and tennis partner, Rick Barrett. While he has productively stayed on the other side of the net in the free will question, his uncanny *wei wu wei* demonstrations have crossed over. Denise Meyer, a fellow participant in this community, has been instrumental in helping me to shape the core ideas in this book, in addition to providing masterful editing through several drafts.

I had the great fortune to have studied philosophy with Melvin Woody, whose engagement with philosophy as a most vital and entertaining enterprise made him the living voice of James to me. That I have answered his *The Embrace of Freedom* with an embrace of determinism is a testament to his never-wavering goal to get us to think for ourselves.

I have also been particularly inspired by the writing of, and conversations I've had with, Lawrence LeShan, Jason Brown, Seth Benardete, David Loy, Whit Blauvelt, Will Johnson, Peter Kingsley, James Austin, Russell Targ, Stephan Schwartz, Leslie Combs, Miranda Shaw, Bernard Haisch, Michael Grosso, and my mother, Big Sur poet Lucy Christopher.

I am grateful as well to SUNY Press for providing a home for Richard Mann's pioneering vision, to my editors, Nancy Ellegate and Ryan Morris, for their patience and professionalism, and to Alan Hewat for his meticulous copyediting.

Finally, my wife, Laura Martocci, more than anyone, guided my first efforts into the semblance of a book and I am eternally grateful for her support throughout, as well as the indulgence of my two daughters, Noa and Quincey, who one day, perhaps, might understand why I found William James the best of company.

Portions of this book were previously published in the *Journal of Consciousness Studies*, the *Journal of Transpersonal Psychology*, and the anthologies *The Volitional Brain: Toward a Neuroscience of Free Will*, *Sciousness*, and *Chromatikon VIII: Annales de la philosophie en procès*.

ONE

William James

A Guide for the Perplexed

> [T]he vividness and clarity of his style no less than the keenness of his analysis roused the imagination of a public in this country which had long been apathetic to the more abstract problems of technical philosophy. . . . [H]e produced a large number of writings which gave ample evidence of his amazing ability to cut through the cumbersome terminology . . . clearing such problems as that of the One and the Many from the dry rot of centuries, and in rendering such problems immediately relevant to practical and personal difficulties.
>
> —*Dictionary of Philosophy* entry on William James

> James's insights on the human mind have been rivaled only by Shakespeare's and Freud's.
>
> —Antonio Damasio, *Descartes' Error*

The inner world of will, self, and time, or the phantoms posing as such, has been extensively traveled by William James, not only in his pioneering transpersonal research, but also in his more mainstream role as the "father of American psychology." An anatomist, psychologist, and Harvard professor, James was one of the clearest and most accessible writers ever to be called a philosopher. Indeed, he defined philosophy as "the search for *clearness* where common people do not even suspect that there is any lack of it" (C3, 409).[1]

Having first aspired to be a painter, James came to see philosophy as an "ugly study" that "de-realized" life (C9, 452). Throughout his professional career, he emphasized direct experience over abstract concepts. While James's ideas have gone in and out of fashion, these renderings of direct experience (including vivid introspections unsurpassed even by his brother Henry) have always had a wide and devoted following among specialists and nonspecialists alike. According to *The Oxford Companion to the Mind*, James's classic work, *The Principles of Psychology* (a virtual anthology of his and other's direct experiences), is "the best-known book in all psychology."[2] Moreover, with James as our guide, questions about free will, self, and time are not mere classroom exercises. As his primary biographer, Ralph Barton Perry, put it:

> Philosophy was never, for James, a detached and dispassionate inquiry into truth; still less was it a form of amusement. It was a quest, the outcome of which was hopefully and fearfully apprehended by a soul on trial and awaiting its sentence.[3]

And his quest took place at the dawn of the era that is still unfolding, the era in which the arbitrator of ultimate insights and concerns is shifting. As James characterized this shift: "'Science' in many minds is genuinely taking the place of religion" (*VRE*, 58).[4] Born just two years after the word *scientist* was first coined, science was still "contested territory" when James came of age.[5] Darwin's big idea was more gauntlet than dogma. James's mystic-minded father, painfully aware that religion was being usurped, encouraged his son to put down his paintbrushes and train to become one of America's first professional scientists. He looked to his son to guide science beyond its "puerile stage of progress" that sought to supplant the divine Absolute with the hypothetical "quasi-unity" of "Nature."[6] That James did in fact pioneer reconciliations between science and religion is one of the reasons he still speaks to us directly.

SONS OF EMERSON

It is not merely the usurping of religion by science that keeps this era open-ended, but how religion has reconfigured itself in response. In a movement that found its first American champion in James's godfather Emerson, for whom the reconciliation of science and religion was central to his calling,[7] traditional Western dualistic modes (God and Man, Heaven and Earth) have been, and continue to be, challenged by Eastern nondual modes.[8] James's insights and research supported this nondual reconfiguration, however much his sympathies did not.

According to the psychologist whom James recruited from Germany to run Harvard's psychology labs, the "fusion-repelling" individualism that informed James's sympathies was a national trait:

> The American popular mind does not at all sympathize with the philosophical idea that individuality is only an appearance, and that we are all fundamentally one being. The American thinks pluralistically, and brings to his metaphysics a firm belief in the absolute significance of the individual.[9]

Such individualism, championed by America's preeminent psychologist, was indeed also championed by America's preeminent essayist, Emerson, and her preeminent poet, Emerson's disciple Whitman. That the same could be said for the era's preeminent philosopher, Nietzsche, just two years younger than James, may only be more confirmation of our national character, since Nietzsche was also a disciple of Emerson.[10] But following the so-called American Century, the firm belief in the absolute significance of the individual—the belief that virtually defined James—is now surely a belief without borders. All the more reason that it is worthy of re-evaluation.

James was not alone in championing this belief while suspecting otherwise. Indeed, Emerson and his two disciples surpassed James himself in their exaltation of individualism, while also championing a nondual transcendence beyond it. All will play key roles here. Whitman's ongoing identification with the cosmic One particularly fascinated James, and he found numerous occasions to engage "the restorer of the eternal natural religion" for "many" (*VRE*, 83). Nietzsche, whom James also took a growing interest in, was a more complicated engagement. When ineptly lumped together with Schopenhauer, and identified with the madness of his later years, he was, to James, poor, pathetic Nietzsche, "with an occasional command of language" (*VRE*, 42; *C8*, 90); but as the author of nondual reconstructions of commonsense reality that James read, Nietzsche may well have influenced

James's similar reconstructions, no less than Emerson who influenced them both. Moreover, at the very end of his life, James became much more sympathetic to Nietzsche, recognizing their shared primal concern, the same concern that his father had tasked him with addressing, and his godfather had already fully addressed: religion's traditional role as our center of gravity could not have its place genuinely taken by evolution and scientific materialism.[11]

In addition to the era's most renowned psychologist, essayist, poet, and philosopher, one of its most renowned novelists will also play a key role. An acquaintance of James, who died in the same year, Mark Twain read *The Principles of Psychology*, as well as *The Varieties of Religious Experience*, championing the investigations of consciousness beyond the margin "made by our professor William James."[12] Most significantly, a powerful experience corroborating the mystical suggestion of "consciousness already there waiting to be uncovered," led Twain to not only join James's American Society for Psychical Research, but to actively participate in it.

While most of what follows will be a direct engagement with James, it is thereby also an engagement with some of the other most insightful minds of his day—his friends and colleagues. For whether relating lab experiments, introspection upon his own mundane experience, or what he deemed the "wild beasts of the philosophic desert"—"religious experiences" and "psychical research"—James was seldom a solo voice (*PU*, 149). And in keeping with James's explicit call to future generations to test the "veridical reality" of what he most daringly proposed, we will also look at the relevant research in neuroscience, physics, psychology, and parapsychology in the century that succeeded him. All of these fields are combined in the vibrant new interdisciplinary field that James as much as anyone helped to establish: consciousness studies. Finally, in the spirit and sometimes the letter of James's most widely read book, *The Varieties of Religious Experience*, the illusion of will, self, and time will be woven into the varieties of spiritual and mystical experience they manifest as.

RADICAL EMPIRICIST

> [W]e have in James's radical empiricism a position that goes right to the heart of the Western viewpoint, exposing its limits. In this he resembles

> . . . the metaphysics of Far Eastern psychology: the Upanishadic *tat* of the Hindu texts; the Theravada Buddhist image of moment consciousness as a string of pearls; the Mahayana Buddhist doctrine of co-dependent origination (*pratityasammutpada*); or Zen suchness (*tathata*).[13]
>
> —Eugene Taylor and Robert Wozniak,
> *Pure Experience, The Response to William James*

In 1903, while lecturing at Harvard on psychology, James spotted a Buddhist monk in his audience.[14] "Take my chair," said James, "you are better equipped to lecture on psychology than I." The monk obliged, and afterward James turned to his students and said: "This is the psychology everybody will be studying twenty-five years from now."[15] The following year James himself helped pave the way toward such a psychology with his doctrine of "radical empiricism"—the construction of reality through direct experience only: nothing experienced left out; nothing not experienced let in (*AWPE*, 1160). This emphasis on direct experience, with a fundamental focus on "plain, unqualified actuality," what James called "pure experience," is the foundation of Buddhist meditation practice, in which each arising moment is not enabled to be more or less than what it is (ibid., 1175).

Evident, as we shall see, in his investigations of self and time, direct experience was James's indispensable starting point in his probing the foundation of them both—the belief in free will, which has no existence, nor can be depicted, outside its confines. "It was . . . through meditating on the phenomenon [of willing] in my own person that I first became convinced of the truth of the doctrine which these pages present," James wrote in *The Principles of Psychology* (*PP2*, 525). Much of this masterpiece is comprised of his personal introspections, but only when he came to the experience of will did he use the more intensified word *meditating* to describe the process. His account of this meditation is among the most significant passages in all Western writing about free will. James himself considered it "to contain in miniature form the data for an entire psychology of volition" (ibid.).

Yet curiously, even as James's popularity continues to grow, this description has been largely ignored or, even worse, casually dismissed. Rollo May, after quoting it in its entirety in his 1969 bestseller, *Love and Will*, rejects it as "unfinished"; but he does so without reflecting upon the basic, irreducible nature of James's subjective account.[16] Biographer Gerald Myers complains that the conclusion James drew from his meditation conflicted with his "typical common-sense defenses of free will," as if challenging common sense were not as essential a duty of a philosopher as defending it.[17] As James himself proclaimed in the *Principles*: to "traverse common sense . . . in philosophy is no insuperable objection" (*PP1*, 304).[18]

And certainly James's conclusion *did* challenge common sense, at least the sense common to mainstream Western thought. To a Zen Buddhist, or even a Christian Quietist, on the other hand, James's conclusion follows naturally from the method he used to reach it. Indeed, given that the form of his meditation, an exercise in direct experience, was similar to the "bare attention" of Buddhist meditation, it is hardly surprising that the key insight he derived from it would be the same that Buddhist practitioners derive from theirs.

Yet it came as a surprise to him. For so radical was James's insight, undermining the very belief in free will he was seeking to uphold, that he himself recoiled from it. Despite openly supporting the Buddhist conception of the nonreality of self, and covertly supporting a radical Buddhist notion of timelessness,[19] James never accepted the nonreality of will that his meditation revealed, and he never integrated it with his other radical insights on the nature of self and time. It was as if the "soul on trial" denied access to a key witness.

But it is only by integrating James's radical insights on will and self—in support of them as phantoms of the inner world—that James's most radical insight can be accessed: time itself is a phantom. The belief in self, as Nietzsche clearly saw, is based on the belief in will. So, too, time, or what James's colleague Dewey called "genuine time," requires a self:

> Genuine time, if it exists as anything else except the measure of motions in space, is all one with the existence of individuals as individuals, with the creative, with the occurrence of unpredictable novelties.[20]

James agreed, and exactly in this all-American language of individuality, creativity, and "unpredictable novelties." But he also, as one James scholar duly noted, remained "too honestly alert to contradictory evidence and desires to fit his texts neatly into any one systematic explanation,"[21] let alone a commonsense one. Will, self, and genuine time were James's desires. But his honest alertness to contradictory evidence pointed him elsewhere.

How experience can be accounted for without will, self, and time is, I argue, James's most significant legacy, however reluctantly, or even obstructively, bequeathed. But the legacy can only be realized by distinguishing what James wanted to believe (based on common sense) from what his deepest insights and researches led him to believe. This discrepancy is most conspicuous in his defense of free will, the foundation of "the absolute significance of the individual." Why James clung to a belief in free will that he as much as anyone helped expose as an illusion begins our journey.

"SOMETHING HITHERTO SOLID WITHIN MY BREAST GAVE WAY ENTIRELY . . . "

Despite his championing of free will, James's own belief was not, as he once declared, "instinctive" (*P*, 537). The summer following his graduation from Harvard Medical School, in fact, he spent in a hammock at his parent's home, swaying to this tune: "I'm swamped in an empirical philosophy. I feel that we are Nature through and through, that we are *wholly* conditioned, that not a wiggle of our will happens save as the result of physical laws" (*C1*, 370). By next year even the swaying almost stopped:

> Whilst in this state of philosophic pessimism and general depression of spirits about my prospects . . . there arose in my mind the image of an epileptic patient whom I had seen in the asylum, a black-haired youth with greenish skin, entirely idiotic, who used to sit all day on one of the benches, or rather shelves, against the wall, with his knees drawn up against his chin, and the coarse gray undershirt, which was his only garment, drawn over them inclosing his entire figure. He sat there like a sort of sculptured Egyptian cat or Peruvian mummy, moving nothing but his black eyes and looking absolutely non-human. This image and my fear entered into a species of combination with each other. *That shape am I,* I felt, potentially. Nothing that I possess can defend me against that fate,

> if the hour for it should strike for me as it struck for him. There was such a horror of him, and such a perception of my own merely momentary discrepancy from him, that it was as if something hitherto solid within my breast gave way entirely, and I became a mass of quivering fear. After this the universe was changed for me altogether. (*VRE*, 149–150)[22]

Having dressed himself in the fashionable mechanistic determinism of his day, James looked in the mirror and saw only his clothes. His belief in a determinism devoid of any spiritual influence implied that we are "*wholly* conditioned," like material objects, completely at the mercy of "physical laws." But it took an image of a human-being-*as*-object before James confronted the full implication of his belief. The "quivering fear" that arose from that confrontation was more than momentary:

> I awoke morning after morning with a horrible dread at the pit of my stomach, and with a sense of the insecurity of life that I never knew before, and that I have never felt since. It was like a revelation; and although the immediate feelings passed away, the experience has made me sympathetic with the morbid feelings of others ever since. It gradually faded, but for months I was unable to go into the dark alone. (Ibid.)

Fear of the dark is not fear of any particular encounter, but rather fear of being surprised by *every* encounter; it is not fear of the unknown so much as fear of one's inadequacy to respond to whatever danger may arise. With this experience, James's belief that "not a wiggle of our will happens save as the result of physical laws" had grown into a feeling: "a horrible dread at the pit of my stomach." This feeling, "like a revelation," gave James "a sense of the insecurity of life that I never knew before," and made for an altogether "changed universe." Then, a few weeks later, a "decisive impression" made on him by the French philosopher Charles Renouvier "freed" him:[23]

> I think that yesterday was a crisis in my life. I finished the first part of Renouvier's second "Essais" and see no reason why his definition of Free Will—"the sustaining of a thought *because I choose to*

> when I might have other thoughts"—need be the definition of an illusion. At any rate, I will assume for the present—until next year—that it is no illusion. My first act of free will shall be to believe in free will. (*L1*, 147)

Rollo May makes much of James's declaration in that last sentence: "He *willed* freedom, made it his fiat."[24] By May's reading of the paragraph, however timid James's first affirmations were, his last one had the "Ta da-da da da da da" triumph of Popeye downing spinach. Such a reading, suggesting that James fashioned his own imperative out of Renouvier's philosophy, would be more convincing if James had formulated that last sentence himself. But it, too, was a direct quote from Renouvier; it was Renouvier who said, "My first act of free will shall be to believe in free will." By "assum[ing] for the present" the belief that free will was not an illusion, and repeating Renouvier's words, was James issuing himself a "fiat," or testing out another man's belief?

Many years later, when James formally addressed the arguments for and against free will, he apparently recalled his own personal struggle:

> When a dreadful object is presented, or when life as a whole turns up its dark abysses to our view, then the worthless ones among us lose their hold on the situation altogether, and either escape from its difficulties by averting their attention, or if they cannot do that, collapse into yielding masses of plaintiveness and fear. (*PP2*, 578)

To a "worthless one," whom he had been in peril of becoming, James contrasts the "heroic mind" of "pure inward willingness." But then, evoking his own "heroic" moment that had lifted *him* from worthlessness, he writes: "[J]ust as our courage is so often a reflex of another's courage, so our faith is apt to be . . . a faith in someone else's faith" (ibid., 579).

Without question, James's born-again affirmation of free will was a decisive, defining moment in his life.[25] But was that affirmation itself an act of willpower, or a reflexive endorsement of a belief he was now, in his changed universe, ready to receive? At the very least, the question this affirmative "decision" begs is this: How much was it a *response* that *came* to James in his altered state, just as the response of helplessness had come to him in his prior state? That a surge of rescuing, purposeful energy attended this thought, and sustained James throughout the rest of his life, is not questioned. What is questioned is the source of this and all such surges. It was a question James came to ask himself. And the answer surprised him.

JAMES'S MEDITATION ON FREE WILL

When I ask people what difference it would make in their life if they didn't believe in free will, most reply that they wouldn't get out of bed. This tells us something right away: people are tired (especially Americans, whose "doing, doing, doing" James, along with his student Theodore Roosevelt, saw as one of the hallmarks of their greatness [C1, 123]).[26] But how in fact *do* we get out of bed? Twenty years after James declared his belief in free will he asked himself this very question. He could, of course, have used any act of deliberation that culminates in an apparent triumph of will. What is especially apt about this example, however, is that it is usually our first deliberate act of the day, following, as it does, a long period of passivity.

Often, to be sure, getting out of bed does not feel mediated by will. It feels, rather, like an automatic response—we are *jolted* upwards—whether this jolt is prompted by the sound of an alarm clock, or the feeling of pressure in our bladder, or the flash of the image of our bus pulling out without us. At other times, however, our movement does indeed seem to resolve a deliberation on whether or not to abandon the cozy environment in which we lie; we have looked at two alternatives and feel we have *chosen* one of them. *There is no feeling of will (let alone verification of its ultimate reality) without such a feeling of having chosen.*

James's meditation served as his paradigm of the feeling of having chosen, of having made a decision and acted upon it—in a word: of having willed. The solid pragmatic philosopher had finally come to test by experience what the shaky youth had accepted on faith:

> We know what it is to get out of bed on a freezing morning in a room without a fire, and how the very vital principle within us protests against the ordeal. Probably most persons have lain on certain mornings for an hour at a time unable to brace themselves to the

> resolve. We think how late we shall be, how the duties of the day will suffer; we say, "I *must* get up, this is ignominious," etc.; but still the warm couch feels too delicious, the cold outside too cruel, and resolution faints away and postpones itself again and again just as it seemed on the verge of bursting the resistance and passing over into the decisive act. Now how do we *ever* get up under such circumstances? If I may generalize from my own experience, we more often than not get up without any struggle or decision at all. We suddenly find that we *have* got up. A fortunate lapse of consciousness occurs; we forget both the warmth and the cold; we fall into some revery connected with the day's life, in the course of which the idea flashes across us, "Hollo! I must lie here no longer"—an idea which at that lucky instant awakens no contradictory or paralyzing suggestions, and consequently produces immediately its appropriate motor effects. It was our acute consciousness of both the warmth and the cold during the period of struggle, which paralyzed our activity then and kept our idea of rising in the condition of *wish* and not of *will*. The moment these inhibitory ideas ceased, the original idea exerted its effects. (*PP2*, 524–525)

As we said, James considered his example to "contain in miniature form the data for an entire psychology of volition." The data can be broken down into three parts. First, thoughts arise. Second, insofar as thoughts have an impulsive power, that power is directly linked to our motor operations. And third, the feeling of will and effort is derivable from the interplay between opposing thoughts.

TWO

Thoughts without a Thinker

> When man studies himself with honest impartiality he observes that he is not the conscious and voluntary artisan either of his feelings or of his thoughts, and that his feelings and his thoughts are only phenomena which happen to him.
>
> —Hubert Benoit, *Zen and the Psychology of Transformation*

> I conceive of man as always spoken to from behind, and unable to turn his head and see the speaker.
>
> —Emerson

Thoughts arise. This becomes strikingly clear if you sit still and bring your awareness to only the movement of your breathing, as in meditation. No matter how hard you try to keep this exclusive focus, you very soon find yourself watching random thoughts, arriving unescorted to consciousness. These thoughts are experienced more as happening *to* us than as being made *by* us. The arising nature of thoughts is so manifest in meditation, in fact, that sitting still with the breath may seem to be not revealing this fundamental truth so much as *concocting* it. Yet it does not take a still, inner environment to experience the arising nature of thoughts. It is, rather, our everyday experience, even if we don't every day assess it as such. Does Mark Twain not speak for us all when he describes his thought process as "racing along from subject to subject—a drifting panorama of ever-changing, ever-dissolving views manufactured by my mind without any help from me—why, it would take me two hours to merely name the multitude of things my mind tallied off and photographed in fifteen minutes?"[1]

Even when you seem to be directing the flow of your thoughts—such as when you are explaining something to someone—you don't know the next word out of your mouth until you say it. And even when you *do* know the next word out of your mouth—such as when you are reciting something—you still don't know the thought that will accompany it. (Actors, for instance, who repeat the same lines every night can never repeat precisely the same thoughts to go along with them.)[2] As the British philosopher Gilbert Ryle says: "One thing that I cannot prepare myself for is the next thought that I am going to think."[3] We may believe that so-called deliberate choices constitute an exception—that *they*, at least, are not so much received as made. James, however, could find nothing in experience that confirmed the "making" of any thought—a deciding thought or otherwise—nothing that confirmed anything other than—as our idiom expresses it—thoughts *occur*. "If we could say in English 'it thinks,' as we say 'it rains' or 'it blows,'" he wrote, "we should be stating the fact most simply and with the minimum of assumption" (*PP1*, 224–225).

And James *was* careful to use such minimum of assumption whenever he characterized the will experience, utilizing such egoless phrases as "things are *really being decided* from one moment to another" and "mental spontaneity . . . select[s]" (*PP1*, 453, 594).[4] Despite his belief in free will, James had no problem reconciling himself to this impersonality of the thought process. Several times throughout the *Principles* he derides the attempts of others to establish an independent "I"—an abiding *subject* or "soul" out of which thoughts come, or in which they inhere:

> It is . . . with the word Soul as with the word Substance in general. To say that phenomena inhere in a substance is at bottom only to record one's protest against the notion that the bare existence of the phenomena is the total truth. A phenomenon would not itself be, we insist, unless there were something *more* than the phenomenon. To the more we give the provisional name of Substance. So . . . [accordingly] we ought certainly to admit that there is more than the bare fact of coexistence of a passing thought with a passing brain-state. But we do not answer the question "What is that more?"

> when we say that it is a "Soul" which the brain-state affects. This kind of more *explains* nothing. . . . The phenomena are enough, the passing Thought [capitalized by James to mean "the present mental state"] itself is the only *verifiable* thinker. (Ibid., 346)

To affirm, as James does, that "[e]very thought *tends* to be part of a personal consciousness," is not to affirm that personal consciousness is a necessary part of consciousness, let alone the *generative* part (ibid., 225; emphasis added). We do not "make a thought" like we "make a pot." The clay pot I make is distinguished from those of my fellow pottery students as having been shaped by my hands, not theirs. There is no dispute about the meaning of the word "make" here. But if I copied an exotic design from the student next to me, there is confusion; and were I to try to sell my pot to an art gallery, there might be litigation. The answer to the question, "Whose hands fashioned this?" answers the question, "Who made this?" except when the origin of the design idea is in doubt. But the origin, ultimately, of all thoughts is in doubt. To say "I make thoughts" is an unwarranted assumption. Rather, "[W]e must simply say '*thought goes on*'" (ibid.).

"PHILOSOPHIZING WITHOUT . . . ASSUMPTIONS"

James's belief that thoughts cannot ultimately be traced to a substance/subject self is shared by empirical-based philosophers East and West. To cite a standard Buddhist example, the phenomena of passing thoughts no more inhere in a substance "I" than the various moments of a twirled, lit torch inhere in a circle of fire. Both the self and the circle of fire are abstracted from, derived from, various moments, and not the other way around. As Krishnamurti puts it: "The I has been created by thought. . . . There is no *you* related to thought."[5] We will have much more to say about this radical view of self later. Here I only want to emphasize that James's meditation on the experience of will is consistent with his belief that thoughts are not generated by an "I." His deliberative thoughts as well as his "deciding" thought arose impersonally, the way he believed all thoughts did at all times, "stating the fact most simply and with the minimum of assumption."

James's dear friend, the British philosopher Shadworth Hodgson, whose writing he called "the greatest mine of philosophic wealth now extant (C2, 43),"[6] took James's free will coach, Renouvier, to task for going beyond the minimum.[7] In a letter to James eight years prior to the publication of the *Principles*, he told him that Renouvier "assumes a spiritual agent working in certain indispensable forms of thought. Where is the foundation for assuming an agent at all?" And he concluded the letter with the admonition "to find the means of philosophizing *without making assumptions*."[8]

James, it would seem, had found precisely such a means in his will paradigm, which assumes neither a deciding "I" nor even a deciding *moment*. He went looking for such a moment but could not find it. Instead of the moment of decision he found a "lapse of consciousness." Out of this lapse "we suddenly find that we *have* got up." Since awareness of the decision came only *after* it had already occurred, consciousness of the decision was not simultaneous with its generation. The decision, the actual deciding moment, occurs, as he says, "without any . . . decision at all." James dilutes this startling discovery with the phrase "more often than not," but obviously, if he had been able at any time to catch himself in the act of *making* a deciding thought, he would not have presented this particular example as his paradigm of the will experience.

Now, it may be argued that James's introspection was inconclusive; or that, lying in bed, he was not fully awake. The "lapse of consciousness" prior to the "flashing" of the deciding thought was filled, he says, by "some revery connected with the day's life"; but had he really hung in there and not "let" his mind drift, or had he "paid" closer attention to the exact content of the revery, might he not then have seen that the idea did not come "flashing" out of nowhere? Had he paid closer attention might he not then have caught himself in the act of "making a thought?"

Rollo May, for one, thinks he can figure out "what went on in that 'fortunate lapse of consciousness'" since "Psychotherapy has brought us a good deal of data about that 'revery' which James did not have."[9] May, of course, does not claim to be able to reconstruct James's revery, but he does claim that it must have contained an essential part of the will process missed by James. May (after Brentano and Tillich) calls that essential part "intentionality," and defines it as the "underlying will" that structures conscious intentions.[10] Although intentionality is the kind of vague abstraction that James's concrete meditation sought to avoid, May believes it can complete what he calls the "unfinished business" in James's will paradigm.[11]

May is undoubtedly correct that there is a realm beyond "conscious intention" where "deeper meanings lie," a realm, as he says, that Freud made "undeniably clear in his use of free association."[12] But he muddles the implications of such a realm (as well as Freud's insight) by suggesting that these deeper meanings come from a self that actively creates them:

> In free association the thoughts and memories and fantasies take their form, their pattern, their meaningful theme (which the patient, or any one of us engaging in free association not on the couch but in normal thinking and creativity, may not at all catch at the moment) from the fact that they are *his* fantasies, *his* associations, coming out of *his* way of perceiving the world and *his* commitments and problems. It is only afterwards that the person himself can see and absorb the meaning that has been in these apparently random, disconnected things he is saying. *Free association is a technique of going beyond mere conscious intention and giving one's self over to the realm of intentionality.*[13]

James once criticized the writing of a philosopher by asking "Who is nimble-witted enough to count . . . the number of times he steps from the known to the knower, and attributes to both whatever properties he finds in either one" (*PP1*, 475)? He could have been talking about May's passage here, in which an active form-making "knower" is continually conflated with a passive, form-taking "known." Such conflation Freud was careful to avoid. As he did not believe in free will, free association was not, for him, a matter of "giving one's self over" but of one's self being taken over, by a will not of one's making. (Later we will have more to say about Freud's view of free association and how it undermines rather than supports the possibility of free will.)

Whatever "meaning" the thoughts of free association may make ("*his* way of perceiving the world and *his* commitments and problems"), they are not evidence that a self shapes thoughts rather than the other way around. Connecting the dots of the known does not connect us to the creative agency of a knower. Whatever "intentionality" means, as long as its "realm" lies "beyond conscious intention" it cannot bolster the argument for free will, which, by definition, must lie within it. Even if May were somehow able to precisely reconstruct all the thoughts that filled James's revery it would be for naught. The content of the revery is irrelevant since "in the course" of it the deciding thought was experienced as being received, as the words "flashes across" indicate. Whatever might be claimed to be going on behind the scenes in the will experience, the lapse of consciousness before the deciding thought is still an irreducible fact of such experience whenever one tries, as James did, to witness it.

Another possible objection to James's paradigm is that it has a design flaw: if you are trying to witness an act of will, "*you*" are occupied by the "trying to witness," and thus miss the role of "you" in the act of will. Such objection, however, begs the question that any meditation on will ultimately poses—namely, whether an active, agent "I" exists in the first place. The only proof of an agent "I" is what can be inferred from the experience of agency. But what if, as Nietzsche says, "will" is not an afterbirth of "I," an autonomous agent; "I" is an afterbirth of will, the experience of autonomy?[14] "Trying to witness" is, itself, ostensibly, an act of will. Thus, referring the action of "trying to witness" to an "I" *assumes* what needs to be proven. The *experience* of will, as we said, is not in question; the question is: What does this experience entail? To answer this question it matters not whether the experience be of trying to do something (such as getting out of bed on a cold morning) or trying to witness the trying. What matters is that some moment of trying be revealed for what it is, stripped of assumptions.

THE GAP BETWEEN THOUGHTS

> Many years ago, I was working with Nisargadatta Maharaj, an Indian teacher. He asked a woman who was audio taping for a new book, "What will be the name of my next book?" She replied, "Beyond Consciousness." He said, "No, Prior to Consciousness. Find out who you are prior to your last thought and stay there."
>
> —Stephen Wolinsky, *Quantum Consciousness*

At the turn of the last century, Karl Marbe, of the University of Würzburg, devised an experiment in which subjects attempted to "catch themselves" in the act of choosing between two impressions. The experiment was concerned with judgment not will, but, like James's meditation, it was, at bottom, an attempt to detect the onset of a decision between two options. The subjects were asked to lift two small weights, which had been placed on a table in front of them, and decide which one was heavier. They indicated their choice by placing the heavier object down. The results startled both Marbe and his subjects, all of whom were trained in introspective psychology. For, contrary to their own expectation, they discovered that while the feeling of the two weights was conscious, as well as placing the heavier one down, *the moment of decision was not*. Julian Jaynes, in his *The Origin of Consciousness in the Breakdown of the Bicameral Mind*, offers a home-kit version of this experiment:

> Take any two unequal objects, such as a pen and pencil or two unequally filled glasses of water, and place them on the desk in front of you. Then, partly closing your eyes to increase your attention to the task, pick up each one with the thumb and forefinger and judge which is heavier. Now introspect on everything you are doing. You will find yourself conscious of the feel of the objects against the skin of your fingers, conscious of the slight downward pressure as you feel the weight of each, conscious of any protuberances on the sides of the objects, and so forth. And now the actual judging of which is heavier. Where is that? Lo! the very act of judgement that one object is heavier than the other is not conscious. *It is somehow given to you by your nervous system.*[15]

Marbe's experiment thus corroborated James's meditation on will. The gap before the "deciding" thought exists.

This gap, which both Marbe and James discovered before the "deciding" thought, meditation reveals to exist before all thoughts. Indeed, "the leading idea of Buddhism," a religion based on meditation, "is that there is no other ultimate reality than separate, instantaneous bits of existence."[16] James had introspected experience into "small enough pulses" to realize that the discontinuity between passing thoughts is mediated by the passing thoughts themselves (*PU*, 129). The "minimal fact" of experience, for James, was a "passing" moment experienced as difference (ibid., 128). But had his introspection deepened into even smaller pulses, he might have realized one more minimal fact about passing, *differing* moments: they do not go "indissolubly" into each other, in a continuous stream or "sheet," (ibid., 130) but, rather, they are separated by a space of non-thought, a space he himself had called the "darkness" "out of" which "the rush of our thought" comes (ibid., 128, 130). In ordinary experience, the space between departing and arriving thoughts is so fleeting as to be an "apparition."[17] In meditation, however, the apparition is real: "If you watch very carefully," says Krishnamurti, "you will see that, though the response, the movement of thought, seems so swift, there are gaps, there are intervals between thoughts. Between two thoughts there is a period of silence which is not related to the thought process."[18] According to Eckhart Tolle such a "gap in the stream of the mind" is the key to enlightenment, insofar as it allows you to "disidentify" from the "voice in your head."[19] In Tibetan Buddhism, where meditation is a widespread daily practice, this gap has a special name: "bardo," literally "in between."[20] Some formal practitioners of meditation have even tried to quantify the frequency of the movements/moments of thought (the word "moment" is derived from the Latin word for "movement," *momentum*): 6,460,000 such moments in twenty-four hours (an average of one arising moment per 13.3 milliseconds), according to the Buddhist Sarvaastivaadins; a sect of Chinese Buddhists puts it at one thought per twenty milliseconds.[21]

James, as we shall see, found other reasons to question the seamless continuity of the stream of thought. But in his meditation on will, the gap he discovered between "deciding" thoughts corroborated his "minimum of assumption" for all thoughts: "it thinks" is more accurate than "I think." Even "deciding" thoughts, thoughts of apparent "I" assertion, do not emerge from an "I," but from a gap.

STREAM OF CONSCIOUSNESS

> The chain of consciousness is a sequence of differents.
> —Shadworth Hodgson, quoted by James in *The Principles of Psychology*[22]

James used the phrase "lapse of consciousness" to describe the gap before the "deciding" thought, but the use of the word "consciousness" can mislead. If we look at his paradigm, we see that it was not his consciousness per se that lapsed, but consciousness of thoughts. James did not black out just prior to his "deciding moment"; he simply witnessed a gap between thoughts. But was not this gap also part of the uninterrupted flow of his "stream of consciousness" (James's most famous phrase)?[23] In fact, it is precisely because the stream of consciousness is an uninterrupted continuity that this gap between thoughts can be perceived *as such*. James illustrates this point well:

> Into the awareness of the thunder itself the awareness of the previous silence creeps and continues; for what we hear when the thunder crashes is not thunder *pure*, but thunder-breaking-upon-silence-and-contrasting-with it. Our feeling of the same objective thunder, coming in this way, is quite different from what it would be were the thunder a continuation of previous thunder. The thunder itself we believe to abolish and exclude the silence; but the feeling of the thunder is also a feeling of the silence as just gone; and it would be difficult to find in the actual concrete consciousness of man a feeling so limited to the present as not to have an inkling of anything that went before. (*PP1*, 240-241)

By this analogy, consciousness without thoughts would be the silence, and consciousness with thoughts would be the "thunder-breaking-upon-silence-and-contrasting-with-it." While thoughts tumble by so quickly one upon the other as to seem contiguous, their perceived distinction from each other implies something other than thoughts in which this distinction plays out. This "something other" is consciousness.

Consciousness, even "actual concrete consciousness," abides; thoughts arise within it. James, like many, sometimes interchanges the words "consciousness" and "thought." His well-worn phrase, "stream of consciousness," for example, is found within a chapter titled "Stream of Thoughts." Watch how he substitutes one word for the other in the following passage from that chapter:

> The transition between the thought of one object and the thought of another is no more a break in the *thought* than a joint in a bamboo is a break in the wood. It is a part of the *consciousness* much as the joint is a part of the *bamboo*. (Ibid., 240; emphases in original)

What else can "the *thought*" in the phrase "no more a break in the *thought*" mean other than "*consciousness*," as used in the last sentence? The two italicized words are, here, equivalent; James begins with the word "thought" but switches to the word "consciousness" by way of clarification. If the transition between the "thought of one object and the thought of another" is analogous to the *joints* in the bamboo, then it is not an "unbroken *thought*" that is the bamboo itself but, as James amends it, "consciousness."

The distinction between breaking thoughts and unbroken consciousness is emphasized by a completely different metaphor that James uses to define the changing pace of the stream:

> When the rate is slow we are aware of the object of our thought in a comparatively restful and stable way. When rapid, we are aware of a passage, a relation, a transition from it, or between it and something else. As we take, in fact, a general view of the wonderful stream of our consciousness, what strikes us first is this different pace of its parts. Like a bird's life, it seems to be made of an alternation of flights and perchings. (Ibid., 243)

The bird perches and flies. But it does not fly away; "comings and goings . . . no more break the flow of the thought that thinks them than they break the time and the space in which they lie" (ibid., 240).

In the East, the distinction between breaking thoughts and "unbroken" consciousness is well known. Indeed, one of the most respected of all Indian metaphysicians, the advaitin ("nondualist") Shankara, came to prominence because of the perceived failure of the Buddhists to adequately distinguish between the arising nature of thoughts and the abiding nature of consciousness in which the moments/movements of thought occur. But the distinction is there for anyone who has either a heightened gift for introspection, like James, or who perseveres in meditation. For it is precisely the existence of this underlying, abiding, "unbroken," witnessing consciousness that the practice of meditation helps make manifest. As Yoga scholar Georg Feuerstein explains:

> Witness-Consciousness, or "Seer" (drashtri) is the pure Awareness (cit) that abides eternally beyond the senses and the mind,

> uninterruptedly apperceiving all the numerous and changeable contents of consciousness. All schools of Hinduism agree that the ultimate Reality is not a condition of stonelike stupor but superconsciousness.
>
> This assertion is not mere speculation but is based on the actual realization of thousands of yogins, and their great discovery is corroborated by the testimony of mystics in other parts of the world.[24]

James's interchanging of the two terms "thought" and "consciousness," as in his bamboo analogy above, helps account for why, in his meditation, he called a lapse of thought a lapse of consciousness. It also may account for why he did not link his observation of the lapse before the deciding thought to his overall sense that thoughts arise impersonally. Clearly, however, his discovery of a lapse before the "deciding" thought forms the center of his paradigm on will. James himself never downplayed the significance of this lapse, nor suggested, as May and others have, that it left his meditation incomplete. Seeking neither to disprove nor to substantiate it by other methods, James, the "radical empiricist" of "direct experience," let the lapse remain in place at the center of his paradigm on will, a period of silence between two thoughts, declaring: "The truth must be admitted that thought works under conditions imposed *ab extra* [from beyond]" (*PP1*, 552).

THREE

Ghostbuster

> [N]o one knows how or by what means the mind moves the body, nor how many various degrees of motion it can impart to the body, nor how quickly it can move it. Thus, when men say that this or that physical action has its origin in the mind, which latter has dominion over the body, they are using words without meaning, or are confessing in specious phraseology that they are ignorant of the cause of the said action, and do not wonder at it.
>
> –Spinoza

In James's paradigm, there were several instances of attention paid to getting out of bed, but only the one that got him up was considered to be an instance of will. As he said, the original idea to get out of bed was, until it got him out, a *wish* not will. Such a distinction between wishing and willing is commonplace. Our sense of autonomous empowerment comes not from what we think but from what we *do*. This is why most discussions of free will do not focus on free thoughts but on free actions. It is in doing, not in thinking about doing, that freewillism is based.

This is true despite the fact that few of our movements feel consciously guided. We are forever discovering the movements we are making only after we have begun to make them. When, for example, we are reading, we may feel, as we get to the bottom of a page, that it is time to move on, but we rarely detect the specific impulse to turn the page. Instead, we find that we *have turned* or *are turning* the page. Similarly, on a hot summer's day, we get a mental picture of a watermelon in our refrigerator and *the next thing we know* we're on the way to the kitchen. Even complicated tasks, such as playing a waltz on the piano, often proceed without a semblance of conscious guidance, since an enduring principle of psychology is that our "nervous system grows to the modes in which it has been exercised."[1] Indeed, after sufficient practice, the amount of attention required to perform complicated tasks becomes almost nil. While beginning pianists must focus on what their fingers are actually doing, accomplished pianists can play a Chopin waltz while reading their e-mail.

"Consciousness," as James puts it, "deserts all processes where it can no longer be of use" (*PP2*, 496). And, since most of our movements are habitual, consciousness is often missing in action. If consciousness is hanging around, *being of use,* then the movement is likely to be either novel or difficult, or at least made in a way that it has not been made before—such as when a newly appointed judge tries to sit with a newly acquired dignity, or when a condemned person, awaiting a last minute pardon, tries to sit on the electric chair as slowly as possible. A novel or difficult moment *feels* consciously guided. To sit "with dignity," or "as slowly as possible" is not simply to move but to *attempt* to move in a specified way. The sense of this attempt to move in a specified way is the sense of conscious guidance all the way down: Pause! Keep head erect! Place hands lightly on knees!, etc.

But of what does any such conscious guidance actually consist? To what extent does the conscious guidance of any movement penetrate into the movement itself? As James puts it, "Whoever says that in raising his arm he is ignorant of how many muscles he contracts, in what order of sequence, and in what degrees of intensity, expressively avows a colossal amount of unconsciousness of the processes of motor discharge" (*PP2*, 499). That we can, and do, consciously guide our movements is a widely believed generalization, but as James says, we cannot "see farther into a generalization than . . . [our] own knowledge of details extends" (*C1*, 122).[2] In James's paradigm, instead of finding any details confirming the conscious initiation of a movement, we find, instead, a blind spot. The movement, *as it is being enacted,* no less than the "decision" to move, feels more like something that *has happened* rather than something that one does.

Like the moment of decision, a movement, immediately after it has been made, is easily construed as having *been* generated by a self-in-charge.

But as the movement is *being* initiated, what we believe to be the execution of our will over our motor responses is no more than automatic responses to the thoughts that have prompted them. "The first point to start from," says James, "in understanding voluntary action and the possible occurrence of it with no fiat or express resolve, is the fact that consciousness is *in its very nature impulsive*" (*PP2*, 526). By impulsive, James does not mean "capricious" but capable of producing an impulse: "We do not have a sensation or a thought and then have to *add* something dynamic to it to get a movement. Every pulse of feeling which we have is the correlate of some neural activity that is already on its way to instigate a movement" (ibid.). Thus, twenty years before the philosopher Gilbert Ryle referred to volition as a "ghost in the machine,"[3] James had concluded that nothing stands between the thought of an act and the act itself except "a supernumerary phenomenon depending on executive ganglia whose function lies outside the mind" (ibid., 560). Between the thought to move and the movement itself no "third order of mental phenomenon" intervenes (ibid., 501).

Not all thoughts of action lead to action. Many thoughts of performing an action—from momentary flashes to extended scenarios—refer to an action not possible in one's immediate circumstance. And even thoughts of actions that *are* possible to be undertaken in one's immediate circumstance do not necessarily lead to actions. As James's example of trying to get out of bed shows, the arising of one thought can inhibit the movement about to be instigated by another. The inhibiting thought need not be antagonistic; it need merely distract. But, says James, once a thought to make a movement "*fills* the mind" unchallenged, or "*stings* us in a certain way," the rest is automatic:

> We may . . . lay it down for certain that every representation of a movement awakens in some degree the actual movement which is its object; and awakens it in a maximum degree whenever it is not kept from so doing by an antagonistic representation present simultaneously to the mind. (Ibid., 564, 568, 526)

James's use of the word *sting*—a word that denotes a distinct bodily feeling—is not poetic license when applied to thoughts. The experience of will is obviously a convergence of thought and feeling; but, as James repeatedly observed, thought *itself* converges with feeling: "[W]hatever elements an act of cognition may imply besides, it at least implies the existence of a *feeling*" (*MT*, 833). No thought enters consciousness other than as a feeling. "Feelings," says James, "are the germ and starting point of cognition, thoughts the developed tree" (*PP1*, 222). Regardless of how plain-feeling a thought may be, such as the thought of a number, it is a feeling nonetheless, a feeling distinctly its own. The thought of the number "3492," for example, *feels* differently than the thought "3493." Some thoughts may seem more neutral than other thoughts, but, depending on their context, all thoughts—all words and images—can register as neutral or otherwise. The feeling, for instance, that registers with the thought of my sister as the answer to a query about whether I have any siblings has a plainer feeling than the feeling that registers with the thought of my sister as someone who can lend me money. But this second thought of my sister is not a neutral feeling/thought composite (like the first) *to which I add* the feeling of relief. Each thought is its own distinct mix.[4] My sister-as-a-fact-of-relation is a *different* thought/feeling composite than my sister-as-benefactor; they each form the composite peculiar to their context. So, too, the word *Yes* strikes consciousness with a different feeling than *Yes?* or *Yes!* Neither *Yes?* nor *Yes!* is experienced as a chord, one of whose notes is the neutral word *Yes* (the word, say, as flashed on TV during *Sesame Street*). Rather, just as the neutral word *Yes* itself, each is experienced as its own distinct note.

For James, the feeling aspect of thoughts was especially evident in relation to conscious movements. "*Movement*," he says, italicizing the entire point, "*is the natural immediate effect of feeling, irrespective of what the quality of feeling may be. It is so in reflex action, it is so in emotional expression, it is so in the voluntary life*" (*PP2*, 527). To illustrate a thought's feeling's "immediate effect" on a movement, try writing your name backwards so that you have the same "beginner's" attention to writing that you had in grammar school. From the thought of writing your name backward to the actual production of letters, myriad responses (of neurons, chemicals, and muscles) come into play. All such responses help relay the thought to the movement. But however coordinated this relay may be, however directed, where is the consciousness of the relay itself? All that consciously affects the shaping of the letters on the page is the "stinging" thought of writing them. This thought, the conscious thought of writing letters, consists of "certain digital sensations, certain alphabetic sounds, of certain appearances on the paper and no others" (ibid., 500). But the work of guiding or prompting the movement ends, is "absolutely completed," with the thought of the movement itself—what James calls the "stable state of the idea" (ibid., 560).

James, as we shall see, addresses the "disconcerting" fact that "no special fiat" of will is invoked by this account (*PP2*, 521). He has, instead, established as a fundamental principal of psychology that the last "mental cue" in all movement—the last conscious, "psychic" antecedent—is never more than the stinging feeling of the kinesthetic thought of the movement (ibid., 496). Whatever outward effect such a feeling may have in our muscles—from waving our arms to wriggling our toes—there is no consciousness of an outgoing *surge* on its way to making the connection. Whether we move our arms away from us or toward us, the feeling in our muscles is always an incoming feeling *after the fact*. James quotes what he calls the "admirably acute" observation of the philosopher Rudolph Lotze on this critical distinction between an outgoing movement and the incoming sensation that *accompanies, but does not precede*, it: the feeling of the movement in our muscles is not the "*force* on its way to produce an effect . . . but only . . . the *sufferance* already produced in our . . . muscles, after the force has, in a manner unobservable to us, exerted upon them its causality" (*PP2*, 523).

No matter how difficult or challenging a movement, no matter what strain of muscles it entails, its only conscious agency is the impulsive power of the thought itself. Any *other* "mental exertion" extraneous to this single-minded thought will only impede it. A woman who struggles for three minutes to weightlift a hundred pounds may well lift twenty times that amount instantly if a car should pin her son under its front wheel. This instantaneous response is not the result of a strong will but a pervasive thought—so pervasive that what James refers to as the "familiar" though "mysterious" "distinction between thought as such, and what it is 'of' or 'about,'" collapses (*PP1*, 296–297). Regardless of what she may have been thinking about just prior to the accident, as soon as her child is pinned she has no other thought than to come to his aid. What fills her mind completely, without a margin, even the margin of the immediate future, is the unified thought/feeling complex to lift the car off her son. The responder has become the response.

That evening, the mother may return to her weights to test her new-found strength, but she won't find it. She will lift, she will feel resistance, and a dialogue with that resistance will ensue. An exclusive, peremptory, unchallenged thought will not fill her mind; and, in the absence of the instantaneous impulsive power that came with that thought earlier in the day, no "super-added 'will force'" will make up the difference (*PP2*, 526). Experiments in James's own time, still cited today, have also shown that extraneous mental exertion greatly reduces the amount of muscle force available.[5]

In the next chapter, we will look with James at the *feeling* of effort and will that accompanies some (but by no means all) of our movements. For now, though, it is enough to note that, despite the feeling of an active will moving things along, no movement, from lifting the front end of a car to lifting its hood, need be, indeed *can* be, referred to any activating agency beyond the impulsive power of the thought itself. James, in agreement with Spinoza, points out that this impulsive power of a thought, the immediate electric connection it makes to our "motor centers," is "a mysterious tie, behind which we cannot go" (*PP2*, 551, 564).

THE HALF-SECOND DELAY

> [H]idden brain-events appear to be "closer" effects than those which consciousness directly aims at.
>
> —William James, *Some Problems of Philosophy*

Since James's time, our capacity to measure neurological responses has, of course, vastly increased. If we cannot go behind the mysterious tie between the thought of movement and its connection to our motor center, we can now at least go behind the skull, into the cerebral cortex, to detect the first impulses of electrical energy that precede all motor activity. We can and we have, but, as with James's meditation on will, and Marbe's experiment on the moment of judgment, the light it has shed on intention has darkened its overall mystery.

Until recently, if we knew nothing else about the electric connection that a thought makes to our motor center, we knew that the conscious thought of movement preceded the movement. Now, thanks to a series of startling experiments, confirming James's fundamental insight on preemptive "hidden brain-events" we can no longer can be sure.

In 1964, two German neurophysiologists, Hans Kornhuber and Luder Deecke, using an EEG, discovered that just before the initiation of every conscious movement the electrical pattern in the cerebral cortex shifts.[6] This shift, which they called the readiness potential, is the first detectable physical manifestation of a movement. But it is detectable only by the EEG. The subjects who are doing the movements have no awareness of it. The average time from the detection of the readiness potential by the EEG to the actual movement is 0.8 of a second.[7] The delay between the readiness potential and the actual movement is thus a measurable gap between the physical inception of a movement and its actualization.

Prior to the onset of any readiness potential, one would naturally expect to find the onset of the thought of the movement—the sequence being:

1. Thought to move (conscious)
2. Readiness Potential, preceding all movement (nonconscious)
3. Movement (conscious)

Given that the readiness potential is nonconscious, however, there is only one way to verify this sequence: compare the precise moment the subjects felt that they had initiated or "willed" the movement with the precise moment their cerebral cortex's electrical energy was initiated (the nonconscious readiness potential). Benjamin Libet, a professor at the University of California, devised an experiment to make such a comparison, and published his results in the journal *Brain*, with the title: "Time of Conscious Intention to Act in Relation to Onset of Cerebral Activity (Readiness-potential)." The experiment, accounts of which have been widely published,[8] went like this: The subjects, hooked to an EEG, sat opposite a clockface with a rotating dot. Their instructions were to move their finger at random, while still observing the rotating dot. They were then to report the time that they felt themselves initiate the finger movement. Like James, in his meditation on will, Libet held that the moment of willing, if it existed at all, existed as an irreducible subjective conscious experience. No amount of wires and gadgets could replace subjective, personal testimony. Libet's experiment, however, enhanced the precision of subjective reporting by the addition of the clock. For it allowed each subject to pinpoint the moment when the initiation of the movement first became conscious—that is, to assign a time, less vague than "now," for the moment of willing.

Since the subjects had been instructed to move their finger, it is a condition of the experiment that some thought or thoughts of moving their finger preceded the movement itself. But what of *the* thought credited with triggering the actual movement? James, as we saw, emphasized the impulsive power of a thought, but by that he meant only that no other conscious agency influencing the movement comes between the thought to move and the movement itself. Moreover, it is not clear from his will paradigm whether the thought to get up preceded, was simultaneous with, or followed the actual movement to get up. His first description puts the consciousness of the action before the consciousness of the decision: "We suddenly find that we *have* got up." His second, longer description, both elaboration and commentary, restores the commonsense temporal order of decision . . . action. The sequence discrepancy between these two descriptions renders the actual sequence ambiguous.

Such ambiguity might seem to be a flaw in his description, but, as it turns out, ambiguity is always precisely what introspection reveals. A drill sergeant barks, "Touch your toes!" to his soldiers, and his words seem to both precede and instigate their bending movement; but tell yourself to bend your finger, and this sequence is not so apparent. The precise moment you will act on your command is held in suspension for a moment or two if not longer; during this interval there will be one or more thoughts of bending your finger. But what happens when your finger first begins to bend? What of the actual thought associated with the actual movement? Can you truly tell whether the thought triggered the movement or the movement triggered the thought? Even if you shorten the command to "Now!," there are various response times to that word, suggesting the intervention of an additional guiding impulse. You can, of course, establish a strict, repetitive sequence of "Now!" (Bend finger), "Now!" (Bend finger) . . . , all of which have the same response time. But in such a strict, rhythmical sequence the additional impulse is either suppressed or subsumed by the rhythmical "Now!"s, whose even, metered repetition ceases to feel like an experience of willing an action. Not "Now!" (Bend finger), "Now!" (Bend finger) "Now!" (Bend finger) . . . so much as "Now!" (Bend finger), "Now!" (Bend finger),

"Now!" (Finger bends), "Now!" (Finger bends). . . . Only the first few movements, in which the response time to the "Now!" is being established, would feel actively willed. But, like all seemingly willed movements, whether or not the actual movement precedes or follows the precise conscious impulse to move is, from the evidence of introspection, ambiguous.

In a sense, this ambiguity could not be otherwise, since watching for the beginning of a willed moment is like watching for the green flag and the checkered flag to drop together. The green flag drops with the it's-*now*-going-to-happen conscious impulse to move, but it is only when the actual movement begins that the checkered flag—marking the transformation from the "condition of wish" to the "condition of will"—drops with it. Thus, while Libet's subjects *were* able to report a conscious initiating impulse after the readiness potential but before (0.2 seconds before) the movement began, they were also able to stop the movement *after* that conscious impulse. Thus, a moment of wishing a movement cannot be distinguished from a moment of willing a movement *until* the movement begins.

Whenever the subjects did abort an it's-*now*-going-to-happen impulse to move, the nonconscious readiness potential was still activated, even though "it looked different toward the end (as action approached) from when the action had been carried out."[9] But to his astonishment, Libet discovered that whether a movement was actualized or not the nonconscious process always began *before* (often a full second before) *any* conscious sense that the movement was being initiated. While the nonconscious readiness potential did not dictate that an action would follow, it always preceded any conscious sense of initiating an it's-*now*-happening movement. As Libet concluded: "Some neuronal activity associated with the eventual performance of the act has started well before any (recallable) conscious initiation or intervention is possible."[10]

This startling result (which has since been repeated by others)[11] comes as less of a surprise when we consider James's data for a psychology of volition. For, if we accept that the "willed" thought, like all thoughts, arises, that it is "somehow given" to consciousness, it follows that it may indeed have a formation of its own prior to the added-on sense of being our own personal thought. If we further accept that thought is, in itself, impulsive, then it may well be, as Libet's experiment suggests, that the initiation of even so-called voluntary movements begins "unconsciously."

To say that our actions begin unconsciously is to say one of two things: either (1) they are initiated by an un- (or sub- or pre-) conscious thought, or (2) they are initiated by no thought at all. If the latter interpretation of Libet's results is correct, then thoughts of making a movement do not initiate movements but merely attach themselves to a movement-in-progress as it passes into consciousness—like a rodeo cowboy jumping down on a horse as soon as it emerges from the corral.[12] But, given how smoothly and seamlessly the conscious intention to move fits with the movement itself, the former interpretation seems more plausible: that the unconscious neuronal activity of the readiness potential originates with some sort of un-, sub- or pre- conscious thought just before it surfaces into consciousness.

What it means for any thought to be sub- or pre- conscious has yet to be resolved. James did not believe that a thought could exist other than as conscious (*PP1*, 162–176). Thoughts *could* occur so "quickly and inattentively that no *memory* of them remains"—one moment "consciously there but the next instant forgotten"—but that is not the same as being subconscious (ibid., 165, 160). Since Freud, it has become customary to speak of sub- or unconscious thoughts as repressed conscious thoughts.[13] But as Sartre, among others, has pointed out, the notion of unconscious thoughts as repressed conscious thoughts raises the question of how someone can repress something that they are not conscious of.[14] Are unconscious thoughts *completely* unacknowledged or are they just infinitesimally fleeting, communicating in an ellipsis of a very few words or a partial image, our knowledge of them obscured by the reactions they trigger—one dim moment of consciousness lost in the glare of the next few brighter ones?

Just such an infinitesimally conscious thought may have passed unnoticed by Libet's subjects. At any rate, the onset of neuronal activity that was detected in their brains was clearly not initiated by an agent "I," since the sense of agency arose only after the initiating impulse began. Thus, when James, in his paradigm of how we will ourselves to get up out of bed, says "[W]e more often than not get up without any struggle or decision at all. We suddenly find that we *have* got up," he was anticipating Libet's results. Unlike May, Libet has perhaps discovered what went on in James's "fortunate lapse of consciousness."

FOUR

The Feeling of Effort

"This. . . . Teaching of yours is indeed wonderful . . .
but if one practices it what experiences will one have?"
One will experience the great and omnipresent Non-effort Root;
One will experience the Non-effort Path, the great transparency. . . .
—Milarepa

Effort is a distraction from what *is*.
—Krishnamurti, *The First and Last Freedom*

The two aspects of the will experience derived from James's will paradigm—thoughts arise, and thoughts themselves (subconscious or otherwise) initiate an action—both point to the same conclusion: what we believe to be acts of will are automatic reactions to stimuli of unascertainable origin. Yet despite the evidence of his own introspection, James did not abandon his belief in will. He granted that thoughts arose impersonally; he granted that thoughts themselves had impulsive power; but those two facts, for him, did not add up to the nonreality of free will. The moment of will, he believed, transpired somewhere in between: *after* the thought arises but *before* it has an effect. Such an in-between positioning is not as contrived as it might seem. Recall that the definition of free will that James had adopted (from Renouvier) in his youth had emphasized not the initiation of a thought but its *sustainment*. What James had declared "need not be the definition of an illusion" was "the sustaining of a thought *because I choose to* when I might have other thoughts." Twenty years later, when he had new reason to suspect that free will might be an illusion after all, this distinction between generating a thought and sustaining it loomed large for him:

> [E]ven though there be a mental spontaneity it can certainly not create ideas or summon them *ex abrupto*. Its power is limited to *selecting* amongst those . . . already introduced. If it can emphasize, reinforce, or protract for a second one of these it can do all that the most eager advocate of free will need demand. (*PP1*, 594)

James identified the power to "emphasize, reinforce, or protract" certain thoughts among those "introduced" to consciousness with "attention," finding there the mental spontaneity commonly associated with will. The question of will thus became, for him, not where thoughts come from, but *how much attention* is paid to them once they arise. Indeed, he declared, "Volition is nothing but attention" (ibid., 447).

James, of course, meant by attention something more than a particular focus at a particular moment, a focus that would hardly be distinguishable from consciousness. Rather, he meant something active (as is implied by attention's root meaning "to stretch toward"). It is the stretch toward (or what he calls the "strain of attention") for which James claimed the power of "*selecting* amongst" thoughts "already introduced" (*PP1*, 594). This position has been echoed by Benjamin Libet as well, who held that even though the nonconscious readiness potential occurs before the conscious thought to move, *another* thought to *block* the move can still prevent the movement from being actualized. "Processes associated with individual responsibility and free will," he writes, "would operate not to initiate a voluntary act but to select and control volitional outcomes."[1]

But to define free will as attention and selection is simply to give more discernible names to a still indiscernible process. For the ultimate source of the selection—attention's power to "emphasize, reinforce, or protract" one thought over another—is no less mysterious than the ultimate source of the thoughts themselves. To acknowledge attention's "mental spontaneity" is to acknowledge *its* ultimate freedom, but not, thereby, "mine." If "it thinks" is "stating the fact most simply and with the minimum of assumption" then so is "it sustains." Just as you cannot know the next thought that will arise, what "it thinks" will think, you cannot know how long any thought that does arise will stay. You can close your eyes and try to concentrate on the image of a full moon, but whether your attention holds that image easily, or whether the glow of the moon begins to fade, or whether thoughts and images gather, like clouds, in front of it, cannot be controlled. Once attention is engaged (by whatever means to whatever thought), there is no way to predict how long before it becomes disengaged. As Twain says: "The mind?—man has no control over it; it does as it pleases. It will take up a subject in spite of him; it will stick to it in spite of him; it will throw it aside in spite of him. It is entirely independent of him."[2] To paraphrase Ryle, one thing I cannot prepare myself for is *when* the next thought that I am going to think will appear. And despite James's dictum that "Volition is nothing but attention," even he allows that "attention *per se,* the *feeling* of attention, need no more fix and retain the ideas than it need bring them" (*PP1*, 450).

This is not to deny that attention, at times, rather than being part of a drifting thought process, feels like an active assertion of will against such drift. Nor is to deny the veto power (stressed by both James and Libet) that attention can have over any act-about-to-happen.[3] Instead of coming into consciousness as just another arising thought, a thought to attend, to *pay* attention,[4] seems to intervene against the whole arising thought process itself. But despite its effect of dispersing all other thoughts and images, a thought-to-attend is itself just another arising thought, following the same protocol as all other thoughts and feelings in being introduced to consciousness. On what grounds can we assert that a rebuking thought to "pay attention" is a stage director, controlling the on-stage action from offstage, rather than merely another on-stage actor, playing the role of a director, who makes an entrance and yells, "Cut"? Is there, in fact, anything in consciousness akin to such an offstage director, standing in a darkened house, watching all that takes place "before the footlights of consciousness" (*PP1*, 450)? (A permanent "witnessing consciousness," a witness with no emotional involvement or even identification with the various thoughts, feelings, and moods that parade in front of it, would, obviously, be no director at all.

Its perspective would be closer to the architect of the theater building who watches a rehearsal from the back of the house without any special interest or even curiosity in the proceedings.)

While the "stretching toward" "strain of attention" is real, what does this reality consist of? To begin with, the strain—anything from a barely conscious beat of focusing to a formal rebuke addressed to one*self*—is felt only when attention is a problem, either in starting up (amidst distractions) or in returning once it has "strayed." Only in such situations do we feel attention *as something distinct from consciousness*. In James's will paradigm, his attending to the thought to get up was a problem because it was juxtaposed with the thought to stay in bed. The two thoughts rotated. Nothing in his paradigm suggested otherwise than that the "strain of attention" he felt was a result of this juxtaposition rather than its own original force. The split or division in his consciousness was a division of *energy*, a "partial neutralization of the brain energy that would otherwise be available for fluent thought" (ibid., 451).[5] Rather than being an original force, the strain of attention, by this analysis, is nothing more than an effect on one thought of a contrary ("inhibitory") thought (or thoughts) "pulling back." What can *feel* like an original force, such as the surge of will-force that James felt in the "lucky instant" when he got out of bed, would be no more than the release of energy from the blocking thought, to stay in bed, into the original thought, to get up. In cases of "antagonistic thoughts," says James, "[w]hen the blocking is released, we feel as if an inward spring were let loose, and this is the additional impulse or *fiat* upon which the act effectively succeeds" (*PP2*, 527).

At the end of his chapter on Will, James, in what threatens to be the start of an infinite regress, writes "that although attention is the first and fundamental thing in volition, *express consent to the reality of what is attended to* is often an additional and quite distinct phenomenon involved" (ibid., 568).[6] James does not define what this "additional phenomenon" is, and "freely confesses" that he is "impotent" to do so (*PP2*, 568). Rather, it is an "experience *sui generis* . . . which we can translate into no simpler terms" (*PP2*, 568–569). Presumably, this experience had already been translated into simplest terms by his paradigm of the will experience and the commentary that followed. His last-minute aside on the concept "express consent" has more, perhaps, to say about his resistance to the implications of that discussion than to a deepened understanding of it.[7]

By the evidence of introspection alone, neither attention nor "express consent to the reality of what is attended to" can be proven to be an active, original force. Nothing in direct experience refutes the passive model of attention, subscribed to by many of James's contemporaries, especially his esteemed colleague F. H. Bradley, who wrote: "Active attention is not primary, either as being there from the first or as supervening, but is a derivative product."[8] James himself in one of his most poetic passages, evoking, again, a stream metaphor, expressed the passive model this way:

> The stream of our thought is like a river. On the whole easy simple flowing predominates in it, the drift of things is with the pull of gravity, and effortless attention is the rule. But at intervals an obstruction, a set-back, a log-jam occurs, stops the current, creates an eddy, and makes them temporarily move the other way. If a real river could feel, it would feel these eddies and set-backs as places of effort. "I am here flowing," it would say, "in the direction of greatest resistance, instead of flowing, as usual, in the direction of least. My effort is what enables me to perform this feat." Really, the effort would only be a passive index that the feat was being performed. The agent would all the while be the total downward drift of the rest of the water, forcing *some* of it upwards in this spot; and although, *on the average*, the direction of least resistance is downwards, that would be no reason for its not being upwards now and then. Just so with our voluntary acts of attention. They are momentary arrests, coupled with a peculiar feeling, of portions of the stream. But the arresting force, instead of being this peculiar feeling itself, may be nothing but the processes by which the collision is produced. (*PP1*, 452)

James offers this striking passive model of attention early on in the *Principles*, in his chapter on Attention. He acknowledges such a model to be "a clear, strong, well-equipped conception . . . fitted to carry conviction" (ibid.). Nonetheless, he states his bias against it, in words recalling the crisis of will he suffered in his youth:

> [T]he whole drama of the voluntary life hinges on the amount of attention, slightly more or slightly less, which rival motor ideas may receive. But the whole feeling of reality, the whole sting and excitement of our voluntary life, depends on our sense that in it things are *really being decided* from one moment to another, and that it is not the dull rattling off of a chain that was forged innumerable ages ago. This appearance, which makes life and history tingle with such a tragic zest, *may* not be an illusion. (Ibid., 453)

Such a statement is, of course, less an argument than a plea. By itself—and James offers no other refutation in his chapter on Attention—this plea for the "excitement of our voluntary life" is hardly "fitted to carry conviction." James himself acknowledges this by stating that his reason for rejecting the passive model of attention is "ethical," and, as such, "hardly suited for introduction into a psychological work" (ibid., 454). Moreover, when James returns to a consideration of attention in his later chapter on Will, he is unable to "equip" an active model. On the contrary, his own paradigm, as well as his other introspective evidence, served instead to equip the already "well-equipped" passive model.

His paradigm uncovered no active control of "the amount of attention, slightly more or slightly less" which the "rival ideas received," but rather a passive witnessing of a neutral process: "[R]esolution [not, in this meticulous introspection, "my" or "our". resolution] faints away and postpones itself again and again just as it seemed on the verge of bursting the resistance and passing over into the decisive act" (*PP2*, 524). His rendering of an impersonal, non-"I"-controlled resolution conforms to his overall sense of the impersonal, arising nature of thoughts. In his paradigm, two conflicting thoughts (or sets of thoughts), defined in relation to each other as resolve and resistance to resolve, battled for predominance like a dogfight in the sky watched by consciousness on the ground below. The dogfight ended when one side dropped out long enough so that the other side, no longer neutralized, "exerted its effects" (ibid., 525).[9] "A mind," says James, "is a system of ideas, each with the excitement it arouses, and with tendencies impulsive and inhibitive, which mutually check or reinforce one another" (*VRE*, 184).

Nothing in James's paradigm suggested that the predominance in consciousness of one thought over another was *generated* by a power of attention;

rather, the predominance in consciousness was *itself* the attention. The first Western psychiatrist trained in Zen meditation, Dr. Hubert Benoit, confirmed this essential aspect of James's paradigm. Calling will an "illusory notion," Benoit, too, could find no "I" *influencing* the battle between resolve and resistance to resolve, no "special inner power . . . exercising a kind of police supervision" over feelings and thoughts.[10] If, for example, I fail to stick to a diet, I might say, "My greed was stronger than I was," but all that can be substantiated, says Benoit, is, "My greed was stronger than my wish to be beautiful."[11] To say otherwise, to suggest that there is some power of attention that proceeds from an "I," conveys, as Bradley says, nothing that can be found "in fact."[12] James all but concedes as much when, at the end of his chapter on Will, he states that "for scientific purposes" one need not give up the view whereby the identification of effort and resistance with our *self* "is an illusion and a trick of speech" (*PP2*, 576).

Schopenhauer, in an amusing illustration, depicts the illusion this way:

> [L]et us imagine a man who, while standing on the street, would say to himself: "It is six o'clock in the evening, the working day is over. Now I can go for a walk, or I can go to the club; I can also climb up the tower to see the sun set; I can go to the theater; I can visit this friend or that one; indeed, I also can run out of the gate, into the wide world, and never return. All of this is strictly up to me, in this I have complete freedom. But still I shall do none of these things now, but with just as free a will I shall go home to my wife." This is exactly as if water spoke to itself: "I can make high waves (yes! in the sea during a storm), I can rush down hill (yes! in the river bed), I can plunge down foaming and gushing (yes! in the waterfall), I can rise freely as a stream of water into the air (yes! in the fountain), I can, finally, boil away and disappear (yes! at a certain temperature); but I am doing none of these things now, and am voluntarily remaining quiet and clear water in the reflecting pond.[13]

Even Buddhists, who deny the existence, and *thereby* the agency, of an "I," can fall prey to this illusion and trick of speech when they urge us to "get control of our minds." Good advice, to be sure. But the advice is ever available while the impulses to take the advice are not. When and how are the impulses to take or resist good advice realized? Both the Buddha and James, as we shall see, shared the insight that whatever motivates the taking and resisting, it is not an "I." Indeed, the deeper that James probed into the nature of the "I" the closer he came to the Buddha's key insight: not only does the "I" not create the welcoming and opposing tendencies of the mind; the welcoming and opposing tendencies of the mind create the "I."

MAKING AN EFFORT: PHYSICAL EXERTION

All of us, to be sure, have moments, even extended moments, when we feel that not only our feelings and thoughts but even our actions are being transmitted through us rather than being generated by us. Dancing can feel this way, as can any improvised activity, such as doodling, or playing a hand drum. At such times, our movements feel like nothing more than reactions to arising stimuli not of our own making; in a word, they feel effortless. The deeper we "lose ourselves" in these activities, the less we experience anything resembling effort and will. Yet no one—besides, perhaps, an enlightened Tai Chi master—routinely lives in such a state. Whatever obscures the absolute beginning of the emergence of a thought, whatever significance one gives to the "lapse of consciousness" that precedes a decision, even granting that a decision has no more epistemological status than an arising stimulus, what of the emphatic feelings of making an active physical effort? Mental exertion is one thing, but what of physical exertion? Can it, too, like the feeling of resolve that initiates some actions, be construed as a derivative product?

Before attempting to answer, we need to distinguish between the words *effort* and *will.* While both words are used to describe the active feeling of influencing a goal ("It takes will," "It takes effort"), only *effort* is used to describe the passive sensation of struggling with the goal ("What an effort this is"). Moreover, this passive meaning of effort is never completely absent from the active meaning. If I say, "It's going to be an effort," I mean both that I am going to have to make an effort and that I am going to *feel the sensation of struggle* when I do. Even in the command, "Make an effort!," the meaning of the word *effort* is blurred by its two usages. "Make an effort!" means, for the most part, to actively make an effort, but it carries, at the same time, the passive sense: "Put yourself in a situation whereby you will experience struggle."

The word *will*, by contrast, both as noun and verb, has no dual meaning or even ambiguity. It has only an active sense. Yet curiously, if not significantly, the word is seldom unambiguously active in its usage. Zeus wills, and the universe responds as if it were a well-tuned Porsche he was driving;[14] we, however, despite the instantaneously impulsive power of a thought, do not, in our language, acknowledge such a direct relationship to our will (whatever we believe it to be). Unlike Zeus, we don't will, we *use* will, suggesting assistance or collaboration, as in the phrase "Use public transportation." Our avoidance of the verb *to will* in depicting our everyday experience, in favor of the less clearly active phrases, "Make an effort" and "Use your will," may, in fact, be a clue to the ultimate nature of will and effort.[15]

Returning to our first act of the day, we can see that, barring illness or injury, the physical effort of getting out of bed is negligible. Yet despite this negligible physical effort, we often find ourselves crawling out of bed as if we woke up on Jupiter with extra gravity to contend with. Sometimes we seem to be fighting physical grogginess, but other times we seem to be fighting nothing more than our own inner reluctance, as in James's paradigm. When this reluctance to move is experienced with the movement itself, the movement becomes an effort. The effort is not the feeling of energy going into the movement upward; nor is it the feeling of energy being siphoned away. Rather, it is both together—the feeling of the energy moving upward *as* it is being siphoned away. It is trying to drive a car with one foot on the accelerator and the other on the brake. Accelerating does not feel like effort, nor does braking—only accelerating *while* braking.

If we leap out of bed because we smell the coffee brewing, or hear the doorbell ringing, or see a fresh field of snow outside our window, we are accelerating without braking. But as long as the contradictory thought of staying in bed is present, and our consciousness is *split* between two courses of action, each one "neutralizing" the "fluent thought" of the other, we may not be able to move at all. When ideas, says James, "*do not* result in action . . . in every . . . case, without exception . . . it is because other ideas simultaneously rob them of their impulsive power" (*PP2*, 525). With a simple experiment, James illustrates how this robbery takes place:

> Try to feel as if you were crooking your finger, whilst keeping it straight. In a minute it will fairly tingle with the imaginary change of position; yet it will not sensibly move, because *its not really moving* is also a part of what you have in mind. Drop *this* idea, think of the movement purely and simply, with all brakes off; and presto! it takes place with no effort at all. (Ibid., 527)

The dynamic of making a physical effort can thus be explained in the same impersonal terms as the dynamic of making a decision, *with the addition of the thought's impulsive power*. The commonplace belief that effort is some sort of a *personal* force comes from confusing the feeling of effort with the efficacy of effort. There is abundant evidence that thoughts alone effect changes in the brain. Pianists, for example, who only *mentally* rehearse the notes they are about to play have been shown to effect the same changes in their motor cortex as when they *actually* play the notes.[16] Such force of thoughts is indeed a neuroplastic "mental force," but it is not to be confused with the *feeling* of force. Even the most dramatic demonstration of a mental force, such as an obsessive/compulsive's victory over the messages launched in conjunction with impaired brain metabolism,[17] fit into James's impersonal paradigm of will.

James, as we saw, got up "without any struggle . . . at all" since "the moment . . . [the] . . . inhibitory ideas ceased, the original idea exerted its effects" (*PP2*, 524–525). But *had* he struggled, his active physical effort could still be interpreted as "a passive index that the feat was being performed." Just as the thought of staying in bed, if it arises immediately after the thought of getting up, can check the thought's initial impulsive power, so can it check the surge of energy that has begun to lift one upward, if it arises just after the movement has begun. If the thought of staying in bed (or any image or variation of this thought) remains before the "footlights of consciousness" long enough, it can trigger an impulse that brings the upward movement-in-progress to a complete standstill. If it does not stay before the footlights of consciousness long enough, then the impulse it triggers will siphon off only *some* of the upward moving energy. It is at this point that continuing out of bed is felt to be a struggle; the feeling of effort has arisen.

SUSTAINED EFFORT

Assuming, at the first feeling of (passive) effort, that you do not respond by "giving up," relaxing the physical muscular contraction producing the movement, what can be said about the feeling of (active) effort by which you seem to persevere? Such sustained (active) effort is, perhaps, easier to reflect upon in relation to an outside force. James, in going from a mental "period of struggle," when he is lying in bed with conflicting thoughts, to a physical movement made "without any struggle," seems to have bypassed the experience of overcoming external pressure. After all, it wasn't the cold *itself* that kept James from getting out of bed, but only his attitude toward that cold. What if, it may be asked, someone had tied James's arms and legs to the bed while he was asleep? His struggle, then, would not have been with the inhibitory power of an internal thought, but rather the restraining force of ropes.

James himself did not give an example of using will and effort against an outside force. He didn't need to. The dynamic of effort and will remains the same whether the obstacle is internal (such as a feeling of reluctance) or external (such as a rope). Whether the restraint is internal or external, the feeling of will and effort (rather than the sensation of mere muscular exertion) can always be explained as the interplay between contradictory ideas or images. An outside restraining force adds no essentially new information to the psychology of volition.

To illustrate, say you awoke one morning to find your arms and legs tied. Undoubtedly your first reaction would be to tug at the ropes. The contraction of your muscles notwithstanding, this first physical response would not be experienced as will or effort. It would feel, rather, like a reflex: an instantaneous reaction to the repugnant feeling of being bound. You would, at first, have had no idea of the actual degree of your bondage, or whether the ropes were even tied to anything else. It would only be after the initial tug, if it did not free you, that a moment of assessment would take place. This assessment would include both the fact of the actual restraint ("Hey, I really am tied down!") and your preliminary estimation of its force. Immediately following this assessment, two thoughts flash by in alternating succession so quickly as to be a whirl: an image of your (objectified) self as bound and an image of your (objectified) self as unbound. Neither of these arising thoughts would be witnessed in detachment, not even the relative detachment in which James witnessed the alternating thoughts of getting up or staying in bed. They would be experienced, rather, with an explosive emotional force. There would not be, as in James's paradigm, a tennis-like volley between two contrasting options. The repugnant thought of your present bound self and the liberating thought of your future unbound self, far from being opposed to each other are, instead, complementary. The energy of one feeds into, rather than siphons off, the energy of the other. Instead of a volley back and forth there is a single smash stroke—the thought to break free—which, without any other mediation, produces a second, intensified physical response.

This second physical response, however, though intensified, would not necessarily feel like active effort. The increased muscle contraction would not feel like active effort unless the ropes offered more resistance than anticipated. For the feeling of active effort is not a function of the muscle force being applied, but of the resistance being overcome. The feeling of active physical effort only arises in conjunction with the feeling of passive physical effort, of struggle—here, the realization (however slight) that the muscle force required to complete the movement has been *underestimated.* Without a moment of *contradicted assessment,* in which your movement would be experienced as a struggle, the force being applied would not be experienced as a force of will.[18]

In the absence of such contradicted assessment (or any other contradictory thought), your movement would not feel like effort, but like an easeful, flowing motion, even a motion assisted by an outside force—such as walking with the wind at your back. If, for instance, after your initial tug, the ropes had, unbeknownst to you, come unhitched, your next use of muscle force would not feel like active effort or a force of will; it would not, in fact, feel like you *were doing* anything at all. Your arms would simply fly up over your head as if by magic. This magical sense of ease would accompany the movement even though your muscle contraction would have been the same as if you had, in actuality, been bound. Likewise, a strong sustained pull that instantly began to loosen the ropes, so that less muscle force was required with each succeeding moment of the tugging, would feel less like a force of will than would a far weaker tug that produced no immediate effect, and required more muscle force in each succeeding moment of the tugging.

THE FLICKERING REALITY OF EFFORT

Assuming that you do not let your arms drop back down at the first indication that you have underestimated the force required to break free, but instead increase the muscle force, such increase would clearly be a continuation of one sustained force. Yet the same cannot be said of the feeling of physical effort (active and passive) that accompanies it. For the feeling of physical effort is always repeated at intervals, however close together those intervals may be so as to seem like one sustained feeling. Unlike the muscle force, the feeling of effort flickers into consciousness with each assessment that the muscle force being applied is inadequate. Try any sustained muscular exertion and you will see that a continuous, unbroken feeling of effort does not exist.

But even a flickering feeling of effort is effort. And the feeling of adding some "oomph" to an action is, like the experience of making a choice, so prevalent that it is seldom isolated for observation, let alone introspection. Nonetheless, any feeling of active effort can be explained in the same impersonal terms as the feeling of will: a unification of brain energy that had been divided—a flowing into one thought of energy that had been divided between two thoughts. As James reluctantly conceded, "The feeling of effort" ["effort" in the sense of "making" an effort, but also, as always, with the passive sense of "undergoing" effort not entirely removed] may indeed be nothing more than "an inert accompaniment and not the active element which it seems" (*PP1*, 452). No one, James believed, could ever prove that a feeling of effort was an "original force": "No measurements are as yet performed (it is safe to say none ever will be performed) which can show that it *contributes* energy to the result" (ibid.; emphasis added).[19]

FIVE

Free Will and Indeterminism

Having found no evidence for free will, James declared that the free will controversy was "insoluble on strictly psychologic grounds" (*PP2*, 572). This was not exactly an admission of defeat, since James believed that there was no psychological proof of determinism either. No psychological evidence, introspective or otherwise, suggests that there is an automatic "push of the past" onto the present. Our actions, before they are made, are "ambiguous or unpredestinate," in a word, "indeterminate" (ibid., 571).

But while James claimed that in "common parlance" indeterminism was the equivalent of saying "*our wills are free*," he himself knew better (ibid.). That no external or internal stimulus commands a predictable sway over attention does not substantiate free will. To accept attention (active or passive) as "an independent 'variable'" is to acknowledge only a radical ignorance concerning it (ibid.). On strictly psychological grounds (as opposed to "ethical" grounds James deemed ill-suited for a psychological work) the "question of *fact* in the free-will controversy" is neither free will nor determinism (*PP1*, 454; *PP2*, 571; emphasis added). It is indeterminism. However much belief in free will gives "the *palpitating* reality to our moral life," or gives the sense that "soul-trying moments" are "decided nowhere else than *here* and *now*," it gives nothing confirmable (*WB*, 594; emphasis added).

But if indeterminism was less than free will, it was more than enough to challenge the physical determinism that dominated psychology in James's lifetime. “Many persons now-a-days,” he wrote in 1878, “seem to think that any conclusion must be very scientific if the arguments in favor of it are all derived from twitching of frog’s legs—especially if the frogs are decapitated—and that, on the other hand, any doctrine chiefly vouched for by the feelings of human beings—with heads on their shoulders—must be benighted and superstitious” (*ML*, 29). For a strict physical determinist, the first determinant of a behavioral response—the originating impulse of the universe—might be unknowable, but the last determinants (the most recent) were believed to be detectable by laboratory experiments.

While James’s endorsement of indeterminism was not an endorsement of free will, it did challenge the dogma of his day (as well as our own) that every action is ultimately determined by material or mechanistic forces. James’s indeterminism was even lying in wait for how determinism evolved soon after his time, through the work of a Russian physiologist and a Viennese psychologist. In the early part of the twentieth century, Pavlov and Freud promoted the belief that behavioral responses are as determinable as physiological ones. In a sense these two, essentially nineteenth-century, theoreticians put the head back on the frog. Nothing in their work refuted the will’s ultimate indeterminacy, or James’s paradigm of how choices are made; but they have supplied the modern imagination with paradigms of their own. Indeed, the names of both men have mutated into deterministic adjectives denoting determined responses. Before moving from James’s indeterminism to a consideration of what we shall call mystical determinism, let us take a quick look at these paradigms, as their common misconstrual still shapes responses to what *any* form of human determinism might mean.

PAVLOV

The belief that human behavior can be explained by physiological responses and that the last (triggering) stimulus to such responses can be isolated has survived to this day through Pavlov’s famous experiments with dogs. After winning a Nobel Prize in 1904 for showing how the secretion of digestive juices in the stomach and pancreas was controlled by the nervous system, Pavlov conducted experiments with digestive juices whose secretion was more conscious—saliva. His famous experiment has so profoundly penetrated our imagination that any consideration of a determined universe readily conjures up the pathetic image of those wired dogs responding with an obedience beyond anything learnable in training school.

The first thing to be said about this image is that it is false. There was, in fact, nothing in Pavlov's experiment that established a deterministic model of behavior. Pavlov demonstrated that just as a hungry dog salivates when given food, it salivates when it *expects* to be given food. His experiment did not, as is commonly believed, establish the existence of conditioned responses. It established only that a dog could learn to associate one event with another. It did not prove a dog's susceptibility to be controlled, but rather its capacity to learn, notwithstanding that the proof of the learning was manifested by a nonconsciously triggered process. The dog did not simply salivate at the sound of the bell. The dog salivated because of what it had *learned* about the bell; after a while, if no food followed the sound of the bell, the dog stopped salivating altogether when the bell rang. That is, the dog could unlearn or disassociate from the stimulus. Its response was thus not fixedly but *provisionally* conditioned, based on experience. "Conditioned response," in fact, with its mechanistic connotation, was not Pavlov's term. "Condition*al* response," with its looser connotation, was what he actually wrote, but it was mistranslated from the original Russian.[1]

This mistranslation, which prevails to this day, has helped to preserve the mistaken conclusion that Pavlov proved the existence of a strictly determined relationship. He did nothing of the sort. The closest thing to a strictly determined response is the *instinctual* response Pavlov *assumed*—namely, that a hungry dog salivates when it believes it is about to be fed. Pavlov did not seek to prove the existence of this response; he accepted it as his starting point only, and then went on to use it in conjunction with a learned, provisional response. The condition*al* association of a bell with food was conjoined with an instinctual response of salivating at the expectation of food. Clearly, the learned, provisional response *triggered* the instinctual response, but it did so without losing its own identity as learned, provisional, conditional.

If Pavlov had wanted to use his sophisticated saliva extraction and measuring equipment to prove that hungry dogs *always* salivate at the near prospect of being fed, that it is an invariable law of nature, both fixedly determined and absolutely determinable, he would have had to experiment with a variety of conditions. He might, for instance, have tested whether dogs "automatically" salivated at the sight of food when they believed their pups were in imminent danger. And while Pavlov never experimented with humans, it would have been interesting to see how an Indian Yogi, or, perhaps, anyone challenged to overturn Pavlov's premise, might have measured up. As it is, despite the popular misconception engendered by Pavlov's experiment, no one has, in fact, ever proven that instinctual responses are fixedly determined.

Nor would it argue against indeterminism or free will if someone did. For no matter how strictly determined instinctual responses prove to be, they do not inform the debate of whether all our actions are ultimately determined or not. Instinctual responses were never at issue. An animal (human or otherwise) can manifest instinctual responses sometimes and indetermined responses at other times. And, as Pavlov's experiment demonstrates, a less determined (provisional) response can also be conjoined with (yet not subsumed by) a more determined (instinctual) response in one sequence. But the mere fact of instinctual responses, or habitual responses, does not rule out indeterminism. Instincts, habits, and indetermined responses coexist compatibly.

In moving beyond a demonstration of how digestive juices are triggered nonconsciously, to a demonstration of how digestive juices are triggered by a learned response, Pavlov seemed to be ushering nineteenth-century material determinism into the realm of behavior. Such a perception, as we have tried to show, is misleading. A bell rang and a dog salivated—not proof of a fixedly determined response, but close enough and haunting enough to repel us from considering any kind of determinism as an explanation for human behavior.

FREUD

At the same time that Pavlov's experiments were misleading us to wonder whether human behavior was anything more than strictly determined effects, his contemporary Freud was trying to prove that strictly determined effects could stretch over many years. While the determinism in Pavlov's work may have been overestimated, the determinism of Freud has been underestimated. Like a true, unabashed, nineteenth-century determinist Freud *openly* disavowed a belief in free will: "[F]aith in undetermined psychical events and in free will," he wrote, "is quite unscientific and must yield to the demand of a determinism whose rule extends over mental life."[2] For Freud, this determinism ruled from the nether world of the unconscious.

It was not a new idea. That unconscious forces dominated, if not determined, conscious life had become part of the zeitgeist of Europe well before Freud. The rage, in fact, of the Berlin salons in 1870 was a thousand-page tome by Eduard von Hartmann entitled *Philosophy of the Unconscious*, detailing this domination. But it was Freud who first promoted the idea that *any* moment in the present could be traced backwards, often very far backwards, to a moment in the past that determined it. It was one thing to suggest that conscious life was rooted in unconscious life. It was another thing to suggest that the root system could be completely exposed.

As it turned out, faith in free will did not yield, not even among Freudians. The faith that early childhood experiences unconsciously controlled adult behavior did not "demand" a belief in absolute determinism. And by the middle of the twentieth century it wasn't determinism so much as Freudianism whose rule extended over mental life, and culture at large.

Nonetheless, blended with our image of Pavlov's dogs, Freud's dramatic (if disputable) evidence linking early childhood experiences to subsequent adult behavior continues to distort how human determinism is perceived. Like Pavlov's bell, the behavioral determinants that Freud discovered were so distinct they were taken for uncaused or *absolute* first causes, separated, themselves, from other determinants. (This illusion of uncaused first causes was heightened by the unspoken assumption of psychoanalysis that dysfunctional behavior is an aberration in the vast, normal course of the universe.)

Since Freud himself was a strict determinist who did not believe in free will, he could hardly acknowledge the existence of any such absolute beginning causes in human behavior. It wasn't only dysfunctional behavior, after all, that Freud believed was determined, but *all* behavior. While the determinants he identified were distinct, distinction does not, in itself, entail separation. The antecedents he discovered to be strictly determining human behavior were themselves, he believed, strictly determined by antecedents of their own.

But by omitting to emphasize his belief in the nonreality of free will, Freud sometimes gave the appearance of having discovered a closed system of determined interactions. This is especially noticeable in his account of free association. Freud was certain that there was no such thing as the spontaneous generation of a thought, and used experiments conducted in so-called free association to prove it: "The association to *numbers* chosen at random are perhaps the most convincing" (he told a roomful of psychologists in his *Introductory Lectures on Psychoanalysis*); "they run off so quickly and proceed with such incredible certainty to a hidden goal that the effect is really staggering."[3] But if, as Freud concluded, someone cannot say a number completely at random "which does not turn out to be closely determined by the immediate circumstances, the characteristics of the subject of the experiment and his situation at the moment,"[4] then one cannot *ask* someone to say a number without that *request* being determined as well. If free association is strictly determined then *every* human response at every moment must be determined. Freud seldom shared this point in his strictly psychological writings, but he believed it nonetheless.

Given his focus on uncovering hitherto unknown determinants to human behavior, Freud's neglecting to remind his readers that whatever determinants he had found must have determinants of their own is understandable. It is possible, however, that Freud was so struck by what he uncovered that he *did* believe, at times, that he had established the existence of absolute beginning causes in human behavior, themselves uncaused. A belief in absolute beginnings poses little problem for those who believe in free will; many moments could be viewed by them as absolute beginnings, coming out of a void. But for a strict determinist such as Freud, to posit an absolute beginning would be tantamount to positing the existence of God, in the Aristotelian sense of an "unmoved mover." Much has been written about how Freudian psychoanalysis has become a modern religion, and perhaps Freud himself believed it – not just metaphorically, but literally.[5]

While we may not know the extent to which Freud viewed his psychological determinism as a religion, we do know that he fervently believed in it as a science. James, who met him in 1909, found him "a man obsessed by fixed ideas" (C9, 334). And indeed, for the rest of his life, Freud never stopped trying to prove that human behavior was as reducible to laws of interaction as matter. But his efforts failed. The linkages he was attempting to make between past experiences and present behavior resisted strict verification. At times Freud complained of the "gross injustice" that psychoanalysis was being held to a higher standard of completeness than other sciences. But by the end of his life he was more conciliatory. Although still insisting that behavioral interactions were as determined as material interactions, he wrote, in 1938, that it would be "entirely in accordance with our expectations if the basic concepts and principles of the new science (instinct, nervous energy, etc.) remain for a considerable time no less indeterminate than those of the older sciences (force, mass, attraction, etc.)."[6]

Almost a century later, the now not-so-new science still remains indeterminate, with some concluding it is more an art form than anything else.[7] Yet even if Freud failed to establish a science, he established a belief: specific behavior in the present is determined by specific, isolatable experiences in the past. It makes little difference that this strict form of determinism resists verification. The possibility that every step forward is no more than a push from behind was made to seem real.

INDETERMINISM

In contrast to the physical determinists of his day, and some later interpreters of Pavlov and Freud, James never lost sight of the fact that whether or not our behavioral responses were ultimately determined (an open question to him on "strictly psychological grounds"), they were not ultimately determin*able*. No psychologist has done more than James to cut through the confusion between the two terms—preserving the possibility of "determined" while undermining the reality of "determinable." Fifty years after James's death, Harvard psychologist Gordon Allport, noting the excesses of deterministic theories in his own time, wrote: "[N]ow that we have recovered from the irreverent shocks administered by Freud, Pavlov, Watson, we begin to perceive that the psychological insights of James have the steadiness of a polar star."[8]

In a sense, James had done for psychology what scientists were soon to do for physics. We now know that matter is energy. Far from the stable substrate of nineteenth-century science, matter has been discovered to be an indeterminable play of subatomic particles. This discovery, the foundation of quantum physics, seems to undermine determinism and, as formulated in Heisenberg's Uncertainty Principle, is often cited in arguments for free will. But quantum physics does not claim that material reality is undetermined. It claims only that it is undetermined *for us*—at the deepest level we can observe it; we cannot even measure the never-completely-at-rest subatomic particles with precision, let alone predict their movement or influence on other particles.[9] There is no evidence that a "push of the past" necessarily influences the movement of subatomic particles any more than it necessarily influences human choice. Nothing at the subatomic level can be proved to be determining anything else. As Fritjof Capra says, "The concept of force is no longer useful in subatomic physics."[10]

James, perhaps more than anyone, rendered the concept of force in the generation of thoughts suspect. And given the complementary nature of the generation of a thought and the generation of a subatomic event, it comes as no surprise that physicists of indeterminism, from Bohr to Henry Stapp, have found James, in Bohr's words, "most wonderful."[11] Indeed, Stapp, Heisenberg's student, *repeatedly* invoked James's indeterminism to support his claim that while our thoughts may be "*entwined* with microphysical . . . elements, they are not completely reducible to them."[12] Subatomic physics, then, has caught up with James's realization that all our thoughts arise, if not out of nowhere, then at least out of no verifiable somewhere. For such radical ignorance of the origin of our thoughts correlates well with our radical ignorance of the origin of subatomic particles:

> The distinction between matter and empty space finally had to be abandoned when it became evident that virtual particles can come into being spontaneously out of the void, without any nucleon or other strongly interacting particle being present. . . . The vacuum is far from empty. On the contrary, it contains an unlimited number of particles which come into being and vanish without end.[13]

That "particles can come into being spontaneously out of the void" may be more than analogous to James's belief in the impersonal nature of the thought process and his discovery of the gap that precedes a so-called deciding thought. Attempts, however, to link the spontaneous indeterminacies of subatomic physics to the indeterminacies of the thought process are doomed from the start.[14] There is no way to causally link two indeterminate processes without compromising the indeterminacy of one of them. A coincidence of indeterminacies is the most you could hope to prove, but prove how? As the philosopher Richard Double put it: "The question of why quantum indeterminacies should occur just when we manifest libertarian free will strikes me as unanswerable."[15]

MYSTICAL DETERMINISM

> Everything is determined, the beginning as well as the end, by forces over which we have no control. It is determined for the insect, as well as for the star. Human beings, vegetables, or cosmic dust, we all dance to a mysterious tune, intoned in the distance by an invisible piper.
>
> —Albert Einstein

That the emergence and disappearance of subatomic particles is not strictly determinable, or that we cannot fix with certainty either what our next thought will be, or the amount of attention that we will bring to it, does not rule out the possibility that all activity—from the movement of electrons to the movement of thoughts—may be part of a larger determined process. Indeterminism thus leaves the door open for the mixture of radical ignorance and faith found in the writing of many mystics. As far back as the sixth century BC, Lao Tzu wrote:

> The surest test if a man be sane
> Is if he accepts life whole, as it is,
> Without needing by measure or touch to understand
> The measureless untouchable source
> Of its images,
> The measureless untouchable source
> Of its substances,
> The source which, while it appears dark emptiness,
> Brims with a quick force
> Farthest away
> And yet nearest at hand
> From oldest time unto this day,

Charging its images with origin:
What more need I know of the origin
Than this?[16]

Belief in an infinite and undefined, but nonetheless determined, process might be called mystical determinism. Mystical determinism is compatible with indeterminism insofar as it disclaims knowledge of the origin of human responses. In contrast with all other forms of determinism, mystical determinism denies that a reason can be found for why any interaction *had* to take place. If a boy throws a rock through a baker's window, determinists might say that he was hungry, or angry at his parents, or, if he had done it in Paris at the end of the eighteenth century, that he was taking one of the last steps in a world democratic dialectical process that began in the ancient world—depending on whether they subscribed to physiological, psychological, or historical determinism. But no matter how much causal evidence is brought to bear, from the standpoint of mystical determinism any connections would remain tentative at best—subunits of an overall determined (yet ultimately incomprehensible) process.

Whereas religious, eschatological determinism sees historical events as divinely plotted, mystical determinism sees historical events as tentative jigsaw puzzle pieces on a mutable board; in the absence of a knowable design, the shape of the pieces, and how they cluster together—that is, one's interpretation of past events—keeps changing. As James himself observes, any given "*this*" that you "think you are doing" can well be a "doing something of which you do not dream. . . . For instance, you think you are but drinking this glass; but you are really creating the liver-cirrhosis that will end your days" (*EA*, 804–805).

No religious script can circumscribe mystical determinism, which allows for the existence of a spiritual force, but not how it came into existence, where it is going, or why.[17] Mystical determinism asks, with Kant, about origin: "What authority have you for inventing an absolutely first state of the world, and therefore an absolute beginning of the ever flowing series of appearances, and so of procuring a resting place for your imagination by setting bounds to limitless nature?"[18] Mystical determinism declares, with Benjamin Paul Blood, the nineteenth-century American mystic who profoundly influenced James,[19] the same futility for those who would rest their imagination on a "last point": "There can be no purpose of eternity. It is process all. The most sublime result, if it appeared as the ultimatum, would go stale in an hour—it could not be endured."[20] And, mystical determinism denies, with Nietzsche, any resting place for the imagination in between:

> One is necessary, one is a piece of fatefulness, one belongs to the whole, one is in the whole; there is nothing which could judge, measure, compare or sentence our being, for that would mean judging, measuring, comparing, or sentencing the whole. But there is nothing beside the whole.[21]

Mystical determinism also challenges James's characterization of determinism as a "dull rattling off of a chain that was forged innumerable ages ago." For if no beginning or end of the chain can be discerned, and our sense of the links—the past, present, and future—is always changing, what sense of being chained remains? It is more like riding a snake. Or perhaps we might say that the chain exists but not the rattling. As a contemporary mystical determinist, Stephen Hawking, put it: "Is everything determined? The answer is yes, it is. But it might as well not be, because we can never know what is determined."[22]

WALKING BACKWARDS TOWARD THE FUTURE

> We live forwards . . . but we understand backwards.
>
> —James, quoting Kierkegaard

Hawking's formulation of an indeterminable determinism is not new to Western thought. The Ancient Greeks, who put the power of Fate above that of Zeus himself, acknowledged, at the same time, our own *un*predestinate perspective in their metaphor for how we move toward the future. We do not, they believed, move forward into the future, as if crossing through a vast field laid out before us. We cannot move forward into the future since we cannot know what the next moment will be until *after* it has occurred. The only way to move into the future is backward, as if sitting in the back of a moving boat, looking out over the wake, seeing the next moment only after we have passed through it. Even a so-called act of precognition, a purported glimpse of a future event, much believed in by the Greeks, can be confirmed as such only after the event has passed. You can believe that such an image will occur, but it is a delusion to believe that it *must* occur, that it is inevitable.[23]

Walking backwards toward the future, with our eyes facing in the opposite direction from which we are moving, we can stare far into what has already passed, lining up recent past events with distant past events for the greater clarification of both; we just can't turn around. All events, no matter how pre*imagined*, are unfore*seen*. Likewise with *any* expectation. All expectations, all plans, are merely conceptions in the *present*. We cannot move toward them as if all that stood between us and their realization were empty space.

Far from being an outmoded curiosity of the Ancient World,[24] walking backwards, as Shadworth Hodgson saw, is not *a* way, but the *only* way, the "compelled" way that we can be said to move in time, insofar as it is the more accurate analogy for how our consciousness unfolds: a "blind and backward course" where each step is not seen as it is taken "but only immediately after it has been taken."[25]

This metaphor of moving backwards toward the future does not, by itself, deny that we can have an *influence* over future events. It is not an abstract denial of cause and effect as set forth by David Hume. Hume's thesis, one of the most unsettling in Western philosophy, is that one event following another never proves that the second event was *caused* by the first event. Even if the same sequence is observed over and over again, such as water coming to a boil when it is heated at 212 degrees Fahrenheit, there is no necessary connection, Hume argued, between the two events. Custom, overwhelmingly witnessed custom, as-yet-to-be-seen-as-otherwise custom, is all you've got. But custom is not causality. That water has always boiled whenever it has been heated to 212 degrees is no absolute guarantee that it will boil the next time it is heated. As James expressed this undermining of a foundation of commonsense reality: "The word 'cause' is . . . an altar to an unknown god; an empty pedestal still marking the place of a hoped-for statue" (*PP2*, 667).[26]

The metaphor of moving backward toward the future encompasses Hume's radical skepticism, but its emphasis is existential. It is less concerned with what we know than how we live. By removing the boundaries of fixed expectations it doesn't restrict knowledge so much as widen possibility. It does not say (even though, in its strictest interpretation, it agrees) that just because water has always boiled when you have heated it on your stove, there is no necessary connection between the two events; it says, rather, that just because you heat water on your stove there is no certainty that the gas will not shut off before it reaches the boiling point, or the cat will not knock over the tea kettle, or any number of other intervening factors, including (at the outer edge of what is now believed possible) that water no longer boils when heated.

SIX

Universe and Nulliverse

Let us imagine . . . a little worm, living in the blood, able to distinguish by sight the particles of blood, lymph, etc., and to reflect on the manner in which each particle, on meeting with another particle, either is repulsed or communicates a portion of its own motion. This little worm would live in the blood, in the same way as we live in a part of the universe, and would consider each particle of blood, not as a part, but as a whole. He would be unable to determine how all the parts are modified by the general nature of the blood and are compelled by it to adapt themselves, so as to stand in a fixed relation to one another.

—Spinoza

[M]any persons talk as if the minutest dose of disconnectedness of one part with another, the smallest modicum of independence, the faintest tremor of ambiguity about the future, for example, would ruin everything, and turn this goodly universe into a sort of insane sand-heap or nulliverse, no universe at all.

—William James, "The Dilemma of Determinism"

"We all have at least the germ of mysticism in us" wrote William James, suggesting, perhaps, by his metaphor, that we should be wary of it spreading (*P*, 553). And James *was* wary. Although sympathetic to accounts of mystical experiences of nonduality, experiences that undermined the commonsense world of active subjects interacting with passive objects, he abhorred the cosmological inferences based on them. To feel at one with the universe did not, for James, imply that the universe *is* one. Such feeling, he believed, was likely relied upon even by those whose defense of oneness was based in logic, such as his colleagues Royce and Bradley:

> [W]hen our idealists recite their arguments for the Absolute, saying that the slightest union admitted anywhere carries logically absolute Oneness with it, and that the slightest separation admitted anywhere logically carries disunion remediless and complete, I cannot help suspecting that the palpable weak places in the intellectual reasonings they use are protected from their own criticism by a mystical feeling that, logic or no logic, absolute Oneness must somehow at any cost be true. (Ibid., 554)

Nothing in mystical feeling, James believed, substantiates that the whole is in each and every part without any "loose play" whatsoever, as expressed, for example, by the Persian mystic Omar Khayyam:

> With earth's first clay they did the last man knead,
> And there of the last harvest sowed the seed.
> And the first morning of creation wrote
> What the last dawn of reckoning shall read. (*WB*, 570, 674)

Calling himself, somewhat coyly, a "pluralistic mystic," James challenged such insistence that all decisions, even the simplest and most trivial, have been determined from eternity. Not the "slightest glimmer of light" is offered, he argued, as to why, say, going down one street instead of another would be "rational and necessary," part of the "nature" of things, and going down the other would be "chance, irrationality, insanity, a horrid gap in nature" (ibid., 574). Therefore, James affirmed, such a belief was "a mere conception fulminated as a dogma and based on no insight into details" (ibid.).

In limiting the inferences that can be drawn from mystical experience, James anticipated his colleague Bertrand Russell's claim that "mysticism expresses an emotion, not a fact."[1] And certainly, mystical determinism, as we have defined it, is not based on any factual "insight into details." But an absence of factual details does not imply an absence of logic. While mystical determinism sees all phenomena as an organic outgrowth of the one spirit of the universe, it makes no claim to understand the direction that the spirit is going—why it produces a mountain here or Paris there. To a mystical determinist, any decision, indeed any *thought*, however seemingly inconsequential, is simply another detail in an unfathomable process—determined yet indetermin*able*.

On the other hand, what "insight into details" suggests that the universe is *not* determined? James's psychological indeterminism does not, as we saw, rule out determinism, only a determinable determinism. Even the "insight into details" from the discipline today that studies apparent "gaps" in nature—chaos theory—would hardly reassure those who, like James, championed "some free play of parts" (*P*, 556).

To be sure, chaos theoreticians have demonstrated that the precise details of apparently regulated phenomena, such as the movement of a pendulum or the formation of a fern leaf, are influenced by so many subtle and disparate factors that it is impossible to predict their *exact* formation in advance. And such an insight into details supports James's belief in an indetermined universe. But these same theoreticians have also shown that seemingly random phenomena, such as avalanches or cloud formations, have, in fact, an underlying order to their movements that can be mathematically ascertained. Through the use of nonlinear "flowing" geometries, many patterns in nature previously considered as arbitrary are now seen as designed. The ultimate course of any apparently chaotic natural phenomenon may be harder to predict than more obviously patterned phenomena (such as the movement of a pendulum), but the evidence increasingly suggests that it is far from random. As James Glieck put it in *Chaos: Making a New Science*, something like "universal laws of chaos" are beginning to emerge.[2]

The dialectic between chance and order that such chaos laws entail is suggested by a vivid metaphor of Blood, a metaphor that James used to introduce the mindset of a radical empiricist:

> The slow round of the engraver's lathe gains but the breath of a hair, but the difference is distributed back over the whole curve, never an instant true,—ever not quite.[3]

"Ever not quite" became, for James, "a herald for the pluralistic philosophical perspective,"[4] a perspective of "real indetermination," affirming that pluralism "triumphs over monism" if even "the smallest morsel of disconnectedness is once found undeniably to exist" (*MT*, 952; *SPP*, 1055). But by the end of his life, as we shall see, he allowed that Blood's mystical beliefs, if not his *own*, required a deeper consideration of the "dialectic circling" between pluralism and monism, a circling that required the inclusion of mystical states, since their "existence" "absolutely overthrows the pretension of non-mystical states to be the sole and ultimate dictators of what we may believe," including, presumably, pluralism's insistence on indetermination, and the "crudity of experience," as an "eternal element" (*APM*, 1304; *VRE*, 385; *WB*, 448).[5]

While mystical feeling "expresses an emotion," mystical belief expresses a fact: the inanimate and animate alike *may* be part of a larger unified process, the course of a statesman no less than a stone:

> "One day in the summer of 1896," recalls Rabbi Joseph Isaac Schneersohn, "my father took me for a walk in the fields. The crops were ripening, a light breeze moved through the sheaves, each ear of corn nodded and whispered to each other. My father said to me: 'See, my son—Divinity! Each moment of every ear of corn, and of every tuft of grass, was anticipated in the primal thought of the first Adam, who could foresee the future of all the generations.'"[6]

The different terms we use to describe how "each moment" of a plant, mineral, animal or human has been influenced depicts our understanding, as far as it goes, only of their different levels of complexity. But just as an adding machine—for all its complexity—is no more spontaneous than an abacus, so, too, farmers *may* have no more actual spontaneity than the ears of corn they harvest. As Schopenhauer put it:

> [T]he action of all existence in this world is always strictly *necessitated* . . . [a]nd . . . it makes no difference whether such an action has been occasioned by causes in the strictest sense of the word, or by stimuli, or finally by motives, for these differences refer only to the grade of the susceptibility of the different kinds of existences.[7]

Regardless of the level of complexity through which influence is effected—whether it be the impulses and intentions that guided Da Vinci as he painted the Last Supper, or the ways the paint and wall cracked in the centuries that followed—all influence may stem from one movement of the universe (literally, "one turning"); "the grade of susceptibility" to be influenced for both animate and inanimate matter being only the surface play of this movement. Who can say what influence is at work beneath this surface play, where even the distinction between animate and inanimate may not apply? The nineteenth-century physicist Gustav Fechner, who James says was "destined . . . to wield more and more influence as time goes on" (*PU*, 64), believed that there was no such thing as inanimate matter. And David Bohm, one of the most eminent quantum theorists of our time, has remarked that based on his observations of the evidence of subatomic movements, he frequently had the impression that the electron sea was "alive."[8]

An even grander unity is suggested by the physics of simultaneity. Following up on theories of Bohm and John Bell, the French physicist Alain Aspect devised an experiment in which a pair of twinned or entangled photons was shown to remain entangled when split apart, with one photon simultaneously registering a change made to the other. In Aspect's experiment the photons were separated by a distance of about four feet; it has since been replicated by others to a distance of seven miles.[9]

Anecdotes about *psychic* simultaneity abound, as well, such as a feeling by a wife that she has been hit on the forehead at the precise moment (it is later learned) that her husband, hundreds of miles away, had been hit on the forehead. Jung, for one, personally experienced this phenomenon. After an unusually restless evening, he went to sleep, only to be "awakened by a feeling of dull pain, as though something had struck my forehead and then the back of my skull." The next day he received a telegram informing him that one of his regular patients had committed suicide by shooting himself. Later, he learned that "the bullet had come to rest in the back wall of the skull."[10]

Directly inspired by Einstein's theory of relativity, Jung called this phenomenon a "synchronicity"—"a relativization of time and space in the unconscious."[11] A well-known controlled experiment has corroborated that such relativizations may indeed be precisely simultaneous. Neurologists hooked two subjects at a time up to EEGs and had them meditate together. In 25 percent of the subjects, a phase coherence in their brain waves was eventually established. Then the subjects were put into soundproofed, electromagnetically isolated chambers (called "Faraday chambers") 14.5 meters apart, and hooked up to individual EEGs. Flashes of light were then flashed at one of the subjects, who registered an electrophysiological response. In 25 percent of those who had established brain wave coherence, as opposed to 0 percent of those who had not, a simultaneous response registered in the other subject.[12] Simultaneous responses mysteriously communicated at a distance have also been detected by one of the founders of lie detection technology, Cleve Backster.[13] Backster conducted experiments with galvanic reactions in white blood cell samples. He showed how such reactions simultaneously corresponded with aggravated feelings of the person that they were extracted from, even though that person was three hundred miles away.[14]

Any confirmable, repeatable simultaneity shakes orthodox science at its core. Most physicists believed in Einstein's speed limit for communication: the speed of light. Einstein himself, who died three decades before Aspect's experiment was conducted, believed that simultaneous influences—indicating communication not only beyond the speed of light but beyond time—would never be found. Thus, when what Einstein had termed "spooky action at a distance" *was* found, it suggested a deeper level of interconnectedness than even that most ardent seeker of a Grand Unified Theory had thought possible. As one preeminent physicist, Basil Hiley, put it: Aspect's experiment "indicates that we must be prepared to consider radically new views of reality."[15] Bell himself, whose theories were the basis of Aspect's experiment, was apparently, like most people, not prepared. He accepted that the easiest scientific interpretation of Aspect's experiment, one that reconciled both quantum physics and special relativity, was the nonreality of free will, but, like James, Bell held to his belief in free will on moral grounds.[16]

It's been almost a century since Einstein and Bohr clashed with each other over the spiritual implications of quantum physics. Einstein, who held that "the profounder sort of scientific mind . . . is possessed by the sense of universal causation" in which "the future . . . is every whit as necessary and determined as the past,"[17] could not abide quantum indeterminism. He famously declared: "God does not play dice with the Universe." James would clearly have approved Bohr's retort: "Don't tell God what to do." It was essentially the same point that James made to those in his day who, he believed, used mystical feeling to support a determinism that "must somehow at any cost be true" (*P*, 554). Neither belief in God's omnipotence, nor a mystical feeling of Oneness, can provide such support, despite the transcendent peace they may encompass; despite the ultimate harmony and reconciliation they imply.

So, too, mystical determinism, as we have defined it thus far, is merely a belief. It has no insight into *why* the most trivial of decisions must be part of a larger order, for the simple reason that it has no abiding idea of what such an order might be; it lacks "rational and necessary" reasons for why even the most *significant* decisions take place. Mystical determinism accepts on *faith* that there are no gaps in nature just as James accepts on *faith* that there are. "Rational and necessary" are irrelevant terms to both these faiths. The only "glimmer of light" into why the most insignificant decision could not have been made other than it was, and why the fly's wing had to fall here and the nutshell had to fall there, comes from a source James knew well but never fully considered.

SEVEN

Precognition

For us believing physicists, this separation between past and future has the value of mere illusion, however tenacious.

—Albert Einstein

A few months ago I had an extraordinarily vivid dream, and waking up repeated it to my wife at once. All I dreamt actually occurred about six weeks afterwards, the details of my dream falling out exactly. There seems to have been no purpose whatsoever in the dream; and one cannot help thinking, what was the good of it? I dreamt that I was asked to dinner by the German Consul-General, and accepting, was ushered into a large room with trophies of East African arms on shields against the walls. (N.B.—I have myself been a great deal in East Africa.) After dinner I went to inspect the arms, and amongst them saw a beautifully gold-mounted sword which I pointed out to the French Vice-Consul—who at that moment joined me—as having probably been a present from the Sultan of Zanzibar to my host the German Consul-General. At that moment the Russian Consul came up too. He pointed out how small was the hilt of the sword and how impossible in consequence it would be for a European to use the weapon, and whilst talking he waved his arm in an excited manner over his head as if he was wielding the sword, and to illustrate what he was saying. At that moment I woke up and marveled so at the vividness of the dream that I woke my wife up too and told it to her. About six weeks afterwards my wife and myself were asked to dine with the German Consul-General; but the dream had long been forgotten by us both. We were shown into a large withdrawing room which I have never been in before, but which somehow seemed familiar to me. Against the walls were some beautiful trophies of East African arms, amongst which was a gold-hilted sword, a gift to my host from the Sultan of Zanzibar. To make a long story short, everything happened exactly as I had dreamt—but I never remembered the dream until the Russian Consul began to wave his arm over his head, when it came back to me like a flash. Without saying a word to the Russian Consul and French Vice-Consul (whom I left standing before the trophy), I walked quickly across to my wife, who was standing at the entrance of a boudoir opening out of the withdrawing room, and said to her: "Do you remember my dream about the Zanzibar arms?" She remembered everything perfectly, and was a witness to its realization. On the spot we informed all the persons concerned of the dream, which naturally much interested them.

—John George Haggard, nineteenth-century British Consul in Trieste, Austria, recorded by the Society for Psychical Research and quoted by F. W. H. Myers in *Human Personality and its Survival of Bodily Death*

However strange may be the phenomenon of precognition, we must not let ourselves be diverted from the truth by the strangeness of appearances. A fact is a fact, even though it may upset our conception of the universe; for our conception of the universe is terribly infantile.

—Charles Richet, Nobel physiologist and co-investigator with William James of psychic phenomena.

James's psychology of volition, as we saw, acknowledges a gap in the decision-making process in which the decision is felt to be received. This gap may be filled by either:

1. a spontaneous generation of thoughts;
2. instinctive, reflexive, or subconscious thoughts;
3. a combination of both; or
4. completely determined thoughts.

It is only when the phenomenon of precognition—specific, photographically detailed visions of the future that later come true—is added to the impersonal, arising nature of the thought process that the last possibility comes most into play.

Along with many other cultures, the two cultures that shaped Western thought—Greek and Judeo-Christian—firmly believed that specific future outcomes could be seen in the present. Precognition did not need to be explained away by an early Greek, Jew, or Christian; prophecy and oracles were at the center of their religious belief. But in the last one hundred years or so, with the rise of technology, the masters of material reality who have now become our masters of higher truth—scientists, or, more precisely, the ruling orthodox sect, scienticisists—have succeeded in sweeping the phenomenon of precognition into a dustbin, a dustbin labeled "occult," "new age," or "squishy." Not that many scientists have reached for the broom; most ignore the evidence altogether. This was as true in James's time as our own, as James duly noted:

> [T]he present condition of opinion regarding [psychical research] is scandalous, there being a mass of testimony, or apparent testimony, about such things, at which the only men capable of a critical judgment— men of scientific education—will not even look. (C3, 105)

It wasn't always so. In the seventeenth century, Robert Boyle, who helped found the Royal Society *specifically* to promote an empirical approach to the natural world, took an active interest in precognition (also called, at the time, "second sight"), due to the many reports of it in Scotland, where it was widely believed in.[1] And James himself had found enthusiastic collaboration in his own day from distinguished scientists, such as Nobel physiologist Charles Richet, and Oliver Lodge, one of the key inventors of wireless technology. His young contemporary Einstein was also to figure as one who would indeed "look." Based on what he felt was compelling evidence for telepathy, Einstein encouraged more research, whether it revealed that such evidence rested on "some unconscious hypnotic influence from person to person" or some other cause "far beyond those which a nature investigator holds to be thinkable."[2] And in our own increasingly technocratic age, significant attempts have been made to make a science of the phenomenon, by conducting repeatable experiments that rely on statistical probabilities.

James's interest in psychical research, as Perry rightly concluded, "was not one of his vagaries, but was central and typical."[3] As founder and president of the American Society for Psychical Research, James waged, in essays and letters to the editor, a lifetime battle on behalf of all parapsychology, which he called "a dog with so few friends at court that almost any stick seems good enough to beat him with" (*EPR*, 217). Repeatedly throughout his career, he attacked, or rather counterattacked, what he called "conservative" scientists who "press . . . with all the weight of . . . [their] authority against the door which certain 'psychical researchers' are threatening to open wide enough to admit a hitherto discredited class of facts" (ibid., 217). His fight on behalf of alternative healers was typical of his determination to keep the door open. The Massachusetts legislature, with the urging of James's professional colleagues, proposed a "Medical Registration Bill," requiring all mental healers to pass a licensing exam. Since this exam would be devised by the medical schools, James knew that it would turn all alternative practitioners into charlatans and criminals overnight. In particular, he was concerned about the banishing of such prominent mind-cure therapists as the Christian Scientists, who viewed their patients as spiritual rather than material beings, with "no separate mind from God."[4] In a passionate and lengthy letter to the *Boston Evening Transcript*, he claimed that such banishment would be a disservice to science:

> I assuredly hold no brief for any of these healers, and must confess that my intellect has been unable to assimilate their theories, so far as I have heard them given. But their *facts* are patent and startling; and anything that interferes with the multiplication of such facts, and with our freest opportunity of observing and studying them, will, I believe, be a public calamity. (*L2*, 69)

James's open-mindedness toward "startling" psychic facts extended to precognition. He was familiar with the British Consul's precognition report quoted above by his psychical research colleague, Frederic Myers, and many more like it. In addition to writing the introduction to Myers's book that anthologized precognitive experiences, James contributed a particularly detailed account submitted to him by one T. F. Ivey, whom he, Myers, and fellow psychical researcher Richard Hodgson corresponded with further, to corroborate. (The original letter sent to James and the further correspondence can be found in the Appendix.) While James did not "hold a brief" for what he called these "mysterious phenomena" of "premonitions" and "clairvoyant visions or impressions," he did hold a theory in support of them, a theory he proposed early in his life, and returned to at the end:

consciousness is not "produced" but exists "ready-made" (*HI*, 1117–1118). We will look more at the theory as first proposed by James, as well as the critical role it plays in his mystical suggestion. But first, we will look at what he called the "unclassifiable" "mystical" phenomenon itself, a phenomenon that, despite its "paradoxical absurdities,"is found "lying broadcast over the surface of history" (*WB*, 681).[5]

Acceptance of divination and precognition may seem unremarkable for a founder and president of a psychical research society. But this particular president had good reason not to broadcast precognition. It was, after all, the one psychic phenomenon that challenged his core belief that "novelty is perpetually entering the world" (*EA*, 810n) (by marked contrast with the determinist Schopenhauer, for whom it comes as no surprise to learn that he devoted considerable attention to precognition in his later years).[6] To accept precognition is to reject that "things are really being decided from one moment to another," and to allow that the world is in some sense "ready-made" (*PP1*, 453; *HI*, 1118). As the most extreme of all psychical phenomena, precognition would also have given James another reason to avoid its public discussion. For as Jung observed on his visit to America, James's belief in "extra-sensory perception" had led him to be "not taken quite seriously" among his colleagues.[7]

But while we will never know what James fully thought about precognition, and will not return to his engagement of it until we look at his mystical suggestion, we can no better inaugurate a discussion of it than by quoting his view of all psychic phenomena, from his essay "The Confidences of a Psychical Researcher":

> For twenty-five years, I have been in touch with the literature of psychical research, and have had acquaintance with numerous "researchers." I have also spent a good many hours (though far fewer than I ought to have spent) in witnessing (or trying to witness) phenomenon. Yet I am theoretically no "further" than I was at the beginning; and I confess that at times I have been tempted to believe that the creator has eternally intended this department of nature to remain *baffling*, to prompt our curiosities and hopes and suspicions all in equal measure, so that although ghosts, and clairvoyances, and raps and messages from spirits, are always seeming to

exist and can never be fully explained away, they also can never be susceptible of full corroboration. (*EPR*, 362)

MONKEYS TYPING, HORSES STOMPING

While abundant evidence for precognition "prompts our curiosities," what prompts our suspicions as well is that there has never been a perfect seer. The greatest rate of accuracy ascertained by a scientific panel for a seer's predictions is 80 percent, for the twentieth-century Bulgarian psychic Vanga Dimitrova.[8] Such ascertainment has yet to be embraced (or even much noticed) beyond that country's borders. And no test of a seer anywhere else has ever come close to such results.

The record, for seers, is spotty, to say the least. Such spottiness is good news for those who, like James, champion indeterminism, since it means that no prediction can ever tell us what *must* lie ahead. Like any other thought of the future, a precognitive image can only be deemed predictive *after the fact*. And even after the fact, what seems like an actual instance of precognition may be something far less.

There are three ways to dismiss any alleged instance of precognition: fraud, a trick of the mind, and coincidence. These explanations are mutually exclusive. If one is true for a particular incident, the others drop out. Take one of the best known alleged instances: Jeane Dixon's vision in the mid-1950s of a blue-eyed president laid out in a casket, and the assassin's name having "O" as the first letter, "s" as the second letter, and a little curve that went straight up as the last letter.[9] If this vision is believed to have been a fraud, then it is not believed to have been either a chance coincidence or a trick of the mind (such as a vaguer vision whose details were exactly constructed only *after* November 22, 1963).

Curiously, however, despite their mutual exclusivity, some combination of the three rebuttals is usually invoked. Where one does not prove persuasive, another is brought forth, and then, if necessary, the third one, only to return again to the first—the process repeating like an endless game of tag. If we begin by being almost completely sure that precognition is a fraud, then become half suspicious that it is a trick of the mind, and, subsequently, three-quarters positive that it is a chance coincidence, we might even seem to be, by some impossible arithmetic, more than wholly convinced that it is not real. At any rate, such an accumulation of suspicions can deter us from scrutinizing each explanation individually, on its own merits.

As for the claim of fraud, there are too many accounts of precognition, under too many varying circumstances, for which the charge of fraud makes no sense. According to the *Harper's Encyclopedia of Mystical and Paranormal Experience*, "precognition is the most frequently reported of all extrasensory perception . . . experiences."[10] Accounts such as the one given at the outset of this chapter are remarkable, but not rare.[11] The suspicion of fraud surrounds people who make a good living from peddling their predictions. Yet by far the greatest number of purported incidents of precognition occur to people out of the blue, taking them completely by surprise. No calculation, no motive for fraud or any kind of gain, can be attached to them. Some of the best documented psychics, such as Vanga Dimitrova, never charged money for their predictions. Even the tabloid tattler herself, Jeane Dixon, did not charge money in the first decades of her career.

The occurrence of purported precognitive images to a wide variety of people in a wide variety of circumstances also makes the charge of a trick of the mind difficult to sustain. An abundance of accounts, verified by a second party, such as in the opening example, make it difficult to believe that in many alleged instances of precognition both the original image and the later realization have not been faithfully reported.

While suspicions of fraud and tricks of the mind are part of a healthy skepticism toward precognition, the health of skepticism needs to be nurtured. Dogmatism has no part in it. As James says, "[N]o source of deception in the investigation of nature . . . can compare with a fixed belief that certain kinds of phenomena are impossible" (C3, 105–106).

In contrast to the claims of fraud and a trick of the mind, however, the charge of chance coincidence cannot easily be set aside. All attempts, in fact, to establish the reality of precognition are "susceptible" to this explanation. This is especially true for laboratory experiments where the subject guesses the immediate future, such as the number that will be chosen by a random number generator. Researchers, for example, at Duke University, the University of Nevada, Princeton, the University of Arizona, and the University of Amsterdam (among others) who have conducted such tests, claim to have established "statistically highly significant results," "beyond chance."[12] But at what point do "statistically highly significant results" become inescapably conclusive results? At what point has "beyond chance" moved beyond the possibility of chance?

It has been said that if a monkey tapped long enough on a typewriter it could write *Hamlet*. For me, the sense of "long enough" that could produce such a result is beyond comprehension. It would be beyond my comprehension if it were only the "Gettysburg Address" we were waiting for. I might well believe that a monkey could tap out a word in a few minutes, a sentence in a few weeks, a paragraph in a few decades. But a play by Shakespeare? A speech by Lincoln? To me that would be not only "beyond chance," but beyond the possibility of chance. And while a monkey typing a paragraph on its first try would not be beyond chance either, such a result would, at the very least, *feel* like something beyond chance. It would give me an eerie jolt that "something's going on."

The philosopher C. J. Ducasse isolated an objective aspect of precognitive images that he claims distinguishes them from other, merely *imagined*, scenes of the future: the photographic accuracy of unusual details that later come to pass, for which one had no present context or reference when the image first arose. He calls such details "extraordinary features." At bottom, they are coincidences too eerie to be considered mere chance:

> If I were to dream tonight that I received a letter from a friend from whom I have not heard for many years—that, by itself, is hardly evidence there was . . . connection between my dream and the advent of the letter. If, however, the letter that I see myself receive in my dream is not an ordinary letter but, let us say, a letter in an oval envelope instead of a rectangular envelope, that itself would be an unusual feature. And if I noticed in addition that, in my dream, this envelope is white on one side and pink on the other, that the stamp is right in the middle of the envelope—all these would be extraordinary features, with strong indication this was not just a matter of chance.[13]

As if it were indeed part of creation's design to "baffle," many of the apparent instances of precognition fall somewhere *between* Ducasse's two examples. Take, for example, a precognitive dream posted on the UK Online Premonitions' Registry on September 5, 2001, by "psychic 1":

> In the last week I've been having a very vivid premonition of a plane—looks like a commercial, passenger aircraft—crashing into a skyscraper and exploding into flames. I think it's in the US—possibly Chigago [*sic*]? I also foresee two deaths taking place in the Royal family, one soon after the other.[14]

Or think of Lincoln's famous dream a few weeks before his assassination, his life's "most startling incident," according to his former law partner and bodyguard, Ward Lamon, who was there with Mrs. Lincoln when her husband first related it:

> About ten days ago, I retired very late. I had been up waiting for important dispatches from the front. I could not have been long in bed when I fell into a slumber, for I was weary. I soon began to dream. There seemed to be a death-like stillness about me. Then I heard subdued sobs, as if a number of people were weeping. I thought I left my bed and wandered downstairs. There the silence was broken by the same pitiful sobbing, but the mourners were invisible. I went from room to room; no living person was in sight, but the same mournful sounds of distress met me as I passed along. I saw light in all the rooms; every object was familiar to me; but where were all the people who were grieving as if their hearts would break? I was puzzled and alarmed. What could be the meaning of all this? Determined to find the cause of a state of things so mysterious and so shocking, I kept on until I arrived at the East Room, which I entered. There I met with a sickening surprise. Before me was a catafalque, on which rested a corpse wrapped in funeral vestments. Around it were stationed soldiers who were acting as guards; and there was a throng of people, gazing mournfully upon the corpse, whose face was covered, others weeping pitifully. "Who is dead in the White House?" I demanded of one of the soldiers, "The President," was his answer; "he was killed by an assassin." Then came a

> loud burst of grief from the crowd, which woke me from my dream. I slept no more that night; and although it was only a dream, I have been strangely annoyed by it ever since.[15]

Given all the enemies he had made as commander-in-chief of an often vicious army, his vision of himself resting in a casket in the White House (even the very East Room in which his casket was later placed) hardly qualifies as an "extraordinary feature," beyond the boundaries of chance. The same can be said for a later president's dream:

> "I don't normally dream," Ronald Reagan told a reporter, "but for a long period of time, before I was ever in government, I had a habit dream. It was always the same thing, maybe a different locale or something, but I evidently had a yen for big rooms. And I would dream that I was in a big mansion, and I could buy it for a song. A man was showing it to me, and I would go from room to room and maybe go into the living room, which was two stories high, and there was a balcony. And, always, it was within my means to buy it. And I had this dream all the time. After we moved into the White House I was *in* the big rooms. And I never had the dream since."[16]

Neither Reagan's nor Lincoln's dream fits Ducasse's criterion of "extraordinary features, with strong indication . . . [it] was not just a matter of chance." Nor does the striking, even startling, dream of "psychic 1." But there are many accounts of precognition that do fit Ducasse's criteria, such as the one we cited at the outset, originally filed with the British Psychical Society, as well as the highly specific dreams of Malcolm Bessent monitored in two controlled studies at the Dream Laboratory of New York's Maimonides Medical Center, and Lawrence LeShan's and Aristed Esser's controlled precognitive experiments with Dutch sensitive Gerard Croiset.[17] One of the most noted precognitive experiments with extraordinary detail was conducted by Harold Puthoff and Russell Targ of the Stanford Research Institute:

> [A]n unusually talented subject named Hella Hammid, a photographer by vocation, was asked to describe the spot Puthoff would be

> visiting one-half hour hence. She concentrated and said she could see him entering "a black iron triangle." The triangle was "bigger than a man," and although she did not know precisely what it was, she could hear a rhythmic squeaking sound occurring "about once a second."
>
> Ten minutes before she did this, Puthoff had set out on a half-hour drive in the Menlo Park and Palo Alto areas. At the end of the half hour, and well after Hammid had recorded her perception of the black iron triangle, Puthoff took out ten sealed envelopes containing ten different target locations. Using a random number generator, he chose one at random. Inside was the address of a small park about six miles from the laboratory. He drove to the park, and when he got there he found a children's swing—the black iron triangle—and walked into its midst. When he sat down in the swing it squeaked rhythmically as it swung back and forth.[18]

Because the arising of a predictive image is itself unpredictable, most alleged instances of "extraordinary featured" precognition elude a controlled investigation of the repeatable trials required for scientific sanction. Like most so-called paranormal experiences, they are, as James said, "capricious, discontinuous and not easily controlled" (*APSPR*, 135).[19] Jung, whose dissertation was entitled *On the Psychology and Pathology of So-Called Occult Phenomena*, and who spent two evenings with James talking about parapsychology, emphasized the same point.[20] "The repeatable experiment is desirable," he wrote, "but inasmuch as most . . . [parapsychological] events are spontaneous and irregular, the experimental method will not be generally applicable."[21] And even when the experimental method *is* applicable, the bar for scientific sanction keeps getting raised. James, pondering why so few scientists will even "*look* at the evidence for telepathy," relates that a "leading biologist" told him that

> even if such a thing were true, scientists ought to band together to keep it suppressed and concealed. It would undo the uniformity of Nature and all sorts of other things without which scientists cannot carry on their pursuits. (*WB*, 463)[22]

While James felt that "no candid mind" could fail to see that the cumulative evidence for telepathy was compelling (*EPR*, 131), he also allowed that "so revolutionary a belief" required "a more overwhelming bulk of testimony than has yet been supplied" (*WB*, 687). This would apply especially to the form of telepathy that Myers, who coined the term, called its "laxity of time relations."[23] Whether or not compelling evidence for such laxity has now been supplied, a bulk of testimony has been offered. According to Dean Radin, a survey of 309 laboratory precognition tests conducted by sixty-two different investigators between 1935 and 1987, consisting of almost two million individual trials by more than fifty thousand subjects, "produced odds against chance of 10^{25} to one—that is ten million billion billion to one."[24]

One of Radin's most intriguing precognitive experiments circumvents an obstacle to repeatability: distortion created by *trying* to predict. Radin's experiment, corroborated by Dick Bierman of the University of Amsterdam and others, does not involve any conscious formulation of precognitive images extraordinary or ordinary. Using a random mix of neutral pictures—such as landscapes—and emotionally charged pictures—such as erotic images—Radin showed that nonconscious processes can also apparently *anticipate* when the emotionally charged images will appear. These nonconscious processes, so-called "orienting responses," are electrodermal skin conductance, heart rate, and blood volumes.[25]

The most renowned experiments employing both conscious and nonconscious orienting responses to future events were published in the *Journal of Personality and Social Psychology* by the highly esteemed psychologist Daryl Bem. The article, entitled "Feeling the Future: Experimental Evidence for Anomalous Retroactive Influences on Cognition and Affect," presented more evidence of what Bierman has called a "puzzling, apparently retrocausal effect" that "seems to suggest that future conscious experience might project backwards in time in the non-conscious realm."[26] But despite the increasing respect given to these experiments, moving from "seems to suggest" to "proves" requires a judgment about statistical probability.

Nobel physicist Brian Josephson, in collaboration with professor of statistics Jessica Utts, has argued that the statistical results of precognitive lab studies have been repeated enough under unimpeachable conditions to be worthy of scientific imprimatur;[27] but it is questionable whether the test of precognition will ever play out on the stage of statistics. For statistical evidence cannot ultimately decide between chance and the unexplainable, as long as each piece of evidence is believed (however stubbornly) to beg the very question it is trying to answer. No matter how many correct hits a subject may get in a lab-controlled card-guessing experiment, our faith in the impossibility of an eerie unknown will likely prevail against our faith in a statistician's theory.[28] If I believe that a monkey has no capacity to communicate ideas through a typewriter, then I will keep ascribing whatever random words it does type to chance until, say, it knocks out a one page description of how it had spent its morning.

On the other hand, even if a monkey typed only one word in a decade, that could not automatically be dismissed as an acausal, chance coincidence. For all we know of their potential brain power, the monkey might have momentarily received ESP stimuli from a human typist down the street. You'd have to set up the experiment so that raindrops or some other inanimate force were affecting the keyboard before you could exclude any explanation other than chance coincidence.[29] As long as an alternative explanation (however remote) can account for a connection between two events, we cannot forever banish the connection to the realm of mere chance. What cannot be fully explained cannot be simply explained away, lest we be like the Houyhnhnm horse/scientists in *Gulliver's Travels*, who stomped their hooves on any evidence that conflicted with their theories. "If we are to judge by the analysis of the past," said James, "when our Science once becomes old-fashioned, it will be more for its omissions of fact . . . than for any fatal lack in its spirit and principles" (*APSPR*, 136).

MARK TWAIN'S DREAM

For the same reason that amassing grammatically correct phrases typed by a monkey may not ultimately convince us of its literacy, amassing accounts of highly specific foreseen events may not ultimately convince us of precognition; in both cases, each piece of evidence might continue to beg the question of chance coincidence. While the dismissal of any precognition becomes more difficult with each succeeding incident that one believes to have happened as reported, the multiplying of accounts can only take us so far.[30] The reality of precognition—as James says of all psychic phenomena—may never, it seems, be "susceptible to full corroboration." Like a spiritual presence it is sometimes sensed to be, precognition will always be accepted, in part, on faith.

Rather, then, than amass accounts of precognition here (accounts readily available elsewhere),[31] I will quote and discuss one compelling incident: Mark Twain's dream of his brother Henry's death, as recorded in his *Autobiography*. Twain had read *The Principles of Psychology* and championed the psychical "investigations made by our professor William James."[32] His own experience left him little choice.

In one sense, Twain's account of a personal psychic experience might seem a preposterous choice to focus on. He was, after all, famous for his hoaxes, deliberately launched to make readers suspicious of unverified newspaper stories, such as his report about the discovery of a three-hundred-year-old petrified man thumbing his nose.[33] But no Twain scholar has ever suggested that Twain perpetrated a hoax here, in this horrific, deeply felt personal tragedy that, as he put it, "blasted my youth and left me an old man before my time."[34] Moreover, we know from independent family sources that he had told this dream to his sister and his mother *before* the fatal trip.[35] Once fulfilled, the dream sparked Twain's lifelong interest in parapsychology.

Let us look, then, at this small jewel in the huge treasure chest of Mark Twain's legacy. The vividness of its images, and the eerie, extraordinary features of its photographically specific details, are typical of many other alleged precognitive dreams—dreams that are anecdotal, or, at least, never "susceptible of full corroboration," but nonetheless the kind of "irregular phenomena" that would "renovate . . . science" if "steadily look[ed] after" (*WB*, 680). The dream occurred while Twain was staying at his mother's house in St. Louis:

> In the morning, when I awoke, I had been dreaming, and the dream was so vivid, so like reality that it deceived me and I thought it *was* real. In the dream I had seen Henry a corpse. He lay in a metallic burial case. He was dressed in a suit of my clothing and on his breast lay a great bouquet of flowers, mostly white roses, with a red rose in the center. The casket stood upon a couple of chairs. I dressed and moved toward that[36] door, thinking I would go in there and

look at it, but I changed my mind. I thought I could not yet bear to meet my mother. I thought I would wait awhile and make some preparation for that ordeal. The house was in Locust Street, a little above Thirteenth, and I walked to Fourteenth and to the middle of the block beyond before it suddenly flashed upon me that there was nothing real about this—it was only a dream. I can still feel something of the grateful upheaval of joy of that moment and I can also still feel the remnant of doubt, the suspicion that maybe it was real after all. I returned to the house almost on a run, flew up the stairs two or three steps at a jump and rushed into that sitting room, and was made glad again, for there was no casket there.[37]

Several months later, as it turned out, Henry did die, along with 1,600 others, in an explosion on board the steamship *Sultana*, downriver on the Mississippi, just below Memphis. It was the biggest maritime disaster in U.S. history.[38] Henry's corpse was laid out with the other victims in a special room in the hospital. According to Twain:

> The coffins provided for the dead were of unpainted white pine, but in this instance some of the ladies of Memphis had made up a fund of sixty dollars and bought a metallic case, and when I . . . entered the dead-room Henry lay in that open case and he was dressed in a suit of my clothing. I recognized instantly that my dream of several weeks before was here exactly reproduced, so far as these details went—and I think I missed one detail, but that one was immediately supplied, for just then an elderly lady entered the place with a large bouquet consisting mainly of white roses, and in the center of it was a red rose and she laid it on his breast.[39]

Twain rejected outright that his memory was playing tricks with him:

> I don't believe that I ever had any doubts whatever concerning the salient points of the dream, for those points are of such a nature that they are *pictures*, and pictures can be remembered, when they are vivid, much better than one can remember remarks and unconcreted facts. Although it has been so many years since I have told

that dream, I can see those pictures now just as clearly defined as if they were before me in this room.[40]

An example of a "remark" that was not well remembered was his telling his mother about the dream. In his *Autobiography* he says that he didn't.[41] His mother and his sister, however, both had vivid recollections of hearing the dream and, before its fulfillment, being "amused that he took it so seriously."[42] Twain scholar Rachel Varble, who had access to his mother's personal papers, corroborates the account of Twain's sister, as related by her grandson.[43]

Twain's dream satisfies Ducasse's criterion of "extraordinary features." Neither the metal coffin, nor the specific arrangement of flowers, nor the corpse being dressed in Twain's own suit, could be considered everyday features of a funeral. Taken all together, along with there being no hint of mortal danger to Twain's brother at the time of his dream, these details are not easily dismissed as chance coincidence.

Nor were the "extraordinary features" of Twain's dream limited to what he saw, but also to *how* he saw it. Like the consul's dream quoted earlier, and like many instances of alleged precognition, Twain's dream, at the time it occurred, appeared to him as something extraordinarily vivid, more than the working of his imagination. Indeed, he so believed in its reality that even after he awoke he proceeded as if it had already occurred. This is additionally significant because it precludes Twain's later, actual encounter with his brother's corpse from having been mere "déjà vu." By walking down the street, coming to the realization that what he thought to be real was only a dream, hastening back to the house, and leaping up the stairs, Twain had, as a reference point, a vivid waking-state corroboration of his dream. If anything, Twain's experience and others like it may help explain déjà vu.[44] Perhaps some instances of déjà vu are the actualization of a previous, dimly recollected precognitive dream—a dream less forcibly impressed upon the imagination than Twain's dream was on his.

Twain's experience also refutes the "trick of the mind" charge commonly alleged against precognition: that the precise details of the image are not remembered but rather *supplanted* by the details later encountered in the actual event. Clearly, this charge does not well serve the facts here. For while the real event was unfolding, Twain caught a discrepancy between it and his dream. This identification of a discrepancy (later resolved) indicates that Twain was holding onto *two* separate experiences, distinct from one another. He did not derive the details of his dream from the reality and somehow re-import these details back into his dream.

Twain was impelled by his experience to begin reading "with avidity" the pamphlets of the British Society for Psychical Research. He became an active member of James's American branch, and published an essay on telepathy that included a less dramatic incident from his life of a knowing "beforehand."[45] It also likely facilitated a spiritual conversion. The quintessential American writer, Twain did not cling to popular Western belief when faced with an experience that contradicted it. He denied free will and accepted predestination. According to his biographer Albert Paine:

> Clemens held that there was no such thing as an accident: that it was all forewritten in the day of the beginning: that every event, however slight, was embryonic in that first instant of created life, and immutably timed to its appearance in the web of destiny. Once on their [Clemens and his friend, Joseph Twichell] travels, when they were on a high bank above a brawling stream, a little girl, who started to run toward them, slipped and rolled under the bottom rail of the protecting fence, her feet momentarily hanging out over the precipice and the tearing torrent below. It seemed a miraculous escape from death, and furnished an illustration for their discussion. The condition of the ground, the force of her fall, the nearness of the fatal edge, all these had grown inevitably out of the first great projection of thought, and the child's fall and its escape had been invested in life's primal atom.[46]

A hard-headed skeptic, Twain had frequently poked fun at glaring inconsistencies in the Bible, and apparently would not accept them in his own spiritual belief. If he could dream such a bizarre, specific scene, without any basis in present reality, six weeks before the scene played itself out, then each moment must be "immutably timed to its appearance in the web of destiny." America's quintessential poet, Walt Whitman, echoed her quintessential novelist, stating:

The universe is duly in order, everything is in its place,
What has arrived is in its place and what awaits shall be in its place.[47]

James, the quintessential American philosopher, attacked these "duly ordered" "effulgent" pictures of absolute and transcendent harmony, frequently satirizing them, as in: "We are but syllables in the mouth of the Lord; if the whole sentence is divine, each syllable is absolutely what it should be, in spite of all appearances" (*PU*, 56).

But he did not attack experiences such as Twain's that supported them.

EIGHT

Fate and Free Will

For all his skepticism toward the Bible, Twain ratified a crucial aspect of it through his belief in predestination. The Judeo-Christian tradition, after all, was built on prophecy. The scroll form of bookmaking, in fact, evolved into our present-day form of cut pages in order to facilitate the checking of prophecies in the Old Testament against events in the New. And fifteen of the dreams recorded in the Bible consist of precognitive prophecy.[1] Of all the miracles in the Bible, nothing is more miraculous than such prophecies, with their suggestion that the future can be seen, not simply guessed at or imagined.

While prophecy is more linked with Islam than either of its two predecessors, it is a common root to all three. The Old Testament is emphatic about its preeminence. In Isaiah, knowledge of the future is God's own gauntlet to distinguish his authenticity from false gods:

> Set forth your case, says the Lord;
> bring your proofs, says the King of Jacob.
> Let them bring them, and tell us
> what is to happen. . . .
> Tell us the former things, what they are
> that we may consider them,

that we may know their outcome;
or declare to us the things to come.
Tell us what is to come hereafter,
that we may know that you are gods.[2]

So, too, a prophet worthy of the name must pass the same test. The knowable future, that manifests God's omniscience, is not a guess: "When a prophet speaks in the name of the Lord, if the word does not come to pass or come true, that is a word which the Lord has not spoken."[3] And explicit belief in precognition has remained part of the Jewish mystical tradition.[4]

Prophecy is also of preeminent significance in the New Testament, which identifies it with "the testimony of Jesus,"[5] and where "a whole family of words associated with God's knowledge of the future" is introduced.[6] In addition to the prophecies in the Old Testament believed to have been fulfilled in the New Testament (and the prophecies in both believed by some to be being fulfilled in our own time) there are examples of Jesus's own prophecy, such as his foretelling to Peter that he (Peter) would renounce him three times before the cock crowed. The specific number and time frame would have us believe that Jesus was not guessing.[7]

Eastern religions, too, embrace prophetic prowess. "If for no other reason save this: whatever he said came true. His words of prophecy have all been fulfilled," is how a chief disciple of one of India's most revered gurus, Shri Ramakrishna, justified his faith in him.[8] Precognition is also "universally accepted in most schools of Buddhism."[9] The Dalai Lama, for example, affirms that on "many occasions" he received "very specific" answers to questions he posed to the trance-induced State Oracle (Nechung), and they always turned out to be correct.[10] The establishment of the Nechung is traced to the eighth-century sage Padmasambhava, author of *The Tibetan Book of the Dead*, whose life was said to have been continually informed by prophecy, including his renowned: "When the iron bird flies and horses run on wheels, the Tibetan people will be scattered like ants across the world, and the Dharma will come to the land of red-faced people."[11]

As we said, not everyone who accepts that the future can sometimes be known in precise detail—divinely inspired or otherwise—accepts the nonreality of free will as a consequence. And certainly, up to a point, it *is* possible to imagine fixed, fated moments coexisting with free will. Fate, in this mixed system, would be like a mother at a playground, who lets her child play freely, interfering only if the child is in danger, or when the time comes to leave—a "fixed" incident, set in advance. Such a mixed system analogy fits the everyday notion of fate as death and taxes: within certain bounds, we can do pretty much as we please.

But the analogy breaks down as soon as the fixed, fated moment is believed to be foreseen in precise, photographic detail, as occurs with so-called precognitive dreams. Returning to our playground, we can see that the fixed incident would not be "the child's stopping play in the late afternoon," but more like "the child's stopping play as the tree's shadow bisects the middle of the playground and the child's hand is reaching for the third rung of the overhang bars." If such is the moment through which the child must pass, what freedom is left to the child? Wouldn't every act and thought of the child that precedes that moment necessarily contribute to the child's being in that precise position at that precise time?

To better understand this logic of precognition, look at one of its most commonly cited instances: a dream of an accident. Let us say that a friend of mine dreams that my white MINI Cooper crashes into a red convertible at a bend in the road on a mountainside, falls off the side of the mountain, and lands in an oak tree. If this dream of "extraordinary features" were later to be actualized—that is, occur as specifically detailed in the dream—how much freedom could I be said to have had? Obviously, much more is entailed than simply how I come to be driving on the fated day. While it takes only one thought to get me into a car, it takes many thoughts to "get" my car to a certain spot at a certain time. Most of the thoughts in my head while I am driving have some slight influence on the pressure that I place on the gas pedal—the pressure that, along with the number of stops, determines whether I will or won't get to the bend in the road at the exact moment that the convertible gets there. Although it is possible to imagine moments of freedom after I get into the car—or even a few miles of undetermined thoughts—this freedom could not, after all, be unrestricted. If certain thoughts caused my pace to slow down to the point that I risked not reaching the fated spot at the same moment as the other car, or caused me to go so fast I would pass the spot before it got there, a new train of thought would have to pop into my head to either speed me up or slow me down. Likewise, I couldn't be allowed to distract myself to the point that I veer off the road; I couldn't decide to pull over for lunch, etc.

And such restrictions on my thoughts while I am driving only take into consideration my own fated moment. If fate—even just an occasional, fated moment—is real, I may well have a critical role to play in others' fated moments, not just the driver of the red convertible. Perhaps my car is fated to speed up so that a state trooper reaches his quota of tickets and, going home early, disrupts a gas station robbery; or my car is fated to slow down near the top of a hill so that another driver, in seeking to pass me, will meet her or his fated end in a head-on collision with a car coming the other way.

Given all these restrictions, it is difficult to see in what sense I would be free for those few miles. Whatever I gained by the invocation of these patches of freedom would be negated by the necessary invocation of a very intrusive agent (an agent something like the ancient Greek Gods, who continually planted thoughts in people's minds with the ease of sending an Instagram). I have given myself a recess from a classroom only to have my every step dogged by a hall monitor.

Moreover, how meaningful could such a recess be if, as it turns out, I am not able to tell the difference between thoughts generated independently of a larger design and thoughts transmitted through me as part of that design? I could never tell, at the time I make what feels like a free choice, whether I am, in fact, altering my fated course or not. A grand resolve to avoid something may not only be keeping me right on track, it may actually be accelerating me toward it. "[E]very man," says Nietzsche, "is himself a piece of fate; when he thinks to resist fate . . . it is precisely fate that is here fulfilling itself."[12] This axiom is illustrated in Arabic culture by the tale of the young man from Isfahan who sees Death beckoning to him in the marketplace. He flees on horseback, riding all day and into the night until he reaches the town of Samarra where he beds down at an inn. But in the middle of the night, death comes knocking at his door:

> "How come you to be here?" demanded the young man, white-faced and trembling; "I saw you only this morning in the market-place in Isfahan." And Death replied: "Why, I have come to collect you, as it is written. For when I saw you this morning in the market-place

in Isfahan, I tried to say that you and I had an appointment tonight in Samarra. But you would not let me speak, and only ran away."[13]

In the West, such an ironic twist of fate is woven into the myth of Oedipus. Upon hearing an oracle prophesy that he would kill his father and marry his mother, Oedipus (not yet having learned that he had been adopted) runs away from home. Then, his first day on the road, he kills a man he does not know to be his real (biological) father. Fate and the *feeling* of free will, including a free-will feeling of fighting fate, are compatible. Not so fate and *actual* free will.

ALTERNATIVE FUTURES

The belief that fated moments can exist in a non-fated universe is widespread. "Karma is simply cause and effect," says hypnotherapist Dr. Bruce Goldberg in *Past Lives, Future Lives*, "'As you sow so shall you reap.'"[14] No matter that the sowing was in Babylon and the reaping is in Brooklyn, *you* are in control of your karma because "the soul always has free will."[15] This free will disclaimer—usually no more than a paragraph or two—can be found in most books that profess belief in karma, fate, and precognition, regardless of its incompatibility with the data these books present.

Such disclaimers convert cosmic mystery into earthly implausibility. "[I]t is my belief," says Harriet Boswell in her chapter on premonitions and precognition in *Master Guide to Psychism*, "that we function under a law which gives us a partial free will and partial fixed incidents which we must undergo,"[16] leaving us to wonder how "fixed" any incident can be if the incidents leading up to it are not. Could a sheriff transporting a prisoner stop for lunch, remove the handcuffs, and tell the captive to meet back at the car in an hour? Yet even the most thoughtful of New Age writers, such as Jungian astrologer Liz Greene, assent, however reluctantly, to this cosmological conundrum: "I have no answers to the fundamental problem of whether we are fated or free," she says in *The Astrology of Fate*. "I am inclined, when faced with such an enormity, to feebly answer, Both."[17]

Whatever leaps of faith, then, these writers make toward a belief in destiny, they tie their ankle first. Enthusiastic investigators of strange phenomena that challenge everyday assumptions about free will, they neglect ordinary evidence that does the same. Some seem unaware that free will is, in fact, only a belief. Like most people today, they accept it as the fundamental given of their existence.

Aware that precognition and free will cannot blend together if each retains its full strength, some writers try to preserve free will by diluting precognition. They still insist that the future exists as a reality that can be known in the present, but they don't insist on the reality *of* that reality. The actual future can be divined, they say, not just guessed at; but there *might* be alternatives, *provided* appropriate acts of will intervene.

Belief in alternative futures has probably been around as long as belief in precognition. (In James's time it was promoted by C. W. Leadbeater, a founder of the Theosophical Society.) Usually it is just presented as a theory, with little elaboration. Like other disclaimers against fate, in books that acknowledge the reality of precognition, it is offered as a brief appendage at the end of the presentation—a plastic (albeit brightly colored) hacksaw to cut the iron chains that have just been forged. Evidence for the theory, when offered, is always the same: a report of a precognitive image that later played out, but at the last moment took a different turn. Frederic Myers offers such evidence in relating the following account of a personal acquaintance:

> The lady had dreamed that she saw her old coachman falling from the top of the carriage to the road, landing on his head. Later that day after a long drive during which she had forgotten completely about her dream . . . she saw the coachman leaning back in his seat, as if he were not well. She called to him to stop the carriage, jumped out, and motioned to a nearby policeman. Just then the coachman swayed and fell off the box. The policeman was by then near enough to catch him and keep him from landing on his head and being severely injured, as the dream had foretold.[18]

Accounts such as these make up the sole evidence for alternative futures.[19] A modern account was given by a particularly strong supporter of the belief, Richard Bach, in his popular autobiographical work, *The Bridge Across Forever*. Like Twain's completely precognitive dream, Bach's semi-precognitive dream is worth dwelling upon insofar as it raises fundamental questions posed by all such accounts. However much the characters and scenes differ in "alternative future" dreams, the plot device remains the same.

Bach's account begins with a dream he had when he was on the verge of ending his relationship with his girlfriend (later, wife) Wookie, the night before he was to compete in an air race. In his dream he is piloting his plane in the race when suddenly another plane crashes into him. The result is as near fatal as dreams allow: "I grab the parachute ripcord, pull it, roll over to see the ground before the parachute opens . . . too late. Wook, I am sorry. So . . . black."[20] Bach wakes from this dream a new man: "I don't want to leave you, little wookie, I never want to leave you . . . I love you."[21]

The next day, Bach is flying in the race when as fate, or something, would have it, there is a midair crash just above his own plane; he only narrowly escapes, and watches it play out from a safe distance:

> Never had I seen a midair collision. At a distance, it was gentle and silent. . . .
>
> All at once I froze in the heat. *I saw this yesterday!* What are the odds against it . . . the only mid-air I've ever seen, coming the day after I lay on the floor of the trailer and watched it in advance!
>
> No, I hadn't watched, it had been *me*, hit by the wing!
>
> Having made the decision to love, had I chosen life instead of death?"[22]

The odds against Bach dreaming of a midair collision the night before he was in an air race in which a collision *did* occur, are surely smaller than he imagines—far smaller, at any rate, than the odds against the alternative explanation that he offers. What sense, after all, can be made of Bach's belief that he had witnessed an actual future scene, but then altered it through his actions? That the future can be known at all, or that it in some sense coexists with the present, is not an easy notion to grasp, except, perhaps, for mystics and theoretical physicists.[23] The notion, however, that there exist alternative futures that can be *divined*, not just imagined, is even harder to fathom.

Perhaps it is because we frequently daydream in something *like* alternative futures that we do not dismiss their existence outright. Both wish-fulfilling and wish-denying images do play out in our minds as alternative endings to a future scenario. Furthermore, as often as not, the actual realization of the scene plays out differently than any we had imagined—an alternative to our alternatives. We are both familiar and comfortable with the idea that the future can easily begin in a way that we have preconceived, and then take a surprising turn of direction.

Such scenarios, however, make poor analogies to alternative futures. To begin with, when a future scene is based on imagination only, we usually feel identified with its outcome. What is important is *our* role, *our* desire, in the scene. Consequently, only what is relevant to that desire is likely to be precisely etched. If, for example, I imagine asking my boss for a raise, I may imagine a specific expression on his face, but I do not imagine the pattern of his tie. By contrast, a striking feature of many purported precognitive visions is the vividness of details unconnected to our desire or "role" in the narrative. (Indeed, our "role" in a precognitive dream is often no more than a walk-on.) Thus, if I have a precognized dream of being in my boss's office, I might see his tie more distinctly than the expression on his face. While scenes of imminent danger are the precognitive images most discussed, innocuous scenes, such as the one reported by the British Consul, are the most common. Such scenes, as he said, seem to have "no purpose whatsoever," and of them "one cannot help think, what was the good of it?" These scenes are "extraordinarily vivid," not because of *what* they show, but *how* they are shown. A particularly compelling account of this sort of purported precognitive image has been recorded by Richard Mann, a professor of psychology at the University of Michigan. In his book, *The Light of Consciousness*, Mann recounts a detailed "scene" that arose while meditating, and was later realized, a scene that "flashed in front of" him with "the smoothness and uncanny fluidity of a scene being photographed by a slowly moving camera," constituted entirely of details to which he had no personal connection.[24]

Rehearsing the future in our imagination (as in a daydream) is like holding a conversation on a time phone. We communicate *to* the future what we wish will happen, and receive *from* that wished-for future reasons why it may not. We then alter our present circumstances to increase our chances for success, and communicate those altered circumstances back to our imagined future. By contrast, a precognitive image is like receiving a text message on a cellphone. It arrives as a completed whole, without any evidence of having consulted us first, unlike ordinary imagination, but in common with heightened inspiration.

More importantly, precognition is *always* distinguished from ordinary imagination by what its alterability implies. For the belief in alternative futures—the belief that a precognized event can be altered—claims more than that the present influences the future; it claims a direct causal link between *specific* points scattered in time—a link not found in any other theories of determinism, outside the excesses of Freudianism. The rigidity of these direct connections between present and future is easily overlooked in the theory since it appears to be completely flexible about what the future will be. The belief attempts to solve the paradox of how free will can be mixed with a fixed future by unfixing the future, but at the same time it fixes a strict relationship between the present and future all its own.

The idea that the will is free within the limits of having to pass through certain specific moments treats the relationship between the ongoing present and the future as water meandering down a mountain, eventually finding its way to the bottom. The belief in alternative futures, on the other hand, sees the ongoing present as water passing through a canal. The fact that the destination of the water might change does not mean that the walls of the canal have become porous. It means only that another canal has been built.

Bach, for example, felt that the decision he had made to stay with his lover changed the specific outcome of the plane crash the next day. He believed that the crash would have happened not as it did, but as he had foreseen it, if he had left her. Thus, as he and other alternative futurists believe, events, in all their detail, run their course, except in certain moments when a change of direction can be introduced. The position of someone facing such moments, says C. W. Leadbeater,

> is somewhat like that of the driver of a train; when he comes to a junction he may have the points set either this way or that, and so can pass on to whichever line he pleases, but when he has passed on to one of them he is compelled to run along the line which he has selected until he reaches another set of points, where again an opportunity of choice is offered to him.[25]

This idea of junction points, with "opportunities of choice" determining highly *specific* outcomes in the future, is the key feature of the theory of alternative futures.

Despite its promotion of an intermittent freedom, however, the theory takes away as much freedom as it grants, by claiming that any given moment is directly, *causally,* connected to another moment that preceded it. The fact that something can intervene to break the connection does not alter the fact *of* the connection. *All* causal connections are subject to intervention. Determinists, on the other hand, who do not believe in any kind of free will, allow that every moment is connected with every other, but they do not make any claim about local causation. Like Hume, they need not accept that any *given* moment has a necessary influence over any other.

Furthermore, even if the highly specific scenarios of precognitive dreams *were* as alterable as virtual reality games, they are seldom scripted for the dreamer alone. Most "opportunities of choice" must, of necessity, be *opportunities of control* over others, of determining *their* course. The highly specific details of precognitive dreams are not a stage set for solo actor. If I can determine a precise future scenario by my present choices and actions, then I must be determining *other* people's choices and actions as well. If, for example, Twain's brother could have chosen not to have taken his fatal boat trip, then he would also have been altering the choice of the old woman to spend part of a future morning procuring white roses.

Alternative futurists, such as Bach and Leadbeater, who would say that Twain's brother was bound to a determined line of action unless he introduced a spontaneous act of will, fail to consider that part of that determined line of action includes the *woman's* responses. It is not just that if Twain's brother "chooses" another mode of transportation then she will not have the *occasion,* a month hence, to bring flowers, but that his choice would *instantly* alter the choreography of her future movements. On the one hand, alternative futurists would allow that she always had the option not to lay white roses on the casket, but on the other hand, they would insist that the precise movements she was to make on that morning could have been altered by the caprice of Twain's brother a month before. His "track switch" would have communicated to a point on her track, down the line. And if free will is assumed to be real, then, as he wavers back and forth between going and not going, he must continually be signaling and canceling her track switch. In other words, he must continually be erasing and etching the fine details of her future every time he changes his mind about his trip.

The most problematical aspect of the alternative future theory, however, is not what it would entail, but how it would exist in the first place. Instead of the relativity of time, the theory of alternative futures posits the relativity of everything. In seeking to explain the mystery of how a precognized image can be realized in most—but not all—of its details, it manufactures a bigger mystery of its own. A time warp of reality is one thing; what is a time warp of a possibility? Such a conundrum of a theory, whether it be called "alternative futures" or "parallel universes," or "many-worlds" is, in the words of physicist Paul Davies, "excess baggage carried to the extreme."[26]

This excess would be easier to accept if there were not a more plausible answer to how a precognized image might later play out differently than originally seen. But as long as a simpler explanation for such a phenomenon exists, alternative futures violate what philosophers call Occam's razor: "Entities are not to be multiplied without necessity."[27] As Bertrand Russell explains this "most fruitful principle in logical analysis": "[I]f everything . . . can be interpreted without assuming this or that hypothetical entity, there is no ground for assuming it."[28] While precognition, despite the perpetual support of some scientists, is not quite a science, it need not therefore become science fiction.

The most plausible interpretation for why a precognitive dream might later play out differently than originally seen is that it is part actual and part imagination. Bach, for example, in his dream, may have precognized the actual future event—the two planes spinning out of control just above him—but then, in a shocked response to the perceived threat, contracted away from the actual time warp, so that the dream continued from that point on as his invention, with its all too plausible scenario of personal doom. Similarly, the woman who thought she foresaw her coachman fall to the ground may have only actually foreseen him begin to fall, recoiled in shock, and completed the scene with her ordinary imagination, supplying it with the all-but-inevitable disastrous result suggested by the context. Robert Ferguson, in his book, *ESP for Everyone*, says: "The literal dream [his phrase for a precognitive dream] is sometimes difficult to differentiate from a dream fantasy."[29] Why then couldn't both exist as part of one dream? As the eminent parapsychologist Louisa E. Rhine wrote in her essay "Precognition and Intervention":

> Even if it be granted that one part of the experience, the one that was fulfilled, had been precognized, it may not be necessary to assume that the averted part was; for it is possible that the origin of the total experience was more complicated, and that the two parts had different origins. Even if the non-averted part were truly cognitive, the other still could have been a rational inference derived from the precognitive impression. Since it is evident from the study of other psi cases that dreamers do often embroider extrasensorially received information, it is only reasonable to ask whether such mental action could be involved in cases like these.[30]

This assumption of mixed origin leaves the integrity of precognition intact. Moreover, it is able to account for instances of precognition where there are inconsistencies between what had been seen and what was later realized without adding any new inconsistencies of its own.[31] At the very least, it removes the ground for assuming the "hypothetical entity" of alternative futures.

KARMA

> Karma . . . I agree in principle with . . . it carries *execution* with it . . . and operates "causally" as partial factor in the natural fact.
>
> —William James, *The Varieties of Religious Experience*

If it is accepted that precognition is real, that no attempt to dilute its reality is satisfactory, then the reality of fate must be considered as well. Like precognition itself, however, most considerations of fate are a diluted or hybrid variety, such as karma. If belief in fate is not as strong today as it has been, belief in the diluted fate of karma has soared. It is almost as if, in the light of renewed interest in precognition, people have begun to inoculate themselves with karma to avoid the disease of fate.

Perpetually de-shackling himself from fate's iron bonds, James celebrated what he saw as the "Buddhistic doctrine of karma" with its emphasis on actions and their consequences, as opposed to the more monistic Vedantic version (*VRE*, 466). And the popular adoption of this term since James's time seems to agree with him. Karma is fate tamed. In place of an unfathomable force, it offers a familiar law: every action has an opposite and equal reaction. In place of one, inexorable, universal will, it allows a will of one's own: only the *re*action is determined; an effect that "I" caused. The determination begins only after "I" have started it going, just as my stepping backwards into a swing *results* in my being propelled forwards. Unlike fate, karma is something I *create*.[32]

As palatable as this hybrid form of fate may be, the problems with it are the same that we encountered in trying to reconcile self-willed actions with precognition: no action takes place in a void, but rather in a context defined by an infinitude of specific details. To be the recipient of karmic law in this life for something I have done previously in a past life would require an extensive collaboration from animate and inanimate forces alike. Karma can never be a simple matter of one event being answered by another, like the movement of a pendulum.

Even if it were possible to exactly correlate our actions to their consequences, we are once again confronted with the reality that all human actions are dependent, directly or indirectly, on our thoughts. Therefore, any instance of "my karma" must entail more than a direct link between a given action and a given consequence; it must entail all the thoughts that lead to both. If, say, it is "my karma" to be reintroduced to someone from a past life with whom I have unfinished business, then, unbeknownst to us both, it is "our karma" to have those ideas pop into our heads that will coordinate our schedules.

Likewise, if a fatal accident is my karma, then so, too, are the thoughts and circumstances that lead me to it. If I am to die in a plane crash (along with, say, two hundred other people who loosened chariot wheels in a past life) I must first have the *idea* to take the trip; and this idea would *not*, presumably, be related to atonement, or, feel, in any way, different from all other thoughts *unrelated* to this karmic connection.

Conspicuous "turns of events" explained as karma are not necessarily or even ordinarily preceded by conspicuous turns of thought. What sense, then, does it make to claim that the ultimate source of the thoughts that inspired me to take a fatal plane ride can be traced back to one moment or event *and no other*? For if karma can inspire me to take a journey I regret, what is to say it didn't inspire me to loosen the chariot wheel in the first place (perhaps to give someone else his or her comeuppance for a past life misdeed) and so on until the meaning of "first place" dissolves?

PRIVATE THOUGHTS AND PUBLIC ACTS

The tendency to restrict fate (insofar as we believe in fate at all) to actions and happenings rather than thoughts is not surprising. Thoughts "of one's own" allow wiggle room in fate's tight squeeze; like the eye of a storm, they seem interior enough to escape being buffeted by a force that nonetheless controls them. If, as Francis Barker says, "[t]he scene of writing and reading is, like the grave, a private place,"[33] how much more private and interior is the scene of our thoughts? By contrast, our actions transpire in a public domain. Actions, we believe, always have consequences, however slight, in the world outside ourselves, unlike thoughts, which, more often than not, appear to remain harmlessly "indoors." Thoughts don't really "count," we believe, unless they lead to an action. "Mrs. Quest was like ninety-nine percent of humanity," says Doris Lessing in her novel *Landlocked*: "if she spent an afternoon jam-making, while her mind was filled with thoughts envious, spiteful, lustful—violent; then she had spent the afternoon making jam."[34]

Even those who believe that such thoughts count, would probably see them as counting only because a strong content has overtaken a faint form. As the jam-making Mrs. Quest's expressions might reveal, some thoughts are exceptionally vivid. Most thoughts, however, are not only hidden from others, they are barely accessible to ourselves. "[T]rains are such magnificent objects we commonly mistake them for destiny," says E. B. White.[35] Thoughts, on the other hand, often seem too fragmentary, fleeting, or insignificant to be part of destiny's vast continuum. Notwithstanding Freud's attempt to prove that no thoughts are random, they often seem but the feeble firings of our individual brains, transpiring completely within a private domain.

Although James dismissed the notion of "the closed individuality of each personal consciousness," of "*being*-an-individual in some inaccessible metaphysical way" (*PP1*, 350), the nonpublic, "interiority" of thoughts has become a cornerstone of identity, especially in the West, with its emphasis on the rights of the individual, and the individual's right to privacy. One consequence of this identity is that it insists on precisely the sort of distinction between private thought and public act that renders fated encounters unintelligible. For belief in fate (including the part-time fated "moments" of karma) is not coherent unless it extends to the private domain of our thoughts no less than the public domain of our actions.

NINE

That Thou Art

> All confess that God is omnipotent; but it seems difficult to explain in what his omnipotence precisely consists.
>
> —Aquinas, *Summa Theologica*

The West's tendency to restrict fate to actions and, at most, only those thoughts that lead to actions, is similar to its tendency to restrict God's omnipotence. Belief in God's omnipotence implies, at the very least, God's potential omniscience and omnipresence. But the West does not readily concede one's every passing thought to be part of either. When we want God to hear what's on our mind, we pray—that is, we *make contact*, as Jimmy Olsen does with Superman. The contact may be to ask for forgiveness, or a favor, or simply to express gratitude, but in all prayer as practiced in the West, even what Twain called the "secret supplications of the heart," the pray-er *initiates* communication.

Not that such pray-ers believe that without such initiating contact God cannot know what's on their minds or in their hearts. Even when God is not being sought, certain of our thoughts may be deemed to be being overheard by God, especially if they are either very loving or very hateful—that is, when, once again, a strong content has overtaken a faint form. Moreover, just as certain thoughts are deemed to be part of destiny's stream, certain thoughts, experienced as inspiration (literally, "to breathe into"), may be deemed to have been *sent* by God to guide us, especially in times of crisis, or while engaged in creative activity. But moments of prayer, or of revealing thoughts, or of "heaven-sent" inspiration, may be distinguished from most other moments in which no connection to God is actively felt or imagined, even though, if God's omniscience is real, that connection is always there. While James's struggling, alcoholic youngest brother, Robertson, once told him: "The only thing in life I am afraid of is the insanity which robs the mind of the thought of God," it could never be a mutual loss (*C1*, 511). As the Psalms say:

> O Lord, thou hast searched me and known me!
> Thou knowest when I sit down and when I rise up;
> thou discernest my thoughts from afar.
> Thou searchest out my path and my lying down,
> and art acquainted with all my ways.
> Even before a word is on my tongue,
> lo, O Lord, thou knowest it altogether.
> Thou dost beset me behind and before,
> and layest thy hand upon me.
> Such knowledge is too wonderful for me;
> it is high, I cannot attain it.[1]

Probably more people strive to feel connected to God than strive to imagine how God's omniscience connects to them. But clearly, a belief in God's omniscience *does* require a leap of imagination as much as faith. How else can we begin to understand the unconditioned degree to which such omniscience might relate to the ever-flowing stream of our consciousness?

The twelfth-century Persian poet Hakim Sanai says that God not only has knowledge "of the inmost thought," he "knows the touch of an ant's foot moving in darkness over a rock."[2] What makes this image so exotic for us is its subtlety. The composite image collapses into itself like the black, multi-layered rectangles of an Ad Reinhardt painting. To the Eastern imagination, however, this collapse is real. Unlike all but the most mystical expressions of Western spirituality, the East is not burdened by the "given" that there are distinct selves separated from God. "[W]hatever states of being there may be," God says in the *Bhagavad Gita*, "be they harmonious, passionate, slothful—know thou that they are all from me alone. *I am not in them; they are in me.*"[3]

In Eastern religions the experience of a separate self is considered a temporary—however persistent—illusion. The most familiar term for this illusion, and the illusions that support it, is the Sanskrit word *maya*—literally, "she who measures." In the divine play (*lila*) of the one underlying, all-embracing reality (*Brahman*), there is a measuring out of apparently individuated selves as if they were acting on their own initiative.[4] It is not that the *world* is an illusion—only the sense of being a separate, autonomous self within it. Emerson, immersed in his vast library of Asian literature, gave perhaps the most cogent English rendering of this state in his poem "Brahma":

> If the red slayer thinks he slays,
> Or if the slain thinks that he is slain,
> They know not well the subtle ways
> I keep, and pass, and turn again.
>
> Far or forgot to me is near;
> Shadow and sunlight are the same;
> The vanished gods to me appear;
> And one to me are shame and fame.
>
> They reckon ill who leave me out;
> When me they fly, I am the wings;
> I am the doubter and the doubt;
> And I the hymn the Brahmin sings.
>
> The strong gods pine for my abode,
> And pine in vain the sacred Seven;
> But thou, meek over good!
> Find me, and turn thy back on heaven.[5]

In notes for a lecture, James wrote, "Even in this world of the mystic One there is something wrong. The rest, the peace, is broken by the maya" (*ML*, 267). Yes. But only "if the red slayer thinks he slays."

The belief that all creation, all agency, transcends self, establishing prime reality as an "impersonal quintessence,"[6] is a foundation of Eastern spirituality. Lao Tzu called this impersonal quintessence the Tao. The Buddha saw the realization of such impersonal consciousness, devoid of self-agency, as enlightenment. The word *nirvana,* meaning "extinguished," refers to this extinguishment of the sense of self (*ahamhara,* "I-ing," and *mamihara,* "mine-ing"); and the impersonal consciousness that remains is called *sunyata*—"void"—that is, void of self, *anatta.*[7] In Hinduism, this impersonal consciousness beyond the three stages of waking, dreaming, and non-dream sleep is called *turya,* or "the fourth," in which the self is dissolved in *brahman,* with the realization *Tat Tvam Asi,* "That thou art"—the Eastern phrase most quoted by the Western determinist philosopher Schopenhauer. The Sufi version of "That thou art" is called "*maqam al-wisal,*" "the station of union," and finds numerous colorful expressions such as:

> When I [Allah] love my servant . . . I become the hearing with which he hears, the seeing with which he sees, the hand with which he grasps, the feet with which he walks, the tongue with which he speaks.[8]

"That thou art" is also the relationship with God (or something like God) that entheogenic drugs facilitate, supporting the conjecture that an entheogenic plant (soma) "was probably the most important source of the vedic religion and philosophy."[9] One such entheogenic experience, with ether, related by a correspondent of James, Frederick Hall, particularly impressed James:

> [T]here flashed through my mind a conversation with a friend in which he, speaking of God as the great immanent spirit, in whom we live and move and have our being, suggested that God could perfectly control all phenomena, yet leave us infallibly convinced that what we saw resulted from natural law and natural law only. Not that this explanation quite fitted the case, not that I had any feeling of God, in the theological sense, but the very atmosphere of this world spoke to me of the oneness and rightness of all things.[10]

James himself, under the influence of the entheogen nitrous oxide, also merged with something like "the great immanent spirit." Experiencing an "intense bewilderment, with nothing particular left to be bewildered at save the bewilderment itself," James seemed to himself to be "spirit become its own object" (*WB*, 679). The universality of unitive experiences such as his and Hall's was emphasized by James when he introduced "That thou art" into *The Varieties of Religious Experience* with the following:

> This overcoming of all the usual barriers between the individual and the Absolute is the great mystic achievement. In mystic states we both become one with the Absolute and we become aware of our oneness. This is the everlasting and triumphant mystical tradition, hardly altered by differences of clime or creed. In Hinduism, in Neoplatonism, in Sufism, in Christian mysticism, in Whitmanism, we find the same recurring note, so that there is about mystical utterances an eternal unanimity which ought to make a critic stop and think, and which brings it about that the mystical classics have, as has been said, neither birthday nor native land. Perpetually telling of the unity of man with God, their speech antedates languages, and they do not grow old. (*VRE*, 378)

As James well knew, to be "entitatively one with god" is a stark contrast to the "monarchial," "external creator" of Western religion, rooted in "dualistic theism, with ourselves represented as a secondary order of substances created by God" (*PU*, 16, 18, 25). The Western imagination, with its more solid and distinct sense of self, has a more solid and distinct sense of God. God is one, declared Judaism, and man, alas, became the other. It is very difficult in the West to eradicate the Sistine Chapel cosmos from our spiritual imagination: God and man as two distinct entities, inhabiting separate realms. (Even the delicate bridge of the finger kiss, uniting God and man, seems to emphasize, as much as bridge, the separateness.)

It is not that the concept of God as a personalized deity is foreign to Eastern religious belief. Hinduism, in particular, abounds in anthropomorphized images of gods. But, with the exception of some overtly dualistic sects, Hinduism sees all deities as manifestations of the one Being, the one Reality. Moreover, in marked contrast to Christian missionary teaching in the East, Hindu belief, as promulgated in the West, mostly through its school of Advaita Vedanta, excludes any overt dualism. Swami Vivekananda, whom James dubbed the "paragon" of the "monistic missionary," emphasized this nondualism when he introduced Hinduism in lecture halls across America, as in this passage cited by James:

> "He who, in this world of many, sees that One; he who in this mass of insentiency sees that One Sentient Being; he who in this world of shadow catches that Reality, unto him belongs eternal peace, unto none else, unto none else!" (*P*, 552, 553)[11]

So, too, although the Buddha has sometimes been prayed to as a deity, the Buddha himself saw his belief as a radical departure from externalized, dualistic, deity worship.

Christian mystics, too, as James well notes, have participated in "the everlasting and triumphant mystical tradition." And along with such celebrated mystics as Meister Eckhart, St. John of the Cross, and Jacob Boehme, Jewish mystics, such as the founder of Hasidism, the Bal Shem Tov, also abound.[12] *Unio mystica*, "becom[ing] one with the Absolute and aware of our oneness," can thus be considered as part of the Judeo-Christian tradition, however much our strong sense of individuated self resists such union. As Jacob Boehme counseled:

> When thou standest still from the thinking and willing of self, the eternal hearing, seeing and speaking will be revealed to thee, and so God heareth and seeth through thee. Thine own hearing, willing and seeing hindreth thee, that thou does not see nor hear God.[13]

Some who acknowledge Jesus's spiritual realization (but not his virgin birth) see him as a mystic, whose "lost years," in his twenties, may have been spent in India. And although the mystical Jesus of the "kingdom of God is within" is overshadowed by the Jesus whose kingdom is above, it can well be asked whether his fundamental message had more to do with Eastern-style mystical dissolution of self than with Western-style exalted pedigree. In John

14:10, for instance, Jesus claims more than a relationship (more than even a filial relationship) to God when he says, "I am in the father and the father is in me." Lest the depth of his self-effacement be missed, he immediately adds: "The words which I say to you from me I do not speak. But the father in me dwelling does his deeds."[14] Even his main quarrel with his fellow Jews can be seen as a quarrel between East and West. Ultimately crucified for the "blasphemy" of claiming to be the son of God, Jesus had earlier narrowly escaped stoning by the Jews for an even bolder claim: "I and the father are one."[15] He escaped that death only by reminding the angered Jews of their own Biblical text: "You are Gods."[16] What did his accusers understand by that reminder? While the God of the Old Testament (the God whom Jesus invokes) may, like the Greek Gods, seem too angry, too jealous, too *human,* to be an agent or agency of a mystical dissolution of self, it is worth remembering that the *name* Yahweh, or Jehovah, derives from the Hebrew root *hayah,* or *hawah,* meaning "to be." This meaning is corroborated by the name that Yahweh gives himself, in Exodus 4:14, a name that may have baffled Moses, but which would have been readily recognizable to mystics and students of Eastern religion. As the Zen scholar/sage D. T. Suzuki said, "'I am that I am,'—whatever its original Hebrew meaning may have been—is the fittest name for God."[17]

But mysticism has been more suspectable than respectable in the formalized religions of the West. The strong Judeo-Christian belief in individuated "I"s creating their own individuated histories, beginning with Abraham's "Going forth," has persisted.[18] Such persistence is somewhat surprising given the equally strong Judeo-Christian belief in God's unabated omnipotence. For if, as Martin Luther (and many) believe, God "does all things according to His immutable, eternal and infallible will," then all things (including the choices we make as well as our feelings about whether we are making those choices ourselves) are also what God "does." In other words, you are (not ultimately distinguishable from) God. That thou art: James's "great mystic achievement." The medieval Christian mystic Meister Eckhart put it this way: "If it is true that God became man, it is also true that man became God . . . and so . . . you haven't got to borrow from God, for he is your own and therefore, whatever you get, you get from yourself."[19] Benjamin Paul Blood affirmed the same nondualism:

> The central truth of the gospel of Jesus is that of himself the creature can do nothing; that God is rather a father than a governor, but more than either he is for his own purpose the inner and inspiring life and light, without which not even a sparrow falls to the ground.[20]

And Blood even quotes Emerson for corroboration:

> The ardors of piety agree at last with the coldest skepticism, that nothing is of us or our works—that all is of God. Nature will not spare us the smallest leaf of laurel. All writing comes by the grace of God, and all doing and having. I would gladly be moral, and keep due metes and bounds, which I dearly love, and allow the most to the will of man; but I have set my heart on honesty in this chapter, and I can see nothing at last, in success or failure, than more or less of vital force supplied by the Eternal.[21]

In overcoming a morbid passivity through a belief in free will, James preferred, as we have emphasized, "tragic zest" to the "perfect sumptuosity of security" provided by radical, spiritual monism, with its "assurance that however disturbed the surface may be, at bottom all is well with the cosmos—central peace abiding at the heart of endless agitation" (*P*, 553; *PU*, 55). A conception of God as the one omnipotent ground of being, "a centre, a Unity of everything" to which all reality can be "traced" struck him as "lazy monism that idly haunts the region of God's name" (*P*, 553; *PU*, 60).[22] Nor did James embrace the Judeo-Christian God, whose "existence is the guarantee of an ideal order that shall be permanently preserved" and through whom "tragedy is only provisional and partial, and shipwreck and dissolution are not the absolutely final things" (*VRE*, 462).

As a pragmatist—one who equated a thought's "significance" with the "conduct" it engenders—James would never sign Nietzsche's death certificate for God, since he believed God's death would terminate, as well, the "maximal stimulating power" of our "moral energy" (*VRE*, 399; *WB*, 615). On the other hand, this same concern for a belief's consequences led James to endorse Nietzsche's dismissal of "other world" salvation, "poisoning our trust in life" (*VRE*, 337). To what he deemed the "serious" question: "Shall the seen world or the unseen world be our chief sphere of adaptation?" James (like Nietzsche) affirmed the former because he scorned the latter (at least as commonly portrayed), and contrasted our "crepuscular natures born for the conflict, the Rembrandtesque moral *chiaroscuro*, the shifting struggle of the sunbeam in the gloom," with the tedium of a vacuous "white-robed harp-playing heaven" (*VRE*, 338; *WB*, 583).

Despite James's enduring interest in the possibilities of an afterlife, the only God he professed "worthy of the name" was "finite"—"*in* the cosmos, not with the cosmos in him"—and would partner with us to combat evil (*PU*, 54). "Us," for James, being that "part of the . . . world experienced . . . with our body as its centre, centre of vision, centre of action, centre of interest" (*EA*, 803n). But, as we shall see, James's end-of-life mystical suggestion offered a radical revision to this zest-questers' cosmos with its individualized centers—a mystic's vision, not only congruent with Frederick Hall's *unio mystica* experience, but based, in part, upon it.

THE ONE IN THE MANY

> No one can strike his roots into eternity without being rid of number.
>
> —Meister Eckhart

The enforced separation between God and man in the Western religious tradition is somewhat ironic given that Western thought was *founded* on the principle of one underlying reality behind the play of appearances. The debate, in the early stages of Greek cosmology, was not whether such a single underlying reality existed, but only what it might be. Anaximander declared it to be some sort of divine, unbounded, infinite substance that "enfolded" and controlled the cosmos. Thales had finitized it into water; Anaxamines said air; both were precursors to Democritus, a post-Socratic who, anticipating twentieth-century physics, envisioned atoms. Heraclitus, restoring the subtlety of Anaximander, proclaimed a fire-like flux to be the underlying reality; Pythagoras, more subtle still, proclaimed it to be a mathematical harmonia. And then there was the only philosopher that Plato referred to as "deep,"[23] Parmenides, who, subtlest of them all, claimed that reality was indivisible; generation and destruction were illusory; and everything that ever was or will be is now, altogether one.[24]

Thus, for all that Christianity tidied up the Greek pantheon it cluttered its cosmos. The rise of modern physics, however, is reuniting us with our cosmologic roots. The all is becoming one again. The theory of relativity proclaims the possibility that the universe (our seemingly separate selves included) is a single, unified field of energy. A wealth of evidence now supports what Einstein first proposed at the beginning of the twentieth century, without "the slightest direct experimental evidence": the equivalency of mass and energy.[25] Today, all matter is believed by physicists to be reducible either to string-like vibrations or to two fundamental particles—quarks and leptons—which, in turn, are nothing more than "points of congealed energy."[26] That is, everything in the universe, from sand to selves, consists, ultimately, of varieties of energy. The sharp distinction between, say, your body and the air that surrounds it is a function of the limited magnification of your eyesight, as neurologist Jill Bolte Taylor learned, with assistance from a stroke in her brain's left hemisphere, the hemisphere that enforces the separating "I" sense:

> I lost my balance and I'm propped up against the wall. And I look down at my arm and I realize that I can no longer define the boundaries of my body. I can't define where I begin and where I end. Because the atoms and the molecules of my arm blended with the atoms and molecules of the wall. And all I could detect was this energy. Energy. And I'm asking myself, "What is wrong with me, what is going on?" And in that moment, my brain chatter, my left hemisphere brain chatter went totally silent. Just like someone took a remote control and pushed the mute button and—total silence.
>
> And at first I was shocked to find myself inside of a silent mind. But then I was immediately captivated by the magnificence of energy around me. And because I could no longer identify the boundaries of my body, I felt enormous and expansive. I felt at one with all the energy that was, and it was beautiful there.[27]

That such de-differentiation cannot be dismissed as a mere "derangement of the brain" is corroborated by Vivekananda. Without a trace of pathology, he had a similar experience when "touched . . . over the heart" by his guru, Ramakrishna: "the houses—rooms, doors, windows, verandahs—the trees, the sun, the moon—all were flying off, shattering into pieces as it were—and ultimately became merged in the Akasha [the ether-like basis and essence of all things in the material world]."[28] If Energy does indeed equal Mass times the Speed of Light squared, then the Trinity seems excessive. Why need there be more than the Holy Spirit? As the contemporary Western mystic Da Free John says: "$E = mc^2$ is the Twentieth Century version of Christ is risen."[29]

"PRIMAL STUFF"

> The world is given to me only once, not one existing and one perceived. Subject and object are only one. The barrier between them cannot be said to have broken down as a result of recent experience in the physical sciences, for this barrier does not exist.
>
> —Erwin Schrödinger, *Mind and Matter*

> Thinkers who first make molecules and then fall down in mute and holy reverence before the awful mystery of how the molecules ever could make them, are far from knowing what it is to cross-question consciousness with any real spirit in their questioning. If I understand you, it is such cross-questioning of consciousness which you want to have done.
>
> —Josiah Royce, in a letter to James

At the same time that Einstein was theorizing matter into energy, James was theorizing everything into experience. Like an Ionian cosmologist, he declared: "There is only one primal stuff or material in the world, a stuff of which everything is composed" (*DCE*, 1142). James called this primal one "pure experience" (*DCE*, 1142). The Ionian Anaxagoras had proposed mind (*nous*) as the primal stuff of reality, but he had only claimed it to be an ultimate *arranger* of matter. James, on the other hand, proclaimed matter itself, matter as "something *behind* physical phenomena," to be a mere "postulate" of thought (*PP1*, 304). He quoted his beloved friend and colleague Josiah Royce on the force of this postulate: "The popular assurance of an external world is the *fixed determination to make one*, now and henceforth" (*PP2*, 318). Such fixedly determined postulates were to be found at all levels of perceived matter, from mountains to molecules. James himself allowed that molecules and atoms could be construed as "pegs in a conceptual arrangement for hanging percepts on . . . so as to predict facts in 'elegant' or expeditious ways" (*SPP*, 1086n). He thus clearly anticipated the direction of quantum physics in the century that followed, where a "comic profusion" of particles has been *first* postulated, and only later "observed" or, rather, "*verified* consistent with the theory":[30]

> An . . . increasingly accepted idea among quantum physicists is that "consciousness" itself configures the experimental target. Consciousness, however, is not so much an activity as it is the ultimate reality, the ineffable substratum . . . out of which "matter" as well as "thought" constructs are carved. Thus what we call "knowledge" per se does not correspond to some interaction between knower and known, because neither the "subject" nor the "object" of cognition are autonomously constituted within the domain of knowing.[31]

James, a psychologist/philosopher not a physicist, knew more about "subjects" and "knowers" than about "objects" and "matter," but none of them, he believed, were autonomously constituted. Just as he believed matter to be a postulate of thought, derived from the ineffable substratum of pure experience, so he believed a thinker behind the thought to be a postulate as well, albeit "*the most fundamental of all the postulates of Psychology*" (*PP1*, 304, 185). Pure experience, in itself, "is no more inner than outer. . . . It *becomes* inner by *belonging* to an inner, it becomes outer by *belonging* to an outer, world" (*ML*, 217). What then of the inner-belonging experience postulated as the thinker, feeler, *willer* "I"? James, the objective anatomist and the subjective philosopher, was particularly well suited to interpret the nature of this postulate: the postulate that Nietzsche called "a fable, a fiction, a play on words."[32]

TEN

Consciousness and Consciousness of Self

> A kind of waking trance I have often had, quite from boyhood, when I have been all alone. This has generally come upon me through repeating my name two or three times to myself silently, till all at once, out of the intensity of the consciousness of individuality, the individual itself seemed to dissolve and fade away into boundless being; and this not a confused state, but the clearest of the clearest and the surest of the surest, the weirdest of the weirdest, utterly beyond words, where death was an almost laughable impossibility, the loss of personality (if so it were) seeming not extinction, but the only true life.
>
> —Alfred Lord Tennyson, in a letter to Benjamin Paul Blood, quoted by James in *The Varieties of Religious Experience*

> There is reality only when the mind is completely free from the . . . experiencer and the experienced.
>
> —Krishnamurti, *The First and Last Freedom*

There is no confusion about what "I" means in a room full of people. It is my body/self, distinct from other body/selves. So, too, the thoughts and feelings that are "my" thoughts and "my" feelings are the thoughts and feelings arising within *my* body/self as opposed to an*other*'s. "The word 'I,'" as James says, "is primarily a noun of position, just like 'this' or 'here'" (EA, 803n).[1]

The sense of a body/self, this/here, *positioning* "I" seems to develop around the age of eighteen months,[2] when all the lobes of the brain have finally become linked by subcortical pathways. It is well developed by the second year when children, placed in front of a mirror, will react to a painted spot on their nose. The presence of a positioning "I" is also revealed in the second year by that most important word: *mine*. When children first start saying "mine," they say it with an emphasis that leaves little doubt about what the word means: "not yours." The sense of otherness is a defining moment in the sense of "I" or "mineness"; it's the flip side of the coin. And whenever "I" am in a room with others, *this* body/self "I," as distinguished from *other* body/self "I"s, is in the room too.

But when a room is empty and I ask, "Who am I?" scanning my body is not of much help. Nor is looking in a mirror, however reassuring such looks may be. "Monkeys," says Malcolm de Chazal, "are superior to men in this: when a monkey looks into a mirror, he sees a monkey." Humans see more. We look *into* a mirror as if it were not a reflecting glass but a window *through* which we observe our *self*—that is, the agent and recipient of all our experience. The very preposition *in* or *into*, rather than *on*, reinforces the sense that we are viewing not merely surface images, but a world and its inhabitants. Indeed, so manifest is our presence in a mirror that some historians have traced the rise of the sense of self (the word *selfish* was not coined until the seventeenth century) to the significant improvement in mirror technology brought on by the use of mercury in the fourteenth century.[3] The expansion, or elaboration, of our reflected outer form into a self comes so naturally that we can easily spend a lifetime looking into mirrors without realizing that the only look we ever get back is dead on. I still remember the shock I felt when, at age thirty-five, I looked straight into the eyes of my reflection, moved my eyes, felt the movement, and yet saw not the slightest quiver in response. Narcissus, apparently, needed a pool of water as much for the ripple as the reflection.

The fact of a body is not the fact of a self. Though stable enough to seem a substance in which experience inheres, the body is more an address than a resident. And a none too certain address at that since, far from being "too, too solid flesh," the body, like all matter, is a swirl of energy, an energy construct. While this energy construct of body may survive in a rarefied form after death, without its bones, sinews, and liquids, and may even reincarnate,[4] such a construct is not a self. For whatever the self may be, it cannot be reduced to an objectifiable entity of energy or matter; insofar as the self exists at all, it must include something nonobjectifiable: consciousness.

SCIOUSNESS AND CONSCIOUSNESS

> Instead . . . of the stream of thought being one of con-sciousness, "thinking its own existence along with whatever else it thinks" . . . it might be better called a stream of Sciousness pure and simple, thinking objects of some of which it makes what it calls a "Me," and only aware of its "pure" Self in an abstract, hypothetic or conceptual way. The sciousness in question would be the Thinker, and the existence of this thinker would be given to us rather as a logical postulate than as that direct inner perception of spiritual activity which we naturally believe ourselves to have.
>
> —William James, *The Principles of Psychology*

> "The Witness"
>
> —James's handwritten annotation next to the word *sciousness* in his own copy of *The Principles of Psychology*.[5]

It is widely believed in the West that consciousness implies a self; that to be conscious (literally, to "know with") is to be a *self* that knows.[6] But James, who devoted most of his life to the study of consciousness, dismissed this belief outright, claiming it to be "a perfectly wanton assumption":

> [N]ot the faintest shadow of reason exists for supposing it true. As well might I contend that I cannot dream without dreaming that I dream, swear without swearing that I swear, deny without denying that I deny, as maintain that I cannot know without knowing that I know. (*PP1*, 274)

Consciousness is always a "knowing" or "witnessing." Sometimes it is a knowing "pure and simple" (*PP1*, 304), without an accompanying sense of "I." Sometimes, "along with" whatever else is known, consciousness has a sense of its "own existence" as knower (ibid.). James labeled consciousness-without-self "*scious*ness," and consciousness-with-self "*con*-sciousness" (ibid.).[7] (From here on the term *consciousness*, without the italicized *con*, will encompass both "sciousness" and "*con*-sciousness," referring to a moment which might be one or the other, or moments alternating between one and the other. In this more general sense, "consciousness" is synonymous with "awareness" and "experience.")

James held that "pure and simple" consciousness, without a "*self*-brand" (*PP1*, 337)[8]—sciousness—was not only a reality, it was the prime reality. For sciousness is not distilled from the "dualistic constitution" of subject-object consciousness (con-sciousness), as oil might be from pigment, but rather a "dualistic constitution" is added to it (*DCE*, 1144). Consciousness and objects have no reality, let alone prime reality, in themselves. Consciousness "in its own right," "felt as a kind of impalpable inner flowing," but "evaporated" to a content-less "estate of pure diaphaneity," is a "non-entity" (ibid.).[9] So, too, is an object devoid of consciousness, existing without any appearance whatsoever, as something "behind phenomena."[10]

When James first introduced "sciousness" as a possible prime reality in the *Principles*, he backed off with the warning that it "traverse[s] common sense," something he felt comfortable doing as a philosopher, but not as a textbook writer for a conservative scientific community (*PP1*, 304). He allowed that he might return to a consideration of sciousness at the conclusion of the book, where he would "indulge in some metaphysical reflections," but it was not until two years later, in his conclusion to his abridged edition of the *Principles*, that he felt emboldened to do so:

> Neither common sense, nor psychology so far as it has yet been written, has ever doubted that the states of consciousness which that science studies are immediate data of experience. "Things" have been doubted, but thoughts and feelings have never been doubted. The outer world, but never the inner world, has been denied. Everyone assumes that we have direct introspective acquaintance with our thinking activity as such, with our consciousness as something inward and contrasted with the outer objects which it knows. Yet I must confess that for my part I cannot feel sure of this conclusion. Whenever I try to become sensible of thinking activity as such, what I catch is some bodily fact, an impression coming from my brow, or head, or throat, or nose. It seems as if consciousness as an inner activity were rather a *postulate* than a sensibly given fact, the

> postulate, namely, of a *knower* as correlative to all this known; and as if "*scious*ness" might be a better word by which to describe it. But "sciousness postulated as a hypothesis" is a practically very different thing from "states of consciousness apprehended with infallible certainty by an inner sense." For one thing, it throws the question of *who the knower really is* wide open. (*PBC*, 432)[11]

Thirteen years later, writing solely as a philosopher, James returned to his "parenthetical digression" of sciousness that "contradict[ed] the fundamental assumption of *every* philosophic school" (*PP1*, 304), openly embracing it. Free at last to fully "indulge . . . metaphysical reflection," he founded a new school of philosophy, called "radical empiricism," and nondual sciousness was its starting point. He even wrote a note to himself to "apologize for my dualistic language in the *Principles*" (*MEN*, 29). James did not continue to use the word *sciousness* in these later essays on radical empiricism, but the concept is clearly there as the "plain, unqualified . . . existence" he comes to call "pure experience," where there is "no self-splitting . . . into consciousness and what the consciousness is 'of'" (*DCE*, 1151). (From here on "sciousness" and "pure experience" will be used interchangeably and in combination.)[12]

Pure and simple sciousness may characterize the experience of newborn babies, who have no consciousness of them*selves*, separate from the exact passing moment,[13] what James calls "one pulse of our life—not conceived so, but felt so" (*PU*, 130). Up until the age of one year, babies will follow almost any visual stimulus; but their eyes seem only to witness, not grasp. One developmental psychologist has called first-year babies "robotic looking machines,"[14] emphasizing what their gaze—from an adult perspective—lacks; if consciousness is only *con*sciousness, then babies have no claim to it. But if consciousness is derived from sciousness, then an adult's gaze can be seen for what *it* lacks: nondivisiveness. Unlike adult *con*sciousness, each movement/moment of baby consciousness is whole: one movement/moment vanishing upon the arrival of the next, as completely as the rattle that drops from their hand drops out of their awareness. James anticipated Piaget's characterization of this essential feature of earliest infancy, lack of object constancy:

> A baby's rattle drops out of his hand, but the baby looks not for it. It has "gone out" for him, as a candle-flame goes out; and it comes back, when you replace it in his hand, as the flame comes back when relit. The idea of its being a "thing," whose permanent existence by itself he might interpolate between its successive apparitions has evidently not occurred to him. It is the same with dogs. Out of sight, out of mind, with them. It is pretty evident that they have no general tendency to interpolate "things." (*P*, 562)

This whole attention to each moment means that babies are not diverted, by either inner or outer influence, from "the instant field of the present" (*AWPE* 1175).[15] Such a nondivertible presence gives them a power no robot shall ever attain. As Emerson puts it:

> Their mind being whole, their eye is as yet unconquered; and when we look into their faces we are disconcerted. Infancy conforms to nobody; all conform to it; so that one babe commonly makes four or five out of the adults who prattle and play to it.[16]

The immediate movement/moment of sciousness may be an adult version of this "whole mind," a state of nondivided attention—consciousness without consciousness of self, completely one-pointed in the ever-arising now. The revered, fifteenth-century Zen master Ikkyū Sōjun apparently believed this when he wrote: "As a baby gets further and further away from birth, it goes further and further away from being Buddha. How sad this is."[17]

James, for his part, found the most compelling evidence for the primacy of wholemind, nondual sciousness not in its being there from the start in babyhood, a controversial hypothesis at best, but in its being accessible afterward, most notably as an occasional side effect of the anaesthetic drug employed by the surgeons of his day: ether. In nineteenth-century America, mass manufacture of ether prompted considerable home experimenting that could induce, as we have already seen, a striking effect: the loss of the sense of "I" *without the loss of awareness*.[18] Thoreau likened it "to exist[ing] in your roots—like a tree in winter," and advised: "If you have an inclination to travel, take the ether. You go beyond the farthest star."[19]

In the *Principles*, James quotes the following firsthand account of such travel:

> During the syncope there is absolute psychic annihilation, the absence of all consciousness; then at the beginning of coming to, one has at a certain moment a vague, limitless, infinite feeling—a sense of existence in general without the least trace of distinction between the me and the not-me. (*PP1*, 273)

To this nondual, etherized experience just before "coming-to," James adds his own personal testimony: "[A]s it [the effect of the chloroform] vanishes I seem to wake to a sense of my own existence as something additional to what had previously been there" (ibid.).[20] Such "lapse of subjectivity," experienced just prior to coming out of anaesthesia, was matched by a lapse of objectivity—in the sense of a stable state of objects—as James went *into* anaesthesia, experiencing all the objects in the room shrinking and receding into the distance (ibid.; *PP2*, 143). But it was the loss of subjectivity within consciousness that impressed him the most. The fact that "many persons . . . at a certain stage in the anaesthetic process" experience objects "whilst the thought of self is lost" (ibid.; *PP1*, 273), led him to conclude that consciousness, or knowing, *itself* was primary, not a knowing that *must* "discriminate between its object and itself" (*PP1*, 275).

Benjamin Paul Blood, whose ether experiences became "cornerstones or landmarks" of James's thought, put the moment of coming-to from the ether state at the center of his mystical vision (*EPh*, 229). Blood called this moment the "Adamic surprise," invoking Adam's consciousness *prior* to his eating from the tree of knowledge:

> There is an invariable and reliable condition (or uncondition) ensuing about the instant of recall from anaesthetic stupor to "coming to," in which the genius of being is revealed. . . . No words may express the imposing certainty of the patient that he is realizing the primordial Adamic surprise of Life.[21]

The serpent's sales pitch notwithstanding, Adam did not gain knowledge when he bit into the apple; he didn't discover fire, or how to graft a tree.

The "knowledge" Adam gained was knowledge of *self*, which is not so much knowledge as *belief*. Under the influence of ether the feelings that this belief are based upon vanish, returning only as one "comes to."[22]

"Comes to" from what? Can blackouts (including dreamless sleep) be confirmed to be other than black-*ins*, of which only the last moment of blackness, before "coming-to," is remembered? What of Tibetan yogis, for example, who remember more? "Taught to develop lucidity first in their dreams and then in their *nondream* sleep," they are able "to remain consciously aware twenty-four hours a day."[23] They black-*in* to dreamless sleep, and know nothing of black*outs*.

Does anyone else? After all, a first-person account of "absolute psychic annihilation" or "the absence of all consciousness" would be tantamount to a description of what does not, indeed *can*not, exist: absolute nothingness. This point was first made by the most influential of the pre-Socratic philosophers, Parmenides. Generally reckoned as the first Western logician, Parmenides is now known to have been a Pholarchos, or "lair leader," who facilitated trance-state healings in caves, and traced his spiritual roots back to India.[24] And it is perhaps in these deep meditative states that he corroborated what the great yoga masters had learned: "absence of all consciousness" is a far more difficult inference to substantiate than an ongoing "undifferentiated darkness" with "some form of awareness."[25]

While it may be possible to experience or imagine the relative absence of anything, it is impossible to experience or imagine absolute nothingness or emptiness. Blackness, silence, the abyss, empty *space*, however large or small, are all relative nothingness, merely. C*on*sciousness, not sciousness, is all that can be said to go out in these gaps—gaps that are no more gaps than "a joint in a bamboo is a break in the wood" (*PP1*, 240). We can easily imagine anything existing without a specific consciousness, and that the entire universe can exist in its manifold splendor without any conscious beings in it; but what can it mean for anything to exist without consciousness *itself*? As Shadworth Hodgson put it: "[T]he least and lowest meaning of the term Being, without which it would be meaningless, is perceivability."[26]

James the metaphysician did not believe such meaninglessness—the meaninglessness of nonbeing—to be beyond consideration. He believed, in fact, that metaphysics was fueled primarily by the equal possibility of the existence and nonexistence of this world (*SPP*, 1002). But James the ether researcher had reason to suspect that there was no "primordial non-entity" beyond perceivability, the barest meaning of the term *Being*.[27] As the ether philosopher himself, Benjamin Paul Blood, declamed: "[W]e shall hardly countenance a not-being which can only be a delusive array of words."[28]

WEST MEETS EAST: SCIOUSNESS AND ZEN

As a researcher of mystical and heightened states of consciousness, James found various occasions to record nondual experiences, both his own (such as his ether and nitrous oxide experiences)[29] and those of others, East and West, such as William Henry Hudson's account of sitting perfectly still in the hills of Patagonia:

> In the state of mind I was in, thought had become impossible. My state was one of *suspense* and *watchfulness*; yet I had no expectation of meeting an adventure, and felt as free from apprehension as I feel now while sitting in a room in London. The state seemed familiar rather than strange, and accompanied by a strong feeling of elation; and I did not know that something had come between me and my intellect until I returned to my former self,—to thinking, and the old insipid existence [again]. (*OCB*, 859)[30]

Or Swami Vivekananda's testifying to the prime reality of nondual consciousness, where "There is no feeling of *I* and yet the mind works" (*VRE*, 361).

Immediately after quoting this passage in *The Varieties of Religious Experience*, James wrote briefly about Buddhist meditation, relying on a German orientalist for his account. He might have done better to have consulted D. T. Suzuki, destined to become the foremost explainer of Zen meditation to the West, and employed at the time as a translator by a colleague of James's.[31] No one was better positioned to bridge a true understanding of Buddhist meditation to James's sciousness, which would blossom two years later as "pure experience." For while James claimed ignorance of Buddhism in *The Varieties of Religious Experience*, his fundamental, emphatically stated, insight that "*to know immediately . . . or intuitively, is for mental content and object to be identical*" explicates Zen monks' attempts to communicate their satori (*MT*, 856). Take, for example, the following:

> When Fa-ch'ang was dying, a squirrel screeched on the roof. "It's just this" he says, "and nothing else."[32]

A sound as startling (yet unthreatening) as a squirrel screeching on the roof bursts *con*sciousness into the "pure experience" of sciousness, insofar as "no dualism of being represented and representing resides in the experience" (*DCE*, 1151). All seeing, tasting, hearing, smelling, touching, thinking, imaging, feeling are reduced to the experience of that screech. If, say, you were watching TV when the squirrel screeched nearby, you could not describe the TV image that coincided with its onset. Likewise, when you bite into a particularly rich piece of chocolate you lose the sensation of how the chocolate feels in your hand; when you see a shooting star, you stop hearing the crickets; and when the answer to a question you have been puzzling over for weeks suddenly bursts into consciousness, you lose complete contact with all external sensations.

The satori bliss of sciousness, or what the Zen tradition interchangeably calls "one thought-instant" (*ekaksana*) and "no-thought-instant" (*aksana*),[33] contrasts sharply with the mild disturbance (from the Latin word *turba* meaning both "commotion" and "mob") of ordinary consciousness. No matter what we are ordinarily conscious of, there is also, as James says, a "staining, fringe, or halo of obscurely felt relation to masses of other imagery" (*PP1*, 478). In the wholemind of sciousness this fringe drops away. Whatever awareness there is, is full awareness. Like the sciousness of the squirrel screech, there is no residue, no experience of self, inhabiting the moment.

While James missed the opportunity to connect his radical, nondual empiricism to a millennium of Japanese spiritual tradition, Suzuki immediately saw the connection and introduced James's writings to his teacher Kitaro Nishida. Nishida not only directly appropriated James's analysis, but also his expression "pure experience" in seeking to translate the direct-experience satori upon which Zen is based.[34] Suzuki, too, appropriated the phrase "pure experience" to define "this most fundamental experience . . . beyond differentiation."[35]

Nondualism was well established in the two strands that wove into Zen: Buddhism and Taoism. Buddhists distinguished between dualistic knowledge—*vi·jna* ("bifurcated·knowing")—and nondual knowledge—*pra·jna* ("springing-up·knowing"). So, too, dualistic perception—*sa·vi·kalpa* ("with·bifurcated·thought construction")—was contrasted with nondual perception—*nir·vi·kalpa* ("without·bifurcated·thought construction").[36] And as for Taoism, Chuang Tzu claimed nondualism—"when 'self' and 'other' lose their contrareity,"—to be "the very essence of Tao."[37] Zen borrowed from these nondual ontologies, but at the same time rejected any borrowed doctrines as the ultimate foundation for truth. Truth in Zen is confirmed by direct experience or not at all.

The British empirical tradition that James adhered to also confirmed its truths by direct experience. Berkeley used it in denying the independent reality of objects. Hume used it in denying the independent reality of subjects. When James used it to confirm what was left, his own tradition converged with Zen. For Zen's "suchness" or "this-as-it-is-ness"[38] is James's pure experience sciousness: "immediate experience in its passing," "a simple *that*," before it is "doubl[ed]" into

1. "a state of mind"
   and
2. "a reality intended thereby." (*DCE*, 1151)

JAMES'S KOAN

> Subjects when disengaged from their objects vanish
> Just as surely as objects,
> When disengaged form their subjects, vanish too.
>
> —Seng-ts'an (Sosan), Third Zen Patriarch

It may seem that a melding of subject and object is inconceivable; that there is a category divide between them that cannot be crossed, let alone eliminated; that a Zen/Jamesian "pure experience," where "there is not yet a subject or an object, and knowing and its object are completely unified,"[39] is not truly conceivable as consciousness, except, at best, as a hallucinogenic haze, or the "blooming, buzzing confusion" that James imagined for a baby's consciousness (*PP1*, 488). Yet we know from Piaget that long after babyhood the "knowing and its object," the "what" of something and the "that" of something, may still be inseparable. In children as old as six, he tells us, "thought is confused with the things themselves, in the sense that the word is part of the thing."[40] For those who would smile at this apparent epistemological naiveté, James has a question—a world-shattering question, much like a koan:

> How, if "subject" and "object" were separated "by the whole diameter of being," and had no attributes in common, could it be so hard to tell, in a presented and recognized material object, what part comes in through the sense organs and what part comes "out of one's own head"? (*DCE*, 1154)

Common sense says that mind and matter are distinct. Common sense says that exterior "material" objects interact with interior consciousness, and that such exterior objects can survive the extinction not only of the subjects who behold them, but of consciousness itself. And despite his "central thesis" that "subjectivity and objectivity are affairs not of what an experience is aboriginally made of, but of its classification," James knew how "indestructible" this "common-sense assumption" was (*PAF*, 1208; *C8*, 552). To "traverse common sense . . . in philosophy" was, we saw, "no insuperable objection" for James; but generating this particular objection to common sense made him at times

> inwardly sick with the fever. . . . It is a sort of madness . . . when it is on you. The total result is to make me admire "Common sense" as having done by far the biggest stroke of genius ever made in philosophy when it reduced the chaos of crude experience to order by its luminous *Denkmittel* [means of thinking] of the stable "thing," and its dualism of thought and matter. (*C7*, 292–293)[41]

And indeed, James's admiration for dualistic common sense stayed with him, despite his own biggest stroke of genius that "things and thoughts are not at all fundamentally heterogeneous" (*N*, 110). Lingering dualism can be found in his formulations of radical empiricism, such as his 1904 essay, "A World of Pure Experience." And it re-emerges with emphasis thereafter.

Indeed, "the dualism of Object and Subject" that the earlier James, *James the psychologist,* said we "must assume" (*PP1*, 220),[42] the later James, *James the pragmatist,* insisted on even more. Applying his "Pragmatic Rule"—"what sensible difference to anybody will its truth make?" (*SPP*, 1013)[43]—James reverts to the default commonsense notion of independent reality, the reality of "ordinary social experience":

> My account of truth is realistic, and follows the epistemological dualism of common sense. Suppose I say to you "The thing exists"—is that true or not? How can you tell? Not till any statement has developed its meaning farther is it determined as being true, false or irrelevant to reality altogether. But if now you ask "what thing?" and I reply "a desk"; if you ask "where?" and I point to a place; if you ask "does it exist materially, or only in imagination?" and I say "materially"; if moreover I say "I mean that desk," and then grasp and shake a desk which you see just as I have described it, you are willing to call my statement true. But you and I are commutable here; we can exchange places; and as you go bail for my desk, so I can go bail for yours. (*MT*, 935)

James tried to shore up this commonsense stand in letters as well, pleading to his colleague Augustus Strong in 1907: "It seems as if the whole world had conspired to insist that I shall not be a realist, in spite of anything I may say to the contrary" (C8, 419).[44] But James's pragmatic reality test, of course, is limited to distinguishing between "private" phenomena and public "shared" phenomena, not disclosing any further reality *behind* phenomena itself.[45] Moreover, James reassured one of his closest colleagues, F. C. S. Schiller, that though there was a pragmatic value in preserving commonsense dualism, it was *not* the final word:

> You write that you shrink a little from my use of independent realities, etc. etc. No need of shrinking! They are an indestructible common-sense assumption, and the discussion is kept on terms more intelligible to the common man if you also assume them. Moreover, in relation to the *individual man* the object *is* an independent reality with which his thought can "agree" only by its pragmatic workings.

> Allowing it prejudges in no whit a final humanistic treatment of the whole of reality thus assumed. (C8, 552)

James had spent years trying to resolve the conflict between the "neutral monism"[46] of his radical empiricism and "indestructible common-sense assumption."[47] He had imagined that his efforts, recorded in a manuscript entitled "The Many and the One," would be his greatest contribution to philosophy. But as the contradictions proved ultimately irreconcilable, he never did or could complete it.[48] And it was only after he abandoned it that James found a way back to his nondualism. We will later see the profound insight that once again led James away from common sense. But it must first be asked: What leads all of us *toward* it?

James is surely right that from a practical and pragmatic standpoint we confront objects as independent realities. But however pragmatic a subject/object, consciousness/matter divide may be, however commonsensical, it is not, thereby, verifiable. Even the feeling of consciousness being generated in the brain, which underlies this common sense, is not universally common. Ancient Egyptians, for example, believed that the brain's sole function was to produce mucus, and they located the mind in the heart; they carefully preserved all the organs of mummies in sacred urns, but discarded the brain as insignificant, and most definitely not the generator of thought. Aristotle, who believed the brain was merely a refrigerator for the body, could not have shown them the error of their ways. Greeks of his day located thoughts and perceptions either in the heart (just like the Egyptians) or the diaphragm (the *phrēn*).[49] While we are no closer, for all our MRIs and fMRIs, to knowing what part of a presented object comes in through our sense organs and what part comes out of our own head, or to knowing a neural location of consciousness, our high tech peep shows prejudice us toward the belief that consciousness is generated deep inside the bony walls of our skulls.

But if the experience of sciousness is the "always 'truth'" prime reality that James, in agreement with Zen, claims it to be, then consciousness is not *of* something (internalized), but *as* something (neither internalized nor externalized) (*DCE*, 1151). There is a useful distinction to be drawn between an object and a mere thought of an object. As James put it, "Mental knives may be sharp, but they won't cut real wood" (ibid., 1155). Mere thoughts of objects are intangible, internal, and inconsequential. "Real," by contrast to merely *mental*, objects are tangible, external, and consequential. Kicking a rock is one way to make the distinction between a mental and a "real" object. It is not, however, as Samuel Johnson famously believed, a way to establish the independent existence of objects themselves. For the touch of his foot on the rock, as James's koan could have helped him understand, did not confirm a realm beyond perception. What part of the touch came in from the rock? What part came out of his own head? This is not to deny that the "world of experience" consists of an objective and subjective part of which the objective part can be "incalculably more extensive" than the subjective part, but "taken alone" as a self-existing objective part, it is a "hollow" and merely "abstract element" of experience (*VRE*, 446, 447).

If full attention, unimpeded by expectation and uninterrupted by emotional reaction, is given to the experience of foot-touching-rock, its hard "objectness" is clearly realized to be an aspect of consciousness. And even if one is driven to penetrate behind this aspect, and all other aspects of an object, the result will be the same, as one of James's contemporaries, the mystic Fitz Hugh Ludlow, realized when confronted with the objectness of a tree:

> But hold! I said to myself; what do I find out in leaning here, which makes me think that I have found a thing? Why, resistance, hardness, to be sure. And it is a fact, these are qualities only. But this is nothing but feeling; let me try the senses of smell and taste. By applying nose and tongue to the tree, I perceived a fresh woody savor—quality still! I put my ear to the tree and struck it: still nothing but quality resulted, the capability to beget sound. I began to be alarmed for the dignity of the Sense, as I saw her chance of proving herself worthy of my past consideration narrowed down to one single organ—the eye. Alas for her! Quality still—a brown tint, a faculty of transmitting certain rays of light, and absorbing others. It seems strange now, but it is true that, with my knife, I began blazing the side of the tree, with a sort of fond flattery of the Sense that, though the qualities lay in the bark, "the thing" was to be detected lurking underneath. In a moment, however, I laughed perplexedly, realizing that I could make the matter no better if I hacked the tree through.[50]

Nor can "'the thing' . . . lurking underneath" be "detected" by our increasing capacity to micro -scope or -hear, regardless of the level of magnification reached. James's colleague Dickinson Miller penetrated wood, not with a knife but with a thought experiment, to reach a similar illumination. Using James's own example of an apparently real "material" desk,[51] he noted that its reality can be variously considered: "a light-brown total or unit," "a wilderness of woody fibre," or even a "host of ordered molecules or atoms." But these various "realities" mean that they are aspects all, and cannot be overlayed without creating a "monstrous medley."[52] To this monstrous medley we can now add "a nucleus surrounded by moving planetary electrons";[53] and "quarks, gluons, preons, or else sets of excitations of strings, etc."[54] What then of matter? As Bohm observes:

> [I]n all of this development of our knowledge, it seems that whatever we have thought of as matter is turning more and more into empty space with an ever more tenuous structure of moving elements. This tendency is carried further by quantum field theory which treats particles as quantised states of a field that extends over the whole of space.[55]

While matter's claim to prime reality in subject/object dualism diminishes the more it is pursued, Touch, such as the first feel of sand between your toes, or a friend's hand on your shoulder, or a Zen master's thwack with a stick, readily manifests as the prime reality of *im*meditaed sciousness. Had Johnson not been preoccupied with trying to distinguish mind from matter, the touch of his foot on the rock might have dispelled the twin illusion on which the distinction is based: an internal consciousness-without-object and an external object-without-consciousness.

PURE ONSENSE

While Zen has an extensive written tradition, it shares, with James, a distrust of words' capacity to convey the prime reality of nondual experience. The account of the ninth-century monk, Xiangyan, is typical: having become frustrated by his efforts to understand Zen through reading, Xiangyan abandoned his studies altogether for meditation; one day, hearing pebbles strike a clump of bamboo, he became enlightened.[56] Or Ikkyū Sōjun, who, while meditating in a boat at night, experienced enlightenment "at the sudden caw of a crow."[57] All such examples of one-pointed (nondual) satori evoke the original enlightenment of the Buddha who, after years of self-torturing meditation, attained enlightenment all of a sudden, in a moment of im•mediated[58] sciousness. The moment occurred after an all-night session under the Bodhi tree, when he "glanced at the planet Venus gleaming in the eastern sky."[59] Philosophers of Zen, such as Nishida, might, with James, write *about* pure experience sciousness, but, like James, they know that words always come too late. For sciousness has a "*naif* immediacy," never knowable as such, but only in "retrospection" (*DCE*, 1151).

Describing never-knowable-as-such im•mediated experience without retrospection seems doomed to confoundment, the kind that prompted Samuel Johnson to remark to Boswell: "Sir, if a man has experienced the inexpressible, he is under no obligation to attempt to express it." James, pen in hand, felt precisely such obligation while under the influence of nitrous oxide. After scribbling some incoherent phrases, he *almost* gave up: "That sounds like nonsense," he wrote, but then reversed himself: "but it's pure *on*sense!" (*WB*, 678). "Pure *on*sense!," like "suchness," brings us as close as a word can to, if not expressing, at least *indicating*, sciousness.

One-pointed, wholemind moments/movements of *on*sense sciousness may be far more frequent than acknowledged. Does the "I" brand our every waking moment, or does it flicker in and out—a flickering that happens so rapidly that the transition from *con*sciousness to sciousness and back to *con*sciousness barely registers? The sense of "I" flickers out, for example, with a red flash at the window; it flickers back in when the red flash "becomes" a cardinal. Like the screech of the squirrel, the sensation of redness, when it first appears, is undefined, unconnected to anything else, unpositioned, without context; and if attention is without definition, position, or context, the sense of "I" is without definition, position or context, which is another way of saying it is no sense of "I" at all. The conversion of the red flash into a cardinal is the reconstitution of the sense of self. But was it an "I" that turned the red flash into a cardinal or did the conceptualization of "cardinal" turn the nonpositioned, noncontextualized sciousness into an "I"?

It is not that names or words always contextualize consciousness. If, for example, after identifying the red flash as a bird, I struggled to remember the name of the bird, the first moment of remembrance might feel as absent of context and self as the initial burst of red color; for a moment it would command full attention. But when it follows immediately upon the one-pointed sensation of redness, the word-thought for the redness, "cardinal," *dis*tracts (literally, "*pulls apart*") the one-pointed sensation of redness into two points: a state of mind, and a reality intended thereby.

Losing the sense of "I" in a one-pointed, wholemind moment of sciousness is not the same as *feeling* lost. As James says, when you are lost in a forest and say, "Where am I?" that is the wrong question. You know where *you* are; you don't know where everything else is. So, too, when a red flash appears outside the window, the "I" sense, oriented in thoughts and feelings of the past and future, drops out in the wonderment of the present moment; but there is no feeling of being lost, since there is no sense of a somewhere else to be.

In the moment just prior to a wholemind moment of sciousness, however, there may be a sense of disorientation, as whatever context had positioned the "I" (the "everything else" of the forest wanderer) lingers. If, say, I am sitting at my desk daydreaming, my "I" positioned within the narrative of that dream, the sudden absence of that narrative, and all its positioning images, in the first moment of the red flash outside my window, may be palpable. Like forest wanderers who feel lost, not because of where they *are*, but because of where they are *not*, there is a palpable presence of an absence. As James noted: "The feeling of an absence is *toto coelo* [by the whole extent of the heavens] other than the absence of a feeling" (*PP1*, 252).[60]

The palpable presence of the absence of a specific "I" context just prior to the onset of a wholemind moment may even be a disorienting blur of fear and enchanted wonder, such as when we are suddenly plunged into darkness. The word *awe*, wonder tinged with fear, is used to describe this blur, felt immediately prior to, and recalled immediately after, a non-"I" moment of sciousness. This disorienting blur is not sustainable, however, since *dis*orientation can only be generated from a sense of orientation that precedes it. Following this disorientation, consciousness either becomes identified with "I" feeling ("It's okay," or "Yikes!") or disidentified (as in nondual awareness). For a sense of disorientation to be sustained, it would have to alternate with a sense of orientation. A sustained feeling of disorientation can only be a continual flickering in and out between "I" and non-"I" feeling—such as you might feel if, say, walking in Manhattan, you suddenly saw a tornado coming up Broadway. A sense of wonder (non-"I" feeling) alternating rapidly with the sense of fear ("I" feeling) in such an encounter contrasts with the sustained feeling of fear induced, say, by a bus speeding out of control toward you, or the sustained feeling of wonder you would feel if that same bus suddenly took off and flew into the sky.

But most of the time the sense of self flickers out and in so rapidly that its absence is not noticed. Daily recalls from dreamless sleep notwithstanding, consciousness seems to be a continuous self-narrative, just as a succession of film frames projected on a screen seems to be one uninterrupted narrative. But whenever we become *completely* absorbed in anything—such as a sunset (just before the response, "How beautiful!"), or dancing (when "the dancer becomes the dance")—that self-narrative is interrupted. "To forget the self," says the ancient Zen master Dōgen, "is to be actualized by myriad things."[61] This remains true even if the self-forgetting be but momentary. As James notes, a "Brooklyner or New Yorker . . . tired or careworn about . . . personal affairs" does not, like the ecstatic Walt Whitman, "soar into the colors of a sunset" (*OCB*, 854).

THE NEITHER-ACTIVE-NOR-PASSIVE SELF

But a self that can be forgotten is still a self. What *is* this self? Nietzsche, as we saw, claimed that the "I" was a *belief* derived from the feeling of will, an "inward fact . . . accepted as given, as *empirical*." The physicist Saul-Paul Sirag, based on his experiences with the total-body anaesthetic drug ketamine, validated Nietzsche's claim. Having, like some ether patients, directly experienced a sustained sciousness state, Sirag observed that the first feeling of the self's return, of *con*sciousness, was a feeling of volition.[62] While we have argued against the reality of will, there is no denying the existence of something that feels like will, what James calls a state of "peculiar *internality* . . . possess[ing] the quality of seeming to be active" (*PBC*, 179). This "seeming to be active," to be making decisions, making things happen—to be *doing*—whatever its actual reality, is a persistent seeming nonetheless, persistent enough to be a foundation of the *sense* of autonomy and self.

Even the feeling of "being done to" only takes shape in *contrast to* the persistent feeling of doing. A "passive" self is a de-*activated* self; without a sense of an active self the sense of a passive self would not exist. In the absence of a belief in an active self, the entire concept of self dissolves. We could say that such self-dissolution renders us mere objects, buffeted about by forces of nature, like leaves blowing in the wind; but here, too, the concept of objects cannot be grasped without the concept of "subjects"—just as "inanimate" has no meaning without "animate." The nonreality of will does not, therefore, entail a passive, determined, object self (such as the catatonic patient who had haunted the younger James) for the very reason that it doesn't entail an active self either. The nonreality of free will entails neither an actual I doing nor an actual I being done to; it only allows for a virtual "I" attached to *feelings* of doing and being done to.

THE BODILY "I"

> While this body clearly exists, clearly realizing this body doesn't exist.
>
> —Zen Master Bunan

If it is true that a belief in self would not exist without the feeling of will, it is equally true that the feeling of will cannot exist without something more than the feeling of being active. While Nietzsche believed that will is the first illusion, from which belief in self is derived, we may well question this order. Even if the "I" is merely an "afterbirth" of the feeling of will, would the feeling of will exist in the first place without the experience of being some sort of an entity, an experience derived in essential part from the feeling (as opposed to the mere fact) of bodily existence? Sirag, too, who returned to a sense of self when he returned to a sense of volition—specifically, moving his hands—returned, at the same time, to a sense of bodily existence, or, at the very least, to a feeling of being an entity.

How pervasive is such a feeling of bodily entityness or existence? As I sit in this chair and write, the points where my body makes contact with other objects—my fingers on the pen, my feet on the floor, my buttocks in the chair, not only enter "my" consciousness as impressions of "my" body but help in an ongoing way, along with more internal sensations, such as a crick in "my" neck or a rumbling in "my" belly, to define what "my" means. As the phantom limb phenomenon attests, bodily feelings do not confirm bodily existence since they could correspond to a part of the body that is no longer there. Nonetheless, all bodily feelings, together with an image of the body constructed from these feelings, as well as the ongoing though partial views of the body, create a positioning thisness and hereness of "I."

Pervasive, however, as such positioning may be, it is not constant. Bodily existence does not imply bodily feeling any more than bodily feeling implies bodily existence: there are both quadriplegics who still feel their limbs, and full-bodied paralytics who feel none of their body. Even under normal conditions, all bodily feelings are intermittent. The pressure in my buttocks from the chair that I am now sitting in, for example, despite being ongoing and uninterrupted, does not consciously register as ongoing. Indeed, most of the time when we sit, the feeling of this pressure fades so far into the background that it would seem to have left consciousness altogether (only to return again).

Even severe pain goes in and out of consciousness. Obviously, the sharper the pain (as in a toothache) the more constant the bodily feeling. But such feeling of constancy (rarely as constant as remembered) is exceptional. Consciousness of bodily feeling, insofar as it exists at all, fades in and out, residing, for the most part, "in the background."

It has been argued that in addition to the background feeling of particular bodily sensations, there is a background feeling for the body as a whole. According to neuroscientist Antonio Damasio, "the background body sense is continuous although one may hardly notice it, since it represents not a specific part of anything in the body but rather an overall state of most everything in it."[63] Although Damasio himself recognizes that the feeling being interpreted as the "sense" of an "overall state" is elusive, he maintains that it is nonetheless there. And certainly some "overall state," however vague, *may* exist, a state that is something more than a collection of felt fragmentary parts. The objectively observable overlay of neuronal and chemical circuits in the "endlessly repeated biological state" that is our body (and, possibly, the less objectifiable energy circuits accessed by acupuncturists and other esoteric healers) may be subjectively sensed as well.[64] This would mean that the positioning *con*sciousness "I" is also the consciousness of a positioning, of a unified circuit of sensations, whether such positioning be an energy construct or an endlessly repeated biological state.[65]

At any rate, whether the body is felt in whole or in part, it is still an intermittent feeling. Frequently recurrent as an overall sense of being in a body may be, it is no more omnipresent than particular body sensations. The body in whole or in part is no more sensed in every moment than that other pervasive localizer of consciousness: time.

Moreover, as Damasio observes, the self's "grounding reference" in the body is not a static imprint, but, rather, "successive organism states, each neurally represented anew, in multiple concerted maps, *moment by moment*, and each anchoring the self that exists *at any one moment*."[66] The concept "self" or "I," the *word* "self" or "I," easily superimposes onto the sight and experience of a body, or onto an internal image of the external body that may (but most often doesn't) exactly match it; likewise, any feelings, thoughts or actions that are perceived as arising in the body are perceived as "my" sensations. "Thought," says James (capitalizing the "T" to indicate "the passing thought"), "is always emphasizing something," and insofar as "I" and "me" are part of that emphasis they are not "mysterious and unexampled," but simply "the bodily life which . . . [the Thought] momentarily feels" (*PP1*, 341).

But the only verifiable self is a self that is sensed *when it is sensed*. The apparent object constancy of the body has no subjective correlate. However much a sense of "I" is linked to an apparently distinct, independently existing body, the sense of "I" itself has no such independent existence, but is always defined by the distinct contexts in which it arises. The "I," insofar as it exists at all, exists only as superimposed; it is like a rider who is no rider unless "in the saddle." As James puts it, "The definitively closed nature of our personal consciousness is probably an average statistical resultant of many conditions, but not an elementary force or fact" (*PP1*, 350).

THE SENSED "I"

The superimposed quality of "I" is even suggested by the word that most aptly describes the "I"'s presence: "sense." To say that the "I" is sensed is to claim for it more concrete reality than is implied by the words *imagined* or *thought*, yet less than is implied by the word *felt*. The use of the word *sense* implies, rather, something between a feeling and a thought, an interpretation of a feeling by a thought, as when we "sense danger." "To sense danger" is to have certain distinct feelings which are instantaneously interpreted as the thought "danger." So, too, the near omnipresent sense of "I" is neither a thought of "I" nor a feeling of "I," but rather an ongoing succession of certain distinct feelings interpreted as "I" in the otherwise nonpossessive stream of sciousness. The fear that arises when a car speeds toward you as you are crossing the street consists of one distinct "I" feeling sense; the anger that arises when it doesn't slow down as it narrowly misses you consists of another; the envy that arises when that car turns out to be an exotic sports car is yet another. Any inner sense of "I" (as opposed to an abstract "I" based on an analogy to the body) is based on a distinct feeling.

Not that the perpetually shifting sense of "I" is like a slide show, with one distinct "I" formation following another. Most of the feelings which constitute the sense of "I" are not experienced of a moment, like a spasm of fear, but as continuous states, like worry or "single-minded" resolve. Different "I" feelings, of whatever duration, mostly blend into each other, making the perpetual shifting of the "I" sense seem less like a slide show and more like a "relatively stable form" in a slowly revolving kaleidoscope (*PP1*, 246).[67] Nonetheless, however overlapping or continuous an "I" sense may be, it is always a particular configuration in a specific context. As David Hume most famously observed, you cannot separate an "I" from some given instance of what the "I" is conscious of, as if it were an empty category that underwent experiences. "For my part," says Hume, "when I enter most intimately into what I call *myself*, I always stumble on some particular perception or other, of heat or cold, light or shade, love or hatred, pain or pleasure. I never can catch *myself* at any time without a perception, and never can observe anything but the perception."[68] The "riddle" of self, as Bradley put it, has "proved too hard for us," for,

> [i]f the self is narrowed to a point which does not change, that point is less than the real self. But anything wider has a "complexion" which "shifts to strange effects," and therefore cannot be oneself.[69]

Now, it might be objected that nothing exists other than in a specific context, with a specific configuration. To deny existence to the self on these grounds is as absurd as to deny existence to the body. For in what sense does the body, or a part of the body, have any "neutral," nonspecifically configured state? While an open palm hand, for example, with the fingers straight up and the thumb at a forty-five degree angle, may *seem* like the hand's neutral state (the hand of a corpse, or the position assumed for hand tracing) which then gets modified into different positions—fist, fingers splayed, pointing—it is still a specific configuration. So, too, the body as a whole can be imagined as a neutral configuration that underlies various distinct attitudes or attributes applied to it—curled up, in motion, hot, cold—but its neutral status is still conceivable only as a specific configuration.

By contrast, however, there is no even *conceivable* neutral, or non-added-on, "I." It *only* exists as "added-on." There is no "open-palm" "I" underlying various modifications. You might say that the "I" of "I fear" is a modification of the "I" of "I envy," but that is as absurd as saying that a hand with fingers splayed wide is a modified fist. While an open palm may serve as a neutral substrate for various hand positions, no thought or sense of "I" exists as a free-floating subject, a neutral substrate of consciousness.

Of course, just as the body forms a pattern—both an "external" form and an "internal" circuit of neural and chemical responses—different "I" moments form patterns as well. The same fears, desires, thoughts, actions recur again and again, with more persistence than any specific person, place, or thing to which they refer. The repetition of feelings, thoughts, and actions (like repetition in any formation) forms a distinct identity. And just as many particles of sand can be identified as something more than the particles themselves (such as a beach or a sandstorm), or many sung notes can be identified as something more than the sum of their parts (a rock song, say, or a requiem), so, too, many moments of self—from affects to aspirations—can be identified as something more than the moments themselves. Distinct patterns of thoughts, feelings, and actions, no less than the distinct patterning of the physical body, render each body/self into a recognizable character, like a character in a movie—an identifiable person "I," or what James calls an "empirical me" (*PP1*, 291, 296). But such an "objectified" empirical me is no less a collection of transient elements on account of such patterning. The various modifications of consciousness do not inhere in any empirical "me" any more than they inhere in a subject "I." Again, this is not to completely deny reality or "substance" to individuals, but to limit what such reality means. Like lions, trees, and stones we may be substances, but, as James says, "all that the word substance means" is "the fact that certain perceptual experiences do seem to *belong together*" (*SPP*, 1045).

THE THINKING "I"

> [The] sense of identity of the knowing subject is held by some philosophers to be the only vehicle by which the world hangs together. It seems hardly necessary to say that a sense of identity of the known object would perform exactly the same unifying function, even if the sense of subjective identity were lost.
>
> —William James, *The Principles of Psychology*

If thoughts about an "I" do not verify its independent existence, what about the fact of thinking itself? The most famous declaration of Western philosophy is "I think, therefore I am." Observing the elusive existence of the self, Descartes sought to verify an "I" through the thought process alone. Even if one doubts that one is thinking, argued Descartes, doubt itself is a form of thinking and therefore thinking prevails; you cannot doubt it out of existence. Descartes is right that *thinking* cannot be doubted out of existence, but what of the existence of the "I" that leaps, in his declaration, from "thinking" to "am?" Has Descartes read more into the evidence than is there? Consider: in the context of his famous sentence, the phrase "I think" depicts no actuality. Descartes meant it to stand for all *possible* instances of thinking something. It is a *formula* for generating specific examples of thinking, rather than a specific example of thinking itself. Without a specific reference (however changeable or provisional), the phrase "I think" has no meaning, let alone actuality. And if the phrase "I think" does not depict an existent fact, it can hardly depict, let alone verify, the existence of one of its components—"I."

If I am thinking I must be thinking *something*, however vague or ill-defined; but no matter what specific something I am thinking, no matter what context the "I think" exists in, the "I" of the "I think" cannot simply be transferred, intact, to the "I" of the "I am." (A point that is more manifest in the original Latin in which it was expressed, *Cogito ergo sum*, where the "I" is not separated from the verbs but exists only *in* the verbs, as a modification of their form.) No matter what actual occasion of "I think" is referred to, by the time you reach the "I" of the "I am," the "I" of the "I think" is no more; it has turned, irrevocably, into "I thought"—a memory of a specific "I-in-context" moment. Such a memory, or any number of them, cannot be transmuted into the abstracted, independently existing "I" of Descartes' "I am."

James, a more perceptive observer of the stream of consciousness than Descartes, declared that there is nothing in the process of thinking that substantiates the independent existence of an "I":

> I may have either acquaintance-with, or knowledge-about, an object O without thinking about myself at all. It suffices for this that I think O, and that it exist. If, in addition to thinking O, I also think that I exist and that I know O, well and good; I then know one more thing, a fact about O, of which I previously was unmindful. That, however, does not prevent me from having already known O a good deal. O *per se,* or O *plus* P, are as good objects of knowledge as O *plus me* is. (*PP1*, 274)

All that the process of thinking ultimately verifies is the existence of a present mental state, which James, as we saw, calls "the passing Thought," and "the only verifiable thinker" (ibid., 346). Meanwhile consciousness continues, unperturbed by having no clearly defined subject to continue as.

JAMES'S "SELF OF SELVES"

Another way of understanding the self as a part-time experience only, a "something additional to what had previously been there," is suggested by a thought experiment which James urged as "the vital point of my whole theory": "*If we fancy some strong emotion, and then try to abstract from our consciousness of it all the feelings of its bodily symptoms, we find we have nothing left behind,* no 'mind-stuff' out of which the emotion can be constituted, and that a cold and neutral state of intellectual perception is all that remains" (*PP2*, 451). To "abstract from" consciousness all sensations ascribable to a body/self would leave the same residue of a neutral, non-"I" witnessing sciousness state accessed under ether.[70] While "emotion dissociated from all bodily feeling is inconceivable," sciousness, by contrast, can and does survive such dissociation (ibid., 452). Such a neutral, mystical non-"I" state might be termed "cold," but "cold" is always a relative term; if my hand feels cold to you, yours will feel warm to me; New York in November would feel balmy to an Eskimo. The coldness James attributes to a neutral state is cold only by contrast to the heat of emotions—that is, feelings that involve a sense of "I."

The more James meditated on the experience of self, the more he believed that this heat or warmth that distinguished it from the coldness of a "neutral state of intellectual perception" was the "*real nucleus*" or "firm basis" on which consciousness of personal identity rested (*PP1*, 341). Whether as an "emphasis" in consciousness, or a sense of consciousness "appropriated" or "intimate," all "I"-consciousness was also, for James, a sense of warmth (ibid.).

That "I"-feeling states are part-time, distinguished from nonemotional or non-"I" states by a feeling of warmth, may be better understood when the point of contrast between "I" and non-"I" is not a rise in temperature but the friction that causes it. *Webster's* defines emotion as a "strong generalized feeling" or "any specific feeling; any of various complex reactions with both psychical and physical manifestations."[71] And James, too, held that all emotional, nonneutral feelings, feelings that *include* the feeling of "I," are "coming to the closest possible quarters with the facts," a feeling of "*some bodily process, for the most part taking place within the head*" (*PP1*, 300). Earlier, we spoke of bodily feeling as an essential component of the sense of self, positioning or anchoring consciousness in "I," a "noun of position." While most feelings in the body contribute to the consciousness of "I" as a "noun of position," *certain specific* bodily sensations, James believed, contribute an active positioning, what might be called a *gerund* of position. James makes much of these specific dynamic bodily sensations, calling them "the 'Self of selves'—the innermost activity of which I am *most distinctly aware*" (ibid., 301). It is these "bodily . . . impressions alone," says James, that support the "postulate" of "consciousness as an inner activity . . . of a *knower*," even though "sciousness," consciousness without such a positioning sense of self, "might . . . better . . . describe" the "*knower* as correlative to all this known" (*PBC*, 432). These core bodily activities James saw as a "coherent group" of "reflexes" or "processes" "furthering or inhibiting the presence of various things" (*PP1*, 302). Specifically, he mentions movements and contractions in the glottis, the eyes, and the brow.

James's focus on bodily activity as the prime source of the feeling of self might seem like a capitulation to the material determinism of his day, a misguided attempt to reduce a subtle interplay of feelings to muscle spasms. It might also be considered as a harbinger of our own day in which an array of neuroscientists seek to locate the self with MRIs and PET scanners. The right frontal lobes, the parietal lobes, the hippocampus, microtubules in the brain's neurons, the synapses *between* neurons, have all been suggested as locations of self.[72] Not surprisingly, these locations change with the frequency of Hollywood's Guide Maps to the Stars. James would no doubt be fascinated by the contemporary light shows that illuminate different parts of the brain's functioning. But he also might point out—as he did to the decapitated-twitching-frog determinists of his own time—that the self cannot be defined by what is not experienced. Antonio Damasio, promoting his theory of a "neural *basis* of self," has praised James's emphasis on the bodily activity that underlies feelings of self as "being well ahead of both his time and ours."[73] But we can be grateful that James was *behind* our times insofar as he relied more on introspection than readouts. For whatever bodily activity may underlie self-feeling, it is only the feeling of that activity, moment to moment, that makes it seem part of a self (*PP1*, 341).

Nonetheless, while such self-feeling always involves more than the bodily activity itself, James believed that bodily activity formed its most "distinct portions." Moreover, he believed that all other aspects of self-feeling might be traceable to bodily activity as well. Let us look at the specific bodily activity of what James calls "*primary* reactions," that "however obscurely recognized as such *may* . . . be the absolute original of my conscious selfhood, the fundamental perception that '*I am*'" (ibid., 302, 341).

James begins his account of the "particulars" of the central nucleus of the self with the arrest of breathing—specifically, in the glottis (*PP1*, 300). The glottis, he says, is like a "sensitive valve, intercepting my breath instantaneously at every mental hesitation or felt aversion to the objects of my thought, and as quickly opening, to let the air pass through my throat and nose, the moment the repugnance is overcome" (ibid., 301). "Mental hesitations" and "felt aversions" underlie, as we saw, the feeling of effort—an emphatic "self" feeling. James was convinced that the interception of breath was a key physiological component of this feeling as well.

The arresting of breath is not, of course, confined to the glottis (nor does James claim it to be); contractions in the diaphragm also play a part. And of all the bodily correlations of self that James mentions, breathing offers the richest opportunity for introspection. Strong, forceful interventions of the breath are rare, but notice the frequency of subtle tugs on the intake of breath, and to what thoughts and feelings they correspond. James himself quotes at length "an experiment of a simple nature" by one of the many other psychologists of his day, David Ferrier, who used direct experience as their primary mode of inquiry:

> If the reader will extend his right arm and hold his forefinger in the position required for pulling the trigger of a pistol, he may without actually moving his finger, but by simply making believe, experience a consciousness of energy put forth. Here, then, is a clear case of consciousness of energy without actual contraction of the muscles either of the one hand or the other, and without any perceptible bodily strain. If the reader will again perform the experiment, and pay careful attention to the condition of his respiration, he will observe that his consciousness of effort coincides with a fixation of the muscles in his chest, and that in proportion to the amount of energy he feels he is putting forth, he is keeping his glottis closed and actively contracting his respiratory muscles. Let him place his finger as before, and *continue breathing* all the time, and he will find that however much he may direct his attention to his finger, he will experience not the slightest trace of consciousness of effort until he has actually moved the finger itself, and then it is referred locally to the muscles in action. It is only when the essential and ever-present respiratory factor is, as it has been, overlooked, that the consciousness of effort can with any degree of plausibility be ascribed to the outgoing current. (*PP2*, 504)

That the self-feeling of effort derives, in essential part, from a contraction of breath is also suggested by selfless states of ecstasy, one of whose chief characteristics is the feeling of nonrestricted breathing. It is especially noticeable in the ecstatic, loss-of-self-feeling experience of an orgasm. The correspondence between sexual and religious ecstasy in this regard is notable. As James says, "[O]ne might almost as well interpret religion as a perversion of the respiratory function. The Bible is full of the language of respiratory oppression" (*VRE*, 19–20).

The sense of noninterference with the breath is also the foundation of impersonal quintessence in Buddhist meditation. As Karlfried Graf Dürckheim writes in his classic account of meditation, *Hara*:

> The first thing that has to be learned is *to let breathing happen*. . . . Just how difficult this is becomes clear when [the meditator] first observes his breathing, for then the effect of the fixing I, interrupting the natural rhythm, becomes immediately apparent. . . . So it is a great and memorable experience when for the first time he succeeds with full consciousness, in allowing the natural, living breath to happen and discovers that it really does come and go, come and go of its own accord.[74]

If most breath contractions are private occasions not readily obvious to others, the second bodily process that James mentions is often more obvious to others than oneself: the movement of eyes, eyelids, and eyebrows, which, James says, "respond very sensitively to every fluctuation in the agreeableness or disagreeableness of what comes before my mind" (*PP1*, 301). So obvious, in fact, are such rapid eye-area movements as a sign of self-feeling—especially of nervousness or worry—that the scarcity of these movements in those who are not feeling this "I" is readily noticed. Videos of the ecstatic mystic Osho, for example, reveal very few eye and eyelid movements. His gaze—not unlike a newborn baby's—seems to absorb each moment whole, without any indication of a behind-the-scenes struggle or divisiveness; yet unlike a baby, sensations of agreeableness and disagreeableness do not play out in his unsettlingly placid gaze.

The third area that James mentions—contractions in the forehead, or brow (the outer coating of the frontal lobes, or prefrontal cortex)—may be the most obvious choice as a locus of self-feeling. Not only is it the newest part of the evolved brain—the part that distinguishes us from apes and all other animals—it is the part of the brain that matures last in childhood. Perhaps more than any other part of the body, contractions in the brow, resulting from tension experienced in the frontal lobes, signal contractions away from a neutral, witnessing sciousness into a feeling of self. As the poet Dylan Thomas, complaining to his agent about having to give recitals of only his own poems, wrote: "An hour of me aloud is hell, and produces large burning spots in front of the mind."[75]

Correlations between self-feeling and the frontal lobes were also made, in James's time, by the German physiologist Paul Flechsig, who found that disease damage to a patient's frontal lobes "deranged" not so much "his perception of . . . objective relations" as his "consciousness of self" (*HI*, 1103). And we know that prefrontal lobotomy patients exhibit a machine-like absence of self, as they "don spectacles simply because they are laid before them, or eat food presented to them, mindlessly and automatically."[76] Brain wave studies have demonstrated how mental stress (a potent conjurer of self-feeling) sharply increases activity in the frontal lobes.[77] Even the subtlest twinge of mental stress can be detected there, as was shown inadvertently by a memory experiment at the University of California. The experiment used dyes (internally digested) and scanning equipment to help locate which parts of the brain are activated during the recall of past images. Traditionally it was believed that memory images were formed in the middle part of the brain (in the hippocampus). According to the study, however, evidence was found that memory also sometimes occurred in the frontal lobe of the brain. But the experimenters overlooked a significant piece of evidence: the hippocampus was activated in all instances of memory, whereas the frontal lobes were shown to be active only "when the subjects were asked to make some effort to recall."[78] Thus, it was not the workings of memory so much as the feeling of effort, a self-feeling, that showed up as an impulse in the frontal lobes. So, too, playing the same keys over and over again on the keyboard, until the playing becomes automatic, will no longer register in a PET scan of the players' prefrontal cortex. But it *will* register if the players suddenly feel that they are making an effort to attend to the action.[79] More recently, neurologists, using a mental processing MRI called a functional or fMRI, were able to track an increase in activity in the frontal lobes when subjects were asked self-referential questions, such as whether certain objects had pleasant or unpleasant associations, and a decrease whenever they were asked non-self-referential questions, such as whether the objects belonged inside or outside.[80]

My own experience, which developed out of an intensive meditation retreat, also physically dramatized the connection between the frontal lobes and the feeling of self. During a week of continuous, blissful, one-pointed sciousness, without a trace of fear or anxiety, my brow felt as if it had no energy impulses coursing through it; and in a mirror I saw that the skin on my forehead had become slack, having relaxed into rows of folds. By contrast, the rest of my body felt more vibrant and energized than ever (with the exception of my genitals, which also, like my forehead, felt energy-less).

While my frontal lobes apparently survived intact during this non-"I" feeling state, some people who have portions of their frontal lobes surgically removed also report feeling an absence of anxiety.[81] Unfortunately, however, a liveliness of responsiveness is absent as well, leaving the patients with a muffled or deadened aspect. And full frontal lobotomies can go even farther in converting an apparent self into an apparent robot.

A quick way to discover how felt impulses in the frontal lobes induce a feeling of self is through a familiar experience: clasping your hands behind your head (as when laying in a hammock, or even just sitting back in a chair). Such a placement of hands, by itself, draws a current of feeling away from the frontal lobes toward the back of the head; this transfer of energy is experienced as a feeling of relaxation, a relaxation away from contracted feelings of self. It is even possible, from this position, to notice the re-formation of contracted self-feelings of "I" and "me" in the return of energy to the frontal lobes.

Since James's self of selves relies on subjective introspection (indeed, introspection about the very feeling of being a subject), his observations function as a guide to our own inquiry. Asserting that "introspection in this field" is "desperately hard," he readily admits that his own details are incomplete and nonconclusive (*PP1*, 301). Henri Bergson, whom James held in the highest esteem, agreed. Bergson, who also had theorized a "system of muscular contraction" to explain emotional states, believed that James, at the very least, had neglected the "irreducible psychic element" in such states.[82] James is clearly vulnerable to such a charge. For even though he acknowledged that "over and above physiological sensations there is an obscurer feeling of something more" (*PP1*, 305), he believed that this "something more" might itself be attributable to physiological processes as well, only "fainter" (ibid.). At any rate, James was impressed enough by the distinctness of the bodily sensations he identified with self-feeling to suggest that these sensations might not only contribute to self-feeling, but cause it. Given the immediate change *away from* a tight feeling of "I" that physical relaxation (such as deeper breathing, or the unfurrowing of a brow) can bring, it is tempting to think that the mere relaxation of all feelings of tension is sufficient to induce an ether-like non-"I" state.

But whether or not all "I"-feelings could ultimately be explained by physiological responses alone, they are never, as Bergson emphasized, experienced as such. Each physical contraction James identifies as the "self of selves" also manifests as an emotion. A knitted brow, for example, is also a knitted feeling, whether that feeling be a skeptical twinge or a steely resolve. Even if introspection confirms physical contractions and a sensation of warmth to be the most distinct aspects of self-feeling, the emotional contractions that accompany them are often all that are experienced *at first*.

CONSCIOUSNESS AS THE WHIRLPOOL OF SCIOUSNESS

> There is no internal self or soul within and independent of the body-mind. The individual body-mind is a modification or Play upon the infinite, All-Pervading, Transcendental Being. The body-mind itself, in its contraction or recoil from the universal pattern of relations, suggests or implies the subjective internal self or independent soul idea.
>
> —Da Free John, *Scientific Proof of the Existence of God Will Soon Be Announced by the White House*

James held that *all* aspects of the experience of self arose "*in* the stream of consciousness" (*PP1*, 299; emphasis added). It could, of course, hardly be otherwise, since his metaphor of the stream of consciousness (not to be confused with a merely haphazard flow of thoughts)[83] was seen by him to be all-encompassing. No experience exists outside the stream.

Nonetheless, at the risk of straining James's metaphor, it might be said that the stream of consciousness flows unimpeded only in the absence of contracted self-feeling, exemplified by Bashō's

Old Pond
Frog jumps in
Sound of the water

and that contracted feelings of self are as much a disturbance *of* the stream as something *in* it—a disturbance rather like a whirlpool, a turning in on itself that creates a formation so distinct it seems separated from that which constitutes it. James himself suggests this possibility in his presentation of the passive model of attention, where he identified the feeling of effort, a contracted self-feeling, with "eddies" in the stream of thought.[84]

The contracted sense of self as an apparently separate formation in a stream of sciousness, the experience of "I"-feeling as sciousness turning in on itself, was vividly described by Suzuki's star pupil, Alan Watts. Traveling away from his sense of self by means of LSD, Watts, like the annata-nauts of the nineteenth century, wrote about what it felt like to return:

> The ego is a kind of flip, a knowing of knowing, a fearing of fearing. It's a curlicue, an extra jazz to experience, a sort of double-take or reverberation, a dithering of consciousness which is the same as anxiety.[85]

Of the many phrases Watts uses to describe the "something additional," turning-in-on-itself sense of "I," let us isolate the word *reverberation*. This is the same word, as it turns out, that James used to describe the feeling of "I" when *he* introspected upon it. As used by James, reverberation is a psychological correlate of the physical contractions he had identified with the self. It does not denote any specific emotion or feeling associated with such contractions, but the one feeling that all the other feelings have in common (*PP1*, 299).

The word *reverberation*, defined by *Webster's* as "to throw back (sound)," literally means "to beat again." What is the nature of this "I" reverberation, this second beat, that accompanies most, but by no means all, states of consciousness, as a feeling of "something additional" to one's own existence? James's introspection on this question begins by setting the stage:

> First of all, I am aware of a constant play of furtherances and hindrances in my thinking, of checks and releases, tendencies which run with desire, and tendencies which run the other way. Among the matters I think of, some range themselves on the side of the thought's interests, while others play an unfriendly part thereto. (Ibid.)

As in his will paradigm, the impersonal nature of this "constant play of furtherances and hindrances" corroborates what James believed to be the "it thinks," impersonal nature of the thought process. The "checks and releases" he describes are *assignable to* but are not *issuing from* an "I." He does not *make* the constant play in his thinking, he merely becomes "aware" of it. A thought (such as the thought to get out of bed) arises; subsequent thoughts may reinforce the thought ("range *themselves*"—like cattle without a cowboy) or obstruct it ("play an unfriendly part"— like directorless actors). For both such "furtherances and hindrances" the reference point of the subsequent thoughts is not a *self*-interest but a (preceding) "*thought*'s interest."

While most people, James believed, would affirm that the "self of all the other selves" is the "*active* element in all consciousness; saying that whatever qualities a man's feelings may possess, or whatever content his thought may include, there is a spiritual something in him which seems to *go out* to meet these qualities and contents, whilst they seem to *come in* to be received by it" (ibid., 297), and while James himself sought to affirm this active element through his defense of free will, the grounds of his defense, as we saw, were not based on what he ultimately knew, but on what he wanted to believe. No one, James knew, could ever prove that the active "spiritual something" that gives or withholds assent to a thought was an "original force."[86]

Now, it may seem that all desire, regardless of whether it is "furthered" or "hindered," manifests contracted self-feeling. Indeed, desire is so identified with self that absence of desire is commonly equated with the absence of self. Socrates, for example, seems almost to be quoting his near contemporary the Buddha when he says "to have no wants is divine." In both East and West, the "peace that surpasseth all understanding" transcends all desire. But a distinction needs to be drawn between desiring and hankering or craving. A desire for something *can* be experienced, in and of itself, as one-pointed, without the second beat "reverberation" of self-feeling. An often quoted maxim of Zen Buddhism is, "When you're hungry, eat; when you're tired, sleep"; and the Buddha himself partook of both activities, for the same reason as everyone else: there was a felt impulse or desire to do so—a desire that presumably did not disrupt his one-pointed, moment-to-moment, enlightenment.

Not even furtherances or hindrances of a desire or a thought's interest need reverberate with contracted self-feeling. The deepening affirmations, for example, that accompany the experience of a favorite symphony or a piece of chocolate may diminish the sense of self to the point that we "lose" ourselves in the experience. So, too, we get "lost" in a thought to the extent that the subsequent thoughts "range themselves" without interruption "on the side of the [antecedent] thought's interests."

Hindrances of a thought's interest, on the other hand, cannot dissolve an "I" in this way, but they, too, do not necessarily emphasize, manifest, or even entail self-feeling. The hindrance of a thought's interest may quite simply be its own, discrete, un-reverberated moment, not experienced as connected through a sense of hindering to the moment before. The thought to stay in bed, for example, even if it followed and hindered the thought to get up, could so completely predominate consciousness, bringing with it a wholly renewed appreciation of the warmth and comfort therein, that the thought of getting up would vanish as quickly and completely as, say, a baseball batter's thought to pull the ball down the third base line, immediately after he has, instead, socked it into the right field bleachers.

Logically, one cannot both get out of, and stay in, bed. Logically, these two thoughts are opposed to each other. But no *emotion* of opposition between them need necessarily arise. In James's will paradigm, when the "original thought" to get out of bed reappeared, it reappeared in relationship to (in context with) the thought that was its opposite. Although it is *possible* for one thought to continue to rotate with an opposing thought without any more feeling of opposition between them than is felt by a skier zigzagging down a hill—turning left one moment, right the next, and then left again—most often, when a pair of opposing thoughts rotates one with the other, a feeling of opposition is there as well. The opposition of one and the other is felt *in* one and the other; it is *how* they are experienced.

In this felt relationship between two opposing thoughts, each turning-toward is also experienced as a turning-from; each turning-from is experienced also as a turning-toward. Either way, it is in this two-pointed connection of welcoming and opposing that James locates the origin of the feeling of self. Not simply "the *constant* play of furtherances and hindrances," but the *reciprocal* or mutual play. Picking up his description from where we left off:

> The *mutual* inconsistencies and agreements, reinforcements and obstructions, which obtain amongst these objective matters reverberate backwards and produce what seem to be incessant reactions of my spontaneity upon them, welcoming or opposing, appropriating or disowning, striving with or against, saying yes or no. This palpitating inward life is, in me, that central nucleus which I just tried to describe in terms that all men might use. (*PP1*, 299; emphasis added)

This "central nucleus," what James refers to as "the central nucleus of the Self," is the kind of nucleus that has become familiar to contemporary physics: a blur of movements. Otherwise, it is no nucleus at all. It has nothing recognizable as a core. James emphasizes its coreless nature by calling it a "palpitating inward life."

THE TEMPORAL LANDSCAPE OF SELF

His free will paradigm gave one example of the systole and diastole of these palpitations, where the rotation of two contradictory desires (to get up or stay in bed) produced a "mutual" relationship between them (*PP2*, 524). The "play of furtherances and hindrances" expresses itself in his paradigm as feelings of "welcoming" or "opposing": a saying "yes" to one thought that is felt as a saying "no" to the other. This "palpitating inward life" of welcoming and opposing is found at the center of every "I"-feeling emotion—which is to say every emotion except the blissful, non-"I" mystical state of one-pointed sciousness, a state with no reverberation of approval or opposition, but only a neutral "whatever is, is." The leap-in-the-air thrill of a victory (as in witnessing a game-winning home run) is felt as a lift from the downward pull of defeat. The let-down feeling of defeat (as when the ball is caught at the top of the wall) is a fall from the uplift feeling of victory. The "opposing," "disowning," "striving against" of negative emotions (anger, fear, hatred, envy, disgust, etc.) is a "saying no" to a present moment of consciousness because it is a "saying yes" to the moment that precedes it. The "welcoming," "appropriating," "striving with" of positive emotions (joy, relief, comfort, etc.) is a "saying yes" to a present moment because it is a "saying no" to its preceding moment.

Take, for example, the negative emotion of anger, an emotion that strongly reverberates with a contracted feeling of self. If each moment of *con*-sciousness were a moment of sciousness instead, then anger would not arise when something contrary to a previous thought's interest arose. In such a non-"I" state you would not feel anger even if, say, returning to your parked car, you found its windshield had been smashed and the GPS stolen. The thought of your intact car might be a vivid image as you are rounding the corner to where it is parked, but it would vanish the instant you saw the car itself. By contrast, without such a wholemind processing of each moment as it comes, a sense of "whatever is, is," the thought of your car being intact would linger, in felt opposition to the sight before you, an opposition that is experienced as anger. Anger is a "saying no," a "striving against" what is, because it is a "saying yes," a "striving for" what *was* but *is no more*. It is precisely in this sense that anger is always a lesson; and to the degree that we stay angry we haven't learned it.[87]

The reverberation of "I"-feeling emotion created by a "mutual inconsistency" between two moments is not merely a reverberation in time. Given the timeless quality of being fully in the moment, without reference to past or future—and hence without the borders that make even the present recognizable as such—the reverberation of "I"-feeling is the construction *of* time: not as an abstract concept, but as a felt relation, a palpitation between two moments.

To the extent that time can be said to exist at all, past, present, and future exist too. Of these three, says James, the present is "the darkest in the whole series," since "nothing can be known *about* it till it be dead and gone" (*PP1*, 341).[88] This darkness was particularly worrisome to Einstein since it meant that the present would never be grasped by science.[89] To mystics, however, this darkness is as it must be, since the essential aspect of the present is that it is not really part of the temporal series at all. The mystic Osho put it this way:

> [T]he present is not part of time. Of course ordinarily in the schools, colleges and the universities you have been told and taught and your dictionaries go on saying again and again that time has three tenses: past, present, and future. That is absolutely wrong—wrong according to those who know. Past and future are in time, but the present is not in time; the present belongs to eternity. Past and future belong to *this*—the world of the relative, change. Between the two penetrates the beyond, the transcendental, and that is the present. *Now* is part of eternity.[90]

With the help of a key insight from an anonymously published book, appropriately titled *The Alternative: A Study in Psychology*, James also disassociated himself from what was "ordinarily" taught. Immortalizing a phrase of its author, E. Robert Kelly, James held that what we commonly think of as the present is a "'specious present,'" "'delusively given as being a time that intervenes between the past and the future (*PP1*, 609).'"[91] Unlike the "immediate existence" of now, with no discernible edges or borders of past or future, such specious present, our "present practically cognized," is, more than a point, or even a "knife blade," "a saddle-back, with a certain breadth of its own on which we sit perched, and from which we look in two directions of time" (*PP1*, 609). The two sides of this duration-block saddle, that combine to form the feeling of the present, are themselves "sub-feelings": a growing-fainter "goes" and a growing-stronger "comes."[92] These sub-feelings are not experienced in isolation from each other, as slices of the specious present, one "retrospective," the other "prospective"; as James says, "We do not first feel one and then feel the other after it, and from the perception of the succession infer an interval of time between, but we seem to feel the interval of time *as a whole* with its two ends *embedded* in it" (ibid., 610; emphases added). Blood compares this two-sided embeddedment of the specious present to "the chimney-sweep, who has neither foothold nor handhold, but climbs by the lateral impact of his elbows and his knees."[93]

James believed that a nonspecious present, or what he called "an *actual* present," a present without two such embedded ends, a present without breadth, "*must* exist, but that it *does* exist can never be a fact of our immediate experience" (*PP1*, 609). But what of "infinite feeling" im•mediated experience—"without the least trace of distinction between the me and the not-me" (ibid., 273)? Even Bradley, who acknowledged that "presence is really the negation of time, and never can properly be given in the series," dismissed only time from the present, not "content."[94] Is there an experienceable non-"saddle-back" present that has "content" but no breadth? Is an onsense moment of *im*mediated sciousness just such a timeless present, a present that, as Blood says, "has no breadth for if it had, that which we seek would be the middle of the breadth?"[95]

Does not a "timeless present"—whether a breadthless moment of immediated sciousness, or the "intuition" of the permanent standing present (a permanence James compares to a "rainbow on the waterfall") depict actual experience (*PP1*, 630)? After all, it is not timelessness that renders a present specious, but the imaginary past/future extensions of its actual "*duration-block*," a block which, like all experiencing, is only experienced in the actual present. However much the experience of the duration-block, with its contents "dawning into its forward end as fast as they fade out of its rearward one" (ibid.), can delude us into thinking that the experience is originating in one other-than-the-present realm (the future), and terminating in another other-than-the-present realm (the past), no reality can be assigned to such marginating experiences, which, by their very definition, never exist in the only realm moments *can* exist: now. The past and future constitute the specious part of the specious present. The actual present, on the other hand, constitutes the actual part of everything, including whatever may be designated a past or future.

We think of the past and the future as distinct domains, continuous within themselves. The most recent past, for example, experienced as a "sub-feeling" of "fading away," is taken as the nearest part of a more distant past, such as a scene from childhood. But as James emphasizes, what makes a distant past distant is not some sort of stretching-out of the near past. There is "no direct 'realizing sense'" of such stretched-out "longer" duration (ibid., 638). Beyond the nearest "immediate consciousness of pastness" (ibid., 650) is a past constituted in an entirely different way: not from an extension of the sub-feeling *perception* of pastness, but from a present *conception*. That is, the past beyond the perceived past of the passing moment is

> known symbolically by names, such as "last week," "1850"; or thought of by events which happened in them, as the year in which we attended such a school, or met with such a loss. So that if we wish to think of a particular past epoch, we must think of a name or other symbol, or else of certain concrete events, associated therewithal. (Ibid.)

The future, too, beyond the perceived nearest "sub-feeling" of "dawning into," is conjured from symbolic markers, such as "tomorrow," and by "certain concrete events" conceived in present time (*PP1*, 650).[96] Often, the images of past and future are the same, or interchangeable, so that, in the absence of a symbolic marker, such as "yesterday" or "tomorrow," or a temporally distinguishing emotional contraction, like regret (for the past) or anxiety (for the future), there is no sensed tense. Perceived changes do not play out in time. Rather, time itself is derived from a hybrid of perceived change—"the short duration of which we are immediately and incessantly sensible"—plus symbolic markers (ibid., 631).

But all moments, whether perceived or conceived (or both) as past, present, or future, only actually exist "now." To probe too deeply into this ever-present now, was, as Alan Watts learned, to miss the obvious:

> One evening, when Eleanor and I were walking home from a meditation session, I began to discuss the method of concentration on the eternal present. Whereupon she said, "Why try to concentrate on it? What else *is* there to be aware of? Your memories are all in the present, just as much as the trees over there. Your thoughts about the future are also in the present. . . . The present is just a constant flow, like the Tao, and there's simply no way of getting out of it." With that remark my whole sense of weight vanished. . . . You could have knocked me over with a feather.[97]

After this satori, Watts's sense of weight returned, even as he continued to mine this insight in all the books he came to write. For it is one thing to understand that the past and future are part of the what-else-*is*-there-to-be-aware-of? ever-present now, and another thing to experience them as such. And rather than being experienced as what they always are—now, *present* moments—the past and the future are most commonly experienced as a pulling-apart, a distraction from the now, into a temporal landscape of di/stances (literally, "to stand apart"). This other-than-the-ever-present-now distracted *con*sciousness is the "palpitating inward life" of self—a moment of (or movement *into*) a feeling of time, away from the timeless, "infinite feeling" sciousness.

What makes sciousness breadthless is not merely the felt absence of temporal borders, but the absence of any "I"-positioning "here/now" to which such borders can refer. Neither the past nor future exist as *actual* alternatives to the present. They exist, rather, as the imaginary temporal landscape that the "I" reverberates as.

We just saw one example of this temporal landscape. In anger, an inconsistency from one moment to the next is experienced as a *mutual* inconsistency that invokes, as much as it relates, two moments in time. This felt temporal relationship applies not only to open anger but to the myriad resentments and frustrations that palpitate more feebly throughout the day. A horn honks outside my study, for instance, breaking the silence that *was* there and, insofar as I am irritated at the interruption, is still there, *in felt opposition* to the sound of the horn. Whether it be the smallest ripple of frustration—such as from writing the wrong date on a check—or open rage—such as from discovering your spouse is having an affair—a relationship between past and present is activated. In all cases of anger, frustration, or resentment, the past is not simply recalled—as just another image in the ever-arising now—it is *revived*, to the point that a distracted, *con*sciousness seems to exist in two different moments of time, represented as two different spaces within a temporal landscape.

The temporal landscaping of distracted *con*sciousness that is anger applies as well to the other, primal negative emotion—fear. While the sense of self, the "palpitating inward life," that arises with anger palpitates between past and present, the sense of self that arises with fear palpitates between present and future. For example, if while walking down a city street I reach for my wallet and discover that it is not there, my initial response is not anger but fear. I stop dead in my tracks and gasp. My step, my very breath is interrupted. Not the revived past that always accompanies an angry "What happened?" but the conjured future that always accompanies a fearful "What *will* happen?" While anger is a striving against "what is" because it is a striving *for* a "what was," fear is a striving against "what is" because it is a striving for a "what shall be." Thus, cancer patients racked with pain, full of the knowledge that they have only a few days to live, may face a gun (possibly their own) with less fear than those filled with thoughts of the future.[98] In all instances of fear, the sense of self that is threatened is a self of the future, just as in all instances of anger the sense of self that is threatened is a self of the past.[99]

Given that the contractile emotions of anger and fear cannot be experienced in one-pointed sciousness, it comes as no surprise that they are absent from accounts of enlightened persons, such as the Buddha. In *The Varieties of Religious Experience*, James quotes the following firsthand account from Richard Bucke's *Cosmic Consciousness*, depicting Bucke's mystical poet friend Walt Whitman: "[H]e never spoke in anger and apparently never was angry. He never exhibited fear, and I do not believe that he ever felt it."[100] While both anger and fear are commonly believed to focus attention, they are, in fact, always a sign that attention is, instead, distracted. As every accomplished martial artist knows, neither anger nor fear facilitates the moment to moment awareness required for self-defense. Indeed, the greater the absorption in the precise movement of, say, a fist coming toward you, rather than in any feeling you might have about it, the greater the chance of avoiding it. For those for whom being in the moment is not an aspiration but a realization, adrenaline is not needed for alertness.

Nor is it only "negative" emotions that distract sciousness. If sciousness is an "infinite feeling" of bliss, then no "positive" emotions can add to this bliss, but must, like negative emotions, distract. This is hardly surprising since, as we saw, "positive" emotions only arise in tandem with "negative" emotions. And insofar as bliss is felt as a "positive" emotion, it *is* felt as a response to, or in a relationship with, a nonblissful or negative emotion. But bliss can also be a trapdoor that drops us out of the positive/negative duality altogether. The surprise scent of a rose, for instance, that comes out of nowhere is a blissful, non-"I" moment of sciousness, fundamentally different than the joy experienced from the scent of a rose sniffed to see if it has a scent.[101] Unlike the blissful scent of a rose that wafts in by surprise, the "positive" feeling we get from the *test* sniff has an additional source: the allayment of a negative feeling (however slight) that it wouldn't have any smell. Although brief moments of bliss, *complete unto themselves*, may be more frequently experienced throughout the day than is commonly suspected, most "positive" feelings are not non-"I" moments of bliss, but, like the test sniff of the rose, are connected to feelings of striving for and against. And even a blissful moment, as it arises, may instantly turn into something to be striven for—its preservation—which is simultaneously a striving against its opposite—non-bliss.

THE UNITY OF "I" FEELING

If the sense of self is only an intermittent (however frequent) occurrence in the stream of consciousness (the sequence of differents that is represented as streaming) what explains the abiding sense of self amongst those differents? How can an "I" of a moment ago[102] be felt to be related to an "I" of three minutes ago, or three decades ago, or the "I" of tomorrow, if there is no one underlying "I"?

Obviously there is an underlying *body*. The fact of a body may not be the fact of an "I," but it is clearly a referent point for past, present, and future "I"s. The body's ever-changing nature does not undermine this referencing capacity. Right now I am sitting in my study at my desk; two hours ago I was in the kitchen putting a bagel in the toaster. A pair of video cameras, placed in each room, would reveal that the hand writing this sentence now was the same hand putting the bagel in the toaster then. My memory would seem to confirm the same.

Yet, while a video camera is a good device for catching a thief, it is a bad analogy for how memory catches the body/self. For although what I saw of my body as I was putting the bagel in the toaster two hours ago—a forearm and a hand—is pretty much what I see now as I glide my pencil across the page, the *re*cognition of my*self* at the toaster is not based on an actual matchup of these two images, past and present, of the same body part. I rarely would see just my forehand and hand in a memory image, as I do in an actual present view. Recognition of my self through body matchups is not based on matching images that would be identical to those taken from a hidden camera taped to my forehead.

The fuller body image that is in memory is never there in the original scene upon which the memory is based. Since we only see aspects of our body in any given moment, any fuller body memory image is *conjured*. Such a conjured, filled-out image, which often includes our back, is more a marker than a memory; it helps position consciousness in the past without having been an actual part of that past. It is *added to,* or *superimposed upon,* what we saw, rather than *being* what we saw.

That we almost always see such conjured body images of self superimposed upon a memory reveals how rarely we re-experience the exact perspective of a "then" in a "now." Rather than exactly relocating into what was experienced, into a "*here*" of the then, the scene appears as a "there," that is, at a distance. Sometimes it is a far distance, like a film's establishing shot; sometimes it is close, just over our shoulder; but whatever the viewpoint, it is a viewpoint that only exists in re-view *now*; it did not exist *then*. While the body does play a key role in this *re*view-point, the body in view, the image of the body as it appears in memory, far from being an authentic recreation, is a spurious stand-in. So, too, such spurious stand-in "I"s are all that appear in future scenarios and daydreams. No matter how many times a future scenario may be rehearsed, the stand-in "I" is viewed from the perspective of a movie director on a flexible dolly crane, not the actor in the scene.

If the body does not reliably link the "I" of now to an "I" of then, the question remains, "What does?" What makes rehearsals and replays possible if there is no underlying "I"? For whether *re*viewed or *pre*viewed, all stand-in "I"s are experienced as related to each other. The *body* of such previews or reviews may be a spurious recreation, but the sense of a unified "I" among them is not. Aware of the shared identity of different "I" moments, James, consistent with his disbelief in a separate, abiding self, accounts for the unity without positing a unifier. The unity of different "I"s is not created by a unifying subject but by a unifying *feeling,* the feeling of warmth—that is, the very feeling that James believed formed the ultimate basis of any given instance of "I" feeling.[103] "The past and present selves compared," says James, "are the same just so far as they *are* the same, and no farther. A uniform feeling of 'warmth' . . . pervades them all; and this is what gives them a *generic* unity and makes them the same in kind" (*PP1*, 335).

The meaning of the word *warmth* flutters between a distinct bodily sensation and a distinct emotion; and just as James fully employed both senses in identifying warmth with the nucleus of self, so, too, he uses both senses in depicting how a past and present self can be compared, "just so far . . . and no farther":

> We hear from our parents various anecdotes about our infant years, but we do not appropriate them as we do our own memories. Those breaches of decorum awaken no blush, those bright sayings no self-complacency. That child is a foreign creature with which our present self is no more identified in feeling than it is with some stranger's living child to-day. . . . We know what he said and did; but no sentiment of his little body, of his emotions, of his psychic strivings as they felt to him, comes up to contribute an element of warmth and intimacy to the narrative we hear, and the main bond of union with our present self thus disappears. It is the same with certain of our dimly-recollected experiences. We hardly know whether to appropriate them or to disown them as fancies, of things read or heard and not lived through. Their animal heat has evaporated; the feelings that accompanied them are so lacking in the recall, or so different from what we now enjoy, that no judgement of identity can be decisively cast. (Ibid., 335–336)

This feeling of warmth, then, is the "brand" by which different memories are identified as belonging to one's "self," "exactly like any one of our other perceptions of sameness among phenomena" (ibid., 334). Such current of feeling, such warmth, such matchups of feelings past and present, unify otherwise isolated moments in the stream of consciousness, providing, as James says, the "*real and verifiable 'personal identity*'" therein (ibid., 336). These matchups are not inferred from their having a common, underlying body/subject, but from their having a common, underlying, *feeling*, a "resemblance in a fundamental respect," a "continuity before the mind of the phenomena compared" (ibid., 334).

PREASSEMBLED THOUGHTS

The feeling of warmth as the basis of generic unity between past and present selves may seem like extreme, bottom-line, material reductionism. James's caveat notwithstanding, can we not go "farther" than this? Beyond a feeling of warmth "branding" different moments as "I" moments, does not the very experience of different moments felt in relation to each other, thoughts and feelings past matched up with thoughts and feelings present, entail the *activity* of some sort of agent self, an activity that brings the different elements together, that *brokers* the relationship? Indeed, even a wholemind moment of sciousness—other than, perhaps, a monolithically perceived patch of color —seems to presuppose an organiz*er*, or at the very least, an organiz*ing*. Do not most images or thoughts, in fact, entail "a manifold of coexisting ideas" that must be actively assembled? James himself asks this very question:

> If . . . the thought be "the pack of cards is on the table," we say "Well, isn't it a thought of the pack of cards? Isn't it of the cards as included in the pack? Isn't it of the table? And of the legs of the table as well? The table has legs—how can you think the table without virtually thinking its legs? Hasn't our thought, then, all these parts—one part for the pack and another for the table? And within the pack-part a part for each card, as within the table part a part for each leg? And isn't each of these parts an idea? And can our thought, then, be anything but an assemblage or pack of ideas, each answering to some element of what it knows?" (Ibid., 278)

But having made the argument for a manifold of coexisting ideas in any thought of more than a single detail, James immediately dismisses it, claiming that "not one of these assumptions is true" (ibid.). To make them is to commit a basic error: confusing a thought with what the thought "can be developed into" (ibid., 279). Although the thought of the pack of cards on the table is a thought about both "the pack of cards" and the "table," the "conscious constitution" of the thought is not one of plurality but of unity (ibid., 278–279). As a whole unit unto itself it is an "entirely different subjective phenomena" than the thought "the pack of cards" or "the table" (ibid., 278). Emphasizing this point with italics, James declares: "*Whatever things are thought in relation are thought from the outset in a unity, in a single pulse of subjectivity, a single psychosis, feeling, or state of mind*" (ibid., 279).

There seems to be no limit to the amount of relations such a single pulse might contain. James quotes Mozart's description of how he composes, bits and pieces coming together in his mind until,

> "At last it gets almost finished in my head, even when it is a long piece, so that I can see the whole of it at a single glance in my mind, as if it were a beautiful painting or a handsome human being; in which way I do not hear it in my imagination at all as a succession—the way it must come later—but all at once, as it were. It is a rare feast! All the inventing and making goes on in me as in a beautiful strong dream. But the best of all is the *hearing of it all at once.*" (*PP1*, 255)[104]

Such "hearing of it all at once" is not to be confused with the ordinary distraction of consciousness into different temporal moments. It has, obviously, more in common with the "tremendous muchness" rapture of a mystical, beyond-self panorama, than with self-feelings of anger, fear, worry, effort, and so forth. Indeed, Mozart's hearing all at once what comes later as a succession is the inverse of a distracted consciousness. For instead of the one-pointed "now" of present consciousness splitting into separate (temporal) moments, separate (temporal) moments fuse into a one-pointed "now." However miraculous such fusion may seem, it is corroborated by the yogic practice of time contemplation "directed towards the immediate realization of ever greater and greater durations and pursued until the whole of time can be experienced *now.*"[105]

But whatever its ultimate complexity, no moment of consciousness is to be confused with what it can later be broken down into. A stab of pain in a tooth, for instance, is not an accretion of different experiences, even if it can later be described as such. So, too, a simple thought, such as "table" (or "cards on table"), does not arise disassembled, like mail order furniture, requiring assembly from an "I." It arrives whole. The more complex the relations within a single thought, the more its preassembled quality is manifest. What kind of assembling process, for example, could possibly deliver an entire sonata "all at once"?

A literary parallel to Mozart's "all at once" is Nabokov's "curious preview." As he told an interviewer:

> Since I always have at the very start a curiously clean preview of the entire novel before me or above me, I find cards especially

> convenient when not following the logical sequence of chapters but preparing instead this or that passage at any point of the novel, and filling the gaps in no special order.[106]

The fact of preassembled complex aggregates in so much artistic creation is why Myers identified the "inspiration of genius" as a "subliminal uprush" that is an "emergence into ordinary consciousness of ideas matured below the threshold."[107]

All thoughts arise—emerge whole, "from the outset in a unity"—and the creative conceptualizations of artists are no exception, despite Bergson's insistence that "creation" is always synonymous with "duration," indeed is what "true duration means," and that the "sprouting and flowering" of works of art entail an "unshrinkable duration, which is one with their essence."[108] As one of the most assiduous contemporary explorers of thought formation, Jason Brown, put it: "Although the artist speaks of insight, of a 'looking-in,' *the concept presents itself for discovery*."[109]

In saying that "things thought in relation are thought *from the outset* in a unity," James is making no claim as to *how* such unity is accomplished. The "how" of such unity remains a mystery—a mystery, he points out, that cannot "be made lighter" by assuming that it happens "inside the mind" (*PP1*, 364). To say, as some philosophers do, that a thought is unified "inside the mind," assumes that there is something *un*unified outside the mind, a "chaotic manifold" that needs to be "reduced to order" (ibid., 363). The most renowned of these philosophers, Kant, called this chaotic manifold "noumena," or objects as they exist in themselves, without the admixture of thought; he then posited a transcendental "I," a *pure* "I," which, though never actually experienced in any way, must still exist in order to convert noumena into recognizable phenomena.[110] In place of the direct experience of an existing unity in thought, Kant thus posited two *un*experienced *concepts*. For James, however, Kant's description of "the facts" was "mythological," and his transcendental "I" (not to be confused with the empirical "me" of a sensed "I") "as ineffectual and windy an abortion as Philosophy can show" (ibid., 365). As James rightly observes, there is no evidence that thoughts come from unknown elements brought together in some sort of "internal machine-shop" in the mind (*PP1*, 363):

> Experiences come on an enormous scale, and if we take them all together, they come in a chaos of incommensurable relations that we can not straighten out. We have to abstract different groups of them, and handle these separately if we are to talk of them at all. But how the experiences ever *get themselves made,* or *why* their characters and relations are just such as they appear, we can not begin to understand. (*HTM*, 1190–1191)

Still, even if there is no chaos of *un*known elements to bring into the known, the presumption persists that *known* elements brought into a relation with each other require a rela*tor* of some sort. How else to account for a unity formed not "from the outset" but from separate moments we experience as time? James's example of the pack of cards on the table, for instance, is presented as a sentence: "The pack of cards is on the table." While the upshot of this sentence is indeed a unified whole, and such a unity, when it occurs at the end of the sentence, occurs "all at once," it is still a gathering of separate moments. Mozart might have experienced an entire sonata "all at once," but most of us cannot make it from "twinkle" to "star" without journeying. The simplest melody (like the simplest sentence), whatever its ultimate unity, unfolds as a *succession.* There may not be "a constant 'self' moving through successive experiences,"[111] but any experience of succession (as opposed to the "all at once" "single glance" of Mozart) seems to entail if not an assembler, at least something more than the assembling itself.

But does it?

JAMES AT BASHŌ'S POND

> Succession is the thing.
>
> –Xenos Clark, in a letter to Benjamin Paul Blood, that Blood shared with James, defining the essence of "the anaesthetic revelation."

When we hear a melody, do the earlier notes hang around until they are pieced together with the later notes, or is the cumulating consciousness of the melody newly reconfigured in each occurrent moment? What of the various images of a poem read? Who or *what* links them together? Look again at Bashō's

Old pond
Frog jumps in
Sound of the water

The three lines are distinct but cumulative: the second line building on the first, the third on the first two. Three different thoughts, one successive experience. But the successive experience of whom? The poet Bashō? On the basis of these three lines we have not the slightest inkling who that might be. The creator of a delightful poem, surely, but the delight is derived from a total vacuuming out of subjective traces. The relating of this scene, in both its parts and its totality, does not depict the history of a subject, in whom the experience inheres, so much as the impersonal modifications of experience itself.[112] There is no question that the three moments of the experience are related to each other. The question is how are they related? A daughter, for example, is, at the same time, both related to her mother and independent of her. She has features that can be *traced back to* her mother but these features reside in her now, completely independently of their source; there is no unifying agency relating each to the other.

So, too, the relationship between the lines in Bashō's poem exists independently of a unifying agency. The "in" of the second line has inherited its meaning from the "pond" of the line before it. In one sense, then, the first line lives in the second line. But that inheritance of meaning in the second line does not imply the continued existence of the first line any more than the hair color that the daughter has inherited from her mother implies that the mother is still alive. The second line *as* written, and *if* read in the spirit in which it is written, is a new moment of sciousness, even if it contains something of a moment that came before it.

Granted, it may take much meditation practice to even glimpse this spirit, in which everything that arises commands undivided attention upon arrival and then vanishes as the next point of focus arrives; and, ultimately, perhaps, grace, to inhabit it fully. As the considered-to-be-enlightened Zen patriarch Huang Po mused about his students: "Why do they not copy me by letting each thought go as though it were nothing, or as though it were a piece of rotten wood, a stone, or the cold ashes of a dead fire?"[113] Why indeed? But even from the vantage point of ordinary consciousness, where each moment of thought is not let go of before the next arrives, relationships between sequential moments are less artificially assigned to the moments themselves than to a go-between unifier.

Take, as James does, by way of illustration, the simplest of sequences—one letter of the alphabet followed by the next. The letter "m" comes before the letter "n," and "n" comes after "m"; but that does not imply that a before-after relationship exists *in between* the two letters, actively linking them. The transitioning between two moments may be protracted enough to suggest such in-between linking is taking place; but whatever transitioning is experienced is, in fact, its own distinct moment in the sequence. James, as we saw, likens all such transitions to "flights of a bird" in between "perchings" (*PP1*, 243). Such transitions are easy to miss, because

> [t]he rush of the thought is so headlong that it almost always brings us up at the conclusion before we can arrest it. Or if our purpose is nimble enough and we do arrest it, it ceases forthwith to be itself. As a snowflake crystal caught in the warm hand is no longer a crystal but a drop, so, instead of catching the feeling of relation moving to its term, we find we have caught some substantive thing, usually the last word we were pronouncing, statically taken, and with its function, tendency, and particular meaning in the sentence quite evaporated. (Ibid.)

James treated such transitional moments as endangered species, and did all he could to preserve the reality of the crystal despite the evidence of the drop. The reality of transitional moments, he felt, was easily overlooked, which is why "we ought to say a feeling of *and*, a feeling of *if*, a feeling of *but*, and a feeling of *by*, quite as readily as we say a feeling of *blue* and *cold*" (*PP1*, 246). But even without such distinct transitional thoughts as "and" or "is followed by," the thought "n" does not require the lingering, active presence of the thought "m" to assume its sequential sense in the recitation of the alphabet. On the contrary, sequential sense, as James says, comes ready-made as its own distinct pulse: "[I]f the plain facts be admitted," says James, "the *pure* idea of 'n' *is never in the mind at all*, when 'm' has once gone before; and . . . the feeling '*n-different-from-m*' is itself an absolutely unique pulse of thought" (ibid., 500).

To believe that succession in thought implies lingering moments that need to be actively unified is to confuse the *feeling of* succession with a thought *about* succession.[114] As the psychologist Wilhelm Volkmann says, in a passage quoted by James, "The thinking of the sequence of B upon A is *another kind of thinking* from that which brought forth A and then brought forth B" (*PP1*, 629; emphasis added). Or, saying the same thing in different words: "[S]uccessive ideas are not yet the idea of succession, because succession *in* thought is not the thought *of* succession" (ibid.). Succession *in* thought, what Kant called "bare succession," is an unreflected-upon "vanishing and recommencing" of thoughts.[115] The thought *of* succession, by contrast, is a *conceptualization* of this vanishing and recommencing. In this conceptualization, the otherwise unreflected-upon transition between different moments is abstracted into still points of thought, spread out in an imaginary row. As Bohm says:

> You can imagine that between this moment now and the next moment there is a stretch; then it is really space by which you are representing time. When you say "ahead of me is the future," that is a spatial analogy. You imagine the future stretches ahead and the past is behind. But the past is nowhere. The future is nowhere. Still, your experience is that "back there" is the past and "ahead of me" is the future.[116]

We take linear time as real, even though at its most fundamental level, as an "internal perception" of flow (*PP1*, 605), it is, as we saw, an amalgam: *actual* feelings, or rather "sub-feelings," of going away and coming toward, mixed with *imaginary* spatialized representations of past and future. Somehow this succession of sub-feelings *in* consciousness (the growing-fainter "goes" and the growing-stronger "comes") gets represented as a temporal landscape *of* succession: a present, always coming out of a past and going into a future. While intuition of time is woven into a linear landscape, the actual dynamic feeling of ongoing consciousness does not "require to know that the sub-feelings come in sequence, first one, then the other; nor to know what coming in sequence means."[117] Past, present, and future are *concepts* which organize successive experience, just as the concept of space organizes coexisting experience. It is not, as we saw James emphasize, that "things come to be thought by us as past . . . because of any 'intrinsic quality' of their own, but rather because they are associated with other things which for us signify pastness" (*PP1*, 605).[118]

We believe that the arrow of time is real, heading toward a future realm and leaving behind a past realm. We are accustomed to seeing emphatically entropic, apparently irreversible, processes—such as a pitcher smashing into bits onto the floor, or a tree shedding its leaves. Only in a comic film do we see smashed bits fly off the floor to form a pitcher, or dried leaves fly up to restore the "bare ruined choirs where late the songbirds sang." While no physical process at their microscopic level would violate any laws of physics if reversed, the absence of a witnessed reversal for so many events at the macroscopic level, such as trees shedding leaves or crockery shattering, as well as the belief that such emphatically entropic processes can never be reversed, constitutes a "folk intuition" of asymmetry.[119] It is this folk intuition that is our inexorably linear arrow of time.[120] As David Bohm puts it, "things succeeding each other in a certain order" is not simply an aspect of time, it is the very basis of time.[121] Time—moving forward in one direction, like a train on a track or an arrow in flight—is not an objective reality of succession, but merely "a concept which is set up by thought to represent succession."[122]

Representations of succession, with imaginary locations of past and future, are readily confusable with experience in succession. But in contrast to a thought *of* succession, an actual experience of thought *in* succession requires no row of imaginary segments spread before and after an imaginarily contemporaneous "I." Even Kant himself saw this:

> An elastic ball which impinges on another similar ball in a straight line communicates to the latter its whole motion, and therefore its whole state (that is, if we take account only of the positions in space). If, then, in analogy with such bodies, we postulate substances such that the one communicates to the other representations together with the consciousness of them, we can conceive a whole series of substances of which the first transmits its state together with its consciousness to the second, the second its own state with that of the preceding substance to the third, and this

> in turn the states of all the preceding substances together with its own consciousness and with their consciousness to another. The last substance would then be conscious of all the states of the previously changed substances, as being its own states, because they would have been transferred to it together with the consciousness of them. And yet it would not have been one and the same person in all these states.[123]

What Kant believed to be possible, James claimed as actual. Introducing Kant's metaphor into the *Principles*, James held that "it is a patent fact of consciousness that a transmission like this actually occurs" (*PP1*, 339); in the stream of thought that is ordinary consciousness, one thought does indeed pass into another without the mediation of an "I":

> Each pulse of cognitive consciousness, each Thought, dies away and is replaced by another. . . . Each later Thought, knowing and including thus the Thoughts which went before, is the final receptacle—and appropriating them is the final owner—of all that they contain and own. Each thought is thus born an owner, and dies owned, transmitting whatever it realized as its self to its own later proprietor. (Ibid.)

It reads like a commentary on Bashō's poem.

If it does not read like an account of ordinary experience it is because ordinary experience assumes more than the impersonal arising of a "sequence of differents." Ordinary experience assumes a thinker generating and connecting passing thoughts, rather than the only "*directly verifiable existent*": "the passing Thought itself" (*PP1*, 401, 346).

"THE DIRECTLY VERIFIABLE EXISTENT"

In the absence of distraction, in which every moment is experienced as "a one thought-instant," the discontinuity between successive thought-instants is not filled by a self, but a gap.[124] In such a "non-regressive satori" state of sciousness, the transmittal process between one thought and another (separated by a momentary gap) is experienced as a simple transition between one moment and the next, "a bare succession . . . always vanishing and recommencing."[125] In ordinary *con*sciousness, by contrast, instead of the vanishing and recommencing of pulses of thoughts *in* succession, such as

> Old pond
> Frog jumps in
> Sound of the water,

a thought *of* succession is present as well. Each moment/movement of thought is experienced not as an "absolutely unique pulse," but as a part of a continuum, with each thought actively relating to other thoughts.

This active relationship with other thoughts, or what James calls "some shading or other of relation" or "inward coloring" (*PP1*, 245), may be as simple as a sense of conjunction:

> Old pond
> And a frog jumps in
> And a sound of the water

or a more complex causal relationship:

> When the frog
> Jumped into the old pond
> There was a splash

In these altered examples, Bashō's one-pointed sciousness *in* succession has been replaced by a *dis*tracted *con*sciousness *of* succession. A "self" no less than a frog has jumped in, just as it more obviously does whenever the sequence is emotionally charged:

> Old pond
> Feels peaceful
> What's that?!
> Wow, a frog!
> There goes the silence!

Ordinary consciousness, as Shaw once said of a feverish pianist, "cannot play even a scale without a crisis in it somewhere." But however much thoughts may whirlpool around in a contraction of *con*sciousness rather than stream in sciousness, there is no independent "I" holding the thoughts together, let alone generating them. On the contrary, the whirl or reverberation of self-feeling *obscures* the arising nature of the impersonal thought process by effectively filling in the gap between one thought and another. Because the stream of consciousness is ordinarily felt *with* "I," it is presumed to be being maintained *by* "I." But no "I" accounts for the coherence between thoughts any more than it accounts for the coherence within a single thought. The unity of relations that exists in any given thought or between thoughts is a fact of experience behind which we cannot go. "If anyone," says James, "urge that I assign no *reason* why the successive passing thoughts should inherit each other's possessions . . . I reply that the reason, if there be any, must lie where all real reasons lie, in the total sense or meaning of the world" (*PP1*, 401).

Despite his freewillism, James's conviction that sense or meaning is not *generated* by an "I" but *conveyed* by a passing thought; that the stream of consciousness creates the "I" (and not the other way around); aligns him squarely with the fundamental axiom of the *Upanishads*, "That thou art." Or, as the great sage of nondualism Shankara expressed it: "If you say that experience depends upon an experiencer, we reply that on our view the experience is itself the experiencer."[126] One thousand years later, James almost seemed to be paraphrasing Shankara when he wrote: "*If the passing thought be the directly verifiable existent which no school has hitherto doubted it to be, then that thought is itself the thinker,* and psychology need not look beyond" (*PP1*, 401).

Of course, Shankara, unlike James, *did* have an answer for "why the passing thoughts should inherit each other's possessions." Like Parmenides, whom he echoes, and Royce and Bradley who echo him, he believed all thoughts, all passing thoughts, are single-sourced in an eternal, changeless witnessing, consciousness, "standing behind everything that is known."[127] For most of his life, James considered such a monistic, eternal, Absolute Self, at best, "an interesting and sublime *hypothesis*" (C8, 402). By deliberate contrast he called his philosophy of the passing thought, his philosophy of direct experience, a "mosaic philosophy" without a "bedding" (*AWPE*,

1180)—in sharp contrast to Vivekananda's "mosaic work set upon God, who is the background of all things."[128] Championing, as we saw, the "as-real-as-anything-else" "directly experienced" "relations that connect experience," James felt he could forego the bedding since it was "as if the pieces clung together by their edges, the transitions experienced between them forming their cement" (*AWPE*, 1160, 1180). But at the very end of his life, as we shall see, James proposed that the mosaic may have a bedding after all; a bedding more unifying than the conjunctive relations that "continue the experiential tissue" at the edges (ibid., 1181);[129] a bedding more unifying than the "unifying feelings of warmth" transmuting "empirical me"s into a single I; a bedding less empty than causality's "pedestal . . . marking the place of a hoped-for statue"; a bedding that, unlike Kant's "windy abortion," does account for how Hume's "successive" "particular perceptions" "*unite* in our thought or consciousness"—the "*loosened*" perceptions whose unity Hume himself felt "hopeless" to give an account.[130]

SCIOUSNESS AS ENLIGHTENMENT

> Having . . . abandoned favoring and opposing. . . .
>
> —The Buddha's description of his Enlightenment in the *Mahatanhasankhaya*

The reverberation of striving for and against, of welcoming and opposing, that generates the sense of self, defines a range within which all emotions arise. Every emotion is found somewhere between them. To focus, however, as James does, exclusively on the movement between the polar opposites of welcoming and opposing is to lose sight of a more fundamental movement—the movement between a neutral state of consciousness and all others—that is, the movement between sciousness and *con*sciousness. The movement between sciousness and *con*sciousness is analogous to the movement of a wave, arising out of a calm sea. As a level sea forms an essential defining contrast to the wave, so, too, sciousness forms an essential defining contrast for all "I"-feeling sensations. As a waveless sea underlies any waves that arise, so, too, sciousness underlies the arising of all "I" feelings.

Another analogy is sound and silence. To describe the feeling of self without reference to sciousness is like describing sound without silence—the silence that forms the contour of any sound that is heard. Just as there can be no sense of sound without a sense of silence, there can be no sense of self without a nonself background to give it definition. "The palpitating inward life" of welcoming and opposing cannot itself give rise to self-feeling any more than the change from soft to loud gives rise to sound. As sound can only be understood in contrast to silence, so, too, the "reverberation" (second beat) of "I" cannot be understood without its first beat, non-"I."

James's omission of neutral consciousness, or sciousness, is what leads him to the oxymoronic conclusion that the "reinforcements and obstructions which obtain amongst . . . objective matters . . . produce what seem to be incessant reactions of my spontaneity." "*Produce* incessant reactions of my spontaneity"? Isn't the defining characteristic of spontaneity the very fact that no known source produces it? James was not witnessing incessantly produced reactions of his spontaneity; he was witnessing the incessant formation of an "I"-sense within the stream of sciousness—what Watts referred to as a "double take" and what they both termed a "reverberation." This "reverberation" is not an *activity* of self, but the very *creation* of self.

The core of that creation—a palpitating inward life of mutually reciprocating feelings of welcoming and opposing—is what the Buddha lost, never to regain, on the day of his enlightenment. As he himself characterized it: "Having . . . abandoned favoring and opposing, whatever feeling he feels, whether pleasant or painful or whether neither-painful-or-pleasant."[131] So, too, the seers of the Upanishads, as well as presumed-to-be-enlightened sages such as Shankara and Ashtavakra, all identified the *non*-"I" state of enlightenment as one in which "the mind does not desire or grieve or reject or accept"[132] Such an enlightened state does not, as we said, entail the *complete* extinction of desire, as is sometimes (erroneously) attributed to it, but, rather, the absence of desire that any given moment be other than it turns out to be. It is the absence of such *hankering* desire in the Buddha, as in other mystics, which corroborates James's sense that "I" feeling is a byproduct of the interplay between feelings of welcoming and opposing; for it is only in the *absence* of these feelings that the wholemind state arises. Like dancers who find themselves "in sync" with the beat of a drum, neither welcoming one beat over another, nor wondering how to respond or how they appear to others, but existing *with* the beat, so that they have no sense of themselves as dancers but only a sense of dance, mystics discover that it is possible to just *be* with each passing moment, leaning neither toward it nor away from it, and having not the slightest sensation that *it* need be otherwise. In such a state, as Whitman says, every event, every encounter "is subdued into sustenance."[133]

James extolled Whitman's moment-to-moment consciousness in a talk he gave to students (*OCB*, 851–854); but a few years later, in a lecture to professors—*The Varieties of Religious Experience*—he turned critical. Ever the pragmatist, James claimed that Whitman's "mystic ontological emotion," free of "all contractile elements," "divert[s] our attention" from hardships, such as "disease and death" (*VRE*, 83, 88). But James's pragmatism is misinformed here. Whitman, a medic during the Civil War, was no such diverter. His poetry is filled with corpses and maggots:

> Behold this compost! behold it well!
> Perhaps every mite has once form'd part of a sick person—yet behold![134]

Indeed, it is precisely because Whitman's poetry is free of all contractile elements that diversion plays no part in it. Only in the enlightened state of pure experience sciousness—free of welcoming and opposing—can one "behold well" every moment.

If James misses the full practical value of such a state in his assessment of Whitman early in *The Varieties of Religious Experience*, he compensates for it later by commending the example of the Christian mystic Catherine of Genoa, an example that can be taken as illustrating his epistemology as much as her spirituality:

> "[S]he took cognizance of things, only as they were presented to her in succession, *moment by moment*." To her holy soul, "the divine moment was the present moment . . . and when the present moment was estimated in itself and in its relations, and when the duty that was involved in it was accomplished, it was permitted to pass away as if it had never been, and to give way to the facts and duties of the moment which came after."[135]

James lamented that his own "constitution" shut him out from mystical experiences (*VRE*, 342). He knew more than he realized.

ELEVEN

Psyche

For my own part I confess that the moment I become metaphysical . . . I find the notion of some sort of an *anima mundi* thinking in all of us to be a more promising hypothesis, in spite of all its difficulties, than that of a lot of absolutely individual souls.

—William James, *The Principles of Psychology*

Psyche is existent, it is even existence itself.

—Carl Jung, *Psychology and Religion*

We got along excellently with regard to the assessment of the religious factor in the psyche.

—Jung, speaking about a long conversation he had with William James, in Bair, *Jung*

"In the beginning," says the Gospel According to John, was not God or man but "logos," defined in the standard Greek lexicon as "*the word* or *that by which the inward thought is expressed.*" The question of how a universal intelligence or logos is connected to the thoughts of individual body/selves was given a very simple answer by Hindu philosophy: through the breath. This was more than a metaphor. The entire Sanskrit alphabet, and all the words formed by it, were thought to be derived from combinations of the sound of inhalation (*Ham*) and the sound of exhalation (*Sa*).[1] And their word for soul, *atman*, is the same as their word for breath.

The identification of the breath with thoughts has its roots in the West as well. The Greek word *psyche* meant soul, life, heart, and mind, but its first meaning was breath, just like another Greek word, *pneuma*, which means breath, spirit, or wind.[2] So, too, the Hebrew word *ruach*, which also means both "spirit" and "wind," was linked to thought. In the original Hebrew alphabet, as well as the related Phoenician alphabet adapted by the Greeks, there were no vowels. For vowels, as "breath uninterrupted" and "breath sounded," were identified by the Hebrews with *ruach*, a force too wild and mysterious to be congealed into written form. Since different vowel sounds would create a different meaning for the same combination of consonants (such as our dud, did, dad), the meaning of the words was the momentary meaning that arose with each sounded breath.[3]

The apparent dichotomy between a still, passive entity (such as written consonants) and a moving, active force (such as breathed vowels) is actually a condition for understanding passive and active on their own terms. There is no sense of active without passive; no sense of passive without active. They are codependent terms, like concave and convex. Likewise, no still moment of consciousness can be completely realized as such without a movement of consciousness.

For James, the movement in the moment of consciousness was just what the ancient spiritual traditions proclaimed it to be. Familiar with *ruach*, which he called the Hebrew's "warm breath of life which animated the dust," and which, along with *pneuma*, he identified as the ancient "ruling conception" of "breath-spirit," James made a direct connection between thought and what he termed "ever the original of spirit"— breath (*EPs*, 316; *DCE*, 1157). Citing no other source than his own "intuitions," which he declared he "must obey," James wrote:

> Let the case be what it may in others, I am as confident as I am of anything that, in myself, the stream of thinking (which I recognize emphatically as a phenomenon) is only a careless name for what, when scrutinized, reveals itself to consist chiefly of the stream of my breathing. The "I think" which Kant says must be able to accompany all my objects, is the "I breathe" which actually does accompany them. (*DCE*, 1157)

James lamented that his intuition would sound "materialistic" to many (ibid.); and he knew that the material sciences of his day could not back him up. Nor could direct observation by itself. The most that direct observation could show is that alterations in breath correspond to alterations in thought.[4] Pushed to elaborate the details of his intuition, James offered only a general observation that "free breathing or oppressed breathing makes our self-consciousness different" (C7, 486). Nonetheless, James never repudiated his intuition that breath was in fact the "essence" of thoughts (*DCE*, 1158).

Whatever the actual relationship between the formation of breath and the formation of thoughts, they have at least one essential feature in common: they are both arising, impersonal, processes. As we have tried to show, thoughts are not made—they *occur*. This is equally true for breaths. Our breathing is autonomous, requiring neither our supervision nor our attention. It arises spontaneously, without effort, and originates beyond the known. As Blood says:

> Every breath that we voluntarily draw is, in the cosmic sense, an irrelevant interference with divine providence. We have no need to *do* it; with or without our volition it will be done.[5]

We cannot take a breath that is not given, nor control what the breath will be. Even if we were to regulate the breath to a uniform pace, as in Yoga *pranayama*, the control we exerted for each breath would not itself be uniform: like trying to keep a kite in the same spot in the air, we would either let the breath do what it will, check its force, or supplement it, depending on each new breath that arose. We are not breathing so much as being breathed.

The link between our mystically determined breathing and the mystically determined thoughts which in turn determine our actions is suggested by the Gospel According to John: "The *pneuma* [wind, breath] bloweth [*pnei*] wherever it listeth, and thou hearest the sound thereof, but canst not tell whence it cometh, and where it leads: so is everyone that is born of the *pneuma*."[6] A similar mystical determinism through the agency of breath is also suggested by the shamanic teaching of the "luminous egg," such as conveyed by Carlos Casteneda's teacher, Don Juan:

> [E]very man is in touch with everything else, not through his hands, though, but through a bunch of long fibers that shoot out from the

> center of his abdomen. Those fibers join a man to his surroundings; they keep his balance; they give him stability. So, as you may *see* some day, a man is a luminous egg whether he's a beggar or a king and there's no way to change anything; or rather, what could be changed in that luminous egg? What?[7]

Even memories—which, like all thoughts, *arise* in consciousness—may ultimately come more from "without" than "within." No relationship has ever been found between damage to a specific part of the brain and a corresponding loss of "stored" (or what James referred to as "secondary") memory. One renowned brain scientist in the middle of the last century, K. S. Lashley, carved out different chunks of rat brain cortex in an attempt to eradicate the rat's memory of a passage through a maze. He was not successful. More recently, measurable changes attributed to learned-task memories have been detected among the one hundred trillion synapses that connect the one hundred billion neurons in the brain; but the memory does not stay where the initial synaptic changes occur.[8] Moreover, these biochemical synaptic changes in memory recall are merely "analogous to," rather than "identical with," what occurred during the initial learning.[9] This suggests that the act of recall *remakes* a memory anew every time, rather than just recalling an original stored trace.[10] As James said about memory in general:

> [R]evival in the mind of an image or copy of the original is obviously not a memory, whatever else it may be; it is simply a duplicate, a second event, having absolutely no connection with the first event except that it happens to resemble it. (*PP1*, 649)

What is now certain is that memories do not reside in the brain like so many bits on a hard drive.[11]

Even if memory moments had a more stable identity with those moments they "happen to resemble," there are no stable storage sites for the memories to reside in. Computer storage analogies fail to consider how radically different the brain is from a machine. There can be no hard drive in the brain, precisely because there is nothing hard, in the sense of fixed. As neurologist Maurice Nicoll put it:

> We know that all living tissue is constantly undergoing changes. There is a continual assimilation and elimination, a constant interchange between cell, blood, and lymph. The material substance of the brain-cells is always being built up anew by this interchange. Let us face the question: Do we really imagine that the past is "coiled up" in the matter of these three-dimensional brain cells that are undergoing such constant changes?[12]

Moreover, while laser scanners isolate different patterns in the brain for memories than for other kinds of thoughts, no instruments can determine whether such memory sites are storage containers, filtration points, or transmitters. As James duly noted, even if the "great psycho-physiological formula" is true, and "thought is a function of the brain," that does not imply that the brain either stores or produces thought.[13] Late-life pronouncements connecting breath and thought notwithstanding, James never denied that thought was a function of the brain; but he adopted his friend and colleague F. C. S. Schiller's proposal that the function was better understood to be one not of production but of *transmission*.[14] In Schiller's words:

> Matter is not that which *produces* consciousness, but that which *limits* it and confines its intensity within certain limits: material organization does not construct consciousness out of arrangement of atoms, but contracts its manifestation within the sphere which it permits.[15]

James concurred.[16] A wider range of observed phenomena could be accounted for, and no observable phenomena excluded, if the brain acted more like a prism, refracting a light from an unknowable beyond, than like a generator, producing the light within (*HI*, 1109–1110).

Acknowledging that Science cannot explain either how the brain might produce *or* transmit a thought (ibid., 1112), James reverts to metaphors instead, such as that of the prism, or, in another metaphor emphasizing that consciousness is not "generated on the spot, in its own peculiar vessel" (ibid.), a pipe organ. The keys of the pipe organ, says James,

> open successively the various pipes and let the wind in the air-chest escape in various ways. The voices of the various pipes are

> constituted by the columns of air trembling as they emerge. But the air is not engendered in the organ. The organ proper, as distinguished from its air-chest, is only an apparatus for letting portions of it loose upon the world in these peculiarly limited shapes. (Ibid., 1110)[17]

Science is no closer today than in James's time to figuring out "the exact process either of transmission or of production" of consciousness; it still has "not the least glimmer of a conjecture or suggestion" to this problem (ibid., 1112). As Blood emphatically put it:

> Consciousness, even as it glows, is a helpless projection from an alien energy, bottomless in its own regard, utterly unqualified to declare or to determine anything as necessary and therefore wholly incompetent to radical explanation.[18]

But science does, today, have more sophisticated technology, offering more sophisticated metaphors, such as this update from William Braud:

> [T]his distinction of brain as producer and transmitter is often expressed picturesquely by asking whether the brain more closely resembles a lightbulb (which is the source of the light it produces, and without which the light can no longer exist) or a television receiver (which modifies and expresses images from electromagnetic fields that exist apart from itself and which later can continue to exist even in the absence of the receiver).[19]

In the middle of the nineteenth century, when Carl Gustav Carus introduced the term *psyche* into the new science of psychology, he was acknowledging how little we ultimately know about where our thoughts come from. The first line of Carus's book *Psyche*, published in 1846, is, "The key to an understanding of the nature of the conscious life of the soul lies in the sphere of the unconscious."[20] Both Jung and Freud embraced Carus's thesis, but only Jung embraced the term. The term *psyche* did not suit Freud, who was reluctant to concede too mysterious an origin to our thoughts.

Unlike Jung, Freud believed that the configuration of the key was derived solely from one's past experiences. This meant, for Freud, that while the unconscious was the key to the conscious, the conscious was the key to the unconscious. Jung split with Freud over this tidiness. In direct opposition to Freud's idea of the unconscious as consisting only of the repressed thoughts of consciousness, Jung saw our unconscious as being fed from a mysterious, inexhaustible source:

> To Freud, the unconscious was a product of consciousness, and the unconscious simply contained the remnants of consciousness; I mean that he saw the unconscious as a sort of storeroom where all the discarded things of consciousness were heaped up and left. To me, however, the unconscious was a matrix, a sort of basis of consciousness, possessing a creative nature and capable of autonomous acts, autonomous intrusions into the consciousness. In other words, I took the existence of the unconscious for a real fact, an autonomous factor that was capable of independent action.[21]

Both consciousness and the unconscious, Jung believed, are created out of the "irrepresentable and transcendental" psyche:

> In reality the psyche is the mother and the maker, the subject and even the possibility of consciousness itself. It reaches so far beyond the boundaries of consciousness that the latter could easily be compared to an island in the ocean. Whereas the island is small and narrow, the ocean is immensely wide and deep and contains a life infinitely surpassing, in kind and degree, anything known on the island.[22]

For Jung, the reach of psyche, "far beyond the boundaries of consciousness," extended to the past and future, "unhampered by the categories of time."[23] He was a champion of the laboratory precognition experiments of Joseph Rhine conducted at Duke University, which, along with his own research, contributed to his belief that his Einstein-inspired "synchronicity" was an "all-pervading factor or principle in the universe."[24] Such a belief in a temporally relativized psyche as "the mother and the maker" underlying consciousness, led him to question whether we all are not just paying, in his phrase, "lip-service to freedom":[25]

> We have got accustomed to saying . . . "*I have* such and such a desire or habit or feeling of resentment," instead of the more veracious "Such and such a desire or habit or feeling of resentment *has me*." The latter formulation would certainly rob us even of the illusion of freedom. But I ask myself whether this would not be better in the end than fuddling ourselves with words.[26]

Robbed of the illusion of freedom, the "small and narrow" island of consciousness sinks beneath the "immensely wide and deep" infinite ocean of psyche. And indeed Jung, an empirical scientist who worked his entire lifetime on this island, began, toward the end of his life, to feel the water rising around him. In the concluding paragraphs of his autobiography he wrote:

> The older I have become, the less I have understood or had insight into or known about myself. . . . There is nothing I am quite sure about. I have no definite convictions—not about anything really. I know only that I was born and exist, and it seems to me that I have been carried along. I exist on the foundation of something I do not know.[27]

THE "MOTHER-SEA"

Jung's destruction of Freud's container for the unconscious was directly influenced by James for whom, as we saw, there was no "definitively closed individuality of our personal consciousness" (*PP1*, 350), no "*being*-an-individual in some accessible metaphysical way."[28] Seven years before meeting Freud and Jung on the same day, James had positioned himself exactly between them in his *Varieties of Religious Experience*. Calling Myers's "discovery" of the "extra marginal" subliminal field "the most important step forward that has occurred in psychology since I have been a student of that science," James wrote:

> [I]n certain subjects at least, there is not only the consciousness of the ordinary field, with its usual centre and margin, but an addition thereto in the shape of a set of memories, thoughts, and feelings which are extra-marginal and outside of the primary consciousness altogether, but yet must be classed as conscious facts of some sort, able to reveal their presence by unmistakable signs. I call this the most important step forward because, unlike the other advances which psychology has made, this discovery has revealed to us an entirely unsuspected peculiarity in the constitution of human nature. No other step forward which psychology has made can proffer any such claim as this. (*VRE*, 218)

Jung, who was familiar with Myers's research,[29] quoted this meta-Freud passage with approval.[30] And yet another harbinger of his break with his mentor's more circumscribed version of the unconscious can be found in a second passage from the *Varieties*, a book Jung knew well:

> It . . . is "scientific" to interpret all otherwise unaccountable invasive alterations of consciousness as results of the tension of subliminal memories reaching the bursting point. But candor obliges me to confess that there are occasional bursts into consciousness of results of which it is not easy to demonstrate any prolonged subconscious incubation. (*VRE*, 215)

This passage illustrates Jung's claim that James's "far-ranging mind made me realize that the horizons of human psychology widen into the immeasurable."[31] And, indeed, years before Jung's break with Freud, James anticipated the metaphor Jung used to explain it: we live on "islands in the sea," James wrote, our "'normal' consciousness" surrounded by a "panpsychic" "mother-sea" (*EPR*, 374). But unlike Jung, who doubted the existence of free will, James felt our connection to this mother-sea to be only "fitful influences from beyond," which "leak in" (ibid.). Although he believed the "I" to be an ongoing process, a manifestation of "passing Thoughts," rather than its own independent entity, he never lived his belief. He maintained an "ear for monistic music," but never lost the keen sense of separation from the Universe that he had professed in his twenties:

> We long for sympathy, for a purely *personal* communication, first with the soul of the world, and then with the soul of our fellows. And happy are they who think, or know, that they have got them! But to those who must confess with bitter anguish that they are perfectly isolated from the soul of the world, and that the closest human love incloses a potential germ of estrangement or hatred, that all *personal* relation is finite, conditional, mixed. . . . (*PP1*, 131)

While James proposed, and in no small measure realized, contributing to the welfare of the world as a "not unfruitful substitute" for feeling estranged from it (ibid.), the equally accomplished Jung required no such substitute. His belief in an autonomous psyche was an affirmation of James's "anima mundi thinking in all of us." Immediately after concluding that he existed "on the foundation of something I do not know," Jung wrote, "In spite of all uncertainties I feel a solidity underlying all existence and a continuity in my mode of being."[32]

The "bitter anguish" that James spoke of for those who were "perfectly isolated from the soul of the world" was not Jung's. Nor was the "germ of estrangement." In feeling the "solidity underlying all existence," Jung felt he shared his cosmic home with everything else, animate and inanimate alike—not as a hierarchical overlord, but as a co-participant in a mystically determined movement of psyche:

> Since psyche and matter are contained in one and the same world, and moreover are in continuous contact with one another and ultimately rest on irrepresentable, transcendental factors, it is not only possible but fairly probable, even, that psyche and matter are two different aspects of one and the same thing.[33]

While such a view gave Jung no more ultimate status for himself than a leaf blowing in the wind, it also gave him a benediction: "The more uncertain I have felt about myself, the more there has grown up in me a feeling of kinship with all things."[34]

Such "kinship with all things," which rises as the sense of self falls, is the only answer one can give to what James saw as the "moral rub" of determinism: one cannot step in to oppose evil, one cannot "take sides" (C3, 100). For while a belief in determinism *does* annul a belief in the agency of self-intervention, it also, thereby, annuls the notion of sides. The less we feel ourselves to be individuated, self-activating beings, the more kinship we will feel with others, even those we most resist (as is reflected in the Dalai Lama's epithet for the people who ravaged and subjugated his homeland: "My friends, the enemy Chinese."). In other words, although a belief in determinism erodes moral agency, it enhances the foundation of all moral behavior: empathy.

TWELVE

Undoing unto Others as Well as Oneself

BEYOND REPENTANCE: THE ABSENCE OF AGENCY IN THE PRESENCE OF EMPATHY

> [A]n acute and prolonged feeling of sinfulness leads to a sense of oppression, whereas the function of a religious life is to *overcome* oppression.
>
> —Nikolay Berdyaev, *Self-knowledge*

> However the creature may seem to himself original and responsible, the true light shows his power to be but secondary from the divine viewpoint, and the remission of his sins is possible only in the truth that the Divine assumes responsibility for them. . . . Let one know that the follies he has committed . . . are not ultimately attributable to him, but rather to the divine purpose, his conscience may drop the ball and chain; for the truth and the light will have set him free.
>
> —Benjamin Paul Blood, *Pluriverse*

While the ultimate origin of our actions may be mysterious, relative determinations *between* events are readily identifiable.[1] Why a child was run over by a car is a different question for pastors than judges. Graveside pastors don't much care whether it was the child's racing after a ball or the driver's racing to beat a red light that caused the fatal accident. Judges very much care, along with other determinations, such as how many drinks the driver had before getting into the car. Pastors, addressing the ultimate question of why, defer the answer to the mysterious ways of the Lord. Judges, addressing the relative question of why, do not defer to ultimate belief systems, including free will and determinism. Even if judges are absolute determinists, they can and must consider the *relative* determinations within a sequence of events. Being an absolute determinist in no way precludes identifying relative determinations.

So, too, even if, as mystical determinists, we believe that our actions are determined by an overall unidentifiable agency, giving us no freedom *to* do other than it wills, we can still speak of a freedom *from* identifiable sub-agencies, and recognize when such freedom has been violated. "If A had not occurred then B would not have followed" makes as much sense to determinists as it does to freewillers. Sitting on a jury with freewillers, determinists could share their reasons for finding a drunk driver innocent of murder. It is not how to justify acquitting, but only convicting, that distinguishes determinists from the rest of the jury.

Now, it might seem that only freewillism—a belief in both freedom from *and* freedom to—allows responsibility to be assigned for actions in the first place. But a moment's reflection reveals that assigning full freedom *for* our actions is far more problematic than removing partial freedom *from* them. For while it is fair to ask: "If there is no free will, how can anyone be held responsible for what they do?" it is equally fair to ask: "How can anyone be held responsible if there *is* free will?" This second question, posed almost exclusively by philosophers, asks how responsibility can be assigned for an action that is free, spontaneous, when such an action is, *by definition,* not connected to anything that came before it: "If a 'free' act be a sheer novelty," says James, "that comes not *from* me, the previous me, but *ex nihilo*, and simply tacks itself onto me, how can *I*, the previous I, be responsible?" (*P*, 538) This was not, for James, a mere exercise in logic; as we have seen, he believed that the relationship between previous and subsequent "I"s was, at best, tenuous.

One way to focus the debate of which (if either) belief system makes responsibility possible is to look not at where an action came from but where it *went*. Taking responsibility for an action hinges less on "owning up" to something you have done wrong, than on seeing the wrong itself *as* wrong. It is the answer to the question "How have 'I' (the objectified 'empirical me' identified with thoughts and actions that occur within my body/self) harmed another (or even 'my' self)?" With or without free will, a behavior has manifested itself through me. Insofar as this behavior (be it from neglect, anger, misinformation, greed, or any number of reasons no longer viewed as justifiable) has harmed another, it is not my free will or lack thereof that makes me see, feel, and acknowledge the harm done, but, rather, the far more powerful and mysterious force of empathy. Without empathy no amount of "owning up" to something is worth anything toward repentance, while with it repentance comes of itself.

Empathy arises whenever the imagined boundaries that distinguish one self from another collapse, such as when we immediately (instinctively?) reach out to another about to jump off a bridge, even at the risk of our life. In such moments we are responding as if that life is our own, which, in the deepest understanding, it is. While empathy is not a moral behavior that can be taught, without it, that most fundamental moral behavioral guide—the Golden Rule—could not be learned. "Do unto others what you would have others do unto you" is, after all, less a strategy for how to relate to others than a formula for questioning how "other" others are. The answer to this questioning is not a thought but a feeling—the feeling of empathy.

To the degree that you truly see the harm done to another through your actions, whatever their ultimate source, your understanding about the harmful effect of the actions has changed. Such a change of understanding, based in empathy, is, in itself, repentance. The Greek word for repentance, in fact, *metanoia,* the word used in the New Testament, originally meant "of a later mind." It did not have the painful self-reverberation of its modern meaning. So, too, the New Testament Greek word for sin, *hamartia,* originally meant, simply, to "miss the mark," or "make an error"; it was the word the Greeks used to describe an arrow missing its target. While "change of mind" and "error" may seem too lightweight to convey the heavy (burdened-with-self) meanings of sin and repentance, they are still adequate to convey the meaning of each word: for in its truest sense, to repent sins is to have a change of mind about an error, the error of causing pain or damage to another whom the feeling of empathy has revealed to be not as "other" as had been imagined.

Although empathy is the foundation of true repentance, its transformative power is rarely acknowledged. Perhaps this is because it is seen as being too "passive" for something as "active" as repentance. Certainly, seeing repentance as ultimately an "effect" of empathy, runs counter to the Western tradition. Our word *repentance*[2] comes from the Latin *poena*, "punishment," and *re*, "again." And as repentance is commonly understood in the West the punishment is indeed repeated; only the person suffering has changed from the victim to the perpetrator. The usual experience associated with repentance is not the feeling of another's pain but one's own: a constricted feeling of "having done wrong." The body is tight; the emotions are wrought; and a sense of self is felt therein.

But self-recrimination is not repentance. It is the pain that one has caused another, not oneself, that is necessary for repentance. If I feel a sense of anguish while repenting a past action then the repentance I am feeling is a cheat. It is a cheat because the anguish brings the scene being repented to a whirring halt, like a film in a theater shutting down in the midst of a screening: the picture dies out, the lights come up on present time. The anguish felt in repenting for a past misdeed does not identify us with that misdeed so much as abort its existence. Notice, for example, the dynamics of the misery-go-round phrase "I can't believe I did that." Often it is accompanied by shut eyes, a turning of the head down into one's hands, and a groan. In such moments the hurtful deed is not being faced, but averted. Our eyelids black out the scene; our groan drowns it out. We are punishing ourselves at the expense of seeing the scene whole. We bring ourselves to the threshold of an understanding only to turn away at the point of entry. Whenever someone says, "I can't believe I did that," I believe them.

True repentance does not re-view a past scene through blinds of anguish. Such a view, no matter how many times it is glimpsed, remains obstructed. True repentance views the scene in question as if through an open window. At such time there is no wincing, no feeling of punishment; just a calm, clear-eyed, neutral, acceptance of reality.[3]

Only to the degree that a past event can be seen for what it was (rather than what it should have been) can the expanding power of empathy (as opposed to the constricting force of shame or guilt) effect the change of mind (*metanoia*) that is true repentance. To the degree that I understand what I did, I am no longer that person. And that is the sign of true repentance: to so fully see and empathize with another's suffering that one feels incapable of doing it again. Even if the suffering was only inflicted on myself, true repentance reveals that "self" to be but the *temporary* confluence of *particular* perceptions and attitudes. All true repentance evolves into repudiation.

Far from being facilitated by a belief in will and self, then, true repentance is more easily realized in their absence. To say, "I did this," or, "I did that," and to mean by this statement more than that the action came through my body/self with its precisely configured feelings and thoughts of the moment, to mean by it that everything that defines the "I" now defined it then, distorts the scene in question by superimposing a still shot upon a moving picture. Any abstracted ("pulled from" different contexts) sense of self will either blur the sense of the past self being reviewed—when it is similar to it, or eclipse it—when it is seen as being different. While repetitions of thoughts, feelings, and actions form patterns objectifiable as a self, any particular action that is being reviewed must be felt in all its particularity before any pattern or general sense can illuminate it. No matter how consolidated a sense of self might be from one moment to the next, to the degree that a past action and the conditions that gave rise to it are understood in a new light, the present "I" is not identified with a past "I." That understanding is the foundation of true repentance. True repentance always speaks thus: "Had I known then what I know now I would have acted otherwise."

If a self-image that is at least partially true can inhibit repentance, a self-image that is false can, obviously, block it completely. When I say, with anguish, "I can't believe I did that," I am saying that the still image of myself does not fit the particular moving picture being re-viewed. Superimposed upon the scene, it is incongruous, out of place, like a snowman in July.

Without a belief in will and self, there is no such blurring, obscuring, or incongruous image, no snowman to melt into the liquid movement of the scene being reviewed—only an action and its consequences, and a response *now to* those consequences. Without a fixed, abstracted image of self, there is more responsibility (literally, "ability to respond") to an action in itself, in its precise particularity. In place of an I, posing as "the elementary force or fact" responsible for the action, there is a precise configuration of the thought, feeling, and circumstance that converged when the action took place.

Such precise configuration allows, as well, for a clearer view of the action's consequences. If I had smashed a lamp in a drunken rage, the turbulence of that rage, like stirred waters, would have obscured the scene and sense of the action. Any insight that provides a clearer sense of what was being experienced at the time also provides a clearer view of the damage and suffering that resulted. "Again punished" is still part of the process of repentance, but instead of self-punishment it is the punishment inflicted upon the other, re-viewed and re-lived in the present with empathy.

The empathic process of metanoia transforms the pang of remorse into an alleviant—the desire to apologize and compensate. Such desire is no more a function of belief in will and self than the process of repentance that preceded it. The desire to apologize and compensate can be felt in the presence or absence of belief in will and self. But differences in belief can affect the motive behind the apology and compensation. With a belief in self and will, apologies and compensations are often attempts to rebuild the toppled statue of self. Without a belief in will and self, compensation serves no other purpose than redress; apology, no other purpose than communicating a realization: conveying to the other that the extent of the harm done has been understood, as well as the conditions that caused it, thereby assuring a greatly reduced likelihood that it will happen again. No apology (however fervid), no amount of compensation (however lavish), can substitute for such an assurance. Nor can such an assurance be conveyed directly. Only the appearance of a true change of mind, *metanoia,* based in understanding and empathy, can convey it. To attempt to assure someone directly, beyond the conveyance of this changed understanding, most often reveals a greater concern for changing that person's understanding than communicating the change in one's own. A true apology has no need of emphasis, no "really"s, as in the ubiquitous "I'm *really* sorry." A plain, straightforward, admission is what is called for. Indeed, it is the very absence of emphasis that underscores the genuineness, the "realness" of the understanding.

But what of crimes such as murder, for which no repentance, no *anything,* can compensate? Critics of determinism are fond of pointing out that punishment is indefensible if free will does not exist. "It wasn't *their* idea to commit the crime so how can you hold them responsible?" The answer is deterrence. All animals and many plants have ways to deter harm. Punishment for a harmful deed—even in the absence of freewillism—is a human form of deterrence. Sometimes people who commit a crime need to be punished (through incarceration) simply to keep them off the streets, in order to prevent a recurrence. More often they need to be punished (through incarceration, fines, or other means) in order to bring to their *own* awareness the harmful nature of their action. (Judges deciding the range of punishment options—from fines and imprisonment to community service—do well to base their decision on which is more conducive to such awareness.) But whatever the specific punishment, insofar as punishment associates harmful actions with undesirable consequences it plays a role in the jurisprudence of determinist and nondeterminist alike. A sense of protection cannot reasonably be abandoned with the assumption of the nonreality of free will.[4] And insofar as punishment is seen as a deterrent it is justifiable. Freewillism need not be part of that justification. As James says: "Instinct and utility between them can safely be trusted to carry on the social business of punishment" (*P*, 538).

The only justification for punishment that would be ruled out is vengeance.

THE MYTH OF WILLPOWER

> It's remarkable how much easier it is to change bad eating habits once the person has become fully conscious of them. You don't have to give orders either. Once a person becomes fully aware of his bad eating habits, he can usually figure out for himself the practical way to change them.
>
> —Diet doctor Henry Jordan, quoted in Bricklin, *The Practical Encyclopedia of Natural Healing*

This insight is indeed remarkable in an age that has so vigorously championed the idea of "willpower." For most of the past century, a publishing industry has been sustained by telling us how to access this power—a power whose existence is taken for granted.[5] Some of those books, such as Rollo May's *Love and Will* or Mark Thurston's *The Paradox of Power*, refer to James's restatement of Renouvier as an example of willpower in action, using the younger James to bolster what the older James could not. As we saw, the source of the power that infused the younger James with a sense of a new direction could have been explained by the older James without the active agency of so-called will or willpower. Nothing in James's psychology of volition supports the existence of either an independent agency or agent as an originating power. All decisions, from choosing a dessert to choosing never to eat dessert again, as well as the experience of power that seems to drive such latter decisions along, can be explained as the interplay of impersonal forces.

For James, no less than the diet doctor quoted above, the power to effect a dramatic behavioral change comes from the full awareness of what the behavior *is*. Beset with having to look after an alcoholic younger brother, James was painfully aware that recovery from such a debilitating condition could involve many false starts. Alcoholics, he came to realize, may try all the willpower in the world to give up drinking, but no change will result unless they first accept that they are, in fact, alcoholics. Full acceptance, and nothing short of it, is the key to change. As James was to emphasize in the *Principles*, in an insight that became the foundation of Alcoholics Anonymous,[6] the decisive moment in any strong resolution—a resolution that changes one's habit or belief—is the moment that one "gets able" to "keep the right *name*" of the belief or habit "unwaveringly present" before one's mind:

> How many excuses does the drunkard find when each new temptation comes! It is . . . poured out and it is a sin to waste it; or others are drinking and it would be churlishness to refuse; or it is . . . just to get through this job . . . or it is Christmas-day . . . etc., etc . . . —it is, in fact, anything you like except being a drunkard. That is the conception that will not stay before the poor soul's attention. But if he once gets able to pick out that way of conceiving, from all the other possible ways of conceiving the various opportunities which occur, if through thick and thin he holds to it that this is being a drunkard and nothing else, he is not likely to remain one long. (*PP2*, 565)

In 1982, a study of four hundred alcoholics confirmed James's insight. The researchers concluded that it is the *shattering* of the sense of a self-in-charge, as when one finds oneself lying drunk in a gutter, that most reliably leads an alcoholic to recovery. As the report emphasized: "Alcoholics who become sober do so *suddenly* under the influence of some crisis situation."[7] Clinical psychiatrists who treat alcoholics sometimes talk of free will as "the key" to recovery, but what they mean by "free" is not the freedom *to* instigate new behavior, but the freedom *from* a distorted view, a *denial* view, of past behavior. The "key" is unlocking the door that shuts out awareness of the full consequences of avoiding recovery.[8] Therapies are designed to enhance the clarity and fullness of the patient's understanding. To help ensure that the understanding once gained will not be compromised, experts in alcoholism denial—other alcoholics in treatment—are enlisted as well.

Successful therapies are thus not designed to instill an offense but to breach a defense. When successful, the decisions that follow are freed *from* the delusional self-image of not-having-a-problem. But the key to gaining such freedom is not turned "at will." It is, rather, a key that turns itself, once it is found, at rock bottom.[9]

The catalyzing capacity of simply seeing a negative state for what it is has wide application. If we apply it to the born-again resolution about free will that James made in his youth, we see that the simply seen negative state was the harrowing image of the patient with catatonia, since it was James's identification with this patient that had induced his crisis of will. Rollo May's discomfort with how James later came to define free will in the *Principles* has him leap over this "right naming" step ("That shape am I"), and the other critical steps by which the young James "got able" to conceive how morbid his view of determinism was: "After the five years in his late twenties and early thirties," goes May's account, "when he was paralyzed with his own depression and scarcely able to will the simplest thing, he decided one day that he could make an act of will to believe in freedom."[10] He decided one day? How spontaneous that sounds. But what happens when James's "act of will" is placed back into context? First, as we saw, there was the "image that rose" in his mind of the catatonic patient. That image James did not choose or will, just as he did not choose or will his body's primal reaction to it. Nor, as the passive voice indicates, did he choose or will the outlook on life that this primal response evoked: "After this the universe *was changed for me* altogether." His decision, then, to accept Renouvier's belief in free will as his own came only *after* his realization that a change had already taken place. Flirting with a belief in a material determinism, a determinism devoid of spirituality or even mystery, proved different than living it. Like the alcoholic who drives off the road into a tree, and subsequently admits, for the first time, to being an alcoholic, James's crisis led him to an awareness of the full implications of what he had come to believe in. As with true repentance, no change is possible without such awareness; while with it, the change seems to come of itself.

Consider, as well, a contemporary true life story by way of further example. Richard Simmons, a TV exercise cheerleader, was, earlier in life, a hundred pounds overweight. No one hectored him into losing it, least of all him*self*. According to his own account, he began losing weight in response to an anonymous note that had been left for him. Having parked his car in the middle of a city, and gone off to attend a meeting, he returned to find a piece of paper on his windshield that said: "Fat people die young. Please don't die."

This note was neither a rebuke nor a rally cry. It made its point without pointing. The first sentence is an impersonal statement of fact whose application to Simmons is only indirectly suggested, in the second sentence. Together, the two sentences form what logicians call an "enthymeme," an implied syllogism. It takes three sentences (in this instance: "Fat people die young. You are fat. Please don't die.") to complete the meaning of an enthymeme even though only two are offered. The missing statement arises automatically as the logical consequence of the other two. For Simmons, this meant that instead of being confronted with the harsh judgment, "You are fat," the conclusion formed itself as an inexorable *fact*, a fact that enabled him to "pick out that way of conceiving from all the other possible ways."[11] Thus Simmons's change of direction was triggered not by an inner resolve but by seeing the manifest truth of his condition.

Had someone confronted him, even benignly, with the truth of his condition, he might have felt shamed and reacted defensively, as if he had been sneered at. Out of such shame he might have "resolved" then and there to change himself. But it is unlikely that real change would have occurred. For his determined resolve "to set things right" would be a defensive reaction, *denying* the condition it sought to change. The Buddhist meditation teacher Dhiravamsa explains it this way: "When an emotional reaction arises, an attempt at rigid self-discipline represses what is actually there so that it can no longer be seen."[12]

The note left on Simmons's windshield provoked insight in part because it did not provoke shame or guilt, and the desire for immediate change these feelings induce. "When the mind," says Dhiravamsa, "wishes to enter the goal as soon as possible . . . [it] tends to become more active.

Instead of opening itself, it gets caught in the desire for achievement and cannot remain aware of its own activities."[13] Standing alone in front of his car, confronted only with an anonymous note, Simmons did not feel rushed by a feeling of shame "to enter the goal as soon as possible." Instead, absent the need to have things be *immediately* different than they were, he "got able" to see the truth of what was. That truth, *in and of itself,* empowered him.

In *The Varieties of Religious Experience,* James cites many conversion experiences in which the antepenultimate moment is one of feeling shame or guilt. But in every case, the penultimate moment is not one of resolve, but of helplessness. Only then did the ultimate moment follow: a total surrender to the truth of one's condition. The "new determination" that ensued was not the ultimate moment of the conversion; it was only the first moment *after* the conversion had already occurred.[14] This paradoxical yet fundamental insight underlies that most effective of long term behavioral change programs, Alcoholics Anonymous. The first of its renowned Twelve Steps, affirming James's fundamental insight, is to state the truth of one's condition. The next two are to disavow a self and a will to deal with it:

1. We admitted we were powerless over alcohol—that our lives had become unmanageable.
2. Came to believe that a Power greater than ourselves could restore us to sanity.
3. Made a decision to turn our will and our lives over to the care of God as we understood Him.

The door to the empowering truth of one's condition cannot be kicked or pried open. It opens effortlessly or not at all. Not only is a "self" taking charge not called for, it may well serve to slam it shut.

THIRTEEN

Belief in Fate Is not Fatalism

. . . a joyous and trusting fatalism . . .

—Nietzsche, *Twilight of the Idols*

The nonreality of free will and the all-consuming reality of a higher will has been acknowledged at one time or another by Hinduism, Taoism, Judaism, Buddhism, Christianity, Islam, the religion of Native Americans, among many other religions. At one time or another, all these religions have identified this higher will as a form of fate. Of the various flowerings of religion, fate is a common root. Indeed, belief in free will has only recently emerged as the dominant, always-accessible, counterforce to any other influence, be it the three, spinning Fates of the Greeks, or the omniscient, omnipotent God of the Judeo-Christian tradition. While the possibility of free will has long been acknowledged, its supremacy has not. In former times, the conundrum, the "unfathomable enigma," was not how free will accommodated fate or divine omnipotence, but how "a thoroughgoing determinism . . . in some mysterious manner, still left men free to exercise discretion."[1]

Some of our most influential writers—Luther, Calvin, Spinoza, Schopenhauer, Nietzsche, Twain, Lincoln, Freud, Tolstoy, and Einstein, to name but a few—solved this enigma by renouncing a belief they viewed as not only extraneous, but erroneous. Nor were they tentative in their renunciations. On the contrary, they expressed it in the strongest possible language.

Tolstoy, for example, concludes *War and Peace* with this unambiguous declaration:

> As in astronomy the new view said: "It is true that we do not feel the movement of the earth, but by admitting its immobility we arrive at absurdity, while by admitting its motion (which we do not feel) we arrive at laws," so also in history the new view says: "It is true that we are not conscious of our dependence, but by admitting our free will we arrive at absurdity. . . . In the first case it was necessary to renounce the consciousness of an unreal immobility in space and to recognize a motion we did not feel; in the present case it is similarly necessary to renounce a freedom that does not exist, and to recognize a dependence of which we are not conscious."[2]

Luther was even more emphatic. In a series of intensely followed debates with Erasmus, who was defending the traditional Vatican line in favor of free will, he declared: "God foreknows nothing contingently, but . . . foresees purposes and does all things according to His immutable, eternal and infallible will. This thunderbolt throws free will flat and utterly dashes it to pieces."[3]

Nietzsche, too, as we have already glimpsed, threw a thunderbolt at free will, creating a wider path of destruction than Luther or Tolstoy:

> People have believed at all times that they knew what a cause is; but whence did we take our knowledge—or more precisely, our faith that we had such knowledge? From the realm of the famous "inner facts," of which not a single one has so far proved to be factual. We believed ourselves to be causal in the act of willing: we thought that here at least we caught causality in the act. Nor did we doubt that all the antecedents of an act, its causes, were to be sought in consciousness and would be found there once sought—as "motives": else one would not have been free and responsible for it. Finally, who would have denied that a thought is caused? that the ego causes the thought?
>
> Of these three "inward facts" which seem to guarantee causality, the first and most persuasive is that of the will as cause. The

> conception of a consciousness ("spirit") as a cause, and later also that of the ego as cause (the "subject"), are only afterbirths: first the causality of the will was firmly accepted as given, as *empirical*.
>
> Meanwhile we have thought better of it. Today we no longer believe a word of all this. The "inner world" is full of phantoms and will-o'-the-wisps: the will is one of them. The will no longer moves anything, hence does not explain anything either—it merely accompanies events; it can also be absent. The so-called *motive*: another error. Merely a surface phenomenon of consciousness, something alongside the deed that is more likely to cover up the antecedents of the deeds than to represent them. And as for the *ego*! That has become a fable, a fiction, a play on words: it has altogether ceased to think, feel, or will![4]

This passage turns Nietzsche's most famous declaration, "God is dead. . . . And we have killed him,"[5] into a murder/suicide—an utter devastation, unless the extinction of two separate entities is required for their resurrection as one. But short of such *unio mystica*, experienced or aspired to, the loss of will and self implied by determinism and inexorable fate is a gloomy prospect for most. The word most commonly used to describe this belief—fatalism—is applied to people who, finding themselves in grim circumstances, accept those circumstances as both not of their making and not in their power to change. If people are pleased with their lives and feel fulfilled, they are not commonly considered fatalists, even if they believe in fate. The more neutral word—determinist—that does not emphasize downturns, would be more apt. On the one hand, determinists accept that they are not masters of their fate. On the other hand, they accept that whatever circumstances they find themselves in can change at any moment. This flexible outlook is shared with freewillers, but it is seldom identified with fatalists.

The distinction between fatalism and determinism is significant, even though the words themselves are sometimes interchanged:

> Krishna is a fatalist, a determinist. He believes that things happen because God has decided them to be so, so nothing can be done about it. . . . If you are poor—God has determined it so. It is your

> fate to be poor; there is no possibility of avoiding it, you cannot escape it. You have to accept it, you have to be satisfied with it.[6]

But such fatalism is not determinism. There is, as we have argued, no such fixed mind-set about the future in determinism. While it is true, as James says, that determinism is a more rigid belief than fatalism, insofar as it affirms "not the impotence but the unthinkability of free-will" (*PP2*, 574); it is less rigid insofar as it does not lock into any fixed scenario. Indeed, determinists' lack of belief in their ability to either control or know their destiny makes them even more open to life's vagaries, to the possibility of change, than those who believe they have access to both. As Nietzsche saw, this openness and allowance for change, experienced as "the enjoyment of all kinds of uncertainties, experimentalisms," is the very "counterweight" to fatalism.[7]

Belief in ultimate powerlessness over destiny was also what empowered those supreme warriors, the samurai, to be fearless in battle.[8] What James characterized as the self's defining "backward reverberation," a "striving with or against"—in contrast to the Buddha's "neither welcoming nor opposing"—was not part of the samurai's armament; while what James defined as fatalism's "solving word in all crises of behavior . . . 'all striving is vain,'" *was* an empowering aspect of their determinism—not, as James imagined, a disempowerment (*WB*, 522). Nevertheless, determinism's acquiescence to the possibility of unavoidable bad fortune can make it seem grim, comfortless: "He who would love God," says the determinist Spinoza, "cannot strive that God should love him in return."[9] It has not been a Gospel of good news.

Spinoza himself did not view determinism as grim, but two other renowned Western determinists, Schopenhauer and Twain, did hold particularly bleak views of the world. Someone who made the mistake of asking James's support to get a statue erected to Schopenhauer received this uncharacteristically scathing rebuke:

> I really *must* decline to stir a finger for the glory of one who studiously lived for no other purpose than to spit upon the lives of me and all that I am for . . . his loud-mouthed pessimism was that of a dog who would rather see the world ten times worse than it is, than lose his chance of barking at it, and whom nothing would

> have unsuited so completely as the removal of care for complaint. (C2, 456)[10]

Twain, too, despite (or, perhaps, due to) all his humor, was a "philosopher of pessimism." In his final years he summed up his outlook on life with the pronouncement: "Anybody that knows anything knows that there was not a single life that was ever lived that was worth living."[11]

Of course abject pessimism is not associated only with determinism. It was Sartre, after all, the champion of freedom as man's essence, who declared, "Man is a useless passion."[12] James, too, was no sunshine optimist. He attacked determinists precisely because he *shared* their bleak worldview. Given how much suffering and evil there was in the world, James believed that determinists, who saw the universe as "one unbending unit of fact," in which "the whole . . . is the only real agent," were guilty of a "monstrous indifferentism" (*WB*, 151; C3, 100). As long as we could feel optimistic about the whole, James argued, as long as we believed that all "cares for complaint" were to be lifted, we wouldn't be concerned whether the world was predetermined or not; we would just "acquiesce in the flow and drift of things, of which . . . [we] found . . . [ourselves] a part, and rejoice that it was such a whole" (C3, 99). But where, outside of palliative religious scenarios, are there grounds for such optimism? Certainly, material determinism, as rampant in James's day as our own, gives no such grounds, nor the philosophical determinism of Schopenhauer.

Mystical determinism[13] also has no grounds for optimism—not because it has grounds for pessimism instead, but precisely because it has grounds for neither. For a "whole" that is immeasurable and inherently incomprehensible cannot be added up at any point for evaluation—good or bad—any more than a landscape painting can be evaluated from one inch away. Up close, Manet's delightful *Luncheon in the Grass* is all black. But a small patch, however compelling in itself, does not disclose the view. Even if all parts of the world are (in one of James's many derisive phrases for the "static absolute") "co-implicated in . . . one logical-aesthetical-teleological unit-picture," they are never seen as such (*P*, 552). The most we can glimpse is how dark and light moments can offset each other. The black moment, for instance, that an American boy in the early part of the nineteenth century experienced when his badly burned leg was amputated (without anaesthesia), turned out to be a decisive factor in the creation of two of his country's greatest writers—William and Henry James. Their father's accident closed the career of a boy who lived for outdoor play, and inaugurated a deeply introspective nature that exerted considerable influence over his two eldest sons.

James allowed that it was possible to "vaguely generalize" from specific examples of bad turned good "into the doctrine that all the evil in the universe is but instrumental to its greater perfection" (*P*, 548). But ultimately, he felt, "the scale of the evil actually in sight defies all human tolerance" (ibid.). The question, though, is whether "the scale of evil" defies all attempts to be placed in perspective. Are we limited, as James held, to a "foreshortened bird's eye view of the perspective of events" (*PU*, 9), or can we attain with Nietzsche such "a height and a bird's eye view" that one "grasps how everything actually happens as it ought to happen: how every kind of 'imperfection' and the suffering to which it gives rise are part of the *highest desirability*."[14]

Earlier, we argued that James had misconstrued Whitman's perpetual affirmation of every moment as avoiding full reality. James himself cautioned that his characterization of all such mystic-minded "quasi-pathological" optimists did not take into consideration "any mystical insight or persuasion that the total frame of things absolutely must be good" (*VRE*, 82, 87). And while cautioning that mystical states "wield no authority due simply to their being mystical states," he allowed that their "optimism" (as well as their "supernaturalism") may turn out to be "the truest of insights into the meaning of this life" (ibid., 386).

"COSMIC INDIFFERENTISM"

> Question: What is the Mind of the ancient Buddha?
> Ch'an Master Wen-I: It is that from which compassion, sympathy, joy, and limitless indifference flow out.
>
> — Tao-yüan (1004/1969), *The Transmission of the Lamp*

For William James, free will "has no meaning unless it be a doctrine of *relief*" (*P*, 539). Like the "religious doctrine" he claimed it to be, free will functioned as a "light" that "grows . . . about us" in the "darkness" of "life's thicket" (ibid.). But as long as one does not settle in an imaginary resting place—let alone a gloomy resting place—to evaluate where life is, is going, or has come from, then a moment-to-moment belief that whatever is, *is*, and is a *given* as is, does not breed despair. Indeed, for Nietzsche, "the boldest, most vital, and most world-affirming human being" is precisely the one "who not only made his peace and learned to get along with whatever was and is but who wills [whatever the ultimate source of 'willing'] to have it again precisely as it was and is to all eternity."[15]

James himself developed a sympathetic understanding of a cosmic "*indifferentism*" under the influence of nitrous oxide, a "Reconciliation of opposites," in which "pessimistic or optimistic attitudes pertain to the mere accidental subjectivity of the moment" (*WB*, 679). He felt "the rapture of beholding a process that was infinite," but then, in "an instantaneous revulsion of mood from rapture to horror . . . the strongest emotion I have ever experienced," something akin to the spiritual crisis of his youth was evoked, as indifferentism became entangled with "pessimistic fatalism" and "depth within depth of impotence" (ibid.). Almost wistfully, he concluded that it would be for others to lose themselves in either a "laugh at the ultimate nothingness," or "a mood of vertiginous amazement at a meaningless infinity" (ibid.).

Ascribing meaninglessness to infinity is somewhat redundant since infinity, by definition, is ultimately beyond meaning, or, at least, comprehension. But the vertigo is real enough. Like standing on the edge of a high precipice, ever so drawn to the vast reach below, it comes from one's finite, meaningful effort encountering an incommensurable magnitude: "ineluctable fate" (ibid.). Such vertigo—like all vertigo—vanishes with a leap. And mystics who have made the leap—or rather, have been leapt—from a faith in will and self, have indeed laughed, but not "at the ultimate nothingness" so much as what they had considered the ultimate somethingness of their self.

Short of this leap, a determinist may well incline more toward gloom than rapture. This is especially true in the West, where determinism has always been more talked about than touched—even for those who most believed in it. Consider, again, Twain. Although Twain was a determinist, to the extent that he identified his enormous early success as a writer with his own personal self, he did not live his belief. To that ultimately unanswerable question "Who am I?" (unanswerable even for someone who believes in free will), Twain had at least a temporary, working response. He was, after all, the most famous writer in America. Everywhere he went people reminded him of who he was. The onset of his pessimism, as Van Wyck Brooks has pointed out in *The Ordeal of Mark Twain*, coincided with the loss of his creativity as a novelist.[16] Later, his pessimism was sustained by financial failures and, toward the end of his life, the loss of his beloved daughter. The fall from grace was all the steeper for Twain because of the height he had reached. Yet his own faith could have helped him to see that it was an illusion to believe that *he* had reached that height—as if by *his* design, especially considering that one of Twain's last essays was an acknowledgment of all the accidental circumstances that had led him to his career.[17] Had he not so strongly identified his success as his own personal triumph, Twain might not have been plunged into despair by his subsequent failure and loss. Like Job, his ordeals might have become the crucible through which he reaffirmed the truest understanding of his profoundest belief.

For to fully live without will and a sense of "I" pushing events along would be to encounter each moment of life with something like the ecstatic wonder known to us only in rare moments of aesthetic or sensual rapture, creative ecstasy, or spiritual awakening: that is, when we feel that we have truly "lost ourselves." Twain knew well the ecstasy (literally "to stand outside [oneself]") of creativity. He did not identify himself as the source of his work. Like many great artists he felt that he was less a maker than a channel:

> As long as a book would write itself, I was a faithful and interested amanuensis and my industry did not flag, but the minute that the book tried to shift to *my* head the labor of contriving its situations, inventing its adventures and conducting its conversations, I put it away and dropped it out of my mind. Then I examined my unfinished properties to see if among them there might not be one whose interest in itself had revived through a couple of years' restful idleness and was ready to take me on again as amanuensis.[18]

In other words, in moments of creation, Twain felt himself to *be* what he believed he actually in all moments *was*—the amanuensis of an impersonal force. This experience of "it" not "I" acting is the same sensation Zen masters feel in the application of their art.

"One day," writes Eugen Herrigel in his classic text, *Zen in the Art of Archery*,

> I asked the Master: "How can the shot be loosed if 'I' do not do it?"
>
> "'It' shoots," he replied.
>
> "I have heard you say that several times before, so let me put it another way: How can I wait self-obliviously for the shot if 'I' am no longer there?"
>
> "'It' waits at the highest tension."
>
> "And who or what is this 'It'?"
>
> "Once you have understood that, you will have no further need of me. And if I tried to give you a clue at the cost of your own experience, I would be the worst of teachers and would deserve to be sacked!"[19]

The difference between a Zen master and a Western artist in relation to the impersonal nature of inspiration is that the Zen master finds it in all aspects of life, even the most seemingly trivial, such as pouring tea. Enlightenment is the extension of such inspiration to every moment. Perhaps if Twain had fully lived his belief, he, too, instead of sinking into despondency might have evolved into a mystic, realizing himself in every moment to be an amanuensis:

> Occasionally several . . . shots came off in close succession and hit the target. But if ever the least flicker of satisfaction showed in my face the Master turned on me with unwonted fierceness. "What are you thinking of" he would cry. "You know already that you should not grieve over bad shots; learn now not to rejoice over the good ones. You must free yourself from the buffetings of pleasure and pain, and learn to rise above them in easy equanimity, to rejoice as though not you but another had shot well. This, too, you must practice unceasingly—you cannot conceive how important it is."[20]

Mystical determinists who fully lived their faith would be freed from the buffetings of welcoming and opposing. For such persons, moments of self-consciousness would be moments of deception, a superimposition of ignorance, while moments of ecstasy—sciousness—would be moments not only of bliss, but of clarity.

This clarity is, in turn, a revelation—a revelation beyond determinism, mystical or otherwise. For it is a revelation not only without an "I"-tag, but what James called the "common-sense dualistic" "time-tag" (*ML*, 255).

FOURTEEN

The Nonreality of Time

> [I]t is not so impossible or even difficult to conceive the universe as it transcends time as has been supposed.
>
> —C. S. Peirce, in an 1898 letter to James

From the moment he had adopted free will, James championed a world that was *what it seemed to be*, a world of "fresh activity-situations," being created as it goes along (*EA*, 810n). "To say that time is an illusion," he wrote, "is only a roundabout manner of saying there is no real plurality, and that the frame of things is an absolute unit. Admit plurality, and time may be its form" (*WB*, 593). James issued this alert to divinity students, prone to contemplating the world as just such a timeless "absolute unit." Indeed, in a different lecture series to divinity students, James's friend William Sturgis Bigelow, a fellow MD with spiritual interests, made just such a case for timelessness.[1] Describing what we now call near-death experiences,[2] Bigelow wrote that

> accumulated states of consciousness sometimes revive simultaneously in a single flash. The events of the whole past are seen down to the most minute and remote details, like a landscape under a flash of lightning.[3]

Bigelow specifically mentions James's teacher and friend Dr. Oliver Wendell Holmes as having "had this experience on one occasion, just before losing consciousness altogether while drowning."[4] More recently, in this very same lecture series to divinity students, Huston Smith also introduced a near-death experience (of a history professor friend, Steve Fanning) that suggested the "frame of things" is indeed a timeless "absolute unit":

> The reality that I was in was more real, more intense, than anything in this current world of ours. It was hyper-reality.
>
> I was in a place. Around me was flatness and barrenness. To talk about a sequence to the experience is to distort it. There was no time there. I now know that time is a convenient fiction for this world, but it did not exist in that one. Everything seemed to be at one moment, even when "events" seemed to occur in a sequence. What seemed to be the sky, the land, and everything was of a pale blue-gray color. It was like being on a raft in the middle of the ocean where sky and sea merge into one monochromatic world, but I felt as though I were standing on firm land. There was only the blue-gray vastness that seemed to stretch endlessly. . . .
>
> The . . . re-experiencing of my life . . . was simultaneous and yet separate and distinct. There was no such thing as the sequence of events that we believe time to be.[5]

James devoted his life to defending accounts such as these. His most popular book, *The Varieties of Religious Experience*, is an anthology of spiritual encounters and self-transcendence. These include the all-at-once, all-in-one visions, such as St. Theresa's: "One day, being in orison, it was granted me to perceive in one instant how all things are seen and contained in God" (*VRE*, 371). And he was familiar with time-collapse near-death experiences through examples in a nineteenth-century textbook that he references in the *Principles*.[6] But from whatever source, revelations of timelessness did not sit well with James who griped: "[I]s not the notion of eternity being given at a stroke to omniscience only just another way of whacking upon us the block universe, and of denying that possibilities exist?" (*WB*, 593). James would not be whacked by what he called the "iron block universe" of determinists. Until, toward the end of his life, he was.

TIMEMASK

> Life, like a dome of many-colored glass, Stains the white radiance of Eternity.
>
> —Shelley, quoted by James in "Human Immortality"

For all his resistance to a block universe, to "the notion of eternity being given at a stroke to omniscience," James had helped prepare the way for its reception. In the same lecture series in which both Bigelow and Smith introduced the time collapse of near-death experiences, James proposed that the world of "natural experience" may be just a "timemask, shattering or refracting the one infinite Thought which is the sole reality into those millions of finite streams of consciousness known to us as our private selves" (*HI*, 1110). It seems a bizarre assertion for him to have made, even to divinity students—the very students whom, on another occasion, he had warned *against* such a timeless universe (*WB*, 593). But James was nothing if not true to experience, and while he declared that "experience as a whole wears the form of a process in time" (*AWPE*, 1169), he questioned whether time itself, time as usually considered, or "*felt*"—"a kind of impalpable inner flowing"—was part of that truth (ibid., 1143).

James quotes a poet's assertion that in a closed-eyed meditative state we can "attend exclusively to the actual passing of time . . . like one who wakes to hear time flowing in the middle of the night, and all things moving to a day of doom" (*PP1*, 619). But, he argued, no such pure time exists. Unlike Bergson, James did not believe in "the flow of real time"[7] any more than he believed that consciousness was an entity. To Bergson's insistence on "real" time as an actual "vital process," such that if "I want to mix a glass of sugar and water, I must, willy nilly, wait until the sugar melts,"[8] and that "[r]eal duration . . . gnaws on things and leaves on them the mark of its tooth,"[9] James countered: there is no "devouring tooth" of time (*PP1*, 628).[10] Time, James believed, was not an innate intuition,[11] but a "patently artificial" "construction" (*P*, 564). From Newton's foundational fiat—"Absolute, True, and Mathematical Time, of itself, and from its own nature, flows equably without regard to anything external"[12]—James declared independence: "We assume for certain purposes one 'objective' Time that aequabiliter fluit [flows evenly], but we don't livingly believe in or realize any such equally-flowing time" (*P*, 566).

What we realize are moments of varying duration, and movements discriminated into varying amounts of successive moments. As Hodgson put it: "[W]henever there is a difference of *feeling* there is a difference of state. Until a difference of feeling occurs, a state continues one and uninterrupted."[13] Any sense of time is based upon some such "difference of feeling." A few years after Hodgson introduced his "sequence of differents," the great physicist/philosopher Ernst Mach, a friend and colleague of James, who shared his radical empirical approach toward time, wrote:

> It is utterly beyond our power to *measure* the changes of things by *time*. Quite the contrary, time is an abstraction at which we arrive by means of the changes of things; made because we are not restricted to any one *definite* measure, all being interconnected.[14]

While accepting that "the *passing* moment is the only thing that ever concretely was or is or shall be," James was well aware of the varying speed—from still to blur—of that passing (*KTT*, 77); of different discriminations of succession under the influence of fatigue, illness, ecstasy, or drugs. In hashish intoxication, for example, he noted that

> there is a curious increase in the apparent time-perspective. We utter a sentence, and ere the end is reached the beginning seems already to date from indefinitely long ago. We enter a short street, and it is as if we should never get to the end of it. (*PP1*, 639–640)

Accidents are perhaps the most common catalyst for extreme time dilation, such as psychiatrist Harold Rosen experienced when his car skidded off the road and turned over twice before landing at the bottom of a hill. The few seconds of that crisis seemed to him as though it took approximately half an hour for each of the four revolutions—side, upside-down, other side, rightside-up—repeated twice.[15]

In other altered states, the opposite effect, as James duly noted, is experienced. Instead of a slowed-downed "finer-grained" succession in which many extra stages of a process are observed, "processes seem to fade rapidly *without* the compensating increase in the subdivisibility of successions" (*PP1*, 640; emphasis added).

And well before Einstein, directly inspired by Mach, had dismantled Newton's absolute time into myriad relative times, James had done the same. Blending his awareness of varying subjective time flows with the computations of the founder of comparative embryology, Karl Ernst von Baer, he wrote:

> We have every reason to think that creatures may possibly differ enormously in the amounts of duration which they intuitively feel, and in the fineness of the events that may fill it. . . . Suppose we were able, within the length of a second, to note 10,000 events distinctly, instead of barely 10, as now; if our life were then destined to hold the same number of impressions, it might be 1000 times as short. We should live less than a month, and personally know nothing of the change of seasons. If born in winter, we should believe in summer as we now believe in the heats of the Carboniferous era. The motions of organic beings would be so slow to our senses as to be inferred, not seen. The sun would stand still in the sky, the moon be almost free from change, and so on. But now reverse the hypothesis and suppose a being to get only one 1000*th* part of the sensations that we get in a given time, and consequently to live 1000 times as long. Winters and summers will be to him like quarters of an hour. Mushrooms and the swifter-growing plants will shoot into being so rapidly as to appear instantaneous creations; annual shrubs will rise and fall from the earth like restlessly boiling-water springs; the motions of animals will be as invisible as are to us the movements of bullets and cannon-balls; the sun will scour through the sky like a meteor, leaving a fiery trail behind him, etc. That such imaginary cases (barring the superhuman longevity) may be realized somewhere in the animal kingdom, it would be rash to deny. (*PP1*, 639)

The slowing down and speeding up of the same content of consciousness suggests the varying speeds that can be applied to the static frames of film. Can the entire content of consciousness, no less than the entire content of cinema, be broken up into still images, separated by intervals? Francis Crick, one of the discoverers of DNA, who launched a second career looking for the foundation of consciousness, concluded, after years of painstaking research with neuroscientist Cristof Koch, that all movements of visual consciousness are indeed derivable from discrete "static snapshots," like a strip of movie film.[16] And neurologist Oliver Sacks, summing up several recent studies of visual consciousness, concluded: "We may find movies convincing precisely because we ourselves break up time and reality much as a movie camera does, into discrete frames, which we then reassemble into an apparently continuous flow."[17]

Exactly analogous with cinema, the conversion of moments into movements can, depending on the speed of the conversion, appear with or without gaps: as a lurching parade or a flowing stream. There are even something like maximum and minimum speed limits for consciousness just as there are for movies. A movie runs at twenty-four frames per second; too much faster creates a whirring blur. And visual perceptual moments themselves have a speed limit: a tenth of a second.[18] Any visual stimulus that vanishes faster than that goes unnoticed, even as a blur. As for a minimum speed limit, just as a celluloid film frame melts if it becomes stalled in a projector for more than a few seconds, so, too, the content of a particular moment of consciousness—whose "minimal pulse" is experienced as a "feeling of change"—does not hang around indefinitely (*KTT*, 77). "Any specific moment of consciousness," according to neuroscientist Ernst Pöppel (in corroboration of Hodgson's primordial "sequence of differents"), "has a survival time of only three seconds."[19]

It is only because film (at twenty-four frames per second) runs within the range of our own ordinary waking beta brain-wave rhythm (fourteen to thirty pulsations, or "bursts of neural energy" per second) that we don't perceive the entirely static nature of its contents.[20] If film is run at sixteen frames per second there would be a flicker effect, and at eight frames per second (corresponding to the lower threshold of our brain's alpha rhythms), it would have the disjointed flow of the nickelodeon. Slow it down to five frames per second (corresponding to the theta rhythm of monks in Zazen)[21] and "the viewer could then begin to distinguish the separate still photographs out of which the illusion of motion is created."[22] No wonder that

Old Pond
Frog jumps in
Sound of the water

sprung out of a culture of meditation, in which monks habitually enter this snapshot-followed-by-snapshot theta state of consciousness. And beyond the three to seven pulses per second of theta are the near-cessation of pulses of delta (the state of deep sleep and much of the first year of infancy, but a state rarely accessed when conscious) where "all motion in what passes for the physical universe has dropped dead still."[23] The sixteenth-century Buddhist monk Han Shan apparently accessed this state immediately upon attaining enlightenment:

> I got up from my meditation bed, prostrated myself before the Buddha shrine and did not have the perception of anything in motion. I lifted the blind and stood in front of the stone steps. Suddenly the wind blew through the trees in the courtyard, and the air was filled with flying leaves which, however, looked motionless. . . . When I went to the back yard to make water, the urine seemed not to be running.[24]

In the West today, such "standstills," showing that the stream of consciousness, and the accompanying sense of time's flow, can be "brought to a halt, stopped dead, for substantial periods,"[25] is a state known mainly as pathology. As Sacks relates:

> Once, I was called to the ward because Mrs. Y [a post-encephalitic patient on the drug L-Dopa] had started a bath, and there was now a flood in the bathroom. I found her standing completely motionless in the middle of the flood.
>
> She jumped when I touched her, and said, "What happened?"
>
> "You tell me," I answered.
>
> She said that she had started to run a bath for herself, and there was an inch of water in the tub . . . and then I touched her, and she suddenly realized that the tub must have run over and caused a flood. But she had been stuck, transfixed, at that perceptual moment when there was just an inch of water in the bath.[26]

Of course, neither the mystic's nor patient's experience of a stilled stream of water is the equivalent of a stilled stream of consciousness. Invariant mental states are, presumably, also constituted of passing moments of maximum three-second durations. As Bergson noted, "even the most stable of internal states," such as "the visual perception of a motionless external object," can never endure as single, but only as repeated rebirths of awareness:

> The object may remain the same, I may look at it from the same side, at the same angle, in the same light; nevertheless the vision I now have of it differs from that which I have just had, even if only because the one is an instant older than the other. My memory is there, which conveys something of the past into the present.[27]

It is not the sequence of differents per se that appears frozen, but the mutability of the apparently external physical world. The startling absence of perceived outward changes overwhelms the presence of the perceived inward changes (as noted by Bergson), creating the momentary illusion of absolute stillness.

In devising a metaphor for consciousness, James rejected the links of a "chain" and a "train" in settling on his linkless "stream"—a continuum, as in a stream of water, in which, as in all continua, "its parts appear as immediate next neighbors, with absolutely nothing between" (*PP1*, 239; *SPP*, 1077). For the same reason, he rejected the metaphor of cinema in the primitive form he knew it as:

> snap-shots taken, as by a kinetoscopic camera . . . insert[ed] in our revolving lantern . . . cannot explain . . . what makes any single phenomenon be or go—you merely dot out the path of appearances which it traverses. For you cannot make continuous being out of discontinuities. . . . The stages into which you analyze a change are states, the change itself goes on between them. It lies along their intervals, inhabits what your definition fails to gather up, and thus eludes conceptual explanation altogether. (*PU*, 106)

But while the jagged images of the kinetoscope support James's claim that "you cannot make continuous being out of discontinuities," today's cinema does not. Moreover, cinema, better than water, accommodates "the different pace of its parts" that James ascribes to our "wonderful stream of consciousness," as well as the gap between thoughts that meditation reveals and James himself had accessed. And, as we shall see, James found another compelling reason for embracing the prime reality of discrete frames, concluding:

> All our sensible experiences, as we get them immediately . . . change by discrete pulses of perception, each of which keeps us saying "more, more, more," or "less, less, less," as the definite increments or diminutions make themselves felt. . . . They come to us in drops. Time itself comes in drops. (*PU*, 104)

But whether pulsed or streamed, the different pace of sensible experience for mayflies and humans, or for humans in altered and unaltered states, implies that there is no absolute clock-time; only consensus time. Brain-damage, accidents, drugs, ecstasy, or space travel at super high speeds, breaks the consensus. For astronauts whizzing by earth, and those in altered states of consciousness sitting in their chairs, the clocks on the walls run at different speeds than for the rest of us. For some patients with Parkinson's disease, for example, the clock on the wall seems to be going "exceptionally fast."[28] For others, the hands move slowly.[29] What then of the "veritable absolute" Bergson ascribed to the "velocity" of "unfoldment" in the universe's "successive states"?[30]

Moreover, although James held that static images could never explain "life . . . in its original coming," some late-life experiences, "mystical in the highest degree," left him wondering whether the world was truly a world of happenings and becomings after all (*PU*, 105; *ASAM*, 1279). As his "data" for free will show, James did not shy from sharing experiences that undercut his core beliefs. And in his brief essay, "A Suggestion About Mysticism," published in the last year of his life, he shared experiences that lent support to the very block universe he had so long opposed. Unbeknownst to him, an epochal insight published five years earlier by a young German physicist had done the same.

"VERIDICAL REVELATION?"

> The falling of the barriers say that there is the dual process . . . the hemming in, the partitioning off, the localizing, the selfing. All that is one process. Now reverse it and say the escape, the unifying, the

> delocalization of the soul that is nearer. Get the thought clear testifying to the existence of a whole.
>
> —Mrs. Willett, sister-in-law of Frederic Myers, and one of Lawrence LeShan's "serious clairvoyants"[31]

In 1905, Einstein published his "Theory of Special Relativity"; two years later, Minkowski derived the concept of space-time from it. James was not aware of the space-time revolution in physics underway (culminating in 1916 with the publication of Einstein's "General Theory of Relativity," in which he formally introduced time as a "fourth dimension"); but in his 1910 essay, written the year he died, knowing the end was near, he promoted its most radical conclusion: the objective world simply *is* rather than *happens*.[32] The phenomenon of precognition that most people bury under the epitaph "too weird to be true" turned out to fit well the worldview of both Einstein and James of this late essay, just as it fits the worldview of the founding philosopher/mystics of the West: Parmenides and Pythagoras.[33]

"Is . . . consciousness already there waiting to be uncovered? and is it a veridical revelation of reality?" (ASAM, 1280). These were the questions with which James concluded his essay. They are the same questions raised by the concept of space-time as well as the phenomenon of precognition. What prompted James to pose these questions were four separate experiences that seemed to "consist" not only in his "uncovering of tracts of *consciousness*" "already there," but "reality" (ASAM, 1279, 1280).

James called these experiences of uncovering a "mystical paroxysm," and characterized them as "very sudden and incomprehensible enlargements of the conscious field, bringing with them a curious sense of cognition of real fact" (ibid., 1273, 1274). Three of the paroxysms "broke in abruptly upon a perfectly commonplace situation," such as while he was engaged in conversation (ibid.). As with his introspection upon free will, James found words at the very edge of the ineffable to describe them:

> What happened each time was that I seemed all at once to be reminded of a past experience; and this reminiscence, ere I could conceive or name it distinctly, developed into something further that belonged with it, this in turn into something further still, and so on, until the process faded out, leaving me amazed at the sudden vision of increasing ranges of distant fact of which I could give

> no articulate account. The mode of consciousness was perceptual, not conceptual—the field expanding so fast that there seemed no time for conception or identification to get in its work. There was a strongly exciting sense that my knowledge of past (or present?) reality was enlarging pulse by pulse, but so rapidly that my intellectual processes could not keep up the pace. The content was thus entirely lost to retrospection—it sank into the limbo into which dreams vanish as we gradually awake. The feeling—I won't call it belief—that I had a sudden opening, had seen through a window, as it were, distant realities that incomprehensibly belonged with my own life, was so acute that that I can not shake it off to-day. (Ibid., 1274–1275)

James had called "a conscious field *plus* its object as felt or thought of *plus* an attitude towards the object *plus* the sense of self to whom the attitude belongs . . . a *full* fact of the *kind* to which all realities whatsoever must belong" (*VRE*, 447). But in his mystical suggestion of "consciousness being uncovered"—*not* generated—"all realities whatsoever" belong to an even fuller fact. The conscious field, plus or minus objects, attitudes toward objects, and a self to whom the attitude belongs, are all absorbed into what James had previously identified as the monistic absolute: "one great all-inclusive fact outside of which is nothing" (*PU*, 21). He compared the process of "uncovering tracts of consciousness" to how our vision appears to uncover tracts of "objects," the field range expanding instantaneously with the "slightest movement of the eye" to an "increasing range of distant fact" because what is *in* the field has "always stood there to be known" (ASAM, 1274). James "prefer[ed] not to set any definite bonds" to the "extent" of such a "transmarginal" field, and only at the end of the essay, as we shall see, introduced the future into its extent (ibid., 1273). But, clearly, such a field would account for the conversions of vast temporal successions into space-like simultaneities, whether it be the retrospective "single flash" time-collapse of Bigelow's near-death experiences, or Mozart's prospective time-collapse, let alone precognition or retrocognition.

James had believed that it was naive to assume that "reality stands ready-made and complete" like a field such as this (*P*, 599).[34] Staring out from his lectern one evening, he told his audience:

> [As] I speak here, I may look ahead *or* to the right *or* to the left, and in either case the intervening space and air . . . enable me to see the faces of a different portion of this audience. My being here is independent of any one set of these faces. (*PU*, 146)

But if consciousness itself is the field, what is the "genuine reality" that James claimed for this "or" or for his "independent being"? (Ibid.).

A SUGGESTION FROM THE ANAESTHETIC REVELATION

In his free will paradigm, and his "minimum of assumption" of "it thinks," James had discovered that the origin of thoughts was unascertainable. In his essay "Human Immortality," he concluded that consciousness, while correlating with brain states, might well originate beyond them, and can no more be explained by them than a radio can explain a symphony. But it was his experience with ether and nitrous oxide, whose "truth has ever since remained unshaken," that James claimed "forbid a premature closing of our accounts with reality" (*VRE*, 349), and to which open account he returned in his mystical suggestion, incorporating the experience of ether.

The correlation between an anaesthetic drug and a time-transcending mystical experience has been traced in the West to the anaesthetic gas that came to replace ether, nitrous oxide, and chloroform: ethylene. Ethylene, rising up naturally through a fault in the earth, is now conjectured to be the secret of Delphi, the agency of the Oracle's trance, in which the future appeared to be accessed.[35] James, as we saw, believed that the "artificial mystic state of mind" induced by nitrous oxide and ether had "metaphysical significance" (*VRE*, 350). By invoking this significance in his essay, he was forbidding a premature closing of his "paroxysms" as being some form of psychosis, and linking them with what had remained for him an unshakable truth of the anaesthetic revelation:

> [Our] normal waking consciousness, rational consciousness as we call it, is but one special type of consciousness, while all about it, parted from it by the filmiest of screens, there lie potential forms of consciousness entirely different. (Ibid., 349)

In addition to Blood, Xenos Clark, and likely himself, as those "persuaded" that in the anaesthetic trance "we have a genuine metaphysical revelation" (ibid.), James clearly would include Frederick Hall, whose eloquent account of being etherized we quoted earlier. It was Hall's full account of that experience with which James concluded "A Suggestion About Mysticism," placing it directly before his claim that "consciousness already there waiting to be uncovered" might be a genuine, "veridical" revelation. Doctors surrounding Hall, talking amongst themselves, believed that they were generating their own thoughts in the ongoing present. But Hall, observing from what he experienced as a privileged and far more comprehensive view, a view beyond arbitrarily marginated linear time, believed otherwise:

> The knowledge of how little [the doctors] actually did see, coupled with their evident feeling that they saw all there was, was funny to the last degree. . . . [They] knew as little of the real causes as does the child who, viewing a passing train and noting its revolving wheels, supposes that they, turning of themselves, give to coaches and locomotive their momentum. Or imagine a man seated in a boat, surrounded by dense fog, and out of the fog seeing a flat stone leap from the crest of one wave to another. *If he had always sat thus,* his explanations must be very crude as compared with those of a man whose eyes could pierce fog, and who saw upon the shore the boy skipping stones. In some such way the remarks of the two physicians seemed to me like the last two "skips" of a stone thrown from my side. All that was essential in the remark *I knew before it was made.* Thus to discover convincingly and for myself, that the things which are unseen are those of real importance, this was sufficiently stimulating. (ASAM, 1279–1280; second emphasis added)

James was aware, too, of other examples of "ether-mysticism" that, like Hall's, "agrees with my formula [of '*reality being uncovered*'] very well" (*WB*, 676; ASAM, 1279). The "tremendously exciting sense of an intense metaphysical illumination" that he claimed as the "keynote" experience for himself and others experimenting with nitrous oxide pierced the fog even more by uncovering a preexisting relatedness behind the apparent many:

> Truth lies open to the view in depth beneath depth of almost blinding evidence. The mind sees all logical relations of being with an apparent subtlety and instantaneity to which its normal consciousness offers no parallel; only as sobriety returns, the feeling of insight fades, and one is left staring vacantly at a few disjointed words and phrases, as one stares at a cadaverous-looking snow-peak from which sunset glow has just fled, or at a black cinder left by an extinguished brand. (*WB*, 676)

Likewise, there was the ether experience of Nobel chemist Sir William Ramsay, published in the *Proceedings of the Society for Psychical Research*, and cited by Blood in a letter to James.[36] Ramsay echoed James's instantaneous seeing of "all logical relations of being" by claiming "one little piece of enormous coherence" for his experience, a coherence in which, as in James's "always stood there to be known," everything was revealed as "having been *always* there."[37] So, too, Blood held that the anaesthetic revelation "brought the comfort of serenity and ancient peace" to all who "have felt sadly the instability of temporal things."[38] In words that Han Shan could affirm, Blood told James: "*I always get a hint of the mystery when the clock stops of itself.*"[39]

"MYSTICAL IN THE HIGHEST DEGREE"

> [The] main point is not that how things will be is settled already, but that, in real truth, the very notions of past, present, and future are flawed, and that all times are just parts of one eternal now. . . . [James] attacked the notion of the closed future mainly by insisting on the looseness of fit between one moment and another, whereas the more ultimate question is whether every moment be not eternally there with its own definite character, whether this be settled for it by "earlier" moments or not.
>
> —T. L. S. Sprigge, *James and Bradley*

Twenty years before James published "A Suggestion About Mysticism," he wrote in the *Principles*: "Most people have probably had dreams which it is hard to imagine not to have been glimpses into an actually existing region of being, perhaps a corner of the 'spiritual world.' And dreams have accordingly in all ages been regarded as revelations" (*PP2*, 294). James's fourth "experience of uncovering," which came to him as he went in and out of dreams, was for him just such a "hard-to-imagine-not-to-have-been" glimpse into a hitherto undisclosed "actually existing region," beyond the local, linear line of commonsense reality:

> I awoke suddenly from my first sleep, which appeared to have been very heavy, in the middle of a dream, in thinking of which I became suddenly confused by the contents of two other dreams that shuffled themselves abruptly in between the parts of the first dream, and of which I couldn't grasp the origin. Whence come *these dreams?* I asked. They were close to *me*, and fresh, as if I had just dreamed them; and yet they were far away from the first dream. The contents of the three had absolutely no connection. One had a cockney atmosphere, it had happened to someone in London. The other two were American. One involved the trying on of a coat (was this the dream I seemed to wake from?) the other was a sort of nightmare and had to do with soldiers. (ASAM, 1276)

Because each dream had a "wholly distinct emotional atmosphere," with a "discontinuous" "individuality" that "repelled" each other, the different dream scenarios were not experienced as a surreal assemblage in one dream, or successive dreams within dreams, but rather each was experienced as its own "dream-system" (ASAM, 1276).[40] "Alternately telescoped into and out of each other," the three dream-systems did not connect to each other or to James's waking life (ibid.). He believed himself to be their "common dreamer" and yet, "quite as distinctly," he felt them "*not* to have been dreamed in succession, in that one sleep" (ibid.).

At first, James considered "the distressing confusion of mind" in his experience to be "the exact opposite of mystical illumination" and thought of several alternative explanations, indeed, diagnoses—"Am I getting into other people's dreams? Is this a 'telepathic' experience? Or an invasion of double (or treble) personality? Or is it a thrombus in a cortical artery? and the beginning of a general mental 'confusion' and disorientation which is going on to develop who knows how far?" (ibid., 1278, 1276–1277). But he then accepted that he might well have just received the profoundest mystical insight of his life:

> [The] exaltation of the sense of relation was mystical (the perplexity all revolved around the fact that the three dreams *both did and did not belong in the most intimate way together*); and the sense that *reality was being uncovered* was mystical in the highest degree. To this day I feel that those extra dreams were dreamed in reality, but when, where, and by whom, I cannot guess. (Ibid., 1279)

James's consideration of such sequence confusion, with its radical "delocalizing"[41] and de-selfing, as "reality being *un*covered" is consistent with his belief that reality as ordinarily experienced is covered by, "wears the form of," linear time (*AWPE*, 1169). "All *felt* times," James wrote, "co-exist and overlap or compenetrate each other . . . vaguely." By "the *artifice* of plotting them on a . . . conceptual time-scale," "cut into numbered instants," "aboriginal confusion" is replaced by the "*notion* of one objective and 'evenly flowing' time" (*PU*, 104; second and third emphases added). In these dreams of "aboriginal confusion" that artifice failed.

Einstein shared James's view that "evenly flowing," linear time was just an artifice, however "natural" such artifice appears.[42] Beyond our common-sense notion of reality—what he termed the "*evolution* of a three-dimensional existence"—Einstein championed the "more natural," preexisting reality of space-time.[43] As one of his ablest disciples, Louis de Broglie, put it:

> In Space-time everything which for each of us constitutes the past, the present and the future is given in block, and the entire collection of events, successive for each one of us, which form the existence of a material particle, is represented by a line, the world-line of the particle . . . each observer, as his time passes, discovers, so to speak, new slices of Space-time which appear to him as successive aspects of the material world, though in reality the ensemble of events constituting Space-time exist prior to his knowledge of them.[44]

Like precognition, James's mystical dreams, "the most intensely peculiar experience of my whole life," seemed to have tapped into (or "uncovered") the more encompassing existence of preexisting space-time reality (*ASAM*, 1275).[45] In those dreams, an "immense spreading of the margin of the field [of consciousness]," James lost his "hold" on his sense of "self," a "sinking, giddying anxiety that one may have when, in the woods, one discovers that one is really 'lost'" (ibid., 1270, 1277). Although he felt himself to be the common dreamer of the "extra" dreams, those dreams did not, as he put it, "*attach*" to his sense of "when," "where," and "by whom" (ibid., 1277–1279). James had lost, in other words, what Einstein called the "reference body" around which successive, linear perspective is constructed.[46] The deeper, or "veridical," reality of a universe where consciousness was already there waiting to be uncovered was not accessible to the relative center that is self, but only when "all was diffusion from [that] . . . center, and foothold swept away, the brace itself disintegrating" (*ASAM*, 1280, 1277). Beyond the narrow field of consciousness-arrayed-around-a-reference-body-self was a "transmarginal panorama" where "vast tracts usually covered are . . . revealed to view" (ibid., 1272, 1274). Insofar as James was perplexed and disturbed by his dreams, he was as if caught between two worlds: one, the ordinarily experienced world of a relatively stable self in a "gradually changing present"; the other, a "suddenly revealed" world beyond the boundary of self, a world of "tremendous *muchness*," revealing what "always stood there to be known" (ibid., 1273, 1274).

RETROCOGNITION

Given that James—the would-be catatonic—was "primarily concerned" to promote a world "still in process," rather than an "'eternal' edition of it ready-made and complete," it is little wonder that he would not connect the dots between the "most intensely peculiar experience of [his] whole life" and his intensely peculiar psychical research (*MT*, 940). But just the year before, in much the same language as "A Suggestion About Mysticism," James proclaimed that psychical research had also pointed to a "continuum of cosmic consciousness" in which all minds "plunge" (*EPR*, 374). And a year before that, James told a room full of philosophy students and professors that while mediumship and other parapsychological phenomena were "perhaps too spook-haunted to interest an academic audience," he found "in . . . abnormal or supernormal facts the strongest suggestions in favor of a superior co-consciousness being possible" (*PU*, 135).[47]

Clearly, "consciousness already there waiting to be uncovered" as in a field that "always stood there to be known" suggests such a superior co-consciousness, plunged into a continuum of cosmic consciousness beyond linear time. What always stands there to be known is not only accessible by precognition, which we have discussed, but its "partial mirror image," retrocognition: the seeing of a *past* event in eerily accurate, vivid detail, that cannot be explained by memory.[48] For the ancient Greeks, as E. R. Dodds has pointed out, divination (*mantikē*), referred to both precognition *and* retrocognition, the "typical diviner" being Homer's Kalchas, "who knew things past, present, and to come."[49] Indeed, says Dodds, the most celebrated seers would sometimes "exhibit supernormal knowledge of past events as evidence that their vision of the future will prove true. The implied assumption is that retrocognition and precognition are manifestations of the same power."[50] James was impressed by such "records of 'supernormal seership'" that the Society for Psychical Research had amassed "of various types and grades," and found the scientific community's outright rejection of them "absurd" (ACC, 243). In the one incident that he, along with a team of researchers, thoroughly investigated, James concluded that the alternative "naturalistic explanations" did not have "the least plausibility" (ibid.). And given that the seer, a New England homemaker named Mrs. Titus, did not seek recognition or payment for her trances, and neither profited from, nor even encouraged, the notoriety that ensued, and that, moreover, the incident was a painful experience for her to endure, trickery or fraud were also not plausible.

The incident (James's complete published investigation of which is available free online) was as follows: In the fall of 1898, Titus had a premonition of a disaster, followed soon after by a sense that it had transpired. Hours later, when a young woman who worked in a local mill was reported missing, she immediately guessed correctly that the woman would be found drowned. Although prone to trances, Titus tried to avoid them because they usually made her ill for some time after (ibid., 236). Nonetheless, she fell into several trances later that day in which she appeared to inhabit the scene of the drowning as it unfolded. She inhabited the scene so thoroughly while entranced that her husband was able to question her on the incident and get answers, but could not get her to respond to anything not related to the scene (ibid.). She even shivered with cold as the early winter morning scene unfolded. Titus neither knew the woman nor had been near the area where the incident occurred, but she saw, in her trance, the woman walking on a bridge and then slip off at a specific spot. In another trance she saw the body of the woman "head down, only one foot with a new rubber showing, and lying in a deep hole" (ibid., 239).

A professional diver from Boston, Brian Sullivan, was hired by the mill owner to search the river. Two days after Titus's trances, in the one and only chance she was given to guide that diver, she pointed to the exact spot the body could be found, and how it would be positioned. Sullivan, who had just concluded a thorough search of the area and found nothing, was highly skeptical and reluctant to search again. But at the urging of the mill owner, he relented:

> "I started down the ladder," he told the investigating committee later, "which extended about five feet under the water. When I swung off the ladder I went sideways and then turned. As I struck the crib work, 10 feet below the ladder, I turned to face the ladder, and my hand struck something. I felt of it, and it felt like a foot. I stopped short where I was:—it is my business to recover bodies in the water, and I am not afraid of them, but in this instance I was afraid of the woman on the bridge. I thought to myself, 'How can any woman come from four miles away and tell me or any other man where I would find this body?' I investigated and felt of her foot, and made sure that it was a body. She was lying in a deep hole head down. It was so dark that I could not see anything. I had to feel entirely." (Ibid.)

When Sullivan was asked by the mill owner what he thought of it he replied: "I did not think, I was stunned" (ibid.). For good reason. The precise details of what Mrs. Titus saw—confirmed by the diver as "absolutely correct"—was an "extraordinary detail" that could not be dismissed as a lucky guess: "She located the place where I was to go down; also told me that the body was lying, head in, in a deep hole, with one foot sticking up, with a new rubber. I was down in about 18 feet of water. It was so dark, nobody could see anything down there" (ibid.).

After his investigation (including cross-examinations) of the various people involved, James concluded that Titus's apparent witnessing, in precise detail, of a past event that she had not been present for, was a "supernormal faculty of seership" (ibid., 243).

JAMES'S WHITE CROW

Precise witnessing of a past event not attended by the witnesser was also the hallmark of the psychic who most impressed James—Leonora Piper, an unassuming Boston housewife and mother, who never set up shop to peddle her prowess.[51] On James's first visit, Piper told him specific details of events that had occurred in his house, including, earlier that day, "my killing of a grey-and-white cat, with ether, and described how it had 'spun round and round' before dying" (*EPR*, 88). Piper accessed her information in a trance and frequently as a medium for specific, recurring spirit "controls," but she never affirmed that her remote information was channeled through them.[52] James himself proposed that her trances might emanate from a "floating mind-stuff in the world," a mind-stuff

> infra-human, yet possessed of fragmentary gleams of superhuman cognition, unable to gather itself together except by taking advantage of the trance states of some existing human organism, and there enjoying a parasitic existence which it prolongs by making itself acceptable and plausible under the improvised name of a "spirit control." (*EPR*, 191)

As with Mrs. Titus and other entranced people James had studied, it was their completely unexplainable access to remote facts, transcending space and time, that he found most significant, affirming it "deliberately, having practically no doubt whatever of its truth," and "well aware of all the liabilities to which this statement exposes me" (*HS*, 268).[53]

James's friend and colleague Theodore Flournoy, a mentor to Jung, believed that genuine clairvoyance, consistent with James's "floating mind-stuff in the world," might come from a universal source that mixes with fabricated localized characters and stories.[54] More recently, Lawrence LeShan, based on extensive research with mediums, proposed that it may be more accurate to speak of their "spirit controls" as "functional entities" rather than as independently existing beings. Writing of the celebrated medium Eileen Garrett,[55] with whom he collaborated, LeShan concluded that asking "*What* her medium was" was less productive than asking "*When* it was." His answer to that question for Garrett might well apply to Piper:

> The "spirit control," emerged "when" Eileen Garrett moves into a particular state of consciousness in the presence of a perceived need of a sitter. When she conceptualizes the world in a particular way (the CR) ["Clairvoyant Reality," LeShan and Garrett's term for the timeless monistic Absolute] and, in this Weltanschauung, conceptualizes . . . [the spirit control] as existing, he exists. Further, he is conceptualized as having certain characteristics. Under these conditions, a *functional entity* with these characteristics comes into existence and functions according to them.[56]

Whatever Piper's actual source, her integrity was vouched for by the most dogged and skeptical of psychical researchers, Richard Hodgson, whose day-to-day scrutiny over fifteen years was so encroaching it amounted to house arrest.[57] James agreed "absolutely" with Hodgson's conclusion that "the hypothesis of fraud cannot be seriously entertained," writing:

> The medium has been under observation, much of the time under close observation, as to most of the conditions of her life, by a large number of persons, eager, many of them, to pounce upon any suspicious circumstance, for fifteen years. During that time *not only has there not been one single suspicious circumstance remarked, but not one suggestion has ever been made from any quarter* which might tend positively to explain how the medium, living the apparent life she leads, could possibly collect information about so many sitters by natural means. (*EPR*, 188)

Calling Piper "the most absolutely baffling thing I know" (ibid., 190), James christened her his "white crow":

> If you wish to upset the law that all crows are black, you must not seek to show that no crows are; it is enough if you prove one single crow to be white. My own white crow is Mrs. Piper. In the trances of this medium, I cannot resist the conviction that knowledge appears which she has never gained by the ordinary waking use of her eyes and ears and wits. What the source of this knowledge may be I know not, and have not the glimmer of an explanatory suggestion to make; but from admitting the fact of such knowledge I can see no escape. (*APSPR*, 131)

But a glimmer, it would seem, did come, years later, in his suggestion of "consciousness already there waiting to be uncovered."

MASTER INFERENCE

> How can you prove whether at this moment we are sleeping, and all our thoughts are a dream; or whether we are awake, and talking to one another in a waking state?
>
> —Plato, *Theatetus*

> Philosophical men . . . have a presentiment that the reality in which we live and have our being is also mere appearance, and that another, quite different reality, lies beneath it.
>
> —Nietzsche, *The Birth of Tragedy*

The suggestion of "consciousness already there waiting to be uncovered" is not so much a theory as a master inference. The inference accommodates not only retrocognition and precognition but James's earlier suggestion of consciousness as a process not generated from the brain but transmitted from a transcendent source.[58] "Consciousness in this process," says James, "does not have to be generated *de novo* [anew] in a vast number of places. It exists already, behind the scenes, coeval with the world" (*HI*, 1113). Speaking from the perspective of a lifelong career investigating consciousness, and well aware how quick the "conveniently 'scientific' head" would be to render his mystical suggestion "bosh" or "rubbish," James concluded his Mystical Suggestion essay with the following prescription:

> [W]e know so little of the noetic value of abnormal mental states of any kind that in my own opinion we had better keep an open mind and collect facts sympathetically for a long time to come. (ASAM, 1280)

In India, a civilization that has for millennia kept an open mind about all aspects of consciousness, including "abnormal mental states," James's master mystical inference can be found in the seminal Sanskrit concept *saksin*: a word that means both witness and field.[59] As many Indian sages, such as Jnaneshwar Maharaj, have affirmed, this "single most important postulate . . . of revelation . . . in experience," the witness/field is the only reality, consciousness uncovering itself:

> The appearance is seen, to be sure;
> But the appearance is in fact
> Nothing but the seer.
> How can something else
> That does not exist be seen.[60]

James, as we saw, handwrote "the Witness" next to the word *sciousness* in his own copy of the *Principles*. He had learned of the prime reality of "the Witness" from a Western metaphysician (E. D. Fawcett) deeply influenced by Vedantic thought.[61] Like *saksin*, not knowable because it is "the element of awareness in all knowing," sciousness is the prime reality of a knowing and witnessing, prior to the distinction of a knowable subject and object.[62] And in his mystical suggestion, where "*Uncovering* . . . [was] the essence of the phenomenon," the prime reality of nondual witnessing became identified, like *saksin*, with a field (ASAM, 1275).[63]

That consciousness *itself* is being uncovered, *revealing nothing other than itself*, was also key to the anaesthetic revelation. Blood emphasized this in *Pluriverse*, citing the experiences of two of its most prominent researchers, Sir Humprey Davy and Sir William Ramsay, as recorded by Ramsay.[64] Emerging from the effects of nitrous oxide, Davy declared, "*with the most intense belief and prophetic manner* . . . 'Nothing exists but thoughts! The universe is composed of impressions, ideas, pleasures and pains.'"[65] Ramsay's comment was: "It is curious that this, with Davy, was an isolated occurrence—with me it was a permanent impression."[66]

The widely-believed-to-be-enlightened sage Ramana Maharshi, putting the all-encompassing reality of consciousness in the starkest possible terms, said: "There is no difference between the dream and the waking states except that the dream is short and the waking long."[67] Beyond the similarity of EEG and EOG (electrooculogram, which measures eye movements) patterns in waking and REM dream sleep,[68] most of us, while dreaming, have experienced subject-object reality indistinguishable from waking reality, no matter how fantastical or surreal many of these dreams later, on reflection, prove to be. As Bradley put it, the "hard division" between "dreamt and waking worlds" is only a question of degree.[69] This indistinguishableness is a remarkable, if seldom reflected-upon, fact, a fact that is critical not just to evaluate but to *conceive* James's mystical suggestion.

Daydreaming and other imaginings, by contrast, do not seal us inside the same dual-seeming world of our waking consciousness. Impressions of specific sights, sounds, smells, and touch can be conjured by imagination, but only nonimagining waking consciousness and sleep-dream consciousness convincingly appear to *manifest* objects and our interactions with them. The most convincing of all such interactions is touch, as in Johnson's kick of the stone, a sensation that imagination alone cannot recreate. But the dreams of sleep can. An imagined pinprick is not confusable with an actual pinprick; but if I awake moments after I have—in a dream—pricked my finger with the tip of a needle, the feeling of the pinprick that I awaken to is indistinguishable from the feeling I would have if I were to have actually just touched it. Dream objects, as James says, even fantastic ones, like a mountain made of gold, "*have a perfectly physical nature or essence*" (*N*, 95; emphasis added).

Dreams are so indistinguishable from waking reality that they raise the question of whether the many disparate aspects of waking reality—a reality, as James argued, in which matter and consciousness are not primarily "heterogeneous"—might also, like a dream, be single-sourced. As Chuang Tze famously asked: "Last night I dreamed I was a butterfly. How do I know that I am not now a butterfly, dreaming I'm a man?" Or as James himself mused: "Hallucinations, illusions, dreams, feel just like reality, until you wake from them. Why may not the whole world be a dream from which we haven't awakened?" (*ML*, 423).

Twain, who had been influenced by James's arguments for transmarginal consciousness,[70] and whose vivid, richly detailed, precognized dream of his brother's death challenged the distinction between waking and dreaming life, ended his writing career with the pronouncement: "[T]here is . . . no universe. . . . It is all a Dream"; and that, *therefore*, everyone and everything was "but a *Thought*." [71]Twain did not, however, as we saw, celebrate this revelation. Unlike its Vedantic metaphysical counterpart, his master inference was not of a single emanation from an eternal source but of a single "Thought, wandering forlorn among the empty eternities." [72]

James's master inference, however tentatively put forth, was, by contrast, of an eternity that was *full*, of consciousness already there waiting to be uncovered (as Twain's own dream corroborated), rather than of consciousness being created *de novo* moment by moment. In the modern era of psychotropic drug resurgence—followed by our current era of resurgence in psychical research—time-displacement experiences and experiments have further corroborated James's mystical revelation as veridical. The stream of consciousness is always a "sequence of differents," but the differents themselves, these experiences and experiments suggest, do indeed coexist, "coeval with the world." The contents of the stream of consciousness, its "events," ultimately reveal themselves to be more like the simultaneous points that constitute the appearance of space, than the fixedly sequential points that constitute the appearance of time. Take, for one of many examples, the following account from the 1950s of British Parliamentarian Christopher Mayhew's experiment with mescaline, which was undertaken at the behest of a doctor friend, Humphrey Osmond, for a BBC documentary on its effects:

> What happened to me between 12:30 and 4 o'clock on Friday, December 2, 1955? After brooding about it for several months, I still think my first, astonishing conviction was right—that on many occasions that afternoon I existed outside time. I don't mean this metaphorically, but literally. I mean that the essential part of me (the part that thinks to itself "this is me") had an existence, quite conscious of itself, enjoying itself, reflecting on its strange experience, in a timeless order of reality outside the world as we know it.
>
> . . .
>
> I was not experiencing events in the normal sequence of time. I was experiencing the events of 3:30 before the events of 3:00; the events of 2:00 after the events of 2:45, and so on. Several events I experienced with an equal degree of reality more than once. . . . All I am saying is that I experienced them, not in the familiar sequence of clock time, but in a different, apparently capricious sequence which was outside my control.[73]

The broadcast of the experiment was never run, due to the fears of religious leaders that a profound spiritual experience was being "had on the cheap."[74] But looking back on it thirty years later, the now Lord Mayhew affirmed it as "a real experience" that took him "beyond absolute time."[75] Had the preeminent religious scholar Mircea Eliade been one of the religious leaders consulted, the broadcast might not only have been run but heavily promoted. Calling Mayhew's written account of the experiment a "prodigious document," Eliade said he "trembled with joy" when he read it, because so many of his own religious studies spoke of "the possibility of abolishing time, and of putting oneself into a trans-temporal condition."[76]

A "trans-temporal condition" well describes the equally remarkable experience of Paul Devereux, the Managing Editor of the archaeology journal *Time and Mind*:

> I was sitting alone in a room that suddenly seemed to fill with people. After a few seconds, the place was mobbed! I blinked my eyes and they all disappeared. I realized that I'd been looking down a corridor of time—down the temporal as well as the spatial axis of the room. The figures weren't all there at one time. It was as if all the people who'd ever been in the room had somehow left an imprint of themselves on the space they'd occupied in that room, and I'd been privy to that composite snapshot.
>
> In that same room later that evening, I was lying down, feeling fairly odd. A friend put his head around the door in a curious way, with his hands gripping its edge, and asked, "are you okay?" I said, "Yeah, sure." Then he vanished into thin air, an apparent hallucination. But half an hour later, this person actually did come to the door, sticking his head around the door in exactly the bizarre, jocular fashion that I'd seen him to do earlier. In this instance I'd been precognitive—looking ahead along the time axis.[77]

EXPLORING SPIRIT

Despite James's appreciation of the noetic value of time-dissolving abnormal mental states—whether it be his own, or those of a seer like Mrs. Titus—and despite his own intuition that time might well be a mask, it was not a mask that he was ready to have removed. Clearly, the younger James would have resisted Einstein's most radical concept: that the separation of time into past, present, and future was "an illusion, however tenacious." Such an apparently block universe would have brought him too close to the haunting image of his youth: the hospital patient who "sat there like a sort of sculptured Egyptian cat or Peruvian mummy, moving nothing but his black eyes and looking absolutely non-human."

But neither a "consciousness already there waiting to be uncovered" yet always in the process of uncovering, nor a space-time in which different sets of coordinates are always in the process of being selected, is aptly depicted as a "block," let alone an "iron block," in which "the whole is in each and every part, and *welds* it with the rest into an absolute unity" (*WB*, 570; emphasis added). There is no such universal catatonia, devoid of all motion, since neither stillness nor motion can exist or be conceived without the other; they, too, are codependent terms, like active and passive.[78] Motion is not eliminated from either account of the universe; only the generation of non-preexisting content. The entire universe as a motionless block is inconceivable.

We saw how James, after he had published his nondual thesis that matter and consciousness were homogeneous, had struggled with this violation of commonsense realism. But on one principle of radical empiricism he never wavered: "Realities are only what they are 'known as'" (*P*, 508).[79] This dictum, as we said, was learned from Shadworth Hodgson, as was the answer to the followup question, "What is the irreducible state of knowing in which reality is known?": a sequence of differents.

Such irreducible "sequence of differents" is what James's greatest protégé, Santayana, insisted on as well when he declared: even if "the realm of truth is indeed eternal and static," there must be something akin to an "exploring spirit" that "may traverse it by one or another narrow path in a thousand directions without adding, removing, or changing a single feature of that indestructible labyrinth."[80] "Flux," writes Santayana, is not "abolished" by this "hypothesis,"

> but only transferred from the panorama of facts to the living spirit which, in gradually discovering them, would be really passing through a succession of different states. All the questions concerning change, time, and existence would recur in respect to this experience and its temporal order.[81]

Since the panorama of facts in James's mystical suggestion preexists any *given* "passing through . . . succession," its uncovering in any moment can run the range from all-at-once inclusiveness, like an omniscient centerpoint of a sphere accessing all its radial endpoints, to a linear temporal landscape, kept in line by an "I" defining what comes before and after *its* centerpoint, the point between past and future. The first is what Royce called the eternal Absolute; the second is the perspective of everyday experience, what Royce called the "perfectly arbitrary limitation of our own special type of consciousness."[82] James's mystical paroxysms fell somewhere in between these two perspectives, with "certain special directions only . . . in the field of reality getting 'suddenly uncovered'" rather than either the unilinear direction of common sense, or the "whole of reality uncovered . . . at once" of "classical mystical experiences" (ASAM, 1275).

Such proposed uncovering of a reality that stood there to be known does not abolish flux; rather, it reinforces the two codependent terms on which the concept of flux is based: stasis and motion.[83] The same codependent equality of foundational terms is emphasized in Tantric Yoga, where *Shiva* and *Shakti* are one and the same entity functioning in different contexts (and only *as* so functioning "*being known*"). Shiva is described as the unchangeable static aspect of the great consciousness, while Shakti represents the dynamic, active side of the same consciousness.[84] Even Christianity, in its early years, recognized an irreducible dualism of motion and stasis: opposing an unchangeable masculine God the Father with the changeable Feminine Holy Spirit.[85]

Such irreducible dualism of motion and stasis is the answer to James's question for which, he believed, "no answer seems possible":

> Why, if one act of knowledge could from one point take in the total perspective, with all mere possibilities abolished, should there ever have been anything more than that act? Why duplicate it by the tedious unrolling, inch by inch, of the foredone reality? (*WB*, 658–659)

Milic Capek (inspired, like James, by Bergson) sought to remove James's tentativeness, upgrading "no answer seems possible" to "Indeed, no answer is possible."[86] But James's irreducible dualism of consciousness uncovering its own preexisting "foredone" contents not only allows for, but demands, a dynamic process, exactly in line with Santayana's Exploring Spirit in the Labyrinth, as opposed to what Capek sees as the "intolerable dualism" of radical relativity, merging "the genuine succession" of "our private 'stream of consciousness'" with "the realm of physical reality devoid of succession."[87] If consciousness *itself* is being uncovered, the *inference* of wholeness, including whatever might be *experienced* as wholeness, is itself just a part. "Private 'streams of consciousness,'" in which "every thought *tends* to be part of a personal consciousness," have no vantage point outside the whole from which a tends-toward-the-personal consciousness could judge its unrolling, as tedious or otherwise, let alone experience it as being duplicated. What Dōgen claimed for an apparently individual perspective, applies, as well, to whatever can be conceived as a whole perspective; in either, duality is denied, other than the duality of a knowing and a known:

> To carry yourself forward and experience myriad things is delusion. That myriad things come forth and experience themselves is awakening.[88]

TIME AS THE EFFECT OF IGNORANCE

> Time is only an illusion produced by the succession of our states of consciousness as we travel through eternal duration, and it does not exist where no consciousness exists in which the illusion can be produced; but "lies asleep."
>
> —H. P. Blavatsky, *The Secret Doctrine*[89]

If we accept, with James, that there is no awareness of time, but only an "awareness of *change*" (*PBC*, 268); that time, as Ernst Mach and Julian Barbour assert, is "nothing but change,"[90] or as we saw Bohm define it: a *construct of thought* to "represent succession";[91] then the question becomes: What is the precise nature of that construct? James's analysis of succession—as neither a concept nor a directly felt experience, *but a combination of the two*—helps deconstruct this "construct." Time is not aboriginal; it's a concoction.

James's skepticism toward objective time is now widely shared not only by physicists but by philosophers, "many" of whom "are suspicious of this notion of the flow of time, the march of time. They doubt whether it is a property of time as opposed to being some feature of human perception."[92] Chief among these is relativity philosopher Adolf Grünbaum, for whom time is nonobjective, and no more independent of perception than color.[93] But like so much modern theorizing about foundational questions of consciousness, his dictum that "coming *into* being is only *coming into present awareness*"[94] could be found in James's richest "philosophic mine,"[95] the writing of Shadworth Hodgson:

> [T]he universe . . . passes from state to state in and through a succession of present moments, every one of which is characterized as present solely by being thought of as existing simultaneously with some moment of an existing consciousness, which is the perception of it.[96]

This notion of time as a "succession of different states" also evokes James's father's spiritual mentor, Swedenborg, in his account of "angel time":

> [W]ith the angels there is no idea of time . . . change of place and distance is only an appearance, according to the state of each one, and according to his change of state.[97]

Cosmologists, from Parmenides to Julian Barbour, who claim that time is an illusion, do not claim that its foundation—the *appearance* of change—is eradicable. Appearance, as Bradley pointed out, is the one thing in the universe that must ultimately stand, because without appearance, there is nothingness, a completely unintelligible concept.[98] And to say that the appearance of change cannot be eliminated is to acknowledge a higher status for that appearance than mere illusion. But what of the reality of time derived from this appearance?

In his end-of-life mystical suggestion, speaking of his own and others' experiences that undermined the veridical reality of linear time, James declared: "We shall not understand these alterations of consciousness either in this generation or in the next" (ASAM, 1280). But a space-time worldview that could, if not explain, at least accommodate, them had already been proposed by his psychical research colleagues Frederic Myers and Sir Oliver

Lodge. Of the accounts of precognition set forth in his book introduced by James, Myers wrote:

> Few . . . have pondered long on these problems of Past and Future without wondering whether Past or Future be in very truth more than a name—whether we may not be apprehending as a stream of sequence that which is an ocean of co-existence, and slicing our subjective years and centuries from timeless and absolute things.[99]

Lodge, a distinguished inventor and physicist, and one of the founders of wireless radio, quoted this passage in his own book defending precognition, or what he termed "prevision."[100] He also had rigorously tested James's "white crow," Leonora Piper, in his home in England, and was astounded at her ability to access precise, minute details of his uncles' distant past, known only to his uncles living far away and who later corroborated them.[101] Soon after those tests, he became the first scientist to propose the absolute relativity of time—the same absolute relativity that Einstein's beloved colleague Gödel (among others) would propose as the logical interpretation of Einstein's theory, and that Einstein himself, as "the believing physicist," came 'round to: a world without time.[102] In 1891, the year that the twelve-year-old Einstein was given his first geometry book, Lodge wrote:

> A luminous and helpful idea is that time is but a relative mode of regarding things; we progress through phenomena at a certain definitive pace, and this subjective advance we interpret in an objective manner, as if events moved necessarily in this order and at this precise rate. But that may be only our mode of regarding them. The events may be in some sense in existence always, both past and future, and it may be we who are arriving at them, not they which are happening. The analogy of a traveler in a railway train is useful; if he could never leave the train nor alter its pace, he would probably consider the landscapes as necessarily successive and be unable to conceive their coexistence.
>
> The analogy of a solid cut into sections is closer. We recognize the universe in sections, and each section we call the present. It is like the string of slices cut by a microtome; it is our way of studying

> the whole. But we may err in supposing that the body only exists in the slices which pass before our microscope in regular order and succession.
>
> We perceive, therefore, a possible fourth dimensional aspect about time, the inexorableness of whose flow may be a natural part of our present limitations.[103]

In the section of the universe, the "once upon a time" we seem to now inhabit, Lodge's and Einstein's most radical view of time is being revived by physicists, as if on James's prophetic schedule to help us "understand" his timeless consciousness "waiting to be uncovered." David Bohm, who had been profoundly influenced by James's merging of thought and thinker into a single totality,[104] writes of the "fundamental law" being an "immense multidimensional ground," whose "projections determine whatever time orders there may be."[105] Physicist Julian Barbour holds that the nonreality of time is the only worldview that reconciles the two foundational theories of physics: relativity and quantum mechanics.[106] Both these theories are scientific in that they have successfully predicted results of testable hypotheses—from the interactions in vast distances considered by relativity theory, to the interactions in infinitesimal spaces considered by quantum theory. But unlike some relativity theorists, quantum theorists have resisted incorporating timelessness, despite their theory's inability to reconcile quantum time with classical time. A notable exception is physicist Carlo Rovelli, who, with his colleagues, "worked out a method to compress multiple quantum events in time into a single event that can be described without reference to time."[107] Echoing James's and Einstein's dismissal of an objective, equally flowing, time, Rovelli concluded: "It is not reality that has a time flow, but our very approximate knowledge of reality. Time is the effect of our ignorance."[108]

FIFTEEN

Eternalism

Nor was it ever, nor will it be, since now it is altogether, one, continuous.
—Parmenides, Fragment 8

You don't look back along time but down through it, like water. Sometimes this comes to the surface, sometimes that. . . . Nothing goes away.
—Margaret Atwood, *Cat's Eye*

The master inference of consciousness uncovering what "always stood there to be known" is called eternalism. It was first expressed in the ancient "Bible of India," the *Bhagavad Gita*:

Of the impermanent
one finds no being;
One finds no non-being
of the permanent.
Indeed, the certainty
of both of these
has been perceived
by seers of the truth.[1]

And it was first echoed in the West by Parmenides, the so-called father of logic, whose disciple, Zeno, created the famous and stubbornly challenging paradoxes exposing the illogic of our commonsense depictions of motion. Plato, who referred to Parmenides as "Father Parmenides," watered it down for his theory of forms, but Plotinus *un*diluted Platonism, restoring Parmenides's vision:

> Life changelessly motionless and ever holding the Universal content in actual presence; not this now and now that other, but always all; not existing now in one mode and now in another, but a consummation without part or interval. All its content is in immediate concentration as at one point; nothing in it ever knows development: all remains identical within itself, knowing nothing of change, forever in a Now, since nothing of it has passed away or will come into being, but what it is now, that it is ever.[2]

Plotinus's monistic vision influenced Augustine and other theologians, leading to the notion of a divine eternalism within Christianity, however controversial. As the only recently un-hereticized Meister Eckhart expressed it:

> Those who do not know . . . will laugh and mock at me and I shall pity them. They like to look at eternal things and consider divine works and to stand in the light of eternity, while their hearts still flutter about in yesterday and today, in space and time.[3]

In James's time, eternalism was introduced both by his colleagues in psychical research, such as Myers and Lodge, and by his two main adversarial colleagues in philosophy, Royce and Bradley.[4] James told Royce that when he composed his Gifford Lectures (published as *The Varieties of Religious Experience*), he did it "with one eye on the page and one eye on you" (C6, 320). The "you" he was staring at was Royce's notion of the "Absolute" or "Eternal Consciousness," which Royce depicted in *his* Gifford lectures a few years later:

> [T]he events of the temporal order . . . are divided, with reference to the point of view of any finite Self, into what *now* is, and what *no longer* is, and what *is to be*, but is *not yet*. These same events, however,

> in so far as they are viewed at once by the Absolute, are for such view, all equally present.[5]

James perpetually tried to "overthrow" Royce's Absolute—"the centre of my gaze, the pole of my mental magnet" (C6, 320), and, as a tentative response to his most profound mystical experience, his own.

Bradley was a member of the so-called Oxford school who saw eternalism as the most logical conclusion to be drawn from metaphysical speculation. [6] Tracing this school of thought back to Parmenides, James held that it falsified reality by relying on "the resources of logical reason alone, or of logical reason drawing rigorous inference from non-subjective facts" (*VRE*, 389). However illogical, for instance, it may be that Achilles can traverse an infinite amount of (ever-dividable) space, it is too rigorous an inference to deny the subjectively observed fact that Achilles does, after all, overtake the tortoise, who set out without any such logical limit to *its* progression.[7] Yet Zeno's paradoxes, all in support of the eternalistic vision of his mentor, Parmenides, still stand[8] and, as we shall see, James himself rethought a fundamental aspect of commonsense time in response to them. Moreover, we now know that the source of the purported rationalism that challenged our commonsense view of time, Parmenides, was more mystic than logician; more shamanic healer than philosophizer. Parmenides's eternalism was not, as James said of his Oxford eternalist successors, "confined . . . too exclusively to thin logical considerations" (*PU*, 149), but came from the very "broadened and thickened up" world that James had urged upon them: the "wild beasts" (for philosophers) of religious and psychical experience.[9]

James's own wild beast mystical suggestion and his transpersonal researches showed how an inference of timelessness could be drawn from experience itself, however extraordinary. And he believed that even those with no direct access to such experience find themselves sympathetic, if not outright drawn, to this inference:

> That doctrine . . . that eternity is timeless, that our "immortality," if we live in the eternal, is not so much future as already now and here, which we find so often expressed to-day in certain philosophic circles, finds its support in a "hear, hear!" or an "amen," which floats up from that mysteriously deeper level. We recognize the passwords to the mystical region as we hear them, but we cannot

> use them ourselves; it alone has the keeping of "the password primeval." (*VRE*, 381)

But for all his resistance to eternalism, James himself accessed the "password primeval" of timeless eternity in the "always stood there to be known" of the second-to-last essay he published in his lifetime.

THE "SECRET OF THE WORLD"

In James's last published essay, however, our reluctant guide to enlightenment returned from "that mysteriously deeper level," bringing, or attempting to bring, his mystic coach, Benjamin Paul Blood, up with him. Early in his career, James had read Blood's drug-induced passwords to the mystical region, which, he said, "fascinated me . . . so 'weirdly' that I am conscious of its having been one of the stepping-stones of my thinking ever since" (*APM*, 1295). And in *The Varieties of Religious Experience* he claimed, as we saw, that the "metaphysical revelation" of drug-induced trances from nitrous oxide might well be "genuine" (*VRE*, 349). But from his initial public response, in his early twenties, to Blood's writing, to his near-deathbed tribute ("A Pluralistic Mystic"), James tried to set limits to this revelation. In his first review, less than five years after his conversion to free will, James proselytized:

> What blunts the mind and weakens the will is no full channel for truth, even if it assist us to a view of a certain aspect of it . . . the faith that comes of willing, the intoxication of moral volition, has a million times better credentials. (*ECR*, 287)

Blood's response to that salvo was not to appear until after his own death, in a posthumous work titled *Pluriverse*, published in 1920, deliberately evoking James's essay title, but repudiating "the conceit of originality" that James had ascribed to pluralism.[10] To James's "ear" Blood's later writings had "a radically pluralistic sound," suggesting to him that "[m]onism can no longer claim to be the only beneficiary of whatever right mysticism may possess to lend *prestige*" (*APM*, 1295). But however pluralistic it may have sounded to James, Blood's pluralism was a celebration of the "*wild*," "game-flavored"

Many, not an overthrow of the One.[11] "The One remains, the many change and pass," wrote Blood, quoting Shelly, and then added: "and every one of us is the One that remains."[12] Like Nietzsche's "get rid of the All . . . shatter the All . . . take . . . back . . . what is nearest, what is ours" circumscribed by a "whole" "there is nothing beside,"[13] Blood's "wild-game-flavored many" is circumscribed by "the One that remains."

Pluriverse does deny that the universe can be known as "an independent Whole and one, a totality within its own comprehension,"[14] but it also denies the ultimate condition for pluralism in James's sense of the word—novelty.[15] Not only does *Pluriverse* deny originality and novelty to its parts, it emphatically denies the novelty that James cared about most—free will.[16] Blood had no problem accommodating "the thoroughgoing causal integration" that James himself had associated with ether revelation (*ASAM*, 1280). Indeed, *Pluriverse* contains one of the strongest attacks on free will in Western literature.[17]

While James read much into Blood's disparagement of "ultimate purpose" and his concordant belief that "[t]hought evolves no longer a centered whole, a One, but rather a numberless many, adjust it how we will" (*APM*, 1304); and saw in Blood a fellow crusader against the excesses of monism, "a sort of 'left-wing' 'voice of defiance,'" Blood was hardly the "man converted from one faith to its opposite" that James suggested at one point, or the "pluralistic mystic" in the sense that James understood pluralism (*APM*, 1304, 1295). Blood's ether revelation was, above all else, a revelation of *being*, not becoming. Like Parmenides, a central figure in *Pluriverse*, Blood concluded that "*it is everything to be.*"[18] And just as Parmenides had held that generation or destruction is no part of that being which is "everything," Blood found "much confirmation," as we saw, in Ramsay's "everything . . . having been *always* there" ether experience of timeless being that he shared with James,[19] and quoted the passage in *Pluriverse.*[20] He never wavered from what James had termed its "monistic insight, in which the *other* in its various forms appears absorbed into the One" (*VRE*, 350).

James's *pre*existing consciousness, "already there waiting to be uncovered," as well as his various transpersonal researches, were revelations of a "totalized world" that he himself had been most reluctant to accept: the "eternalist" world of Parmenides, characterized by James as "all that is *not* is from eternity impossible, and all that *is* is necessary" (*P*, 603). But as Blood noted, James "showed but faint partiality among metaphysical theories";[21] metaphysical *revelation* was what he most "fully believed."[22] And just as Parmenides's revelation was based on an experienced mystical insight, rather than a theory, James, too, based his proposed revelation on mystical insight, which he further linked with the "anaesthetic revelation" of ether. Blood claimed that the "insight of the anaesthetic revelation" was, for James, "the secret of the world."[23] At the very least, it was what James believed all veridical mystical experiences to be: "windows through which the mind looks out upon a more extensive and inclusive world" (*VRE*, 385).

James worried that Blood's dialectic between the one (that remains) and the many (that change and pass) might be "too pure for me to catch" (*APM*, 1304). But his mystical suggestion had caught it exactly. "Consciousness already there waiting to be uncovered" is but a restatement of what James had quoted as the anaesthetic revelation's "real secret":

> the formula by which the "now" keeps exfoliating out of itself, yet never escapes. . . . The truth is that we travel on a journey that was accomplished before we set out.[24]

HOLOGRAPHIC UNIVERSE AND THE "CONTINUITY OF ADJACENTS"

> In my view, self-transcendency is everywhere denied. Instead of it, and performing the same function, we have the continuity of adjacents. It is clear that too much attention cannot be brought to bear upon this notion.
>
> —William James, *Manuscript Lectures*

We see evidence of change everywhere, but as anyone who has passed back and forth in front of a holographic, sequenced image of a glass shattering can attest, evidence of change is not evidence of generation and destruction. It may only be evidence of a change in perspective. In James's proposed veridical revelation of ultimate reality, the universe itself is like a hologram, or what Frederic Myers called "a cosmic picture gallery,"[25] in an endless process of being uncovered, but in which nothing causes or *becomes* something else. As you move your head from side to side in front of a holographic sequenced image of a glass shattering, shards fly out and fuse back in two complementary sequences that confirm their fixed adjacency. But might the moments that constituted the actual shattering from which the image was derived also likewise be "*neighboring* segments of change,"[26] fixedly adjacent to each other? Might they too, in Jason Brown's phrase, be "serialized in situ prior to actualization?"[27]

That all reality may be such a *fixed* continuity of adjacents (not the merely *provisional* continuity with which James sought to render the universe cohesive) was proposed by James's contemporary John McTaggart, the most celebrated time-denier since Zeno.[28] McTaggart denied that events change, flow into each other, or cause each other, but he allowed that they might nonetheless be arranged with each other in a "permanent relations of terms," such as the alphabet, or the Great Charter preceding the Reform Bill.[29] Such relations, like the hologram of shattering glass, define an order but not a direction:

> Events have an order. They are, let us say, in the order M, N, O, P. And they are therefore *not* in the order M, O, N, P, or O, N, M, P, or in any other possible order. But that they have this order no more implies that there is any change than the order of the letters of the alphabet, or of the Peers on the Parliament Roll, implies any change.[30]

If consciousness is being uncovered, then something like such an order, an order with fixed adjacencies, but with "no direction *of its own*,"[31] might be what the "exploring spirit" (the knowing half of consciousness) uncovers as its other half (the known). The mostly *seeming* one-way direction of such uncovering, with its *appearance* of causation from one event to another, while consistent with the "big bang," is no less consistent with what has been theorized as a possible coming reverse of direction in "the big crunch," perhaps in a never-ending oscillation. A one-way direction order of succession, tracing fixed adjacencies with no direction of their own, is also coherent with both James's mystical suggestion and the ancient belief of cyclical eternal recurrence, introduced to the West by Pythagoras:

> If one may believe the Pythagoreans, the same things will recur exactly, and I shall be holding my pointer and talking to you as you sit there, and everything else will be exactly as it is now.[32]

However much the *known* half of consciousness, perceived as objectified things, sensations, or ideas, may seem to be causing or becoming other known moments, in a directional flow witnessed by the *knowing* half; however much causation itself is, as James says, "one of the forms in which experience *appears* as a continuous flow" (*SPP*, 1083; emphasis added), nothing can ultimately be said to be causing or *becoming* something else. As Dōgen emphasizes:

> When firewood becomes ashes it never returns to being firewood. But we should not take the view that what is latterly ashes was formerly firewood. What we should understand is that, according to the doctrine of Buddhism, firewood stays at the position of firewood. . . . There are former and later stages, but these stages are clearly cut. . . . They are like winter and spring, and in Buddhism we do not consider that winter becomes spring or that spring becomes summer.[33]

Despite his championing of agency and novelty, James, too, knew that generation, destruction, and becoming are not ultimately verifiable events. The only verifiable "events," the only events that truly "happen," are "transitions and arrivals (or terminations)" (*AWPE*, 1170). And his mystical suggestion went farther: beyond the illusion of becoming, of generation and destruction, it may well be that consciousness merely uncovers what is, pre-existing, "ready-made."

Our everyday concept of generation and destruction requires material objects. Mere ideas, mere perceptions, mere phenomena, even though they flash in and out of view, exist in a timeless realm of non-change since they can recur intact indefinitely. Only material objects, as "something behind physical phenomena," can be said to be subject to the process of generation and destruction; not only are material objects subject to apparent ravages of time, they are what makes the conventional sense of time, as a force to be reckoned with, gotten under control, or submitted to, possible. Indeed, for Einstein the very "concept of the material object must precede our concept . . . of time."[34] But what if, as James proposed, and physicists have re-proposed ever since, there are no material objects "behind" phenomena? What *if* the speculation James derived from his psychical research, and others, today, continue to derive from their research, is true: "human experiences, on its material as well as its mental side," are "only an extract from the larger psycho-physical world" (*APSPR*, 374–375)?[35]

Parmenides, who dismissed the reality of conventional time, also dismissed the concept of the material object that supported it. In words echoed by the Eastern traditions of meditation from which he sprang, he declared: "The same thing exists for both thinking and for being."[36] Like Parmenides, James, too, denied the independence of material objects that is conventional time's essential prop:

> Things and thoughts are not at all fundamentally heterogeneous; they are made of one and the same stuff, stuff which cannot be defined as such but only experienced; and which one can call, if one wishes, the stuff of experience in general. (*N*, 110)

"Subjects" knowing, "things" known, are "roles" played, says James, not "ontological" facts (ibid.). "Consciousness, as it is ordinarily understood, does not exist, any more than does Matter" (ibid., 109). Consciousness and matter as they are ordinarily understood are created, destroyed, or transformed in time. *Genuine* consciousness, which includes that aspect of consciousness called matter, cannot be created, destroyed, or transformed. The most that it can be is "uncovered."

INFINITELY VARIED RELATIONS: CONSCIOUSNESS UNBOUND

James, as we saw, envisioned prime reality not as an objectified world appearing to a subject self, but as a "monism" of "pure experiences," a stream of sciousness, "thinking objects of some of which it makes what it calls a 'Me,' and only aware of its 'pure' Self in an abstract, hypothetic or conceptual way" (*PP1*, 304). These pure experiences "exist and succeed one another" and "enter into infinitely varied relations" (*N*, 105), "throw . . . [ing] the question of *who the knower really is* wide open" (*PBC*, 432). In the *Principles*,[37] he recorded a friend's "hasheesh-delirium" that revealed just how infinitely varied a monism of "pure experiences" could be, freed from the ordinary constraints of a subject-self experiencing non-subject objects:

> Any animal or thing that I thought of could be made the being which held my mind. I thought of a fox, and instantly I was transformed into that animal. I could distinctly feel myself a fox, could see my long ears and bushy tail, and by a sort of introvision felt that my complete anatomy was that of a fox. Suddenly the point of vision changed. My eyes seemed to be located at the back of my mouth; I looked out between the parted lips, saw the two rows of pointed teeth, and, closing my mouth with a snap, saw—nothing. I was next transformed into a bombshell, felt my size, weight, and thickness, and experienced the sensation of being shot up out of a giant mortar, looking down upon the earth, bursting and falling back in a shower of iron fragments.
>
> Into countless other objects was I transformed, many of them so absurd that I am unable to conceive what suggested them. For example, I was a little china doll, deep down in a bottle of olive oil, next moment a stick of twisted candy, then a skeleton inclosed in a whirling coffin, and so on ad infinitum. (*PP2*, 122)

That consciousness can transcend the "this" and "here" *positioning* body/self "I" (flesh or astral) was made clear to Krishnamurti, as well, in *his* mystical paroxysm:

> On the first day, while I was in that state [of great physical pain] and more conscious of the things around me, I had the . . . most extraordinary experience. There was a man mending the road; that man was myself; the pickaxe he held was myself; the very stone which he was breaking up was a part of me; the tender blade of grass was my very being, and the tree beside the man was myself. I almost could feel and think like the roadmender, and I could feel the wind passing through the tree, and the little ant on the blade of grass I could feel. The birds, the dust, and the very noise were a part of me. Just then there was a car passing by at some distance; I was the driver, the engine, and the tires; as the car went further away from me, I

> was going away from myself. I was in everything, or rather everything was in me, inanimate and animate, the mountain, the worm, and all breathing things.[38]

Stanislav Grof—another MD, like James, who followed the trail of psychology to the transpersonal—researched and helped induce (first with LSD and later with breathing exercises) many such states that "cross boundaries separating us from various animal species," as well as allow us to "experience processes in the botanical kingdom and in the inorganic world."[39] Grof called these boundary-crossing states "holotropic"—that is, "oriented toward wholeness" and "transcend[ing] the narrow boundaries of the body ego."[40] Corroborating James's mystical suggestion, Grof holds that "holotropic states" access an "unchangeable" "cosmic . . . plenum" void of "concrete manifest form" or thingness, yet "responsible for all aspects of creation, not just the raw material for the phenomenal world."[41]

The dispersal of "I" into a succession of myriad objects, animate and inanimate alike, as in the examples above, is less a migration than a dissolution of individuated, body-dependent (flesh or astral) "I"s into free-ranging consciousness. Such dissolution coheres with James's deconstruction of both terms *soul* and *I* in the *Principles*, later emphasized in his radical empiricism, and brought to a crescendo in his mystical suggestion. In the middle of this trajectory, between the publication of the *Principles*, in 1890, and the publication of "A Suggestion About Mysticism," in 1910, James described a world absent individuated selves and souls, but full of varied relations. He designated it Buddhist, but it applies to his own most radical vision as well—a world not generated but uncovered; where change is only perspectival:

> For . . . [Buddhists] the soul is only a succession of fields of consciousness: yet there is found in each field a part, or sub-field, which figures as focal and contains the excitement, and from which, as from a centre, the aim seems to be taken. Talking of this part, we involuntarily apply words of perspective to distinguish it from the rest, words like "here," "this," "now," "mine," or "me"; and we ascribe to the other parts the positions "there," "then," "that," "his" or "thine," "it," "not me." But a "here" can change to a "there," and a "there" become a "here," and what was "mine" and what was "not mine" change their places. (*VRE*, 182)

The Varieties of Religious Experience, from which this quote comes, listed, as we saw, other examples of self-dissolution along the lines of Krishnamurti's "I . . . in everything . . . everything . . . in me." Reluctant guide that he was, James, as late as 1909, overlooked both his transpersonal research and radical empirical evidence to hold that the "world experienced (otherwise called the 'field of consciousness') comes at all times with our body at its centre" (*EA*, 803n). A more nuanced perspective, simultaneously offered, lists body awareness as one among several perpetual aspects of the experienced world:

> In the pulse of inner life immediately present now in each of us is a little past, a little future, a little awareness of our own body, of each other's persons, of . . . sublimities . . . , of the earth's geography and the direction of history, of truth and error, of good and bad, and of who knows how much more? (*PU*, 129)

Our awareness of "our own body" and "the earth's geography" is fundamental to our sense of consciousness bound. Some astronauts, thrown off both centers (earthless and weightless) have experienced "how much more" awareness there can be to a consciousness unbound. Moonwalker Edgar Mitchell quotes "a little known report in a technical journal"[42] that

> records the experiences of two Russian cosmonauts living aboard the Mir spacecraft for six months. Their concerns about official reaction to the experience requires their anonymity. . . . They each, but not simultaneously, experienced dream and waking states featuring extraordinary perceptions. They also experienced distorted time perception during these events. The cosmonauts frequently perceived themselves as other creatures on Earth, including dinosaurs, other humans and extraterrestrials. They discussed these experiences in great detail, including hearing voices, instructions and precognitive predictions about their spacecraft's future problems, which were all subsequently fulfilled. They experienced these events as though the information originated outside themselves. With good reason they could not report these events to their controllers nor to the medical monitors for fear of mental disqualification and loss of flight status.[43]

Mitchell himself, during his own mission, had also experienced an epiphany in space of felt-interconnectedness with everything, and later founded the *Noetic Institute* to foster holistic research that challenged scientistic dualism.[44] He invokes "the quantum hologram" as the only "framework to explain these events within the context of science, without resorting to hallucination and mental dysfunction."[45]

A GROWING CONSENSUS?

The co-founder of string theory, Leonard Susskind, as well as Nobel physicist Gerard 't Hooft, have also proposed that the universe may be a hologram. And last year—again as if on James's "not-in-this-generation-or-in-the-next" schedule for explaining how consciousness may be the uncovering of a preexisting field, such as a hologram—a dramatic astrological prediction was verified by using the cosmic holographic model. The eminent astrophysicist Craig Hogan[46] used the holographic model to predict that a giant laser interferometer, searching for gravitational waves, would detect a specifically located, and otherwise inexplicable, noise. According to the theory, this noise manifests "the fundamental limit of space-time—the point where space-time stops behaving like the smooth continuum Einstein described and instead dissolves into 'grains.'"[47] Many more experiments will need to be run before there is broad-based support for Hogan's explanation of this anomalous discovery at the edge of the known universe. But the conceivability of a holographic universe is growing.

Cautions abound, of course. In his monumental *The Road to Reality*, Roger Penrose notes wryly that the "'holographic conjecture' . . . has somehow [especially by string theorists] got promoted to the *holographic principle*."[48] And historian Wouter Hanegraaff, after offering a concise account of how the holographic paradigm evolved in New Age thought, suggests illicit mutation:

> Nobody seems to notice, rather surprisingly, that the holographic model, "if taken to its logical conclusions" does not imply that the holographic blur is the "true" reality. The True reality in actual holography is the original object. This object is transformed into

> frequencies, and these frequencies are then reconverted into an illusory image.[49]

James's mystical suggestion of consciousness uncovering *itself* precludes these two realities, as well as the problem, first noted by Stephen Braude, of how frequencies in a fixed "antecedently isolable arrangement," with no consciousness contextualization, could be the "building blocks" for contextualizing "experiential reality."[50] At the very least, the experience of a holographic cat—one moment resting in its picture frame, and the next reaching a paw out into the room toward you, then retreating again within the frame, repeatable endlessly—offers radical new options for describing "transformations in the form or representation of information,"[51] a primary task of physicists as well as mystic-minded philosophers.

And such options are critical to reevaluate James's mystical suggestion which, however consistent with his previously expressed views on the relation between consciousness and reality, has been ignored by scholars as if it were a detour into senility.[52] While a younger James would have viewed this mystical suggestion as a most unattractive, radical idealism, akin to what he dubbed Hegel's "absolute block whose parts have no loose play," he had also declared that "new discriminations or discoveries" might well bring him around (*WB*, 674, 673). Ultimately left still doubting by his own discriminations and discoveries, what might James have made of those by contemporary physicists in support of a timeless, holographic universe, affirming his mystical suggestion as a veridical revelation?

DAVID BOHM

Bohm, who introduced the holographic metaphor into cosmology, chose it because he believed that all appearances were indeed "projections of a single totality."[53] But just as James insisted that the universe was irreducibly dynamic, that is, a never-at-rest "sequence of differents," Bohm recognized that a static hologram was an inadequate analogy for the universe. He therefore divided the universe into a functional duality: the implicate order (a potential, submanifested, extractable, field of experience that was beyond thought-constructed linear time) and the explicate order (the manifest world of thought-constructed linear time). He proposed the term *holomovement* for their convergence. Such holomovement, which Bohm at times identified with God, was of a universe in process. But like Santayana's "exploring spirit" of a static field, and James's "consciousness being uncovered," the holomovement does not generate, but merely "*unfolds* into a sequence of moments that is not completely derivable from what came earlier in this sequence or set of such sequences."[54]

Ultimately, Bohm's hologram was, for him, just a metaphor. When blended with the concept of the holomovement, it stood for a deeper and more comprehensive reality "too subtle" to depict otherwise.[55] James, who saw the absolute as "foreign to our powers either of apprehension or of appreciation," also, like Bohm, resorted to a metaphor to depict *his* most comprehensive view of reality, a metaphor that anticipated his late-life mystical suggestion insofar as it reconciled the world of "finite multifariousness," where things appear to "really happen," with an eternal One (*ML*, 411; *PU*, 28). The metaphor was of radii emanating from one central point, like Bohm's "projections of a single totality." Similar in its all-encompassing nature to a cosmological hologram, it is even closer to one of the first cosmological metaphors in Western philosophy.

PARMENIDES'S SPHERE

> The eye is the first circle; the horizon which it forms is the second; and throughout nature this primary figure is repeated without end. It is the highest emblem in the cipher of the world. St. Augustine described the nature of God as a circle whose centre was everywhere and its circumference nowhere. We are all our lifetime reading the copious sense of this first of forms.
>
> —Emerson

> Hogan realised that the holographic principle changes everything. If space-time is a grainy hologram, then you can think of the universe as a sphere whose outer surface is papered in Planck length-sized squares, each containing one bit of information.
>
> —Marcus Chown, "Our World May Be a Giant Hologram"

The *sine qua non* of all spiritual transformation, James discovered, is peace. What does *not* vary in the varieties of religious experience, what is "central" to all of them, "is the loss of all the worry, the sense that all is ultimately well with one, the peace, the harmony, the *willingness to be*, even though the outer conditions should remain the same" (*VRE*, 228). So, too, the "higher" mystical states "tell of the supremacy of the ideal, of vastness, of union, of safety, and of rest" (ibid., 386). Blood experienced his anaesthetic, eternalistic revelation as "divine composure," "serenity and ancient peace," in which triumphs and tribulations "recline," and "the majestic and the absurd are of equal dignity."[56] And such equality of all moments underlies the profoundest peace of all, the peace of Parmenides, expressed through one of the most enduring representations of divine composure. No moment, Parmenides held, is smaller or larger than any other, for all moments are but points on a "perfectly rounded sphere," that is, "from a center equally matched everywhere."[57]

What exactly Parmenides meant by this cosmic sphere has been long debated. Elsewhere Parmenides refers to the ὄγκος (*ongkos*), "mass," of the sphere, leading some scholars to downplay the significance of the sphere's surface's equidistance from a central point, and up-play the sphere's entire undifferentiated solidity, as if it were a stone ball. But as the eminent Parmenidean scholar, Alexander Mourelatos, has argued:

> There can be little doubt that ὄγκος is Parmenides' word for three-dimensional spread. And since ὄγκος is the basis of the comparison, it is also clear that the relevant feature of the sphere is not weight or balance but shape. The fact that ὄγκος is anticipated in the text by "of a ball nicely circular from every side" makes it certain that the analogy dwells on the external curvature of the sphere.[58]

Moreover, a sphere's solidity turns out to be a natural complement of its "external curvature." "[I]n a curve," said James, unlike a "myriad-sided polygon," "the same direction is never followed" (*MT*, 815).[59] A sphere's surface is one continuous, uninterrupted curve. That is the ideal, anyway. For there is no such thing, no such apparently objectifiable thing, either in Parmenides's day or our own, as a perfect sphere. Even the roundest of balls is but a myriad-sided polygon, with its surface not precisely "equally matched" from its center. The same direction, however infinitesimally, *is*, somewhere, followed. The most perfectly machined steel ball would, if magnified a thousand times, reveal peaks and valleys. Nature, especially at the outer limits of size observable in the solar system—the sun and the electron—comes closest, but not quite.[60] It would take an infinite amount of radii streaming from the center to achieve a perfect circle, or its three-dimensional variety, the sphere. Anything less than an infinite amount of radii would create a facet: a straight, same-direction, line between at least two of the radial endpoints. But since in a perfect sphere there are no such radial gaps, a true sphere—"from a center equally matched everywhere"—radially speaking, is a solid.

The ideal (mathematical) concept of a facetless sphere, then, entails a spatial infinitesimal: every point on a perfect sphere's surface is, by definition, equidistant from its centerpoint; but between any two of those points, *an infinite number of other points must always intervene*, the radial gap getting tighter and tighter toward a never-quite-arrived-at seamless continuum. Infinity manifests as well in a sphere's or circle's construction, where the ratio of the diameter to its circumference is infinite π. The commonsense, dualistic philosopher Aristotle rejected any model of reality based on infinity.[61] (And the absence in the dualistic world of perfectly spherical objects would seem to support this rejection of actualized infinity.) Mystic-minded nondual philosophers, such as Plotinus, however, saw infinity as reality's very ground.[62] James, in response to Parmenides's chief disciple, fell somewhere in between.

ZENO AND JAMES: BEYOND THE CONTINUUM

> Zeno's argument conclusive. Continuity is only an ideal construction. In actual experience, there are "thresholds," and change is always by finite increments.
>
> —William James

> We feel in possession and in control of the continuum . . . it will hardly ever be dropped in abstract geometry; but it may very well turn out to be out of place for physical space and physical time.
>
> —Erwin Schrödinger

All of Zeno's paradoxes,[63] as we said, were devised to challenge commonsense dualism, the commonsense worldview that his teacher and father-by-adoption,[64] Parmenides, had claimed to be illusory. The two most well-known paradoxes are the arrow in flight and Achilles's race with a tortoise. Both of these left a profound impression on Western philosophy, and on James, leading him to revise his fundamental view of reality.

The arrow paradox shows that an arrow in apparent flight is never in actual motion, because it is always in some particular spot, occupying a space exactly equivalent to itself, at any given moment. You cannot arbitrarily select some of the points on the trajectory as the only markers of where the arrow is flying to and from; all the transition points in between must be included as destinations. In other words, the arrow is always, without exception, at some particular spot. But if the arrow is always at some particular spot, then the arrow is always still.

The race paradox[65] also challenges our everyday sense of motion, but from the standpoint of the space the motion is taking place in: an apparent continuum. The tortoise sets out first, traveling a certain length. To overtake the tortoise, Achilles must pass through that same length. But he cannot pass through the whole of that length until he passes through 1/2 of it; and he cannot pass through 1/2 of it until he passes through 1/2 of that 1/2, 1/4, and then 1/2 of that 1/4, 1/8, 1/2 of 1/8, 1/16, and so on. To catch up with the tortoise, Achilles must pass through an infinite number of such units—units, says James, whose capacity to be "separately conceived" as "elements with other elements between them *ad infinitum*" is essential to the very concept of a continuum (*SPP*, 1027).

Clearly, the arrow is *perceived* to move from one point to the next; and Achilles is *perceived* to win the race; everyone, including Zeno and James, agrees on that. Perception is not the issue. Conception is. Either the concept of motion or the concept of the "divisible ad infinitum" continuum must give (ibid., 1069). James, ever wary of a concept's propensity to "de-realize" experience, compared the conceptual analysis of the arrow's flight to the futile effort of "seizing a spinning top to catch its motion" (*PP1*, 244). Since discrete moments do not occur in such spinning motion *as perceived*, "motion cannot truly occur as [Zeno in his arrow paradox has] thus discretely constituted [it]" (*SPP*, 1062). What version, what *concept* of reality, then, *does* allow for the arrow's perceived flight and Achilles's perceived triumph?

Before answering, it is worth again noting that Zeno's paradoxes are still as much in play today as they have always been. Bertrand Russell, as James duly noted, took them most seriously, as did James himself. Most recently, Joseph Mazur wrote of these race and arrow paradoxes, collectively referred to as "the motion paradox":

> It would be wonderful to have an answer that would explain away the paradox, an argument about continuity perhaps, or a trick to untangle the infinitesimal fabric of the continuous line. But our only answer seems to still be Zeno's. He said it twenty-four centuries ago. If we were to ask him why we see the arrow leave the bow and hit the target, he would still respond, "Mere appearance of change. Motion is an illusion . . . "[66]

That motion, or at least *things* moving, *is* an illusion, as in Parmenides's and James's eternalistic revelation, is what Zeno had set out to demonstrate. In making a fundamental challenge to our everyday sense of motion, the paradoxes challenge the common sense that says that consciousness, far from uncovering itself, exists independently of space and matter. If space and matter existed independently from consciousness, then matter, our body especially included, would move through space; movements that consciousness either witnesses or not. But such a commonsense conception of independently existing space is of a continuum, infinitely divisible, a space that is *in*conceivable as something to finitely venture through. In such an infinitely divisible continuum, neither the arrow, nor Achilles (nor the tortoise, for that matter) moves.

In addition to his mystical suggestion, which he never linked to Zeno's paradoxes, James had an explicit response, not to the reality of motion, but to the reality of a continuum. His response did not "untangle the infinitesimal fabric of the continuous line" so much as *cut* it. James was aware that Zeno's paradoxes not only fail to account for the perception of motion, they cast "no ray of light" on how *any* experiences "*get made*" (*PU*, 107). But he also recognized that the commonsense view of how things get made did not illuminate the paradox of an unbroken continuum, necessarily conceptually decomposable into ever smaller units. But what if there were no such continuum? After all, the Greek solution to the continuum paradox was the atomic theory, in which matter is conceived not as a continuum but as a compilation of "discrete particles, which themselves do not change, but recede from each other or come closer together, leaving more or less empty space between them."[67] James's response, too, was a version of discrete atomisim:

> If in the natural world there were no other way of getting things save by such successive addition of their logically involved fractions, no complete units or whole things would ever come into being, for the fractions' sum would always leave a remainder. But in point of fact nature doesn't make eggs by making first half an egg, then a quarter, then an eighth, etc., and adding them together. She either makes a whole egg at once or none at all, and so of all her other units. (*PU*, 103)[68]

That things get made "whole" accommodates James's prime reality of nondualism, in which consciousness and matter are not of "disparate essence" and the apparent stream of consciousness is reconfigured into "sections" or "bits" of "sciousness," as actually experienced in the ongoing satori "whole mind" state

> Old Pond
> Frog jumps in
> Sound of the water. (*N*, 107; *PP1*, 304)

Even without accepting James's nondual premise that objects and consciousness are homogenous, the most apparently continuous parts of the stream of consciousness—perceived-to-be external, motionless, solid objects, such as mountains—are repeated bits or pulses. "Substance," says James, only "means that a definite group of sensations will recur" (*SPP*, 1014). Such recurrence, as Jason Brown points out, underlies all substance solidity:

> In order for an object to exist as a "solid" . . . it must recur over successive durations. This is true for all perceptions, though it is more emphatic in some modalities than others. It may not be obvious that a tree, like any visual object, must be perceived over a succession of occasions for it to be perceived at all.[69]

Whatever the illusion of solidity, or the illusion of seamless continuity, all "perception changes pulsewise," says James, however much those pulses "continue each other and melt their bounds" (*SPP*, 1027). This fundamental pulsing cannot be disguised, or at least is "more obvious when, instead of old things changing, they cease, or when altogether new things come" (*PU*, 104). It is by just such a conversion of moments-changing into moments-ceasing-and-arising that meditation penetrates the disguise of seamlessness, as in the Tibetan insight of the bardo gap between each moment.[70]

For Buddhism, the fact that all moments arise, wholly and discretely, as instantaneous bits of existence, rules out anything "assumed to be enduring and eternal," from the "simple stability of empirical objects" to "God."[71] But James's mystical suggestion—a suggestion fortified by his and others' transpersonal researches and experiences—allows for a different accommodation: consciousness is uncovering its own already-formed and nonchanging moments, rather than uncovering a process of change outside itself. If consciousness were uncovering a process of change outside itself, then "one phase of a thing must needs come into being before another phase can come" (*PU*, 103). Such a gradual phase process, James saw, is precisely where "Zeno's paradox gives trouble," because the process would be "infinitely divisible," rendering the simplest processes impotent: "If a bottle had to be emptied by an infinite number of successive decrements, it is mathematically impossible that the emptying should ever positively terminate" (ibid.).

QUANTUM PULSE

Abandoning his radical empirical principle of not talking about anything outside of experience, James first presents his reconfiguration of the universe as pulsing rather than *streaming* as if it were a law of things unto themselves:

> In point of fact . . . bottles and coffee-pots empty *themselves* by a finite number of decrements, each of definite amount. Either a whole drop emerges or nothing emerges from the spout. (Ibid., 103–104; emphasis added)

And he continues his abandonment of radical empiricism in contrasting real time to perceived time:

> If all change went thus drop-wise, so to speak, if real time sprouted or grew by units of duration of determinate amount, *just as our perceptions of it* grow by pulses, there would be no zenonian paradoxes . . . to trouble us. (Ibid., 104; emphasis added)

But whether he conceived reality as dual or nondual, James's "innate fear of Zeno," as one commentator dubbed it, remained intact.[72]

It is, though, a well-based fear. For James's Zenoan-inspired flight from a continuum-based reality paralleled the quantum revolution in physics of his day. A few years before James had rendered his stream of consciousness into drops, both heat energy and light had been revealed to be discrete pulses, rather than the continua they appeared as. "The energy of a beam of light emanating from a certain point," wrote Einstein, in the discovery that launched the quantum revolution,[73] "is not distributed continuously in an ever increasing volume, but is made up of a finite number of indivisible quanta of energy that are absorbed or emitted only as wholes."[74] The quantum revolution, which has now evolved into an uneasy co-orthodoxy with relativity, is still, like James, respectful of Zeno.[75]

Physicist Julian Barbour, as we said, holds that timelessness alone reconciles quantum theory and relativity. And so, too, timelessness reconciles James's discrete pulses, "which in themselves do not involve change"[76] with his proposed veridical revelation. As James declared, "Time itself comes in drops," but from the perspective of his mystical suggestion, the kind of drops or "steps" suitable to a world "being uncovered," "already made," "coming wholly when they do come, or coming not at all" (*SPP*, 1076). It is such drops, each moment as it arises, that return us to a consideration of the sphere, with the drops considered as radial endpoints.

JAMES'S "MORE REALLY CENTRAL SELF"

> Just as in the centre of a circle there is a single point at which all the radii meet, so one who . . . reach[es] God recognizes in him, by a direct

> awareness and without formulating thoughts, all the essences of created objects.
>
> –Maximus the Confessor

If the universe is indeed a sphere, and all moments, as both Parmenides's and James's mystical suggestions agree, do not undergo generation and destruction, like wildflowers in a field, but are, rather, preexisting, like the field itself, then the center of the sphere connects to all moments and all moments are connected to each other through it–forming a "whole" that "never was or will be but exists now, altogether, one."[77] One name for the sphere's circumference is appearance. One name for the center is God.

Not God the Father, "not a God," as Parmenides's Eleatic predecessor Xenophanes[78] taught, "at all like mortals in body or in thought,"[79] but "eternal and one, and similar in all directions and spherical and sentient in all its parts."[80] While we smile today at Zeus's many erotic escapades, we are still catching up with this other kind of Greek God who sees, thinks and hears "whole," and who "completely without toil . . . shakes all things by mind's thought," and "always abides in the same place, not moving at all."[81] A God for whom it would be "unfitting" to "travel to different places at different times."[82] If the universe is the sphere that both Xenophanes and Parmenides (in anticipation of Einstein) conceived it to be,[83] then everything can be conceived as radial endpoints of a centerpoint God.[84] These endpoints may well feel themselves in any given moment to be their own centers, "severally alive on their own accounts," believing themselves to be "things *per se,*" "quite otherwise" than mere endpoints (*PU*, 79), but a momentary center's "separately graspable essence" is not proof of actual separation.[85]

This spiritual cosmology of the Eleatics was derived, in essential part, from the East.[86] Xenophanes's "motionless," "toilless" God who "shakes all things by mind's thought" is, in India, akin to God the Self, God the Witness, the God of Vivekananda: "impersonal, omnipresent," of whom, as we saw earlier, "everyone is but a manifestation," and through whom dualism's object-without-consciousness "mass of insentiency" is sublated into "one sentient being."[87] In a lecture at Harvard that James likely attended,[88] Vivekananda invoked the same shape for this omnipresence as Xenophanes and Parmenides and other mystics, West and East: "God is a circle whose center is everywhere and whose circumference is nowhere"–that is, no identifiable somewhere.[89] However unidentified with, or removed from, this one centerpoint we might feel ourselves to be, however not radii of any circle, let alone this one circle, with its one centerpoint, "each of us," Vivekananda asserts, "is moving towards" this center "along one of these radii" and "it is certain that all of us *must* reach that center. And at the center, where all the radii meet, all our differences will cease."[90]

For James, "God," like "cause" and "soul," was one of those concepts whose "image-part . . . is so faint . . . their whole value seems to be functional" (*SPP*, 1013). Since God suggests "no definite picture," its "significance" consists entirely in its "*tendency*," in "the further turn" which it "may give to our action or our thought" (ibid.). We thus "cannot rest in the contemplation of . . . [the] form" of God, as we can rest in the contemplation of a form for which we have a "definite picture," such as—James offers—a "circle" (ibid.). But years before he posed his late-life mystical suggestion of consciousness being uncovered, James merged the contemplatible image of a circle with divine functionality, creating a mandala (the Sanskrit word for circle) with radii projecting out from a Godlike centerpoint, coming as close as he ever would to his father's "only true god" as a "partaker of our own nature to the very brim."[91] Despite his persistent belief that "we are invincibly parts . . . and must always apprehend the absolute as if it were a foreign being," he subdued both parts and foreignness in this image, fulfilling his own early injunction that "the notion . . . of a Spirit of the world which thinks through us . . . must be considered" (*PU*, 23; *PP1*, 215):

> Every bit of us at every moment is part and parcel of a wider self, it quivers along various radii like the wind-rose on a compass, and the actual in it is continuously one with possibles not yet in our present sight. And just as we are co-conscious with our own momentary margin, may not we ourselves form the margin of some more really central self in things which is co-conscious with the whole of us? May not you and I be confluent in a higher consciousness, and confluently active there, tho we now know it not? (*PU*, 131)

James here invokes how a circle is constructed, or can be verified to have been constructed—radii reaching out in all directions from a centerpoint—rather than evoking the result of that construction—the curved circumference that can be derived from it. The circumference, the outer edge of the compass, is an incidental part of the construction; it does not bind the open-ended radii, reaching out an unfathomable distance, but only suggests their equidistance from the centerpoint. Compared with the Hindu centerpoint image of the Bindu dot, a timeless point that is considered to be the source of all manifestation, James's image hovers between the "absolute plurality or independent finite souls" that he had identified with Hindu dualism and the "illusion of finite personality" "dwell[ing]" apart from the one "self" that he identified with Hindu monism (*PAP*, 316).

But combined with his mystical suggestion, it hovers no more, as the "confluently active" radii become the confluently activated. The one consciousness, already there being uncovered, is divided functionally into the knowing and the known, with the knowing (centerpoint) activating the known (circumference).[92] Each radius is precisely what it is, and never more than what it is, so that there is no thickening or layering in each recurrent activation, just as there is none in a looped film's endless journey through a projector, or the full moon's periodic beam upon a lake. Although from the perspective of commonsense duality "I" might be increasingly enriched by each glimpsed moonglow or by each repeated viewing of a film, this wind-rosed mandala of consciousness being uncovered has no such cumulating vantage point. As in Nietzsche's "highest formula of affirmation," "eternal recurrence," "existence *as it is*," "recurring inevitably without any finale of nothingness,"[93] there is no "neutral *substratum*" in which thoughts originate or inhere, just as there is none in James's "passing thought."[94]

Despite their shared wariness of mystical experience, both James and Nietzsche formulated complementary worldviews inspired by their "ecstatically lived-through possibility of thought," worldviews so radical that they both explicitly designated their acceptance to future generations only.[95] That most James scholars feel about James's mystically inspired worldview what most Nietzsche scholars feel about Nietzsche's—"his most puzzling and least compelling idea"—suggests that future has not yet arrived.[96] To approach James's mystical suggestion, you have to go beyond his mass of testimony in defense of common sense. So, too, we are "forced to 'go beyond'" Nietzsche's writings, published or unpublished, on eternal recurrence, since, "if one adheres strictly to what Nietzsche wrote about eternal return, it is impossible to 'solve' the enormous problems inherent in this thought," a thought that may well be less "a rational conception than a mystical revelation."[97] But might emphasizing Nietzsche's most radical insights, insights that we have shown throughout that he shared with James, open new possibilities for interpretation? And might that interpretation reflect back on James? Legal scholar Sir Frederick Pollock told James that he found Nietzsche's eternal recurrence "the oddest form of 'spiritual comfort'" (C8, 622). Might the same be said for James's mystical suggestion, and for the same reason?

UNIVERSE (FROM "UNUS" ONE AND VERSUS "TURNING")

> [A] circle . . . is inevitable if this be a universe.
>
> —William James

> circulus vitiosus deus?
>
> —Nietzsche, *Beyond Good & Evil*[98]

> It will certainly accept your own measure of your doing and being, whether you sneak about and deny your own name, or, whether you see your work produced to the concave sphere of the heavens, one with the revolution of the stars.
>
> —Emerson, "Spiritual Laws."[99]

While Nietzsche could have had the mystically suggestionless James in mind when he scorned "those who would like to force on the world the ability for *eternal novelty*,"[100] James, in the very last months of his life, had a "vital insight into" Nietzsche that, as we said, gave him "much more sympathy" with him (C9, 540). James never specifies the insight beyond identifying its source—an essay by his friend Julius Goldstein entitled "The Keynote to the Work of Nietzsche."[101] But that keynote, the essay's almost exclusive focus, is the crisis that Nietzsche perceived stemming from "the death of God," and it introduced some of Nietzsche's most fervid passages to the English-speaking world, proclaiming that crisis as "ever on the brink of a catastrophe, continually stumbling . . . backwards, sidewards, forwards in every direction. . . . Are we not straying through a never-ending Naught? Is it not getting colder? Does not the darkness grow deeper and deeper?"[102]

Such abject chaos is what Eliade called the "terror of history" for which, he asserts, the ancient myth of eternal recurrence was an antidote, long before Nietzsche "revivified"[103] it as follows:

> What, if some day or night a demon were to steal after you into your loneliest loneliness and say to you: "This life as you now live it and have lived it, you will have to live once more and innumerable times more". . . . Would you not throw yourself down and gnash your teeth and curse the demon who spoke thus? Or have you once experienced a tremendous moment when you would have answered him: "You are a god and never have I heard anything more divine."[104]

James likely agreed with the characterization of eternal recurrence as a "naïve formula," the characterization made by Daniel Halevy in the biography James read.[105] But might James also have come to see eternal recurrence in a more positive light, as did Halevy himself, who later emphasized its "mark of eternity" on each instant lived?[106] This same, more mystical, perspective was evoked by James scholar Eugene Fontinell as well when he characterized eternally recurring moments as possessing "an eternal depth that lends to this life a significance denied by the [escapist] eternalist and missed by the hedonist."[107] Since James, like Nietzsche, was disdainful of otherworldly salvation, he could embrace Nietzsche's "world as it is, without subtraction [or] exception," while rejecting his world "without selection."[108] But from the perspective of his wind-rosed mandala the world *is* preselected, along Nietzsche's "new path to a 'Yes' . . . eternal circulation": "beyond good and evil without a goal, unless the joy of the circle is itself a goal, and without will, unless a ring feels goodwill toward itself."[109]

HEROIC MONISM

> My formula for greatness in a human being is amor fati: that one wants nothing to be different, not forward, not backward, not in all eternity. Not merely bear what is necessary, still less conceal it—all idealism is mendaciousness in the face of what is necessary—but love it.
>
> —Nietzsche, *Genealogy of Morals*

Nietzsche's "great *cultivating* idea" of eternal recurrence, that "makes everything break open,"[110] contains a paradox particularly challenging for James: heroic monism. For whereas James saw monism as inevitably bestowing the "slumber of nonentity" on its participants (*P*, 615), Nietzsche saw self-erasure[111] as essential to the eternal recurrence's most supremely functioning "overman," part Caesar/part Christ.[112] But it was a paradox James had encountered, though never fully engaged, in the wide-awake paragon of monism *and* social revolution, Vivekananda, as well as Nietzsche's iconoclastic mentor Emerson, and Nietzsche's iconclastic spiritual brother (via Emerson) Whitman.[113] Whitman, who exudes "the radiating apotheosis of life" that Nietzsche "set forth" as the "quintessence" of the teaching of eternal recurrence,[114] draws his iconoclasm from the same monistic well, proclaiming: the "whole referring, yet each distinct and in its place"—a "duly ordered" configuration for everything that is arriving, has arrived, and "awaits" arrival.[115] Realizing, as well, that nothing could be "duly ordered" unless such ordering could not be undone by the ordered or the orderer, Whitman ratifies Nietzsche's "right to erase" oneself, and Emerson's "If the red slayer thinks he slays," with his declaration: "the simple, compact, well-joined scheme, myself disintegrated, every one disintegrated, yet part of the scheme."[116]

Such a "well-joined scheme" of "every one disintegrated" in "a duly ordered universe" is far from James's chiefly advocated "scheme of uncertified possibilities," in a world of "real adventure, with real danger" (*P*, 618, 614). But it is near to the "tranquil confidence in the right ordering of the Whole," that he had gleamed in his troubled youth (*C1*, 140), as well as the divine wind-rose and mystical suggestions gleamed in his final years. For the well-joined scheme of a wind-rosed mandala is a version of eternal recurrence, where every moment repeats itself exactly, though always in its apparent "original sensible givenness" (*PU*, 126); the radial endpoints disintegrated as agent selves, yet supremely well-joined with everything else;[117] connected not through lines between them, for there are no facets on a circle, but through a mutual centerpoint defined by their own distal margin.[118] Such a well-joined scheme is not, for sure, "the strung-along unfinished world in time" that James persistently held as the "rival" to absolute monism; but neither is it the "very ambiguous" appearance of a monistic reality that James claimed for "only a few mystics" (*PU*, 62). Rather, it allows for the same pluralistic appearance that James claimed for "everyone": a processing of the "immediately given" "*in the shape not of an all but of a set of eaches*" (ibid.); experiential moments "next to each other" that "cohere and compenetrate" while remaining "in a certain sense 'their own others'" (ibid., 227). And in proposing that the "eaches" manifest "pulsewise," "coming wholly when they do come or coming not at all," James reinforces Nietzsche's foundational belief that "every successive phenomenon" is "completely atomistic," "terminal," and "causes nothing."[119]

"Ring out, ring out my mournful rhymes, but ring the fuller minstrel in," was how James, two years before he died, concluded his lectures promoting his pluralistic universe (*PU*, 149).[120] Had he lived longer, had he read the books of Nietzsche he had ordered in the last months of his life, following his resurgence of interest in him,[121] and just after he had published his "A Suggestion About Mysticism," James might have engaged what is surely the fullest minstreling of any philosopher, eternal recurrence, Nietzsche's "greatest elevation of the consciousness of strength in man,"[122] a minstreling that rings out all the "mournful rhymes," without contraction, *thereby* ringing the fullest minstreling in, as in the lines of Emerson with which Nietzsche introduced the book that introduced eternal recurrence: "To the poet and sage, all things are friendly and hallowed, all experiences profitable, all days holy, all men divine."[123] Had James engaged Nietzsche's ecstatic vision of eternal recurrence, a vision supported by his own transpersonal researches, he might have seen it as an ultimate "state of assurance," such as that which we saw accompanied spiritual conversions: "the *willingness to be*, even though the outer conditions should remain the same" (*VRE*, 228).[124] For while James had identified the capacity "to stand ready" "whatever the conditions be" with "Blood's revelation," he also allowed that it "seems to resemble . . . Nietzsche's *amor fati*," which Nietzsche himself identified with his eternally circulating Yes path (*APM*, 1312).[125]

More significantly, James's "consciousness already there waiting to be uncovered" affirms eternal recurrence's "closest approximation of a world of becoming to a world of being," where the "character of being" is thereby "impos[ed] upon becoming"; in a cycle that does not *itself* become, being the cycle that "all becoming is within."[126] For both James in his mystical suggestion, and Nietzsche in his "high point of the meditation,"[127] this Parmenidean-Heraclitian fusion is not a colorless, static reduction but rather a vivid, flowing amalgamation, in which the being of the whole, whether as "already there waiting" or eternal recurrence, is impressed upon each moment of uncovering or recurring. This impress of being upon becoming, of a fixed whole upon individual parts, is what allows for the paradox of Nietzsche's "artists' metaphysics": "the sunlight in the gloom," where "midnight is also noon; pain is also a joy; a curse is also a blessing."[128] It is a paradox that James-the-artist could perhaps have embraced more readily than James-the-philosopher, for it is artists, as Nietzsche says, "*imposing* artists," who, by letting "*harmony* sound forth from every conflict," transcend the "the ugly and disharmonic" with a "justification of the world as an aesthetic phenomenon."[129]

As it turns out, James treated eternal recurrence the way his own mystical suggestion has been treated: with disregard.[130] But the exponential acceleration of the "terror of history" in the century that has followed Nietzsche and James, the terror that Eliade identified as eternal recurrence's original rationale, prompts this consideration: if a few people with nuclear weapons can eliminate half the world's population in a second, such a holocaust is due either to a divine order or no divine order; but if there were anything like the dynamic partnership in which James originally conceived his divine wind-rose, the "marginal" status of his freewilling radial endpoints to a "more really central self in things" is jeopardized.[131] On the other hand, combined with his mystical suggestion, and corroborated by a lifetime of radical research of "consciousness beyond the margin," research that James saw as the "chosen instruments for a new era of faith" (C2, 499), the centerpoint and the radii configure an eternally recurrent process that fulfills what Eliade claims as the dream that has most obsessed the human spirit: "to coincide with the All, to recover Unity, to re-establish the initial nonduality, to abolish time and creation (i.e., the multiplicity and heterogeneity of the cosmos)."[132]

Reluctant guide that he was, forever in flight from the morbid monism of his youth, James took only hokey-pokey steps toward any such holistic vision. But we need not step back with him. To realize ourselves in every moment as the eternally recurring "margin of some more really central self" is to substitute an anxious subject-self, forging a linear path in an indifferent object-universe, for what James allowed "may turn out to be the most acceptable of all hypotheses": "total union, with one knower, one origin, and a universe consolidated in every conceivable way" (*P*, 556).

THE END

APPENDIX

This firsthand account of a vivid premonition and precognition investigated by William James and Richard Hodgson appeared in Frederic Myers's *Human Personality and Its Survival of Bodily Death.* Some of Myers's commentary is included as well.

Forney, Texas, February 1, 1894
Prof. William James

Dear Sir,

Replying to your request, I find it hard for me to present to you the "premonition" as it impressed me.

In the first place I will state that I am, or have been, in perfect health. I am not in the least superstitious and am not subject to hallucinations, and have never taken but little interest in the investigation of such phenomena. Three years ago last December my son, then eighteen years of age, left home to accept a position in a drug-house in an adjoining county. I was perfectly willing for him to go, and never felt a moment's uneasiness about him. Last summer I took an extended trip east and was gone some time. During my absence I never once felt the least apprehension about my son or any member of my family. I am naturally of a buoyant disposition. Some time last fall, in a vague and indescribable way I became dissatisfied about my son. I can't say I was uneasy—only dissatisfied—though I cannot tell why, I wrote him several letters—more than I had written him the entire three years of his absence. Early in November he came home on a visit, and after he left, I seemed to get more troubled and dissatisfied about him; it was not uneasiness or apprehension as to any danger, simply I was dissatisfied and troubled about him. I cannot explain my feelings. As near as I can remember, I felt just as I did after my father's death, when I was quite a small boy. It seemed that the light had suddenly gone out of my life and there was nothing left for me to live for. A weight like a mill-stone seemed crushing out my life. I remarked often to my friends that living seemed to have lost its attraction for me. As December wore along this feeling became intensified, and in some way my son seemed to be the centre of it all. Often I would awake in the night thinking about him, and so impressed with the emptiness and hollowness of life that I could not sleep. On the morning of the 19th of December I awoke some time before day. It seemed that I had reached a crisis. I got up and kindled a fire without disturbing any member of my family. In all my life I do not remember ever doing such a thing before. I sat down by the fire to think. I cannot explain the awful weight that oppressed me. I did not know what it was, nor what was the matter with me, yet in no way did I anticipate trouble or danger to my son. About 7 A.M. my wife awoke, and sitting in the bed, told me a dream that was strangely impressing her,—in fact, it caused her to awake.

"I thought," she said, "that you were in a strange place, and among people I had never seen before. It was a large family of people, with several small children who were going to school and a grown-up daughter. I came to the place in a wagon, but you were there already. I thought you were very intimate with the family. The large girl sat in your lap and put her arms round your neck and kissed you repeatedly. While I was wondering where you had met these people to become so intimate with them, you suddenly dropped over and died. And I awoke."

I replied to her that I felt wretched enough to wish the dream a reality; that I was so troubled about Walter that life had become a burden. After breakfast I got my writing material, and called my daughter and told her to write Walter a letter at once and tell him to come home. To be sure and get her letter off by the first mail train. I then rode out to one of my farms for recreation. About 12 M. I received a dispatch to the effect that my son was badly hurt and was unconscious. I boarded a freight train and hurried at once to the scene, with the understanding that my wife and daughter come later on the passenger. Now, right here comes in a remarkable feature in that strange matter. Through some misunderstanding they failed to catch the train and had to get private conveyance and come directly across the country. By their changing horses at each little town, they were enabled to reach my son by 11 o'clock at night. The accident had happened near the residence of a most excellent farmer, whose daughter my son had been long visiting. To the house of this gentleman he was taken, as it was not only near by, but was the house of his best friends. He had a large family of children who were all deeply attached to my son. Of a truth, I could not say that we suffered more than did those people because of my son's death. When my wife entered the room where our boy lay unconscious, this girl I speak of was standing at the head of his bed weeping. She gave a glance around, and then whispered in my ear, "This is my dream! This is the room I saw you in—these are the people I dreamed of." Even her trip there in a wagon was a verification of her dream, and the family were just such people as she described to me—"very plain, but most excellent country people." The very nature of the country through which she traveled was in perfect fulfillment of her dream, as was also the scenery surrounding the house.

In conclusion I will say that the heaviness of feeling that so oppressed me has all disappeared. I have never felt that peculiar, that indescribable weight that was crushing out my very life, since Sunday morning, the 17th of December. Of course, I feel sad because of my loss, but it is altogether a different feeling.—T. F. Ivey

Mrs. Ivey adds the following corroboration:

February 14th 1894.
Prof. James,

It was after daylight on the morning of 17th December 1893, that I had the dream. I thought that I was at a strange place. I had gone there in a wagon. I had no recollection of my husband going with me, but he was there and seemed to be a particular friend of the family. It was a large family, and I was very much struck with their manner and dress and general appearance, I observed the house closely and the scantiness of its furniture and the slipshod way it seemed to be kept. The children were getting lessons and would go to my husband for assistance. The largest one of the children, a girl about budding into womanhood, sat on my husband's lap and was very affectionate. I was not the least jealous of this girl, only I wondered how in the world came my husband so intimate with those people whom I had never seen or even heard of before. They did not seem to pay any attention to me, but to devote themselves entirely to my husband, who seemed to be the centre of attraction. Suddenly my husband dropped over and died,—and then I seemed to be at home, and awoke.

About 12 M. the same day, we got a telegram from Copeville, Tex., that our son was fatally injured, and to come at once. My husband went immediately on a freight train. Through some misunderstanding I had to go in a private conveyance across the country. As soon as I entered the house I thought of my dream, for it was all just as I had dreamt, even the house and its surroundings. The peculiar dress and manner of the people, their scantiness of furniture and negligent housekeeping, even to the children getting their lessons and the larger girl who wept over our son like her heart would break all were just as I had dreamed that very morning. No one could have told that the dead boy was not their son instead of ours. We learned that he was indeed an intimate and most particular friend of the family; that he spent more of his time there than anywhere else; that all the children looked on him as a brother and that the larger girl loved him more than a brother. With the single exception of putting my husband in place of my son, the dream was a real and vivid anticipation of the actual.—A. L. IVEY.

Even this great inaccuracy—the substitution of the husband for the son—does not, I think, destroy the impression of a true relation between the actual and the visionary scene.

In a subsequent letter Mr. Ivey gives some further particulars:

Forney, Texas, April 20th, 1895.
Mr. Richard Hodgson,

Dear Sir,

Replying to yours of the 12th inst., I will say:

1st. My son was hurt about 11.30 A.M. Sunday, December 17th, 1893.

2nd. I woke about 3 A.M. the same morning, but not being able to go back to sleep from some undefinable cause, I got up about 4 o'clock and kindled a fire and remained up.

3rd. He was returning from church with two other young men in a buggy when the horses took fright, and, running away, came in contact with a tree which, striking my son, produced the fatal injuries from which he died.

4th. The blow produced concussion of the brain, from which he was unconscious the greater part of the time. He died about 1 A.M., Tuesday 19th.

After more than a year I know of nothing I can add to the letter I wrote Prof. James. I believe it contained as near the truth as it was possible for me to write. As near as I can remember, for six weeks or more before the accident I was to a great extent two different distinct persons. During the day, I was my normal self-satisfied interested in my business and going along as usual. But at night I was altogether another person. I would generally take a short nap and then awake with the most awful feeling of weight and depression that it is possible to conceive of. I could seldom sleep all night (though I am usually a sound sleeper), I would lie and toss vainly trying to sleep feeling all the time that there was nothing more to live for—that all that was worth living for had gone out of my life—that I had lived too long—and that my life was nothing henceforth but a burden. When I would awake after a short nap, I felt like I imagine a person must feel who was to have been hanged that day and realised the dreadful fact immediately after awakening. This expresses it better than anything I can think of. I once called the attention of a friend to my singular condition—it was something unusual in my life—I couldn't understand it—I remarked to him that I was so low-spirited as soon as I went to bed that I could not rest, and that I could see no sense in it, as my business was in good condition. I thought possibly that I was going to be sick, as I was only troubled at night and was as cheerful and full of life during the day as I usually am. I don't know, for some time, that this state of mind was in any way associated with my son, but gradually he became the centre, as it were, around which the awfulness seemed to crystallise. On Sunday morning, December 17th, I awoke about 3 o'clock, and the feeling was so heavy that I could not stand it and got up and made me a fire. As soon as breakfast was over I got pen and paper and ordered my daughter to write to Walter to come home at once.

I remember well walking the floor after breakfast; and, turning to a friend who was at my house, I remarked to him, "Jo, I am troubled to death about Walter—I see ahead of him—and there is ruin." I then called my daughter, and, getting material and placing it on the table before her, ordered her to write to Walter then to come home at once.

Understand though, I never dreamed of any accident happening to him that day. I never thought of his getting hurt, or I would have telegraphed to him. I was simply troubled to death about him and couldn't tell why. It never once crossed my mind that he was in any danger at all. I had no premonition of any evil happening to him. I was simply troubled to death, and he seemed to be the centre of it. I am a farmer. Buckle says that farmers and sailors are the most superstitious of people. Possibly this may be true, but I don't think I am the least so. I never had anything in the way of a premonition in my life before, though I once had a remarkable experience in connection with my first child who died at nine years of age; still it was in no sense a premonition. In the whole range of human experience I know of no class of phenomena so inexplicable as premonitions. Even if Spiritualism be true, I cannot see how spirit intercourse can explain it.—T. F. Ivey[1]

ABBREVIATIONS FOR JAMES TEXTS

ACC James, William (1907a/1986), "A Case of Clairvoyance," in *Essays in Psychical Research* (Cambridge: Harvard University Press)

ACRWE James, William (1903/1987), "Address at the Centenary of Ralph Waldo Emerson, May 25, 1903," in *William James: Writings 1902–1910* (New York: Library of America)

APM James, William (1910b/1987), "A Pluralistic Mystic," in *William James: Writings 1902–1910* (New York: Library of America)

APSPR James, William (1896/1986), "Address of the President before the Society for Psychical Research," in *Essays in Psychical Research* (Cambridge: Harvard University Press)

ASAM James, William (1910a/1987), "A Suggestion About Mysticism," in *William James: Writings 1902–1910* (New York: Library of America)

AWPE James, William (1904b/1987), "A World of Pure Experience," in *William James: Writings 1902–1910* (New York: Library of America)

C1 Skrupskelis, I., & Berkeley, E., editors (1995), *The Correspondence of William James*, Vol. 4 (Charlottesville: University of Virginia)

C2 Skrupskelis, I., & Berkeley, E., editors (1995), *The Correspondence of William James*, Vol. 5 (Charlottesville: University of Virginia)

C3	Skrupskelis, I., & Berkeley, E., editors (1998), *The Correspondence of William James*, Vol. 6 (Charlottesville: University of Virginia)
C4	Skrupskelis, I., & Berkeley, E., editors (1999), *The Correspondence of William James*, Vol. 7 (Charlottesville: University of Virginia)
C5	Skrupskelis, I., & Berkeley, E., editors (2000), *The Correspondence of William James*, Vol. 8 (Charlottesville: University of Virginia)
C6	Skrupskelis, I., & Berkeley, E., editors (2001), *The Correspondence of William James*, Vol. 9 (Charlottesville: University of Virginia)
C7	Skrupskelis, I. K., & Berkeley, E., editors (2002), *The Correspondence of William James*, Vol. 10 (Charlottesville: University of Virginia)
C8	Skrupskelis, I. K., & Berkeley, E., editors (2003), *The Correspondence of William James*, Vol. 11 (Charlottesville: University of Virginia)
C9	Skrupskelis, I. K., & Berkeley, E., editors (2004), *The Correspondence of William James*, Vol. 12 (Charlottesville: University of Virginia)
DCE	James, William (1904a/1987), "Does 'Consciousness' Exist?," in *William James: Writings 1902–1910* (New York: Library of America)
EA	James, William (1905a/1987), "The Experience of Activity," in *William James: Writings 1902–1910* (New York: Library of America)
ECR	James, William (1987), *Essays, Comments, and Reviews*, edited by Frederick H. Burkhardt & Fredson Bowers (Cambridge: Harvard University Press)
EPh	James, William (1978), *Essays in Philosophy* (Cambridge: Harvard University Press)
EPR	James, William (1986), *Essays in Psychical Research* (Cambridge: Harvard University Press)
EPs	James, William (1984), *Essays in Psychology* (Cambridge: Harvard University Press)
ERE	James, William (1912/2003), *Essays in Radical Empiricism* (Mineola, NY: Dover)

HI James, William (1898/1992), "Human Immortality," in *William James: Writings 1878–1899* (New York: Library of America)

HS James, William (1890b/1984), "The Hidden Self," in *Essays in Psychology* (Cambridge: Harvard University Press)

HTM James, William (1905d/1987), "How Two Minds Can Know One Thing," in *William James: Writings 1902–1910* (New York: Library of America)

ILR James, William (1882/1982), "Introduction to the Literary Remains of the Late Henry James," in *Essays in Religion and Philosophy* (Cambridge: Harvard University Press)

KTT James, William (1894a/1983), "The Knowing of Things Together," in *Essays in Philosophy* (Cambridge: Harvard University Press)

L James, William (1920), *The Letters of William James*, Vols. I-II (Boston: The Atlantic Monthly Press)

MEN James, William (1988a), *Manuscripts, Essays and Notes* (Cambridge: Harvard University Press)

ML James, William (1988b), *Manuscript Lectures* (Cambridge: Harvard University Press)

MT James, William (1909a/1987), *The Meaning of Truth: A Sequel to Pragmatism*, in *William James: Writings 1902–1910* (New York: Library of America)

N James, William (1905c/2005), "The Notion of Consciousness," translated by Jonathan Bricklin in *Sciousness*, 89–111 (Eirini Press)

OCB James, William (1899/1992), "On A Certain Blindness in Human Beings," in *Talks to Teachers on Psychology and to Students on Some of Life's Ideals*, in *William James: Writings 1878–1899* (New York: Library of America)

P James, William (1907b/1987), *Pragmatism: A New Name for Some Old Ways of Thinking*, in *William James: Writings 1902–1910* (New York: Library of America)

PAF James, William (1905b/1987), "The Place of Affectional Facts in a World of Pure Experience," in *William James: Writings 1902–1910* (New York: Library of America)

PAP James, William (1894b/1984), "Person and Personality," in *Essays in Psychology* (Cambridge: Harvard University Press)

PBC James, William (1892/1992), *Psychology: Briefer Course*, in *William James: Writings 1878–1899* (New York: Library of America)

PP James, William (1890a), *The Principles of Psychology*, Vols. I–II (New York: Henry Holt and Company)

PU James, William (1909/1978), *The Works of William James: A Pluralistic Universe* (Cambridge: Harvard University Press)

SPP James, William (1911/1987), *Some Problems of Philosophy*, in *William James: Writings 1902–1910* (New York: Library of America)

TT James, William (1899/1992), *Talks to Teachers on Psychology and to Students on Some of Life's Ideals*, in *William James: Writings 1878–1899* (New York: Library of America)

VRE James, William (1902/1987), *The Varieties of Religious Experience*, in *William James: Writings 1902–1910* (New York: Library of America)

WB James, William (1897/1992), *The Will to Believe and Other Essays in Popular Philosophy*, in *William James: Writings 1878–1899* (New York: Library of America)

NOTES

PREFACE

1. Zohar, 1983, 118.
2. The philosopher Karl Popper recalled a discussion he had with Einstein in 1950: "I tried to persuade him to give up his determinism, which amounted to the view that the world was a four dimensional Parmenidean block universe in which change was a human illusion, or very nearly so. (He agreed that this had been his view, and while discussing it I called him 'Parmenides')" (Popper, 1992, 2). See, too, Petkov: "[O]nly the block universe view does not contradict the experimental evidence which supports special relativity" (Petkov, 2006, 210).
3. Needleman, 1976, 89.
4. Ibid., 89–90.
5. However much he and other physicists were aware of this demand. As we read in the journal *Foundation of Physics*: "It seems that Einstein's view of the life of an individual was as follows. If the difference between past, present, and future is an illusion, i.e., the four-dimensional space-time is a "block Universe" without motion or change, then each individual is a collection of myriad of selves, distributed along his history, each occurrence persisting on the world line, experiencing indefinitely the particular event of that moment. Each of these momentary persons,

according to our experience would possess memory of the previous ones, and would therefore believe himself identical with them; yet they would all exist separately, as single pictures in a film. Placing the past, present and future on the same footing this way, destroys the notion of the unity of the self, rendering it a mere illusion as well" (Horwitz, Arshansky, & Elizur, 1988, 1189).

6. Scotton, Chinen, & Battista, 1996, 21.
7. See Whitehead, 1925, 205.
8. Tart, 2009, 135–136. Compare philosopher David Ray Griffin's "real dilemma" of being "forced to choose between dogmatically denying the evidence [for precognition] or accepting a radically incoherent theory" (Griffin, 1997, 92).
9. Nietzsche, 1889/1976, 494–495.
10. Rumi, 13th cy./1995, 281.

CHAPTER 1: WILLIAM JAMES: A GUIDE FOR THE PERPLEXED

1. It was "the clearness of his mind," along with the "complete absence of intellectual prejudices" that impressed a young Carl Jung, who spent two "delightful" evenings with James, mostly discussing "parapsychology" and the "psychology of religious experience" (Jung, 2014, 92).
2. Gregory, 1987, 395.
3. Perry, 1935, Vol. I, 323.
4. America's first professional science school, the Lawrence Scientific School at Harvard, was founded when James was five years old. He enrolled when he was nineteen.
5. Croce, 1995, 61.
6. James, Henry, Sr. (*C1*, 204, 205).
7. See Laura Walls's *Emerson's Life in Science: The Culture of Truth.*
8. In addition to Advaita and Buddhism, introduced to America in James's lifetime, America's first homegrown nondual movement, Christian Science, had a significant following and commanded James's respect.
9. Hugo Munsterberg, in Bjork, 1983, 58.
10. Nietzsche called Emerson "the author richest in thought in this century" (Brobjer, 2008, 25), was "stimulated" by him "every year of his life" and annotated his books "more heavily than perhaps any other" (ibid., 22).

11. James's change of mind was prompted by Julius Goldstein's essay, entitled "The Keynote to the Work of Nietzsche." See p. 268.
12. Gillman, 1989, 136.
13. Much of what follows is an elaboration of this premise.
14. Anagarka Dharmapala.
15. Fields, 1981, 135. Nietzsche, too, foresaw the ascendency of Buddhism in the West, calling it "a hundred times more realistic than Christianity" (Nietzsche, 1889/1976, 586).
16. May, 1969, 221, 222.
17. Myers, 1986, 366.
18. Elsewhere James wrote: "Some one has said that the art of philosophizing is to see the strange as if it were familiar and the familiar as if it were strange" (*ECR*, 380).
19. Especially as expressed by Dōgen.
20. Dewey, 1998, 225.
21. Seigfried, 1990, 393.
22. Presented in *The Varieties of Religious Experience* as the experience of a Frenchman, James later revealed that it was, in fact, his own experience. (See *L1*, 145). It was his son Henry who later figured out the probable time that the experience occurred (ibid., 147). This timing has been accepted by most biographers. A notable exception is the psychiatrist Howard Feinstein who, in his *Becoming William James*, proposed a date two years later, 1872 (Feinstein, 1986, 241). Feinstein's reasons for changing the date are not, I believe, wellfounded. He points to the "internal evidence" of a letter James wrote to his brother Robertson in 1874 about a "philosophical" crisis he had undergone around the time of Robertson's visit to their home in 1872. But James's mentioning to Robertson of such a crisis—surely one of several, if not many, that he underwent—does not mean that he was referring to the cataclysmic crisis that his son had dated as occurring, rather, in 1870. In fact, it can*not* mean it, since *James's characterization of his 1872 crisis does not match the* Varieties *account at all.* James explicitly tells Robertson that the 1872 crisis was "philosophical" and "did not deal with my personal relations to God" (*C1*, 489). But clearly this crisis did. How else can Feinstein interpret: "I have always thought that this experience of melancholia of mine had a religious bearing. . . . I mean that the fear was so invasive and powerful that, if I had not clung to scripture-texts like The eternal

God is my refuge, etc., I am the Resurrection and the Life, etc., I think I should have grown really insane" (*VRE*, 150–151)?

23. James dedicated his last book, published posthumously, to Renouvier. The dedication read, in part, "[H]e [Charles Renouvier] was one of the greatest of philosophic characters, and but for the decisive impression made on me in the seventies by his masterly advocacy of pluralism, I might never have got free from the monistic superstition under which I had grown up" (*SPP*, 980).
24. May, 1969, 270.
25. Although Howard Feinstein, in his *Becoming William James*, has questioned it. Feinstein argues that other writers may have had even more influence than Renouvier in getting James through his crisis (see Feinstein, 1986, 307–312). But while other writers undoubtedly deserve more such credit than they have been given, Renouvier's decisive influence in turning James around can never be diminished. At the end of his life, in addition to the tribute to Renouvier above, James wrote to the philosopher James Ward: "I think the centre of my whole *Anschauung* [a mode of view, contemplation], since years ago I read Renouvier, has been the belief that something is *doing* in the universe, and that *novelty* is real" (C9, 278).
26. Roosevelt, 1899, 3. James tried to infuse his brother Henry, who had emigrated to England, with this American ideal, urging him not to write against "the grain of my own impulses," but rather "with great vigor and decisiveness in the action." To which his brother replied tartly: "I mean to try to produce some uncanny form of thing, in fiction, that will gratify you, as Brother—but let me say, dear William, that I shall greatly be humiliated if you *do* like it, & thereby lump it, in your affection, with things, of the current age, that I have heard you express admiration for" (William & Henry James, 1997, 463, 466–467).

CHAPTER 2: THOUGHTS WITHOUT A THINKER

1. Twain, quoted in Brooks, 1933, 264. See, too, James: "Who can count all the silly fancies, the grotesque suppositions, the utterly irrelevant reflections he makes in the course of a day? Who can swear that his

prejudices and irrational beliefs constitute a less bulky part of his mental furniture than his clarified opinions?" (*PP1*, 552).

2. Nor would they want to, since the illusion of undergoing an original experience is paramount to their success.
3. Ryle, 1949, 197.
4. By contrast, Rollo May, in his account of will, repeatedly leaps from the experience of intention "in consciousness" to an "I" intending.
5. Krishnamurti, 1979, 73.
6. Hodgson's "method of attacking problems by asking what their terms are 'known as,'" made him one of James's two inspirations for Pragmatism, the other being Peirce (C9, 401).
7. C2, 276.
8. Ibid. In the Preface to his *Principles*, where James acknowledges the "inspiration" he has received from five writers, Hodgson is listed directly after Renouvier.
9. May, 1969, 222.
10. Ibid., 223–224, 253.
11. Ibid., 222.
12. Ibid., 235.
13. Ibid.
14. Nietzsche, 1889/1976, 494.
15. Jaynes, 1976, 37; emphasis added.
16. Stcherbatsky, 1930, 80.
17. James uses the phrase of the mystic who influenced him the most, Paul Benjamin Blood: "apparition of difference." He quotes it without attribution in his essay "The Continuity of Experience," and then quotes it again, with attribution, in his homage to Blood, "A Pluralistic Mystic." Blood refers to "*the apparition of difference*" as the "curtain" between "the process of becoming" and "the process of departing" (*APM*, 1298).
18. Krishnamurti, 1954, 226.
19. Tolle, 1997, 21.
20. While this term is more familiar to Westerners as the Tibetan name for the in-between state between death and rebirth, in Tibet it more fundamentally refers to what meditation reveals: "At the death of each moment there is a gap, a discontinuity, before the arising of the next" (Ray, 2001, 330, 333).

21. Hameroff & Penrose, 1996, 20.
22. The whole passage, quoted by James with the tag "Such a description as this can awaken no possible protest from any one" is as follows:

> I go straight to the facts, without saying I go to perception, or sensation, or thought, or any special mode at all. What I find when I look at my consciousness at all is that what I cannot divest myself of, or not have in consciousness, if I have any consciousness at all, is a sequence of different feelings. I may shut my eyes and keep perfectly still, and try not to contribute anything of my own will; but whether I think or do not think, whether I perceive external things or not, I always have a succession of different feelings. Anything else that I may have also, of a more special character, comes in as parts of this succession. Not to have the succession of different feelings is not to be conscious at all. . . . The chain of consciousness is a sequence of differents (*PP1*, 230). Compare Aristotle: "One thing after another is always coming into existence." (206a22–23)

23. Though not, as is commonly assumed, coined by him. The phrase was used as early as 1840 by William Douwes Zoethout in his *A Textbook of Physiology*, and was undoubtedly encountered by James in Alexander Bain's *The Senses and Intellect*, published in 1855.
24. Feuerstein, 1989, 13.

CHAPTER 3. GHOSTBUSTER

1. W. B. Carpenter, quoted by James (*PP1*, 112).
2. From a letter to his father in praise of the zoologist Louis Agassiz, whom he was accompanying on an expedition to Brazil. It was Agassiz who, he says, taught him "the difference between all possible abstractionists and all livers in the light of the world's concrete fullness" (*ECR*, 50).
3. Ryle, 1949, 63.
4. As Jason Brown puts it: "Affect is not an energy that invades and charges an idea. . . . Affect is not applied to cognition from without, rather it . . .

changes—is *inwardly* present—at each level in cognition" (Brown, 1977, 126).

5. Pashler, 1988, 387.
6. Norretranders, 1998, 213–214.
7. Ibid., 215.
8. See, for example, Tor Norretranders's *The User Illusion*, Libet's own edited anthology, *The Volitional Brain*, or Michael Pauen's *Scientific American* article "Does Free Will Arise Freely?"
9. Norretranders, 1998, 243.
10. Libet, 1985, 536.
11. See Keller & Heckhausen, 1990.
12. Psychologist Dan Wegner, in his delightful book, *The Illusion of Conscious Will*, gives many accounts of experiments in which subjects believed that they were initiating the movement of objects that were, in fact, being initiated by the experimenter. See Wegner, 2002.
13. Freud himself never used the term *subconscious*, preferring, instead, *preconscious* for any thoughts that easily come into and go out of consciousness, and *unconscious* for thoughts that are repressed.
14. Sartre, 1956, 52.

CHAPTER 4. THE FEELING OF EFFORT

1. Libet, 1985, 538.
2. Brooks, 1933, 264.
3. "'Thou shalt refrain, renounce, abstain!' This often requires a great effort of will power, and, physiologically considered, is just as positive a nerve function as is motor discharge" (*TT*, 729). For Libet on will as veto power, see Norretranders, 1998, 242–250. The most obvious response to this rescue mission was well stated by Max Velmans: "Libet has shown that the experienced intention to perform an act is preceded by cerebral initiation. Why should the experienced decision to veto that intention, or to actively or passively promote its completion, be any different?" (Velmans, 1991, 705).
4. A curious phrase, suggesting not making or creating but somehow giving over that which is there.

5. Although this quote is logically linked with the quote at the end of this paragraph, it appears in his earlier section on the passive model of attention where he allows that it is "fitted to carry conviction," but is not to his liking. However, by the time James revisits the passive model, he has embraced it as a description of "what happens in deliberative action," albeit "warning the reader" that this "introspective account of symptoms and phenomena" does not address the issue of causal agency (*PP2*, 528–529).
6. Previously, in his chapter "The Perception of Reality," James had proposed that the consent to believe in free will, a consent he had emphatically given in his youth, was not an additional phenomenon that accompanied instances of willing, but the underlying belief of all instances of will.
7. And two years later, his deepened understanding was reflected in his summary of that commentary:

> We can . . . ignore the free-will question in psychology. . . . [T]he operation of free effort, if it existed, could only be to hold some one ideal object, or part of an object, a little longer or a little more intensely before the mind. Amongst the alternatives which present themselves as genuine possibles, it would thus make one effective. And although such quickening of one idea might be morally and historically momentous, yet, if considered dynamically, it would be an operation amongst those physiological infinitesimals which an actual science must forever neglect. (*PBC*, 424)

8. Bradley, 1886, 305.
9. James gives the following vivid account of how the same impersonal process plays out far from the safety of one's bed:

> Sometimes no emotional state is sovereign, but many contrary ones are mixed together. In that case one hears both "yeses" and "noes," and the "will" is called on then to solve the conflict. Take a soldier, for example, with his dread of cowardice impelling him to advance, his fears impelling him to run, and his

> propensities to imitation pushing him towards various courses if his comrades offer various examples. His person becomes the seat of a mass of interferences; and he may for a time simply waver, because no one emotion prevails. There is a pitch of intensity, though, which, if any emotion reach it, enthrones that one as alone effective and sweeps its antagonists and all their inhibitions away. The fury of his comrades' charge, once entered on, will give this pitch of courage to the soldier; the panic of their rout will give this pitch of fear. In these sovereign excitements, things ordinarily impossible grow natural because the inhibitions are annulled. Their "no! no!" not only is not heard, it does not exist. Obstacles are then like tissue-paper hoops to the circus rider—no impediment; the flood is higher than the dam they make. (*VRE*, 242)

10. Benoit, 1955/1990, 203.
11. Ibid.
12. Bradley, 1886, 315.
13. Schopenhauer, 1839, 43. For Einstein, this seminal thought of Schopenhauer's, encountered in his youth, that we can do what we will but cannot *will* what we will, was a "real inspiration" that "accompan[ied]" him "in all situations throughout [his] life" as an "unfailing wellspring of tolerance" (Einstein in Isaacson, 2004, 391).
14. As James says of turning a faucet for water or pressing a button for a "Kodak-picture," "We hardly need to do more than the wishing" (*P*, 614).
15. Gilbert Ryle lists it as his first objection against the reality of will: "No one ever says such things as that at 10 a.m. he was occupied in willing this or that, or that he performed five quick and easy volitions and two slow and difficult volitions between midday and lunch-time" (Ryle, 1949, 64).
16. Schwartz, 2002, 217.
17. See Schwartz, 2002.
18. The same dynamic would apply to internal physical restraints, such as experienced by a biochemically imbalanced obsessive/compulsive patient.

19. In *The Mind and the Brain: Neuroplasticity and the Power of Mental Force*, Jeffrey Schwartz accurately notes that "James . . . despaired of the possibility of scientifically demonstrating the efficacy of will" (Schwartz, 2002, 259). But he misrepresents the degree of James's doubt toward free will. James *wanted* the feeling of effort to contribute energy to results, but he never claimed that he had *any* kind of proof that it does. This point might be missed by those who read of James's "idea that the 'feeling of effort' is an 'active element which . . . contributes energy' to bodily action" (ibid., 259). The full quote of that emphatic language (which is *not*, as Schwartz has it, in James's chapter on "Will," but, rather, in his earlier chapter on "Attention") is the same quote used here: "The feeling of effort certainly *may* be an inert accompaniment and not the active element which it seems. No measurements are as yet performed (it is safe to say none ever will be performed) which can show that it contributes energy to the result" (*PP1*, 452).

CHAPTER 5. FREE WILL AND INDETERMINISM

1. Gregory, 1987, 159.
2. Freud, 1916, 106.
3. Ibid., 107.
4. Ibid.
5. This is how some, at any rate, interpret Freud's fainting spell when Jung told him about an ancient Egyptian pharaoh who had tried to supplant God. Here is the last part of Jung's account of the incident:

   > [O]ther pharaohs [I told Freud] had replaced the names of their actual or divine forefathers on monuments and statues by their own, feeling that they had a right to do so since they were incarnations of the same god. Yet they, I pointed out, had inaugurated neither a new style nor a new religion.
   >
   > At that moment Freud slid off his chair in a faint. (Jung, 1961, 157)

6. Freud, 1964, XXIII, 159.

7. See, for example, *Freud Evaluated: The Completed Arc*, by Malcom Macmillan.
8. Allport, quoted by Allen, 1975, 517.
9. Electrons cannot be observed without interference because the minimum requirement of observation is at least one quantum of light, and any quantum of light collides with the electron and disturbs its motion.
10. Capra, 1984, 203.
11. Bohr particularly admired James, saying of him, "I thought he was most wonderful" (Pais, 1991, 424).
12. Stapp, in Libet, 1999, 160.
13. Capra, 1984, 208–209. "Take any volume of space and take away everything else—in other words, create a vacuum—and what you are left with is . . . permeated by . . . ceaseless electromagnetic waves. . . . The vacuum as a condition of complete emptiness, as an absolute void, does not exist" (Haisch, 2006, 70).
14. Henry Stapp, John Eccles, Roger Penrose, and Stuart Hameroff are among those who have tried to find a causal correlation between the two indeterminacies. David Hodgson gives a good summation of their attempts in *The Oxford Handbook of Free Will* (Kane, 2002, 85–110).
15. Double, 1991, 221.
16. Lao Tzu, 1972, 49.
17. As Roger Penrose put it: "The world might . . . be deterministic but *non-computable*" (Penrose, 1999, 170). The suggestion was echoed by Stephen Wolfram, who writes of the will's "computational irreducibility" (Wolfram, 2002, 1136).
18. Kant, 1787/1965, 412.
19. A debt James acknowledged in his last published essay.
20. Blood, quoted by James (*APM*, 1310).
21. Nietzsche, 1889/1976, 500–501.
22. Hawking, 1993, 139.
23. The Greek word *atë*, often used in their tragedies, means infatuation, delusion, and doom. To stride forwards toward an expectation as if what you see is what you get is to fall a victim to *atë*. It is as foolhardy as striding backwards through a forest; if each step does not anticipate the unknown, you will frequently bump your head.

24. Or the (recently discovered) "primitive" conception of a remote tribe in the Andean Highlands. See Nuñez & Sweetser, 2006.
25. Hodgson, 1865, 191, 190. While James borrowed heavily from Hodgson's description of how consciousness unfolded, it is an open question how much Kierkegaard's quote, which James quoted four times, can be used to map this same perspective. See Stewart, 2012, 89–95.
26. See also Bertrand Russell "[T]he reason physics has ceased to look for causes is that, in fact, there are no such things. The law of causality, I believe, like much that passes muster among philosophers, is a relic of a bygone age" (Russell, 1963, 263).

CHAPTER 6. UNIVERSE AND NULLIVERSE

1. Russell, 1935, 194.
2. Gleick, 1988, 314.
3. Blood, quoted by James (*WB*, 448).
4. Barnard, 1997, 33.
5. Ibid., 31.
6. Weiner, 1969/1992, 155.
7. Schopenhauer, 1818/1886, 66.
8. Talbot, 1991, 38.
9. Nadeau & Kafatos, 1999, 3.
10. Aziz, 1990, 171.
11. Jung, 1961, 138. Jung had a series of dinners with Einstein in Switzerland, between the years 1909 and 1913, in which Einstein communicated his theory of relativity, providing Jung with the "stimulus" that "led me to . . . my thesis of psychic synchronicity" (Mann, 1997, 16).
12. Grinberg-Zylberbaum & Ramos, 1987.
13. Backster's earlier work with plants was featured in the book, *The Secret Life of Plants*.
14. Jensen, 1997, 7.
15. Hiley, 1983, 19.
16. See Price, 1997, 232.
17. Einstein, 1954, 40.

CHAPTER 7. PRECOGNITION

1. A friend of Samuel Pepys, Dr. George Hickes, wrote to him about Second Sight: "I told you, when I was in Scotland, I never met with any learned man, either among the Divines or Lawyers, who doubted of the thing" (Pepys, 17th cy./1884, 20). But see Hunter for an account of the "genuine modernizing impulse," beginning in the Restoration Era, where a "cutting edge of skepticism" played out as scathing attacks on all accounts of second sight. While Boyle and other scientists were trying to isolate material science from supernatural phenomena as a way to preserve both, the coffee house "culture of wit" that first arose in the late seventeenth century and continues to this day, discouraged all supernatural reports, without regard to source or verification. In this regard, as Hunter notes, "it may be that the legacy of the 'wits' was in the long term more powerful than that of the scientists" (Hunter, 2001, 49).
2. Einstein, in Sinclair, 1930/2011, xi.
3. Perry, 1935, Vol. II, 155.
4. Eddy, 1906, 475.
5. James's list of these phenomena begins with "divination".
6. Well before the Society for Psychical Research got under way, Schopenhauer had published long essays filled with accounts of spirits, clairvoyance, and precognition, including a personal accident with an inkwell that a maid had dreamed (and had told another maid the moment she woke up what she had dreamed) the night before. Schopenhauer was particularly impressed by how an accident, that "depended on the most trivial slip of my hand," could be precognized, and saw it as confirming "the truth of my proposition that all that happens necessarily happens" (Schopenhauer, 17th cy./1851/1974, 254).
7. Jung, 2014, 92.
8. See Ostrander & Schroeder, 1971, 275. Well known throughout the Balkans, Vanga was reported to have been consulted by more than a million people, including Brezhnev and Gorbachev. When she died in 1996, the prime minister, Zhan Videnov, said: "She lived not for herself but the people. That made her a living saint for us" (*The London Times*, August 14, 1996, 7).

9. An investigative report of Jeane Dixon which corroborates her predictions in the forties and fifties was written by Newsweek editor Jess Stearn in 1963, just *before* her most famous prediction came true, and thus before she had converted whatever might have been a prowess into a profession, and became a caricature (see Stearn, 1963, 38–50; see, also, Vaughan, 1973, and Brian, 1976).
10. Guiley, 1991, 463.
11. One of the most earnest researchers into precognition, aeronautics engineer John Dunne, argued that precognitive glimpses may be far more prevalent than we realize: "Dreams," he writes, "are mostly about trivial things which happen everyday of one's life. Such a dream, even if it were, in actual fact, related to tomorrow's event, would naturally be attributed to yesterday's similar incident" (Dunne, 1927, 61).
12. See Rhine, 1949; Jahn & Dunne, 1987; Radin, 1997, 2006, 2013; Schmidt, 1975; and Bierman, 2002.
13. Ducasse, quoted in Stearn, 1963, 7.
14. http://www.ukpsychics.com/prem2.html, as of March 2015. Larry Dossey devotes an entire chapter to 9/11 premonitions in his book *The Power of Premonitions*.
15. Lamon, 1911, 114–116. Lincoln may have been predisposed to accept precognition based on his Baptist faith in the nonreality of free will (see Guezlo, 1999).
16. Reagan, quoted by Ed Klein, 1990, 6. Reagan repeatedly talked about this dream. See, for example, Deaver, 2001, 144.
17. See Ullman, Krippner, & Vaughn, 1973; LeShan, 2009, 57–62.
18. Talbot, 1991, 206–207. For a BBC segment on Targ and Hammid see http://www.youtube.com/watch?v=OGtT8CVwNoM, as of March 2015. One of Puthoff and Targ's most intriguing remote viewing investigations was with Burbank Police Commissioner Pat Price. Price gave a highly accurate and detailed description of the target site, a swimming pool complex at Rinconada Park. But he also saw "what seemed to be a water purification plant" that included water storage tanks. Years later, however, Targ received the Annual Report of the City of Palo Alto, celebrating its centennial year, that showed a picture of a new municipal waterworks that was built on the site of the present Rinconada Park in 1913. Targ's account includes pictures from that report, together with

Price's drawing. As Targ put it: "For years, we had assumed that Price had simply made up an erroneous water purification plant and water tanks. In reality, he had looked sixty years back in time and told us what had been there before the swimming-pool complex was built!" (Targ, 2012, 61–62).

19. On the same point in a letter to Myers, James wrote: "[T]he facts are *so* discontinuous so far that possibly all our generation can do may be to get 'em called facts" (C4, 140).
20. Rosenzweig, 1992, 81.
21. Jung, 1981, 156.
22. An attitude in marked contrast to the scientist Einstein, who effected the most profound reimagining of nature's uniformity since Newton, and *did* look at evidence for telepathy.
23. Targ also sees precognition as a form of telepathy, the two together being a direct experience of "spacious awareness . . . transcending time and space . . . that corresponds to our deepest and most *fundamental essence* . . . [that] people have known for millennia . . . [however] nonphysical and nonconceptual, i.e. presently ineffable" (Targ, 2012, 240–241).
24. Radin, 2006, 162.
25. In addition to Radin and Bierman, Kathy Dalton, University of Edinburgh; Richard Broughton, Rhine Research Center; Adrian Parker, University of Gothenburg, Sweden; among others. See Radin, 2006, 161–180, for a survey of orienting response experiments up to 2006. A recent "meta-analysis" of twenty-six experiments, published between 1978 and 2010, that were not looking specifically for predictive anticipatory activity but had data before, during, and after a reaction to a stimulus, also suggested that "unconscious physiological processing occurs seconds before a person perceives a meaningful stimulus that should be, in all normal ways, unpredictable" (Mossbridge, Tressoldi, & Utts, 2014). An updated summary of predictive orienting response experiments that includes a concise review and explanation of meta-analyses can be found in Radin, 2013, 130–169.
26. Bierman, 2002, 140.
27. Josephson and Utts, http://www.tcm.phy.cam.ac.uk/~bdj10/psi/tucson.html, as of March 2015.
28. Though Utts has made a forcible argument in support of two key

validating elements of such statistical analysis:

> [A]nomalous cognition . . . has been replicated in a number of forms across laboratories and cultures. The various experiments in which it has been observed have been different enough that if some subtle methodological problems can explain the results, then there would have to be a different explanation for each type of experiment, yet the impact would have to be similar across experiments and laboratories. If fraud were responsible, similarly, it would require an equivalent amount of fraud on the part of a large number of experimenters or an even larger number of subjects. (Utts, 1996, 23)

29. And perhaps not even then, since, as Bohm and others have argued, there may be no such thing as completely inanimate matter (see p. 67).
30. Of the many predictions of the most famous seer, Nostradamus, only a dozen or so can be taken as possibly realized. However, a historian has recently suggested that most of those plausible realizations are less renderable as chance hits when considered as a connected series of a specific era. His "A-List" of detailed verses traces French history from the Revolution through the rise and fall of Napoleon (see Ashe).
31. See F.W.H. Myers, 1903b; Rogers, 1916; Saltmarsh, 1938/2004; Stearn, 1963; LeShan, 2009; and Dossey, 2009, to name but a few.
32. Gillman, 1989, 136.
33. See Rasmussen, 1995, 204.
34. Twain, 1853–1866/1988, 81.
35. See Webster, 1946, 37; Varble, 1964, 239–240; and Hoffman 2006, 53.
36. The second story sitting room. Immediately prior to this passage, Twain had described this room as the place where family members were reposed.
37. Twain, 1961, 108.
38. The actual explosion occurred three weeks after his brother's dream. Henry, who was severely burned by the blast, died two months later.
39. Twain, 1961, 110.
40. Ibid.
41. Ibid., 107.

42. Webster (the grandson of his sister), 1946, 37.
43. See Varble, 1964, 239–240.
44. James describes déjà vu as "sudden invasions of vaguely reminiscent consciousness . . . bring[ing] a sense of mystery and of the metaphysical duality of things, and the feeling of an enlargement of perception which seems imminent but which never completes itself" (*VRE*, 346).
45. Twain, 2000, 1–86.
46. Paine, 1912, 628.
47. Whitman, 1882, 331.

CHAPTER 8. FATE AND FREE WILL

1. Krippner, Bogzaran, & de Carvalho, 2002, 115.
2. Isaiah 14: 21–23.
3. Deuteronomy 18:22.
4. See Heschel, 1996, 6, 27, 48; Hoffman & Schacter-Shalom, 2012, 135, 139. The American mystic Andrew Jackson Davis, mentioned by James in *The Varieties of Religious Experience*, put it this way: "That there was a perfect harmony throughout the Jewish writings—that prophecy and fulfilment fitted into each other like joints in human anatomy—was doubted by no intelligent descendant of Abraham" (Davis, 1860, 133).
5. "The testimony of Jesus is the spirit of prophecy." *Revelations* 19:10.
6. "foreknow" (*proginōskō*), "foreknowledge" (*prognōsis*), "foresee" (*prooraō*), "foreordain" (*proorizō*), and "foretell" (*promarturomai, prokatangellō*). See Craig, 2001, 244.
7. Matthew 26: 33-34, 69-75.
8. Nikhilananda, 2008, 23. James's friend Swami Vivekananda, who introduced much of the West to Yoga and nondualism, was the recipient of one of those prophecies; on his very first visit to Ramakrishna he was told by the guru that he would "be famous across the seas" (ibid., 85).
9. Wallace, 2011, 306.
10. Dalai Lama, 1991, 214.
11. Das, 1998, 23. See, also, Yeshe, 2004.
12. Nietzsche, 1878/1996, 325.
13. Greene, 1989, 1.

14. Goldberg, 1982, 25, 33.
15. Ibid., 26.
16. Boswell, 1969, 79.
17. Greene, 1989, 9.
18. Myers, 1903a, 103.
19. See Louisa Rhine, 1955, for a nuanced analysis of intervention scenarios.
20. Bach, 1984, 225.
21. Ibid.
22. Ibid., 230–231.
23. See, for example, Julian Barbour's *The End of Time.*
24. Mann, 1984, 43–49.
25. Leadbeater, 1968, 167.
26. Davies, 1992, 190.
27. This is how Occam's original phrase—"It is vain to do with more what can be done with fewer"—is usually paraphrased.
28. Russell, 1945, 472.
29. Ferguson, 1989, 173.
30. Rhine, 1955, 30.
31. Though simple enough an explanation, it is not an obvious choice for even the most advanced researchers of precognition. Russell Targ, for example, after he had presented the evidence for precognition at the New York Open Center, held out for the possibility of free will, based on what he saw as the unreliability of precognitive dreams to always play out as seen. In a long afternoon discussion the following day, I introduced the concept of the mixed dream to him, and he acknowledged it as a viable alternative to "alternative futures."
32. For Buddhists, the creation of karma ends with nirvana; with the extinguishment of self through nirvana comes the end of reincarnation. Any implication of linear progression, however, is undermined by the Buddha's capacity of recognizing *all* of his past reincarnations, a capacity he claimed that he alone had attained. For such a complete recapitulation in reverse time, as Eliade notes, "exhausts" temporal duration, bringing one to the beginning of time itself, that is "nontime, eternity" (Eliade, 1969, 185).
33. Barker, 1995, 2.

34. Lessing, 1965, 89.
35. Tropp, 1992, 334.

CHAPTER 9. THAT THOU ART

1. Psalms 139:1–6.
2. Sanai, 1974, 24.
3. *Bhagavad Gita*, 7.12; emphasis added.
4. The Ancient Greek *Moira* (literally, "the apportioners"), or Fates, also "measured out" individuated selves. But these selves, unlike those created through maya, were believed to be actual, not apparent. Nietzsche credited both Heraclitian "play" and Vedantic *lila* as a "predecessor" to his worldview "beyond good and evil" (Nietzsche, 1980, Vol. 11, 26).
5. Emerson, 1903–04, VIII, 195. See also his declaration in his essay "The Oversoul":

> We live in succession, in division, in parts, in particles. Meantime within man is the soul of the whole; the wise silence; the universal beauty, to which every part and particle is equally related; the eternal One. And this deep power in which we exist, and whose beatitude is all accessible to us, is not only self-sufficing and perfect in every hour, but the act of seeing and the thing seen, the seer and the spectacle, the subject and the object, are one. (Emerson, 1903–04, II, 269)

Ever enlightenment's reluctant guide, James tried to incorporate both the "radical monism" and the "radical individualism" of his godfather in the first draft of his talk for the Emerson Centennial in 1903. But other than furtive references to Emerson's nondualism, such as "each of us is an angle" in the "eternal vision" of the "great Cosmic Intellect," he "abandoned the draft" and "started over. . . . This time with an emphasis . . . firmly on Emerson's individuality and his teaching of individualism" (*ACRWE*, 1121; Richardson, 2006, 434–435). But one year later, the nondualism he had suppressed emerged, as we shall see, in his epochal essay "Does Consciousness Exist?"

6. In Georg Feuerstein's phrase. Feuerstein, 1989, 2.
7. Suñña Sutta 35.85.
8. *Sahih-al-Bukhari* 81:38, translated and cited by Sells, 1996, 69.
9. Grof, 1998, 261.
10. Hall, letter to James, in Carus, 1909, 737, 738 and C9, 619.
11. In Advaita Vedanta, the school of Hinduism Vivekananda was aligned with, this "one sentient being" is identified as Brahman: "that state of being where all subject-object distinctions are obliterated. . . . [T]he self-effulgent light . . . that is . . . a necessary condition for the very possibility of the perceiving process" (Gupta, 1998, 63).
12. See Moshe Idel (Idel, 1988, 1–31), for the restoration of the extreme form of unio mystica—union with God as opposed to merely communion—in the Jewish tradition, a union that had been denied by his teacher Gershom Scholem.
13. Jakob Boehme, quoted by Bucke, 1901/1969, 187.
14. John 10:14.
15. John 10:30.
16. John 10:34.
17. Suzuki, 1954, 168. Ramana Maharshi, quoted this same "I am that I am" passage as a fit depiction of the one "Self," or God, which he identified as "Simple Being" (Maharshi, 1968, 401).
18. Thomas Cahill, in his excellent book *The Gifts of the Jews*, has argued that free will is one of their gifts (see Cahill). But it's worth noting that the two most renowned Jewish thinkers, Spinoza and Einstein, tried to give it back. According to Professor Yehuda I. Gellman of Ben-Gurion University, the question of free will has never been a settled question in Judaism. The Essenes, for example, did not believe in it. Nor did the Hasidim for whom "the consciousness of free will was only part of the illusion of creaturely separateness that has no basis in reality. Free will is only an appearance. When we cognize from within the appearance we experience our free will. However, were one to achieve the *bittul ha-yesh*, the nullifying of selfness, of a separate consciousness, then free will would disappear along with the consciousness of separateness" (Gellman, 2009, 2).
19. Eckhart, 13th cy./1941, 244.
20. Blood, 1920, 191.

21. Emerson, quoted by Blood, 1920, 202–203.
22. He even accused one of his most cherished theorists, Fechner, of this laziness, for letting "the usual monistic talk about him pass unchallenged" (*PU*, 133).
23. "*Bathos*." This observation was made during a lecture by Seth Benardete, long before computer search engines made it easily verifiable.
24. The chronological order is Thales, Anaximander, Anaximanes, Pythagoras, Heraclitus, Parmenides, Democritus.
25. Hoffman, 1973, 84.
26. See Close, Marten, & Sutton, 1987, 8.
27. Taylor, 2008.
28. Vivekananda, 1970–1973, V, 292.
29. John, 1980, 269.
30. Scaruffi, 2002.
31. Raschke, 1982, 232.
32. See p. 203.

CHAPTER 10.
CONSCIOUSNESS AND CONSCIOUSNESS OF SELF

1. Though "here" is mostly thought of as an adverb, it is also a noun, defined as such in Webster's as "Immediacy in space, abstracted from the other qualities and relations of the immediate experience."
2. Piaget & Inhelder, 1969, 13.
3. MacFarlane & Martin, 2002, 72.
4. According to Da Free John, a remembered sense of self from a past life "obviously is not dependent on *this* [present] body . . . [b]ut possibly a more subtle aspect of the body, or body-mind, also tacitly identified as 'self,' survives death and becomes reassociated with phenomenal conditions of bodily existence upon rebirth" (John, 1983, 185). The capacity for the same "soul" to travel from body to body, so-called metempsychosis, was a commonplace teaching in the East and was introduced to the West by the sixth-century "mixed theologian" (in Aristotle's depiction) Pherekydes of Syros (Barnes, 1983, 606), but was popularized by Pythagoras, who may have been his pupil (Philip, 1966, 188). Though

identified mostly with reincarnation, it was not restricted to human bodies, but could include migrations into other animal forms as well.

5. Burkhardt, 1981, 1449.
6. For an excellent treatise on the significance of nondual consciousness in the East, see Loy, 1998.
7. It was here that James handwrote "the witness" in the margin. See p. 119.
8. Or what Brian Lancaster has called an "'I'-tag" (see Lancaster, 1991, xii, and throughout).
9. In a manuscript version, James says that consciousness as a pigmentless "menstruum" "in which the states of mind float . . . is too diaphanous to be the ghost of a gas even" (*MEN*, 28).
10. See p. 115.
11. Only the original version of *The Principles of Psychology* retains James's proposed, but not in that book actualized, sciousness agenda: "At the conclusion of the volume, however, I may permit myself to revert again to the doubts here provisionally mooted, and will indulge in some metaphysical reflections suggested by them" (*PP1*, 305).
12. In addition to replacing "sciousness," "pure experience" was also used by James in the more general sense of "directly lived experience."
13. See James, *PP1*, 320–321.
14. See Carter, 2000, 23.
15. Defined by James as "Undifferentiated into thing and thought" (*AWPE*, 1175).
16. Emerson, 1903–04, II, 48. According to Henry James, Sr., Emerson himself possessed a somewhat similar, almost mystic power of attraction:

> I find in no man, especially no man equally famous, anything like the exquisite, unaffected, perfectly unconscious deference he pays to every other man's freedom. . . . He seems to me absolutely void of covetousness; entertains no clandestine designs upon any one; would not if he could impose his sway upon you; is destitute of all persuasive arts; has no resources either of flattery or command; is so ignorant, indeed, of all our accustomed devices in this sort, and so estranged from our ordinary

corrupt manners in general, as to appear to most people utterly inexpansive; and yet he draws all men unto him, is sure of their spontaneous homage. (James, Sr., 1857, 54)

17. Ikkyū Sōjun, quoted by Harada-Roshi, 1997, 7. Sokei-an, the first Zen master to settle in America, and both teacher and father-in-law of Alan Watts, put it this way: "[C]onsider the mind of an infant; he doesn't know the words papa or mama, he doesn't know his own existence, he doesn't know the outside world; nevertheless he has his own mind, pure and empty. We can discover that mind in this world through meditation. The attainment of this pure and empty mind is true samadhi. And this is Buddhism" (Sokei-an, 1940/1954, 1).
18. James Austin, in his magisterial *Zen and the Brain*, trivializes the use of ether to attain spiritual enlightenment by quoting one of Dr. Oliver Wendell Holmes's encounters with it: "A strong smell of turpentine pervades throughout" (Austin, 1998, 239). But Austin fails to add that Holmes himself was not satisfied with that result and tried again. Of that second effort, Holmes wrote: "I felt . . . that I really had seen the secret of the universe. . . . Put Jesus Christ into a Brahma press and that's what you will get" (Holmes, quoted by Blood, 1920, 231). Holmes was a family friend of the Jameses, taught William at Harvard, and is one of the signatories on his Medical Diploma.
19. Thoreau, 1848–1851/1990, 218.
20. Chloroform is an anaesthetic frequently mixed with ether.
21. Blood, quoted by James (*APM*, 1306). The last sentence, also quoted in an extended footnote in the *Varieties* (352), is attributed by Blood himself to fellow anaesthetic revelationist Xenos Clark, along with all but the last two paragraphs of passages that James attributes to Blood in that same footnote (see Blood, 1920, 233, 235). The footnote includes a long letter from Clark to James, and selections from a pamphlet by Blood called "Tennyson's Trances and the Anaesthetic Revelation." Curiously, in attributing the pamphlet passages to Clark, Blood neglects to mention that a key passage of Clark's letter is, according to Clark himself, a quote from Blood. Continuing the lively footnote existence that both these two American originals have enjoyed, I quote that intriguing passage here: "In the first place, Mr. Blood and I agree that the

revelation is, if anything, non-emotional. It is utterly flat. It is, as Mr. Blood says, 'the one sole and sufficient insight why, or not why, but how, the present is pushed on by the past, and sucked forward by the vacuity of the future. Its inevitableness defeats all attempts at stopping or accounting for it. It is all precedence and presupposition, and questioning is in regard to it forever too late. It is an initiation of the past'" (*VRE*, 351n).

22. Frederic Myers believed that the movement from the nitrous oxide state of "impersonal consciousness" to where the "personality itself, and the specialized senses severally, seem to define themselves," could be seen "not only as an advance and a development, but as a loss and a limitation" (F. W. H. Myers, in Kelly et al., 2007, 543).

23. Walsh & Vaughan, 1992, 198; emphasis added. Stephen Laberge, the first scientist to empirically confirm lucid dreaming by having the dreamer signal while in REM sleep, relates the following account with a Tibetan teacher: "I took a workshop from Tarthang Tulku, a Tibetan Buddhist, at Esalen and I was surprised at the topic of the workshop, which was essentially asking us to maintain consciousness throughout the twenty-four hours. Tarthang's English was limited at the time, he'd just arrived from India, and he would repeatedly say nothing more than, 'This dream!' and laugh. He was trying to get us to think of our current experience as a dream and to see what it had in common with our nocturnal experiences" (Laberge, 2008).

24. See Kingsley, 1999. Kingsley's restoration of Parmenides's Eastern spiritual origins uproots more than two millennia of misunderstanding, beginning with Plato, and epitomized by Aristotle's characterization of Parmenides's argument as "merely contentious" because his "premise" was "false" and his "conclusions" did "not follow." See Aristotle (5 167b). Parmenides's thematic connections to Indian thought had been commented on by others before Kingsley, including by James's beloved friend and polyglot scholar, Thomas Davidson (Davidson, 1870, 13). Also more than a century ago, German Sanskritist Richard Garbe observed: "The most striking resemblance—I am almost tempted to say sameness—is that between the doctrine of the All-One in the Upanishads and the philosophy of the Eleatics. . . . Parmenides holds that reality is due alone to this universal being, neither created nor to be destroyed, and omnipresent; further, that everything which exists in multiplicity and

is subject to mutability is not real; that thinking and being are identical. All these doctrines are congruent with the chief contents of the Upanishads and of the Vedanta system, founded upon the latter. Quite remarkable, too, in Parmenides and in the Upanishads, is the agreement in style of presentation; in both we find a lofty, forceful, graphical mode of expression, and the employment of verse to this end . . . I therefore do not consider it an anachronism to trace the philosophy of the Eleatics to India" (Garbe, 1897, 32).

More recently, but prior to Kingsley's compelling case for Parmenides's actual Eastern and mystical roots, German scholar Marcel Hinze had also made an extended argument that Parmenides was more mystic than logician. According to Hinze, Parmenides's text "exhibits numerous characteristic features, which also characterize the Indian Yoga. I even believe that this . . . poem represents, in this respect, a unique phenomenon in world literature: neither in old literature nor in new, have I met a text which shows in so concise a space such a great number of facts from the sphere of yoga-philosophy in a proper right context" (Hinze, 1979, 85).

25. Gupta, 1998, 27. See also Bricklin, 2006.
26. Hodgson, 1898, I, 455. Meaning, by perceivability, that which can be perceived either through the senses or the mind, as in imagination.
27. "Attempts are sometimes made to banish the question [of being] rather than to give it an answer. Those who ask it, we are told, extend illegitimately to the whole of being the contrast to supposed alternative non-being which only particular beings possess. These indeed, were not, and now are. But being in general, or in some shape, always was, and you cannot rightly bring the whole of it into relation with a primordial nonentity. . . . Non-being is not, said Parmenides and Zeno; only being is" (*SPP*, 1003).
28. Blood, 1920, 153. Or as Shadworth Hodgson put it, total nonexistence, or "pure nothing . . . is a concept-name and not a concept" (Hodgson, 1865, 347).
29. Due to its asphyxial properties, nitrous oxide was not considered safe until it was mixed with oxygen. But once mixed, its effects appeared to be the same as ether, both in its "initial sensations" and in the "main features" of deep anaesthetics (Hewitt, 1901, 71).
30. In this same account, from his *Idle Days in Patagonia*, Hudson wrote,

"My mind had suddenly transformed itself from a thinking machine into a machine for some other unknown purpose. To think was like setting in motion a noisy engine in my brain" (Hudson, 1893, 216).

31. Paul Carus. Suzuki also later married a student of James's, Beatrice Erskine, who helped him with his translations.
32. Watts, 1957, 201.
33. Suzuki, 1996, 268.
34. For more about the relationship between James, Nishida, and Suzuki, as well as reasons to suspect James exaggerated his ignorance of Buddhism, see Taylor, 1978.
35. Loy, 1998, 136.
36. Ibid., 42–43.
37. Ibid., 34.
38. Suzuki, 1959/1973, 16.
39. Nishida, 1990, 4.
40. Piaget, 1965, 38.
41. Compare Santayana, who wrote of "oscillat[ing] between . . . a solipsism of the living moment, and a materialism posited as a presupposition of conventional sanity" (Santayana, 1945, 16).
42. Along with "their pre-established harmony" (*PP1*, 220).
43. James's sense of pragmatism's value ranged from just "a method of carrying on abstract discussion" (*MT*, 857) to "a sort of *surrogate* of religion" (*C8*, 276).
44. Previously James had written Strong that "the reality known exists independently of the knower's idea and as conceived, if the conception be a true one. I can see that some bad parturient phrases of my radical empiricism might lead to an opposite interpretation, but if so they must be expunged" (*C8*, 372). James is being disingenuous here. His radical empirical essays contained more than phrases. See, especially, his 1905 lecture the "Notion of Consciousness," for example, delivered before an international audience of his peers (*N*, 89–111).
45. See p. 115.
46. A phrase coined by Russell after hearing James lecture. See Taylor, 1996.
47. Dickinson Miller, to whom James confessed his great turmoil over the conflict (see above), and Boyd Bode had made James keenly aware that he couldn't have it both ways.

48. See Moller, 2008. Whitehead, for one, believed that was a good thing, as the "ever-present complexity and possibility" always implicit in James's writing about human experience was best left not "filled out" (Price, 1954, 337–338).
49. Notable exceptions included Alcmaeon, Hippocrates, and Plato. To this day, the root word *phrēn* is used in medical words indicating either the diaphragm or the mind.
50. Ludlow, 292.
51. See p. 129.
52. Miller, in Taylor, 1996, 185.
53. Bohm & Hiley, 1993, 322. Bohm makes the same point as Miller, but begins a step earlier. As you walk around a round table, he noted, its changing shape looks elliptical; and to this changing elliptical *appearance* we oppose its nonchanging, rigid, circular *essence*. This essence is but a thought except that "this thought is projected into our immediate experience so that the table even *appears* to be circular" (ibid.).
54. Ibid.
55. Ibid.
56. See Cleary, 2001, 265.
57. Fischer-Schreiber et al., 1994, 154.
58. Turning the adjective into a participle, to directly oppose the participle "mediated."
59. Kapleau, 1980, 31.
60. The palpable presence of an absence, such as the "presence" of one's missing car in the parking space from which it has been stolen or towed, has been aptly described by Sartre in *Being and Nothingness* (Sartre, 1956, 6–12).
61. Dōgen, in Tanahashi, 1985, 70.
62. Wolf, 1995, 314–315.
63. Damasio, 1994, 152.
64. Ibid., 236.
65. Neuroscientist Joseph Ledoux has argued for an "I"-positioning that is in between electricity and matter: the shaping of the synaptic organization in the brain. (See Ledoux, 2002).
66. Damasio, 1994, 235; emphasis added.
67. "In a kaleidoscope revolving at a uniform rate, although the figures

are always rearranging themselves, there are instants during which the transformation seems minute and interstitial and almost absent, followed by others when it shoots with magical rapidity, relatively stable forms thus alternating with forms we should not distinguish if seen again" (*PP1*, 246).

68. Hume, 1826, 321. A later Edinburgh philosopher, J. R. Smythies, claimed that Hume failed to find the "I" in his search because the "I" was what was "doing this searching." The "I," he says, can never be found in a collection of thoughts and images and sensations, but only as the experience of what the collection belongs to, relates to, is presented to, is observed by. Admitting that such experience is "hard to describe," Smythies proves his point by claiming, "All I can say is that I am aware of my own existence separate from my thoughts, my images, and my sensations," which fails to distinguish omnipresent and ineradicable "witnessing" from the *added-on* sense of ownership of the witnessed (Koestler & Smythies, 1971, 234).
69. Bradley, 1893/1968, 81.
70. The "reduction" of self-feeling to muscle sensations is built into one of the most ancient of all languages, Sanskrit, where the word for emotions, *dugraha,* literally means "cramp" or "spasm." So, too, the English word for one of the most pronounced "I"-feeling states, "worry," comes from the Anglo-Saxon word for "strangle."
71. *Webster's Dictionary.*
72. See Hameroff and Penrose, 1996, for microtubules; Ledoux, 2002, for synapses.
73. Damasio, 1994, 244, 129.
74. Dürckheim, 1989, 153.
75. Thomas, 1985, 729.
76. Schwartz, 2002, 312.
77. Luria, 1973, 275.
78. *The New York Times*, Nov. 11, 1991, 1. Luria, too, had long ago pointed out that lesions in the frontal lobes do not impair memory but, rather, "the active effort required for voluntary recall" (Luria, 1973, 211).
79. Dick Passingham's experiment, presented in Schwartz, 2002, 334–335.
80. Gusnard, Akbudak, Shulman, & Raichle, 2001.

81. Damasio, 1994, 60. An operation called a "prefrontal leucotomy."
82. Bergson, 1910, 29.
83. As in the popular usage of the term after James.
84. See p. 39.
85. Watts, 1962, 72.
86. See p. 47.
87. Needless to say the belief in the illusion of will, a disbelief in ultimate preemptive control over events, facilitates this lesson. The determinist Einstein explicitly stated it kept him from "losing my temper" (Brian, 1996, 233).
88. James credits his colleague Shadworth Hodgson with the terminology "darkest."
89. Einstein, in a conversation recalled by Rudolf Carnap, in Nahin, 1993/1999, 204.
90. Osho, 1984, 366.
91. James added obfuscation to anonymity by identifying E. Robert Kelly as E. R. Clay.
92. Shadworth Hodgson, quoted by James (*PP1*, 607).
93. Blood, 1920, 122.
94. Bradley, 1883/1994, 43. Bradley's direct quote is: "It is not the time that can ever be present, but only the content."
95. Blood, quoted by James (*APM*, 1298).
96. Though James himself does not complete the symmetry.
97. Watts, 1973, 152–153.
98. Pain cannot be experienced as sciousness, as we have defined it, but there are many testimonies of transcending pain through transcending a feeling of self. Yogis and Christian martyrs alike could identify with the final sermon of the besieged sixteenth-century Zen abbot Kwaisen who, along with his fellow monks, was locked into a room that was then set on fire. Sitting cross-legged with them in front of the image of the Buddha, the abbot spoke these words as the flames closed in on them: "For a peaceful meditation, we need not go to the mountains and streams. When thoughts are quieted down, fire itself is cool and refreshing" (Suzuki, 1959/1973, 79).
99. Anger can involve the loss of a future scenario, but what fuels the anger is clinging to the sense of what the future *was* supposed to be. If I am

training to be a concert pianist and lose my hand in a subway door accident, I am angry not about the loss of a future self I imagine myself to be, but the self I *had imagined* I was going to be.

100. Bucke, quoted by James (*VRE*, 83). How *enlightened* Whitman remained throughout his lifetime is arguable. In his old age, however, he recalled the ecstatic state of his younger years, in which, "the whole body is elevated to a state by others unknown—inwardly and outwardly illuminated, purified," and, in a "marvelous transformation from the old timorousness . . . [s]orrows and disappointments cease—there is no more borrowing trouble in advance . . . a man realizes the venerable myth—he is a god walking the earth" (Whitman, quoted in Allen, 1975, 194). If this testimony, corroborated, in part, by his friends and acquaintances, is not enough to convince us that Whitman did experience something like, if not equivalent to, the Buddha's enlightenment, there are the many photographs of the man, which confirm his own words about how "the marvelous transformation" altered his appearance: "A singular charm, more than beauty, flickers out of, and over, the face—a curious transparency beams in the eyes, both in the iris and the white" (ibid.).
101. James quotes Emerson's example of such a blissful moment coming out of nowhere: "Crossing a bare common in snow puddles, at twilight, under a clouded sky, without having in my thoughts any occurrence of special good fortune, I have enjoyed a perfect exhilaration. I am glad to the brink of fear" (*OCB*, 856).
102. However such moment is conceived, whether in a conventional temporal sense or as "a particular choice of coordinate in the description of the location of a space-time event" (Penrose, 1989, 384).
103. See pp. 142–149.
104. Although the authority of this passage has been questioned, it is congruent with Mozart's wife's depiction of how he composed. (See Niemetschek, 1798/2006).
105. Coomaraswamy, 1947/2001, 47.
106. Dembo, 1972, 40.
107. Myers, 1903a, 120.
108. Bergson, 1911, 343, 341.
109. Brown, 1977, 163.

110. About this conversion, James wryly notes: "Although Kant's name for it—the 'original transcendental synthetic Unity of Apperception'—is so long, our consciousness about it is, according to him, short enough" (*PP1*, 362).
111. Watts, 1957, 123.
112. Bashō was a serious student of Zen, who did a year of meditation practice under Rinzai master Butchō (Dumoulin, 2005, 349). Santayana identified "impersonality," "the power of losing itself in its object," as the hallmark of genius in poetry (Santayana, 1910, 34).
113. Huang Po, 1958, 61.
114. Any pre-known sequence, such as the alphabet, is, as it plays out, actually both at once: a thought in *and* of succession. "N-different-from-m" may be an "absolutely unique pulse of thought" but it is not an unanticipated thought, such as "n-different-from-w."
115. Kant, 1787/1965, 214. Compare Buddhist "bare attention" (Thera, 30–45).
116. Bohm, 1992/1994, 232.
117. Shadworth Hodgson, quoted by James (*PP1*, 607.).
118. James writes "Many things," rather than "all" things, but does not give any example of an exception.
119. Price, 1997, 152. As Feynman points out, the apparent irreversibility of a film of an egg splattering on the sidewalk is due only to the insufficient microscopic detail of the images which, if enhanced, would allow the film to be run backward without any apparent violation of the laws of physics. "If we see the egg splattering on the sidewalk and the shell cracking open, and so on, then we will surely say 'That is irreversible, because if we run the moving picture backwards the egg will all collect together and the shell will go back together, and that is obviously ridiculous!' But if we look at the individual atoms themselves, the laws look completely reversible. This is, of course, a much harder discovery to have made, but apparently it is true that the fundamental physical laws, on a microscopic and fundamental level, are completely reversible in time!" (Feynman, 2013, 52–53).
120. Recently, physicist Lee Smolin has argued that the presence of certain time arrows (such as the "thermodynamic arrow" of entropy, or the expanding universe's "cosmological arrow," or the emergence and proliferation of black holes "black-hole arrow") suggests that however

"time-symmetric" the fundamental laws of physics may be, "the initial conditions of our universe appear to have been finely tuned to produce a universe that is asymmetric in time" (Smolin, 2013, 204, 206). But such apparent asymmetric arrows presuppose, rather than mandate, an absolute starting point—the big bang, say, rather than a cyclical or oscillating process. As the philosopher John McTaggart pointed out in his classic 1908 essay, "The Unreality of Time," however reversible a process or series may be (such as the series of natural numbers), when there is only one end, it "seems the more natural to us . . . to have that end as a beginning than as a termination" (McTaggart, 1908, 462).

121. Bohm, 1992/1994, 227.
122. Ibid.; Bohm acknowledges Leibniz as the first to see time this way, but compare Aristotle's "Time is the enumeration of motion" (*Physica* IV.10–14).
123. Kant, 1787/1965, 342n.
124. Suzuki, 1959/1973, 268.
125. For "non-regressive satori," see Loy, 1998, 150. See, too, the visual aid of three ovals side-by-side-by-side, representing this state, that a Theravada monk sketched for him (ibid., 144–145).
126. Shankara, 1982, 80.
127. Gupta, 1998, 25. See Shrivasanda for a comparison between Bradley and Shankara. Shankara also loosens the "vise" of Bradley's "intellectualist difficulty," which James attempted to loosen with the aid of Bergson. James depicts this "difficulty" as follows: "the impossibility of understanding how 'your' experience and 'mine,' which 'as such' are defined as not conscious of each other, can nevertheless at the same time be members of a world-experience defined expressly as having all its parts co-conscious, or known together. The definitions are contradictory, so the things defined can in no way be united" (*PU,* 100).
128. Vivekananda, 1970–73, V, 11.
129. "Radical empiricism takes conjunctive relations at their face-value, holding them to be as real as the terms united by them" (*PU*, 126).
130. Hume, 1826, 558, 559.
131. *Mahatanhasankhaya*, Sutta 38, in Nanamoli & Bodhi, 1995, 360.
132. Ashtavakra, 1940, 61.

133. Whitman, quoted by Allen, 1975, 194. Compare, too, Nietzsche's assessment of their fellow mentor, Emerson: "His mind always finds reasons for being contented, and even grateful" (1889/1976, 36).
134. Whitman, 1882, 294.
135. T. C. Upham, quoted by James (*VRE*, 265). Compare the Sufi *ibn waqtihi*, "a son of the moment," meaning that one "is completely occupied with the religious obligation of his present state, carrying out what is demanded of him at the time. It is said that one who embraces poverty has concern neither for the moment past nor for the moment to come. He is concerned only with the present moment in which he finds himself" (Sells, 1996, 100). It is also said by the Sufis that "to be preoccupied with a past moment is to lose a second moment" (ibid.).

CHAPTER 11. PSYCHE

1. Muktananda, p. 1978, 47.
2. This meaning is not without controversy among classicists. The first Greek/English lexicographer, Alfred Liddell (father of the real life Alice in Wonderland), whose lexicon is the standard (and practically exclusive) English lexicon of the Ancient Greek language, determined that breath was the original meaning of psyche. A modern editor of a revised version disagreed for lack of evidence. Any scholar who does not accept the classical references that support Liddell's definition (including the verbal form of the word which indisputably meant "to breathe" or "to blow") might consider a compelling modern one: it is an everyday term for breath in use in Greece today.
3. See Abram, 1997, 239–250.
4. Even James's close colleague Charles Sanders Peirce, who pointed out to James that he can only think when he *holds* his breath, was thereby acknowledging this (C7, 484, 485).
5. Blood, 1920, 241.
6. John: 3.
7. Casteneda, 1971, 23. While some critics claim Don Juan to be a pure fiction, Casteneda himself maintained that he was real.

8. Rose, 2005, 208.
9. Ibid., 161–162.
10. Ibid., 162.
11. Ibid., 208. For "serious difficulties" with the reality of engrams, not overcome by recent experiments with fear recall in rats (Liu, et al.), see, among others, Heil (1978) and Braude (2014, 1–26).
12. Nicoll, 1952/1976, 116.
13. See James (*HI*, 1104–1121).
14. In the *Principles*, James does emphasize what he calls "the total brain process." There is plenty in that seminal work to make a Cartesian dualist happy. James, however, is not one of them. He accepts "the ascertainment of a blank unmediated correspondence, term for term, of the succession of states of consciousness with the succession of total brain-processes" only as a "provisional halting place" to keep his psychology "non-metaphysical" (*PP1*, 182). One biographer, Gerald Myers, has even suggested that James had adopted this provisional dualism in the *Principles* because to do otherwise would have been a "strategic error" in a "textbook in which psychology was at last presented as a natural science" (Myers, 1986, 55).
15. Schiller, 1891/1994, 289.
16. Quoting this and other passages of Schiller in his essay "Human Immortality" (*HI*, 1120).
17. James had used the same metaphor four years earlier when he characterized the brain as the chief obstacle to realizing the transcendentalists' "oversoul": "As the pipes of an organ let the pressing mass of air escape only in single notes, so do our brains, the organ pipes of the infinite, keep back everything but the slender threads of truth to which they may be pervious. As they obstruct more, the insulation increases, as they obstruct less it disappears" (*KTT*, 86).
18. Blood, 1920, xxxvi.
19. William Braud in Joseph, 2002, 132. See, too, biologist Rupert Sheldrake, who believes that our behavior is organized by "morphic fields" surrounding the body that "no more leave material traces in the brain . . . than the programs to which a radio set is tuned leave traces in the set" (Sheldrake, 1988/1995, 198–199).

20. Carus, 1846/1989, 1.
21. Jung, in Evans, 1976, 134.
22. Jung, 1999, 243.
23. Jung, 2014, 151.
24. Ibid., 167.
25. Jung, 1950, 87.
26. Ibid.
27. Jung, 1961, 358.
28. See p. 102.
29. Having cited him as early as his dissertation.
30. Jung, 1969, 167.
31. Ibid., 125.
32. Jung, 1961, 358.
33. Jung, 1973b, 213.
34. Jung, 1961, 359. Compare the following passage from Thoreau, quoted by James as one of his varieties of religious experience: "Every little pine-needle expanded and swelled with sympathy and befriended me. I was so distinctly made aware of the presence of something kindred to me, that I thought no place could ever be strange to me again" (*VRE*, 252).

CHAPTER 12. UNDOING UNTO OTHERS AS WELL AS ONESELF

1. Even if not, as Hume argued, ultimately provable.
2. French, *repentir*; Spanish, *arrepentirse*.
3. Anita Hill, in her notorious televised appearance before the Senate Judiciary Committee, seemed to have this acceptance. As she acknowledged before the nation her own misjudgments (along with her steadfast accusations), she did not seem constrained by contrition but opened up by her acceptance of a reality whose specific details she, perhaps for the first time, had come to fully acknowledge.
4. A story is told of a man in the nineteenth century, a determinist, about to make a journey out through a wilderness filled with bears. His nephew comes across him as he is cleaning his gun and asks, teasingly: "Why are you taking your gun. If your time comes, there is nothing you

can do about it, right?" Without looking up the man replies: "Maybe it's the bear's time."

5. Norman Vincent Peale's phrase, "the power of positive thinking," the title of his epochal best-seller, has so saturated the collective consciousness of our culture that it is easy to forget that the power he was promoting was not of self but of God.
6. In crediting James as "a founder of Alcoholics Anonymous," Bill W. explicitly references only the calamity-helplessness-surrender dynamic in *The Varieties of Religious Experience*, not this most obvious precedent. (W., 2005, 150–152).
7. Smith, 1999, 7; emphasis added, citing the study of Valiant G.E., Milofsky E.S. (1982), "Natural history of male alcoholism IV: Paths to recovery," *Archives of General Psychiatry* 39(2): 127–133.
8. Ibid., 4.
9. Ibid., 1–7.
10. May, 1969, 197.
11. Ibid.
12. Dhiravamsa, 1989, 123.
13. Ibid., 31–32.
14. See James (*VRE*, 177–238).

CHAPTER 13. BELIEF IN FATE IS NOT FATALISM

1. Trachtenberg, 1939/2004, 208. In Medieval Judaism, writes Trachtenberg, "the deterministic view of life . . . governed the masses. . . . [I]t was . . . the general view that 'nothing ever happens to a man except at God's command.'" He then quotes renowned twelfth-century Jewish mystic Eleazar of Worms: God "decrees who shall be a scholar, and how much and for how long he shall study, and whether he will compose one, or two, or three books" and "just how many steps he will take in his lifetime, and how many men his eyes will behold" (ibid., 209).
2. Tolstoy, 1942, 1351.
3. Luther, 1990, 106. Luther had, of course, strong scriptural support for invoking God's omniscience and omnipotence (which cannot coincide with free will). Isaiah 45:7, for instance, states: "I form the light, and

create darkness; I make peace, and create evil; I the LORD do all these [things]."

4. Nietzsche, 1889/1976, 494–495.
5. Nietzsche, 1882/2010, 181.
6. Osho, 1983, 220.
7. Nietzsche, 1901/1967, 546.
8. Suzuki, 1959/1973, 188.
9. Spinoza, 17th cy./1883, 265.
10. Nonetheless, in the same letter, James conceded that there was a deep kernel of truth to Schopenhauer's system. The same rabid reaction to Schopenhauer is also in evidence in *The Varieties of Religious Experience*, where, lumping him with his youthful follower Nietzsche, James sneered: "The sallies of the two German authors remind one, half the time, of the sick shriekings of two dying rats" (*VRE*, 42). But the pairing is inept, as Nietzsche is James's ally in this denunciation, attacking the "world-denying" idol of his student days, and promoting instead his own "ideal of the boldest, most vital, and most world-affirming human being" (Nietzsche, in Heidegger, 1961, 64).
11. Brooks, 1933, 257.
12. Sartre, 1956, 615.
13. See pp. 57–59.
14. Nietzsche, 1901/1967, 520.
15. Nietzsche, 1886/1989, 68. Nietzsche's passionate promotion of eternal recurrence as a reality, rather than merely a doctrine he had been familiar with and written about as a Greek scholar, came to him suddenly during a walk in the woods, as he approached "a powerful pyramidal rock" (Nietzsche, 1908/2010, 295). The original mystical insight of this ecstatic vision supersedes the implausible physics he later tried to supplement it with: finite matter rearranging itself in infinite time into perpetually recurring exact replicas (see Nehamas, 1985, 144–145); see also, Kaufmann: Nietzsche's "reasons for not publishing a proof [based on physics] presumably included his own sense that his efforts were inadequate" (1950, 327). For such added-on physics were not "presuppositions *that would have to be true* if it were true" (Nietzsche, 1901/1967, 545; emphasis added). The only presupposition of physics "that would have to be true" is what Bohm identified as physics' real fact: an "order of

succession" (Bohm, 1992/1994, 233). The physics that does support eternal recurrence, special relativity, emerged five years after Nietzsche's death [see Fraassen (1962) contra Capek (1960)]. Attempts to construe Nietzsche's "highest formula of affirmation" as a "thought-experiment" (Arendt), a "pretend" game (Sartre) (Lukacher, 1998, for both, 117), or, most recently, a "grand fiction" (Panaïoti, 2013, 128) run counter to "the strong emotion of the discovery" that left him "bathed in tears" for a long time (Halevy, 1911, 231). His beloved companion Lou Andreas-Salomé's account of how he experienced it confirms as much: "To me the hours are unforgettable in which he first confided it to me, as a secret, as something he unspeakably dreaded to see verified . . . : only with a soft voice and with all signs of the deepest horror did he speak of it. And in fact he suffered so deeply from life that the certainty of the eternal recurrence of life had to entail something ghastly for him" (Lou Andreas-Salomé in Löwith, 1997, 197–198). These are not the expressions of experiment, pretend, or fiction.

16. Brooks, 1933, 14.
17. "Turning Point," first published in 1910, Twain, 2000, 477–485.
18. Twain, 1961, 288. In his acceptance letter to the American Psychical Society, Twain dwelled on his persistent feeling of being "a mere amanuensis," and, when writing letters, an amanuensis linked to a common source with others (see Horn, 1996, 162–164).
19. Herrigel, 1971, 58–59.
20. Ibid., 69.

CHAPTER 14. THE NONREALITY OF TIME

1. After studying with Louis Pasteur for five years, Bigelow became one of the first Americans to live in Japan, and played a major role in introducing Japanese art and culture to his homeland. He later converted to Buddhism.
2. A term coined thirty years ago by another MD, Raymond Moody. In 2001, the esteemed medical journal *The Lancet* published an article by Dutch cardiologist Pim van Lommel corroborating that such

experiences do transpire during periods of clinical death, when the brain's EEG has flatlined (see Lommel, 2001).

3. Bigelow, 1908, 14–15.
4. Ibid., 15.
5. Steven Fanning, quoted by Huston Smith, 2001–02, 14. See, too, Lommel's accounts of NDE experiences in which "[t]ime no longer plays a role; everything exists in an eternal present" (Lommel, 2010, 224).
6. Dr. Winslow Forbes's *Obscure Diseases of the Mind* (published in 1866) relates time-collapse experiences in relation to incidents of near-death by asphyxiation, such as the following:

> A gentleman, during an attack of acute mental depression, hung himself. A short period only elapsed before he was cut down. He was subsequently brought to me for advice, and placed for a time under my medical supervision. He ultimately recovered. He often related to me the strange mental visions that floated in his mind during the few minutes or (in all probability) seconds he continued suspended, and temporarily deprived of consciousness. They were of the most pleasing character. The scenes of his early life were in their minutest particular revived. He was taken to the cottage in which he was born, interchanged tokens of affection with his beloved parents, gambolled once more with the companions of his childhood on the village green, and again
>
> "Whispered the lover's tale, Beneath the milk-white thorn, that scents the evening gale."
>
> Incidents connected with the school in which he received his early instruction were reproduced to his mind. He once again renewed acquaintance, and shook hands with the loved and dearly cherished companions of his boyhood. The remembrance of faces (known when a child) that had been (as he supposed) entirely obliterated from his memory, was restored to his recollection in a most remarkably truthful and vivid manner. During that critical second of time (when it may be reasonably presumed he was struggling with death), every trifling and

> minute circumstance connected with his past life was presented to his mind like so many charming pictorial sketches and paintings. (Forbes, 1866, 285)

7. Myers, 1986, 155.
8. Bergson, 1911, 9.
9. Ibid., 52.
10. "Succession, time per se, is no force. Our talk about its devouring tooth, etc., is elliptical. Its contents are what devour" (*PP1*, 628).
11. As Kant had asserted.
12. Newton, 1687/2002, 6.
13. Hodgson, 1878, 290.
14. Mach, 1919, 222. Thanking Mach for dedicating a book to him, James wrote that he hoped they both would continue to "contribute jointly to the establishment of the truly philosophical way of thinking—which I believe to be 'on the whole' *our* way!" (C7, 72).
15. Cooper & Erickson, 1959, 16. An attempt to experimentally verify the subjective perception of slowed-down time in frightening situations was attempted utilizing a "perception chronometer" of flashing numbers, too fast to be read under normal circumstances, strapped to the wrists of subjects falling from a fifty-foot tower into a safety net. The experiment yielded some positive correlations, but not enough for the experimenters to conclude that the falling subjects had gained "increased discrimination capacities in the time domain" (Stetson, Fiesta, & Eagleman, 2007, 3). But as one commentator noted, some of the misses are very close indeed given the wide range of 1–100 (such as 98 for 96 and 56 for 50), and, much more to the point, subjects who know "they were not in danger of dying" cannot be equated with a real "near-death situation" where "the outcome is far from certain" (Peake, 2012, 153).
16. Crick & Koch, 2003, 122.
17. Sacks, in Folger & Weiner, 2005, 221 (Sacks particularly relied on the studies of Dale Purves). John Stroud was the first to revive the pulse hypothesis, proposing "a fixed psychological moment within which all ongoing cognition would be integrated in non-overlapping pulses" (Hunt, 1995, 247).
18. Baars & Gage, 2010, 7. One hundred milliseconds, or one-tenth of

a second, "about the rate of individual alpha and theta waves," is "the order of magnitude required to become conscious of a sensory stimulus" (ibid.).

19. Pöppel, 1988, 62.
20. Floyd, 1974, 262.
21. See Austin, 1998, 89.
22. Floyd, 1974, 261.
23. Ibid., 263.
24. Luk, 1971, 77.
25. Sacks, in Folger & Weiner, 2005, 220.
26. Ibid., 219–220.
27. Bergson, 1911, 2.
28. Sacks, citing neurologist William Gooddy, in Zaleski & Lopez, 2005, 160.
29. Ibid., 160–162. Sacks gives a vivid account of two such contrasting patients.
30. Bergson, 1911, 358.
31. LeShan, 1974, 35. "A serious clairvoyant is an individual who has been shown over a period of years of intensive study to be able, under strictest laboratory conditions, to acquire information from other than known channels and about whom there has never been the slightest evidence of chicanery. Typical among these are Mrs. Piper, Mrs. Willett, and Eileen Garrett" (ibid., 260). While James believed that psychologists were beginning to recognize the investigation of mediums "as an urgent task" (*EPs*, 321), LeShan was one of the few psychologists of the last century who felt this urgency. His first grant was to investigate why intelligent people believed in the paranormal. More than sixty years later, he is still finding the reasons.
32. In Hermann Weyl's formulation of Einstein's theory of relativity: "The objective world simply is, it does not happen. Only to the gaze of my consciousness, crawling upward along the life line of my body, does a section of this world come to life as a fleeting image in space which continuously changes in time" (Weyl, 1963, 116).
33. "Pythagoras," said Empedocles, "whenever he reached out with all his thinking organs . . . easily saw each of all the things which are in ten or twenty human lifetimes" (Inwood, 2001, 83).

34. In agreement with what he called Lotze's "deep suggestion" that "our descriptions may themselves be important additions to reality" and that "previous reality itself be there, far less for the purpose of reappearing unaltered in our knowledge, than for the very purpose of stimulating our minds to such additions as shall enhance the universe's total value" (*P*, 599).
35. See Broad, 2006, for the ethelyne hypothesis, and the compelling case to be made for the authenticity of some of the Delphic visions, revising the pre-archaeological critiques of Parke, Wormell, and Fontenrose.
36. Blood, C9, 104.
37. Ramsay, "Partial Anaesthesia," *Proceedings of the Society for Psychical Research*, 9 (January 1894); emphasis in original. Compare Ramsay's ether experience with contemporary accounts of Ayahuasca, such as the following by one of its foremost researchers, Benny Shanon: "What does the experience of eternity consist in? . . . Ayahuasca brings people to a realm that is above all times. Thus, from the perspective of the eternal, everything that has ever happened, as well as everything that will ever happen, all have an equal temporal status. In a certain sense, they are all there and one only has to look at them. This, I suspect, is what is meant when the term *sub specie aeternitatis* is invoked: A perspective is taken by which all that will have happened at all times is co-present. In this limit situation, the temporal may, in a fashion, be reduced to the spatial" (Shanon, 2001, 47).
38. Blood, 1874, 35.
39. Blood, C2, 230.
40. See Krippner, Bogzaran, & de Carvalho, 2002, 77–82, for examples of successive dreams within dreams.
41. In Mrs. Willett's word. See p. 219–220.
42. Einstein, 1961, 150.
43. Ibid.
44. de Broglie, quoted in Schilpp, 1974, 114.
45. James did not interchange mystical and psychical. While he allowed that mystical states were states in which "the mind ascend[s] to a more enveloping point of view" (*VRE*, 385), he held that their hallmark was "ineffability" (ibid., 343 and ff.). The "definiteness of what was perceived" in his own "mystical paroxysm" he thought of as "unmystical," along with

the "distressing confusion of mind" (*ASAM*, 1278). But his overall sense of the experience, as his title emphasizes, was mystical, however much he resisted it. James historian Daniel W. Bjork saw James's struggle with these dreams as part of his lifelong "masterful strategy to stay poised between science and art, between the mystically appealing unbounded unconscious and the hazards of falling into its abyss" (Bjork, 1983, 157). Bjork dubbed James "the compromised scientist." But that is only half the story. The other half, as we have tried to show here, is that James was a compromised mystic. As Barnard astutely observed: "[T]he Tantric and Sufi belief that a mystic could also be highly successful in the everyday work-world was never part of James's understanding of the possibilities of mysticism" (Barnard, 1997, 72).

46. Einstein, 1961, 26.
47. A step forward from the younger James's confession: "I myself am convinced of supernormal cognition. Supernormal healing. But not a vestige of a theory" (*ML*, 71).
48. Barrington, Stevenson, & Weaver, 2005, 131.
49. Dodds, 1973, 160.
50. Ibid. and fn.
51. For an excellent account of Piper see Blum and Tymn. Both of these lowly speculative, highly researched books serve to rebut Martin Gardner's highly speculative, lowly researched essay "How Mrs. Piper Bamboozled William James" (Gardner, 2004, 252–262). For a detailed analysis of Gardner's bamboozling, fitting James's description of "critics who, refusing to come to any close quarters with the facts, survey them at long range and summarily dispose of them at a convenient distance by the abstract name of fraud" (*EPR*, 191), see Prescott and G. Taylor. Piper is one of LeShan's "serious clairvoyants" (see endnote 323n31).
52. Sage, 1904, 128–130.
53. By stark contrast, the French school of neurologists (led by Janet) investigating trances ignored the profound implications of accessing this remote transmarginal realm (Taylor, 1996, 46). Janet and Charcot saw such trances as "disintegrations of personality," diametrically opposed to the holistic vision of Myers, who believed that the "splitting-up of our total individuality has . . . taken place already, and before our supraliminal memory begins" (Myers, 1892, 472). Whereas the French school saw

transmarginal trances like "cracks in a plate," Myers compared them to "fissures . . . of the earth's crust," that "testify to unknown depths and a volcanic power beneath them" (ibid.).

54. See Kelly et al., 2007, 359–360.
55. "Of all [clairvoyantly] gifted people, no one offered herself as willingly, regularly, and extensively for scientific investigation" (Mayer, 2007, 266).
56. LeShan, 1974, 225; emphasis added. Even the spirit control, George Pellew (aka George Pelham), who most convinced Hodgson and Myers that he was an actual (deceased) person, corroborated this timeless clairvoyant reality. Speaking through Piper, Pellew asserted that he had "lost" the "idea of time," and when asked during a session if he could witness what friends of his were doing in their home now, he gave a detailed report, later verified by them, but instead of the activities of that day, they turned out to be the activities of yesterday (Tymn, 2013, 70–71).
57. Debra Blum, in her recent *Ghost Hunters: William James and the Search for Scientific Proof of Life after Death*, gives an excellent account of Hodgson's work with Mrs. Piper.
58. See pp. 181–182.
59. In his essay "The Concept of Saksin in Advaita Vedanta," Andrew Fort "differentiates two conceptions of saksin: saksin as witness, an eternal, passive observer, and saksin as field, the context or 'space' for all contents or form" (Fort, 1984, 277).
60. Gupta, 1998, 66, Jnaneshwar, 1979, 57.
61. Burkhardt, 1981, 1449.
62. Gupta, 1998, 17.
63. Most Jamesean commentators, perhaps uncomfortable with his mystical leanings, have passed over "sciousness" in silence let alone accord it this prime reality. But not the colleague with whom James felt a most special affinity. A month before James died, he wrote to the psychologist Theodore Flournoy: "Through all these years I have wished I might live nearer to you and see more of you and exchange more ideas, for we seem two men particularly *faits pour nous comprendre*" (C9, 569). Seven years later, Flournoy published his book *The Philosophy of William James*,

emphasizing the key concept of "sciousness," and its role in the mystical music that James had an ear for:

> [P]rimordial facts . . . pure experiences are entirely objective, simple phenomena of "sciousness" and not of "consciousness." This means that [James] holds that the distinction between self and non-self, implied in the word "consciousness," from which we are in a normal state unable to free ourselves, is not primary, but results from a subsequent construction, from a conceptual sorting out and classifying of the primitive experiences. One can get some idea of this "sciousness" from the fact that the mystics, and some people on coming out from under the influence of anaesthetics (particularly of nitrous oxide), tell of a state in which all sense of the "me" is abolished, and where there is nothing but the purely objective intuition of something present (the world, God, or whatever it may be). (Flournoy, 1917, 98)

For an attempt to construe sciousness absent this transpersonal perspective see Natsoulas, 2013.

64. In the same article cited previously. See 324n37.
65. Davy, in Blood, 1920, 221. Davy, one of the early explorers of nitrous oxide, was the first to discover its analgesic properties.
66. Ibid.
67. Ramana Maharshi, in Osborne, 1996, 193.
68. Freeman, 2003, 198–199.
69. Bradley, 1914, 48. As Bradley also observed: "There are moods in which our daylight world seems to have lost actuality, where the reflection and what it mirrors have equal force, and we ourselves seem hardly more than one of the things we contemplate" (460).
70. See Gillman, 1989.
71. Twain, 2011, 187.
72. Ibid. See also p. 205.
73. Mayhew in Hartocollis, 1983, 131.
74. According to the BBC video documentary (available on YouTube as of March 2015), about the event, with excerpts from the original planned broadcast and an interview with the principle participants.

75. Ibid.
76. Eliade, 1989a, 157.
77. Paul Devereux in Hayes, 2000, 317.
78. Parmenides uses words for motion, *kinetos,* and trembling, *tremo* (attached with an alpha privative) to depict motionless, *akinetos,* and steadfast, *atremos.*
79. See Barton Perry's Preface to *Essays in Radical Empiricism* (*ERE*, vi).
80. Santayana, 1930, 75.
81. Ibid. Philosopher of time Milic Capek derides Santayana's general tendency as a philosopher to merge apparently irreconcilable views: "It would be an interesting game to find for nearly any of Santayana's views an opposite one—if not on the same page, at least in the same chapter or the same book" (Capek, 1987, 588). But his criticism of Santayana's views on time as "incoherent and improvised" (ibid.) never engages the coherent reconciliation of opposites of this "labyrinth" and "exploring spirit."
82. Royce, 1920, 142.
83. See p. 136.
84. Hinze, 1979, 36.
85. "Up until the end of the second century at least, the universal Church remained united in one basic sense; they all accepted the supremacy of the Father. They all regarded God the Father Almighty as alone supreme, immutable, ineffable and without beginning" (Buckley, 1978, 114). This neo-Platonic, via Parmenides, exaltation of God-the-immutable was also affirmed by the greatest medieval theologian, Thomas Aquinas: "God does not move at all, and so cannot be measured by time; neither does he exist 'before or after' or no longer exist after having existed, nor can any succession be found in Him" (Aquinas, *Summa Contra Gentiles* 1.14).
86. Capek, 1987, 584.
87. Capek, in Cobb Jr., 1977, 55, 58. Capek's appreciation of Santayana's key insight might also have fostered a less contemptuous dismissal of Aquinas's "almost pathetic" attempt "to reinject life and personality into his static divine substance" (Capek, 1951, 18).
88. Dōgen, in Tanahashi, 1985, 69.
89. Blavatsky, 1888/2009. A heavily marked version of *The Secret Doctrine* was allegedly found on Einstein's desk after he died (http://

theosnet.ning.com/profiles/blog/show?id=3055387%3ABlogPost%3A30653&commentId=3055387%3AComment%3A30972&xg_source=activity). James and his psychical research colleagues believed that their own Richard Hodgson had exposed Blavatsky as a fraud, but subsequent research has called this exposure into question (http://www.theosociety.org/pasadena/hpb-spr/hpbspr-h.html).

90. Barbour, 1999, 2. For Mach, see p. 214.
91. See p. 170.
92. Dowden, 2007, 4.
93. Grünbaum, 1968, 7.
94. Grünbaum, 1963, 329.
95. See p. 16.
96. Hodgson, 1898, IV, 350.
97. Swedenborg, 1749/1910, 78.
98. "Appearance without reality would be impossible, for what then could appear? And reality without appearance would be nothing, for there certainly is nothing outside appearance" (Bradley, 1893/1968, 432).
99. Myers, 1903b, 273.
100. Lodge, 1900, 105. Prevision is generally understood as a precognition limited to visual images. See Ducasse, 1951, 204.
101. For an excellent account of Lodge's experiments, see Blum, 2006.
102. See Yourgrau, 2006.
103. Lodge, 1891/1892, 554.
104. Peat, 1987, 168.
105. Bohm, 1980, 209.
106. See Barbour, 1999. Kaku, among others, believes that the only viable candidate for the unification of quantum theory and relativity is superstring theory. Kaku, 2004, 225.
107. Gefter, 2008.
108. Ibid.

CHAPTER 15. ETERNALISM

1. Verse 2.6, translated by Graham M. Schweig (Schweig, 2007, 40).
2. Plotinus, 3rd cy./1991, 216. "For both Parmenides and Plotinus, the supreme reality is the one, wholly undifferentiated" (Ustinova, 2009, 216).

3. Eckhart, 13th cy./1941, 73.
4. As he was composing his *Varieties of Religious Experience* lectures, James wrote to Royce:

> When I compose my Gifford lectures mentally, 'tis with the design exclusively of overthrowing your system, and ruining your peace. I lead a parasitic life upon you, for my highest flight of ambitious ideality is to become your conqueror, and go down into history as such, you and I rolled in one another's arms and silent (or rather loquacious still) in one last death-grapple of an embrace. (C6, 320)

5. Royce, 1920, 141.
6. Even though Bradley most often held this view "in reserve," as Sprigge notes:

> Some of Bradley's obscurities stem, I suspect, from the fact that while he was committed to the eternalistic view, he thought it more "way out" than we are inclined to do since Einstein and so often reverts to discussing things from a supposedly more common-sense perspective for which only the present is real. (Sprigge, 1993, 477–478)

7. As Blood puts it: "Let Achilles himself propose the paradox, that he cannot overtake the tortoise, and we see at once that to be a philosopher he has to be a knave; the mathematical requirement of the feat is wholly impertinent to its empirical accomplishment" (Blood, 1920, 178).
8. See Mazur (2007) and Kennedy (2003), 96–103.
9. See p. 4. Denied Kingsley's revisionist perspective, even the Greek scholar Nietzsche saw Parmenides as having concocted a "purest absolutely bloodless abstraction, unclouded by any reality" (Nietzsche, 1996, 69).
10. Blood, 1920, 241.
11. Blood, quoted by James (*APM*, 1312).
12. Blood, quoted by James (*APM* 1303). Blood's quote is from the same

stanza of Shelley's poem *Adonais* as James's earlier quoted passage. The whole stanza is as follows:

> The One remains, the Many change and pass;
> Heaven's light for ever shines, Earth's shadows fly;
> Life, like a dome of many-colored glass,
> Stains the white radiance of Eternity.

In an essay entitled "Timelessness and Romanticism," tracing the fundamental role of timelessness in writers from Blake to Proust, George Poulet relates the following precognitive encounter of Shelley, experienced while walking with a friend in Oxford, as he turned the corner of a lane:

> "The scene was," Shelley said, "a tame uninteresting assemblage of objects. . . . The effect which it produced on me was not such as could have been expected. I suddenly remembered to have seen that exact scene in some dream of long . . . " And there he stops suddenly, adding in a footnote some time afterwards: "Here I was obliged to leave off, overcome by thrilling horror." "I remember well," comments Mary Shelley, "his coming to me from writing it, pale and agitated, to seek refuge in conversation from the fearful emotions it excited." (Poulet, 1954, 3)

13. Nietzsche, 1901/1967, 181.
14. Blood, 1920, 82.
15. "Towards . . . the reality or unreality of novelty . . . the pragmatic difference between monism and pluralism seems to converge" (*SPP*, 1055).
16. See *SPP*, 1054.
17. See Blood, 1920, 182–203. Blood quotes Emerson's challenge to free will and concludes with this quote from Meister Eckhart: "All error and depravity come from God's creatures presuming to be or do something on their own account" (203). Blood's first book was entitled *Optimism: The Lesson of the Ages. A Compendium of Democratic Theology, Designed To Illustrate Necessities Whereby All Things Are As They Are, And To Reconcile The Discontents Of Men With The Perfect Love and Power of Ever-Present God* (see Blood, 1860).

18. Blood, 1920, 244. In James's first draft of his essay, he correctly identified Blood's Parmenidean manifesto—"There is no reason for what is not; but for what there is reason, that is and ever was" (Blood, quoted by James in *APM*, 1301)—as "timeless" (*EPh*, 308); but apparently James could not tolerate the dissonance with what he admitted to be his "*pro domo mea*" ("for my house") version of Blood (*APM*, 1296), and changed "timeless" to "vibrant" (*EPh*, 308).
19. Blood, in a letter to James (C9, 104).
20. Blood, 1920, 220.
21. Blood, quoted by Marks, 1953, 112.
22. Ibid. James affirmed as much when, in support of physchical research, he wrote: "Abstract considerations will not do in a year what the glimpse into a world of new phenomenal posibilities . . . will do in an instant" (C2, 499).
23. Ibid.
24. Xenos Clark, Blood's co-revelationist, quoted by James (*VRE*, 351n).
25. Myers, 1903a, 142.
26. Brown, 1996, 30.
27. Brown, 2010, 75.
28. James considered him "the most extraordinary person," capable of "formal perfection" but "of such pure abstraction that it is impossible for me to think of his thought as having any connection at all with reality" (C9, 304). How much reality had caught up with McTaggart's anti-time abstractions, the first published in 1908, the same year that Minkowski coined the concept space-time, is debatable. McTaggart claimed that two *fixed* series are necessary for the commonsense view of time—an "A" series of past present and future, and a "B" series of before and after. But, he argued, only the "B" series is fixed: what comes before, once it has come before, will have always come before; but what is past, present, and future keeps changing. Whether or not this argument is, as James felt, "pure abstraction" merely, it has generated a cottage industry of responses. These myriad responses, many of them starting points for their authors' own theories about time's reality, defy even summarization in a book not itself devoted to a logical analysis of time. But McTaggart's almost completely ignored preamble to his theory is well worth recalling here:

> It doubtless seems highly paradoxical to assert that Time is unreal, and that all statements which involve its reality are erroneous. Such an assertion involves a far greater departure from the natural position of mankind than is involved in the assertion of the unreality of Space or of the unreality of Matter. So decisive a breach with that natural position is not to be lightly accepted. And yet in all ages the belief in the unreality of time has proved singularly attractive. In the philosophy and religion of the East we find that this doctrine is of cardinal importance. And in the West, where philosophy and religion are less closely connected, we find that the same doctrine continually recurs, both among philosophers and among theologians. Theology never holds itself apart from mysticism for any long period, and almost all mysticism denies the reality of time. (McTaggart, 1908, 457)

29. McTaggart, 1908, 462–463. McTaggart called the permanent relation of terms the "C series" (463). While McTaggart's A and B series have received the most attention among philosophers of time, see Vorenkamp, 1995, for an acute analysis of McTaggart's C series as it relates to Dōgen.
30. Ibid., 462.
31. Ibid.
32. Aristotle's pupil Eudemus, *Phys*. fr. 27 = DK 58B34. Just one of several ancient sources from which Nietzsche, the Greek professor, acknowledges the Pythagoreans as conceiving such recurrence, "repeated down to the minutest detail . . . with graphic *exactitude*" (Nietzsche, 1990, 97). George Stack makes a compelling argument that Nietzsche might also have been influenced by his mentor Emerson, citing several passages of Emerson affirming the empowering embrace of Fate, as well as passages that had earned him the epithet "the circular philosopher," such as the "inexplicable" "continuity" of the "web of God," which is always "a circular power returning to itself" (Stack, 1992, 208).
33. Dōgen, quoted in Watts, 1957, 123.
34. Einstein, 1954, 141.
35. Lynne McTaggart's book *The Field* is a comprehensive survey of the

evidence that our manifest world is extracted from a submanifested electromagnetic field, known as the zero-point field or the quantum state vacuum. Occasionally, though, this master inference of an objectifiable matter/energy substrate (however subtle) underlying all other states assumes a full nondualism, consistent with James's fullest expression of nondualism. Of the Princeton psychical researcher Robert Jahn, for instance, she writes: "He kicked around the most radical idea . . . there may be no distinction between mental and the physical. There might be only one—the Field" (McTaggart, 2002, 121).

36. Parmenides, Fragment 3, translated by the author. This fragment, together with his "all together one, continuous" fragment 8:15, emphasizes a monism of content but is neutral (*pace* Sorabji, 1983, 107–108) in respect to any potential unfoldment, cyclical, or otherwise.
37. Before he had elaborated the monism of pure experience.
38. Krishnamurti in Luytens, 2003, 42.
39. Grof, 1992, 18.
40. Ibid., 2.
41. Grof, 1998, 30, 33.
42. Krichevskii, 1996, 66-69.
43. Mitchell, 2001.
44. Ibid.
45. Ibid.
46. Director of the Center for Particle Astrophysics at the DOE's Fermi National Accelerator Laboratory and professor of astronomy and astrophysics at the University of Chicago.
47. Chown, 2009.
48. Penrose, 2005, 920.
49. Hanegraaff, 1998, 141.
50. Braude, 1981, 54, 55.
51. Hogan, in Hubris, 2012.
52. One notable exception is Eugene Taylor's perceptive account in an interview by the French philosopher Thibaud Trochu (Trochu, 2008, 11). Forman, Barnard, Simon and Fontinell are others.
53. Bohm, 1980, 266. Like Jung's inspiration for synchronicity, Bohm's conversion to transcendent interconnectedness was inspired by a direct talk with Einstein. (Einstein invited Bohm for a talk after Bohm sent

him his classic textbook on quantum physics) (Jammer, 1999, 227–228).

54. Bohm, 1980, 212; emphasis added.
55. While physicists and even a prominent neuroscientist, Karl Pribram, have found the holographic paradigm central to their research, "Bohm took pains to point out that his holographic example was but a shadow of what he meant by the implicate order" (Peat, 1987, 260–261).
56. Blood, 1874, 35, 34.
57. Parmenides, Fragment 8, line 46, translated by the author.
58. Mourelatos, 2008, 126.
59. Perhaps the most inspired architect of James's time, Gaudí, held that "[t]he straight line belongs to Man. The curved line to God."
60. A recently concluded decade-long experiment at Imperial College of London discovered that "the electron differs from being perfectly round by less than 0.000000000000000000000000001 cm." (http://www3.imperial.ac.uk/newsandeventspggrp/imperialcollege/newssummary/news_26-5-2011-8-58-6). And, more recently, scientists at the University of Hawaii, able to measure the dimensions of the sun accurately for the first time, were "shocked" to find that "scaled to the size of a beachball," the diameters between its poles and at its equator differed less than the width of a human hair (http://www.guardian.co.uk/science/2012/aug/16/sun-perfect-sphere-nature).
61. "The infinite does not have, even potentially, the independent being which the finite has" (206b15-16).
62. Tubbs, 2008, 53.
63. Presumably more than forty, only nine of which have survived.
64. See Kingsley, 2003, 295, against Burnet, 1910, 323.
65. The colorful characters of the Achilles/tortoise race paradox are often used, as James does here, to illustrate another of Zeno's paradoxes, the half-stepping dichotomy paradox. Aristotle believed that these two paradoxes, were essentially making the same point.
66. Mazur, 2007, 219.
67. Schrödinger, 1954, 62.
68. This last lecture series, devoted to a more common sense view of reality, was sandwiched by his essays on nondualism before, and his mystical suggestion after.
69. Brown, 2010, 54. This dissolution of objective solidity is echoed by

Julian Barbour: "We think things persist in time because structures persist, and we mistake the structure for substance. But looking for enduring substance is like looking for time. It slips through your fingers" (1999, 49).

70. Tibetans weave the bardo revelation of discretely arising moments with the revelation of prophecy. See p. 90. For divination as an "inseparable part of traditional Tibetan life" see Roney-Dougal, 2013. One of the people responsible for the apparent fulfillment of their most renowned prophecy (see "the iron bird," p. 90), American Buddhist meditation teacher Joseph Goldstein, has also begun weaving the bardo revelation of discretely arising moments with moments out of time. Writing of the "critical place of understanding" in which "we begin to see with extraordinary clarity the momentary rise and fall of all phenomena," he likens the mind in this advanced meditative state to "a shining piece of crystal"; but a crystal, it seems, that has become holographied: "At this stage distant memories may arise in the mind and, for some people, even recollections of past lives" (Goldstein, 2002, 163–164).
71. Stcherbatsky, 1930/1962, 80.
72. See Gale, 2005, 221.
73. And earned him the Nobel Prize more than a decade later. According to the astrophysicist John Gribbin, this very sentence "marks the true beginning of the quantum revolution" (Gribbin, 2002, 511).
74. Barbour, 1999, 187.
75. de Broglie, who first identified the wave properties of matter, also linked Zeno's arrow paradox with the "element of discontinuity" introduced into the Universe by the "quantum of action" (de Broglie, 1939, 255).
76. Field, 1981, 270.
77. Parmenides, Fragment 6, lines 4–6, translated by the author.
78. Reputed to have been a Pythagorean.
79. Xenophanes, in Lesher, 1992, 97.
80. Xenophanes, quoted by Hippolytus, in Guthrie, 1979, 377. Also quoted, with variations, by Diogenes Laertius, Theodoret, and others (ibid.). Scholars, though, disagree as to whether the idea originated with Xenophanes, or was later attributed to him by these ancient sources in order to align him more with Parmenides. See Lesher, 1992, 101–102.
81. Ibid. Compare Aristotle's "unmoved mover."

82. Ibid.
83. Not all scholars agree that Xenophanes saw the universe as a sphere. (But see, among others, Guthrie, Gilbert, and Cornford.)
84. Compare, too, here, the God that Nietzsche didn't kill, the God "around" whom "everything becomes—what? Perhaps 'world'?" Nietzsche, 1886/1989, 90); God as "a center of power from which the world, so to speak, radiates" (Stambaugh, 1972, 100).
85. Sprigge, 1983, 259.
86. See Kingsley, 1999, for the Eastern roots of Eleatic spirituality.
87. Vivekananda, quoted by James (*P*, 553).
88. See Chattopadhyaya, 1999, 360–361, for an extended analysis of the evidence.
89. Vivekananda, 1970–73, V, 271. This precise circle metaphor, of obscure origin, though frequently referred to Empedocles, first appeared in the twelfth-century *Book of the Twenty-Four Philosophers*.
90. Vivekananda, 1970–73, II, 381.
91. James, Sr., 1885, 96–97.
92. This functional division of consciousness into a knowing and a known allows for range of emphasis, from an absorption in the known (or many knowns at once) on the circumference that obscures the knowing function, to an absorption into the knowing of the centerpoint. The latter would provide what Forman criticizes as a missing element of James's suggestion, insofar as it would account for "mystical experiences that are apparently devoid of objective content (for instance the *nirvikalpa samadhi* of the Hindu *yogi*)" (Forman, 1997, 181).
93. Nietzsche, 1901/1967, 35.
94. Nietzsche, 1887/2010, 45. "[F]alse introspection . . . believes in . . . a subject-substratum in which every act of thinking . . . has its origin" (Nietzsche, 1901/1967, 264).
95. The quoted phrase, Martin Buber's delineation of Nietzsche's inspired idea (Buber, 2001, 35), also applies to James's. For Nietzsche's wariness of mysticism see Nietzsche (1887/2010), 95–96. See Gutmann, 1954, 842, for Nietzsche's renowned Sils Maria experience as a "tremendous moment of mystic experience"; also Nishitani, 1990, 59. For Nietzsche as mystic, see Stambaugh, 1994. For Nietzsche as "above all, a mystic" see Coomaraswamy, 1924, 115, and Bataille's strong conviction that

without experiencing a Zarathustra-like "dazzling dissolution into totality" Nietzsche's "words are just a maze of contradictions" (Bataille, 1945/2004, xxviii). Whereas James's mystical experiences occurred late in life, and he described them in considerable detail, but made only a brief suggestion of how they would radically reconfigure reality if their deepest implications proved true, Nietzsche's Zarathustran "experiences" occurred early, and were "share[d] with nobody" (Nietzsche, 1969, 254), but he repeatedly expounded on what he saw as their implication.

96. Loeb, in Gemes & Richardson, 2013, 645. Nietzsche himself was concerned that hiding the ultimate, experiential source of his insight may have contributed to rendering it "unintelligible" (Nietzsche, 1969, 254).
97. Stambaugh, 1972, 103. Fink, 2003, 80.
98. Nietzsche, 1886/1989, 68. "The ideal of the most high-spirited, alive, and world-affirming human being who has not only come to terms and learned to get along with whatever was and is, but who wants to have *just what was and is* repeated into all eternity, shouting insatiably *da capo,* not only to himself but to the whole play and spectacle, and not only to a spectacle but at bottom to Him who needs precisely this spectacle—and who makes it necessary: because again and again he needs himself—and makes himself necessary—What? And this wouldn't be—*circulus vitiosus deus?*" (ibid.).
99. Believed to have been one of the sources that inspired Nietzsche to adopt "eternal recurrence" (see Brobjer, 2008, 121).
100. Nietzsche, 1901/1967, 564.
101. See Goldstein, 1902.
102. Ibid., 221.
103. Eliade, 1955, 146.
104. Nietzsche, 1882/2010, 273.
105. Halevy, 1911, 349, which James would have read in the original French. Halevy also conflates Nietzsche's mystical inception of the idea with Nietzsche's *truly* naive belief that scientific materialism could support it (Halevy, 1911, 231).
106. Halevy, 1944, 269.
107. Fontinell, 1986, 178. See, too, Poulet, 1967, 159.

108. Nietzsche, 1901/1967, 536.
109. Ibid., 536, 550.
110. Ibid., 544.
111. Nietzsche, 1901/1967, 544. Disregarding his proto-Nazi sister's anachronous placement of the 1884 aphorism (in which he proclaims for many "the right to erase themselves") immediately after the 1885 aphorism depicting eternal recurrence as a "hammer," which "breaks and removes degenerate and decaying races" (ibid.), and reading instead "the right to erase themselves" with Klossowski's overall interpretation of eternal recurrence as the self "emptied", "a series of infinite vibrations of being" Klossowski, 1998, 66, (72).
112. Nietzsche, 1901/1967, 513. Nietzsche's "characterizations of Jesus as lovingly accepting of all things and of Caesar as the embodiment of the conquering will mean that the fusion of the two in one, Caesar with the soul of Christ, involves a will which conquers by reaching out to infinity, by extending its willing forever, and which at the same time merely wills the infinite repetition—and thus, its own loving acceptance—of everything most glorious, most painful, or most boring" (Austin, 1986, 146). Without such a construal of the ultimate will to power, Nietzsche's foundational "love of the whole, and . . . love of everything with everything within the whole, remains a mystery wrapped in a riddle" (Desmond, 2008, 235). And we are left with the all-too-familiar caricature of Nietzsche's "transvaluation of all values" such as Paul Carus's "appeals to all wild impulses and a clamour for the right of self-assertion" (Carus, 1907, 230).
113. However much James preferred both Emerson and Whitman "suitably shorn" of their monism (Oliver, 3). For James's attempts with Emerson, see endnote 301n5; for Whitman, see James (*P*, 606–610).
114. According to Lou Andreas-Salomé (Löwith, 1997, 128).
115. Whitman, 1882a/2001, 485, 331.
116. Ibid., 199.
117. Compare Harry Hunt's "pragmatic effect" of the belief in eternal recurrence: "an in-the-world version of an attunement to and acceptance of the unfolding here and now" (Hunt, 2012, 130).
118. Such a mystical vision coheres with what Bohm identified as "the best way to look at physics": "an abstract representation which allows you

to keep track of the order of succession" (Bohm, 1992/1994, 232–233). It also coheres with Nietzsche's assertion that science's attempt "to fathom the innermost essence of things with the aid of causality" is an "illusory notion" (Nietzsche, 1871/2010, 132).

119. Nietzsche, 1901/1967, 265.
120. Quoting Tennyson.
121. See C9, 538–539.
122. Nietzsche, 1901/1967, 546. That Nietzsche's monistic vision elevated his consciousness, as attested by one of the most remarkable sustained outpourings of writing ever known, without, it seems, elevating his entire being, as did the monistic vision of Vivekananda and Whitman, is affirmed by Lou Andreas-Salomé:

> The quintessence of the teaching of the return, the radiating apotheosis of life that Nietzsche afterward set forth, forms such a profound contrast with his own tortured perception of life that it charms us like an eerie mask. . . . Everything that Nietzsche thought, felt, lived after the genesis of his idea of the return, arises from this discord within himself, and moves between "cursing with gnashed teeth the demon of the eternity of life" and the expectation of that "tremendous moment" which gives one the strength to pronounce the words, "You are a god and never did I hear anything more divine." (Löwith, 1997, 197–198)

123. Nietzsche, 1882/2010, 8.
124. Not to be confused with James's caricature of a "mystical monism shutting its eyes on the concretes of life, for the sake of its abstract rapture" (C3, 99).
125. Nietzsche, 1901/1967, 536.
126. Nietzsche, 1901/1967, 330; 1980, Vol. 9, 502.
127. Nietzsche, 1901/1967, 330.
128. Nietzsche, 1883/1997, 263.
129. Nietzsche, 1871/2010, 141.
130. Even James's friend Schiller (who corrected the spelling of Nietzsche in James's manuscript of *Varieties*) neglected to mention eternal

recurrence in his extensive article on Nietzsche for the *Encyclopedia Britannica* (Schiller, 1911, 672). Kaufmann, by contrast, seeing eternal recurrence as the "climax to his whole philosophy," regards this disregard by "most interpreters of Nietzsche's thought" as "perilous" (Kaufmann, 1950, 307). Kaufmann locates the source of this disregard in Nietzsche's contradictory "dual vision" of eternal recurrence with his "overman" (ibid.). But the contradiction only applies to a fledgling will-to-power "strong-man" overman, not the wise overman of the "all-comprehensive synthesis," who "submits to the circularity of all that happens" (Löwith, 1997, 101). Such distorted over-regard of the will to power (as in Carus's caricature) is, as Laurence Lampert noted, "one of the greatest single causes of the misinterpretation of Nietzsche's teaching" insofar as Nietzsche's "clearly definitive teaching on eternal return" is "rendered obsolete" by his "clearly provisional teaching on the superman" (Lampert, 1986, 258).

131. For the resurgence of the terror of history in the Nuclear Age, what Eliade called our "terrorized epoch" "par excellence," see Eliade, 1989b, 129–130 and 2010, 104.

132. Eliade, 1969, 99.

APPENDIX

1. Myers, 1903a, 402–405.

BIBLIOGRAPHY

Abram, David. (1997). *The Spell of the Sensuous: Perception and Language in a More-Than-Human World.* New York: Vintage.

Allen, Gay Wilson. (1975). *The New Walt Whitman Handbook.* New York: New York University Press.

Ashe, Geoffrey. (1977). *Encyclopedia of Prophecy.* Santa Barbara: ABC-CLIO.

Ashtavakra. (uncertain dates/1940). *Ashtavakra Samhita* (also known as *Ashtavakra Gita*). Translated by Swami Nityaswarupananda. Himalayas, India: Advaita Ashrama.

Atwood, Margaret. (1989). *Cat's Eye.* New York: Bantam Books.

Austin, James H. (1998). *Zen and the Brain.* Cambridge: MIT Press.

Austin, Scott. (1986). *Parmenides: Being, Bounds, and Logic.* New Haven: Yale University Press.

Aziz, Robert. (1990). C.G. *Jung's Psychology of Religion and Synchronicity.* Albany: State University of New York Press.

Baars, Bernard J., & Gage, Nicole M. (2010). *Cognition, Brain, and Consciousness: Introduction to Cognitive Neuroscience.* Oxford: Academic Press.

Bach, Richard. (1984). *The Bridge Across Forever.* New York: William Morrow.

Bair, Deidre. (2003). *Jung.* Boston: Little, Brown.

Bannerjee, Devendra. (1954). "The Indian Origin of Nietzsche's Theory of the Eternal Return." *German Life and Letters,* 7(3), 161–169.

Barbour, Julian. (1999). *The End of Time: The Next Revolution in Physics.* Oxford: Oxford University Press.

Barbour, Julian. (2009). "The Nature of Time," http://arxiv.org/PS_cache/arxiv/pdf/0903/0903.3489v1.pdf, as of October 2009.

Barker, Francis. (1995). *The Tremulous Private Body: Essays on Subjection.* Ann Arbor: University of Michigan Press.

Barnard, G. William. (1997). *Exploring Unseen Worlds: William James and the Philosophy of Mysticism.* Albany: State University of New York Press).

Barnes, Jonathan. (1983). *The Presocratic Philosophers.* London: Routledge.

Barrington, Mary, Stevenson, Ian, & Weaver, Zofia. (2005). *A World in a Grain of Sand: The Clairvoyance of Stefan Ossowiecki.* Jefferson, NC: McFarland.

Bataille, Georges. (1945/2004). *On Nietzsche.* Translated by Bruce Boone. London: Continuum.

Bem, Daryl. (2011). *Journal of Personality and Social Psychology, 100,* 407–425.

Benoit, Hubert. (1955/1990). *Zen and the Psychology of Transformation.* Rochester, VT: Inner Traditions International.

Bergson, Henri. (1910). *Time and Free Will.* New York: The MacMillan Company.

Bergson, Henri. (1911). *Creative Evolution.* Translated by Arthur Mitchell. New York: Henry Holt.

Bierman, Dick. (2002). *Tucson 2002: Toward a Science of Consciousness: Conference Research Abstracts.* Devon, UK: *Journal of Consciousness Studies.*

Bierman, Dick. (As of Spring 2002). http://www.psy.uva.nl/resedu/pn/pubs/bierman/1998/tucson/tucson3.html.

Bigelow, William Sturgis. (1908). *Buddhism and Immortality.* Boston: Houghton, Mifflin.

Bjork, Daniel W. (1983). *The Compromised Scientist: William James in the Development of American Psychology.* New York: Columbia University Press.

Blavatsky, H. P. (1888/2009). *The Secret Doctrine.* New York: Jeremy P. Tarcher.

Blood, Benjamin Paul. (1860). *Optimism.* Boston: Bela Marsh.

Blood, Benjamin Paul. (1874). *The Anæsthetic Revelation and the Gist of Philosophy.* Amsterdam, New York: Published by the Author; digitalized by Harvard University. Full text available on Google Book Search.

Blood, Benjamin Paul. (1920). *Pluriverse*. Boston: Marshall Jones Company.

Blum, Deborah. (2006). *Ghost Hunters: William James and the Search for Scientific Proof of Life after Death*. New York: Penguin.

Bohm, David. (1980). *Wholeness and the Implicate Order*. London: Routledge.

Bohm, David. (1992/1994). *Thought as a System*. New York: Routledge.

Bohm, David, & Hiley, Basil. (1993). *The Undivided Universe*. London: Routledge.

Boswell, Harriet. (1969). *Master Guide to Psychism*. New York: Lancer.

Bradley, F. H. (1883/1994). "The Principles of Logic." In Allard, J., & Stock G., (Eds.), *Writings on Logic and Metaphysics*. Oxford: Oxford University Press.

Bradley, F. H. (1886). "Is There Any Special Activity of Attention?" *Mind*, 43, 305–323.

Bradley, F. H. (1893/1968). *Appearance and Reality*. Oxford: Clarendon Press.

Bradley, F. H. (1914). *Essays on Truth and Reality*. Oxford: Clarendon Press.

Bradley, F. H. (1995). *Writings on Logic and Metaphysics*. Oxford: Clarendon Press.

Braude, Stephen. (1981). "The Holographic Analysis of Near-Death Experiences: The Perpetuation of Some Deep Mistakes," *Essence, 5*(1), 53–63.

Braude, Stephen E. (2014). *Crimes of Reason: On Mind, Nature, and the Paranormal*. Lanham, Md.: Rowman & Littlefield.

Brian, Denis. (1976). *Jeane Dixon: The Witnesses*. New York: Doubleday.

Brian, Denis. (1996). *Einstein: A Life*. New York: Wiley.

Bricklin, Jonathan. (2006). "Switched-Off Consciousness: Clarifying What It Cannot Mean," *Journal of Consciousness Studies, 13*(4), 16–17.

Bricklin, Jonathan. (2007). *Sciousness*. Guilford, CT: Eirini Press.

Bricklin, Mark. (1977). *The Practical Encyclopedia of Natural Healing*. Emmaus, PA: Rodale Press.

Broad, William J. (2006). *The Oracle: The Lost Secrets and Hidden Messages of Ancient Delphi*. New York: Penguin.

Brobjer, Thomas H. (2008). *Nietzsche's Philosophical Context: An Intellectual Biography*. Chicago: University of Illinois Press.

Broglie, Louis de. (1939). *Matter and Light in the New Physics*. Translated by W. H. Johnson. New York: Dover.

Brooks, Van Wyck. (1933). *The Ordeal of Mark Twain*. New York: E. P. Dutton.

Brown, Jason W. (1977). *Mind, Brain, and Consciousness: The Neuropsychology of Cognition*. New York: Academic Press.

Brown, Jason W. (1996). *Time, Will, and Mental Process*. New York: Plenum.

Brown, Jason W. (2010). *Neuropsychological Foundations of Conscious Experience*. Belgium: Les Éditions Chromatika.

Buber, Martin. (2001). *Meetings: Autobiographical Fragments*. London: Routledge.

Bucke, Richard. (1901/1969). *Cosmic Consciousness*. New York: E. P. Dutton.

Buckley, J. R. (1978). *Second Century Orthodoxy*. Cornwall, UK.

Burkhardt, Frederick, (Ed.). (1981). *The Works of William James: The Principles of Psychology*, Vol. III. Cambridge: Harvard University Press.

Burnet, John. (1910). *Early Greek Philosophy*. Cambridge: Andover-Harvard Theological Library.

Cahill, Thomas. (1998). *The Gifts of the Jews*. New York: Doubleday.

Capek, Milic. (1951). "The Doctrine of Necessity Re-Examined," *The Review of Metaphysics, 5*(1), 11–54.

Capek, Milic. (1960). "The Theory of Eternal Recurrence in Modern Philosophy of Science, with Special Reference to C.S. Peirce," *The Journal of Philosophy, 57* (9), 289–296.

Capek, Milic. (1987). "Review of Time and Reality in American Philosophy by Bertrand P. Helm," *Transactions of the Charles S. Peirce Society, 23*(4) (Fall), 579–597.

Capra, Fritjof. (1984). *The Tao of Physics*. New York: Bantam.

Carter, Rita. (2000). *Mapping the Mind*. Berkeley: University of California Press.

Carus, Carl Gustav. (1846/1989). *Psyche*. Dallas: Spring Publications.

Carus, Paul. (1907). "Friedrich Nietzsche," *The Monist, 17*(2), 230–251.

Carus, Paul. (1909). *The Open Court*, Vol. XXIII. Chicago: The Open Court Publishing Co.

Casteneda, Carlos. (1971). *A Separate Reality*. New York: Simon & Schuster.

Chattopadhyaya, Rajagopal. (1999). *Swami Vivekananda in India: A Corrective Biography*. Delhi: Motilal Banarsidass.

Chown, Marcus. (2009). "Our World May Be a Giant Hologram," *New Scientist, 2691* (January).

Cleary, Thomas. (2001). *Classics of Buddhism and Zen*, Vol. 4. Boston: Shambhala.

Close, Frank, Marten, Michael, & Sutton, Christine. (1987). *The Particle Explosion*. New York: Oxford University Press.

Cobb Jr., John, & Griffin, David R. (1977). *Mind in Nature: The Interface of Science and Philosophy*. Washington, DC: University of America Press.

Coomaraswamy, Ananda K. (1924/1985). *The Dance of Siva*. Mineola, NY: Dover.

Coomaraswamy, Ananda K. (1947/2001). *Time and Eternity*. New Delhi: Munshiram Manoharlal Publishers.

Cooper, Linn, & Erickson, Milton. (1959). *Time Distortion in Hypnosis*. Wales: Crown House Publishing.

Craig, William Lane. (2001). *Time and Eternity*. Wheaton, IL: Crossway Books.

Crick, Francis, & Koch, Cristof. (2003). "A Framework for Consciousness," *Nature Neuroscience*, 6(2), 119–126.

Croce, Paul Jerome. (1995). *Science and Religion in the Era of William James: Eclipse of Certainty, 1820–1880*. Chapel Hill: The University of North Carolina Press.

Dalai Lama 14. (1991). *Freedom in Exile*. New York: Harper Collins.

Damasio, Antonio R. (1994). *Descartes' Error*. New York: Grosset/Putnam.

Das, Lama Surya. (1998). *Awakening the Buddha Within: Tibetan Wisdom for the Western World*. New York: Doubleday.

Davidson, Thomas. (1870). "Parmenides," *The Journal of Speculative Philosophy* 4(1), 1–16.

Davies, Paul. (1992). *The Mind of God*. New York: Simon & Schuster.

Davies, Paul. (1996). *About Time*. New York: Simon & Schuster.

Davis, Andrew Jackson. (1860). *The Great Harmonia: Being a Progressive Revelation of the Eternal Principles Which Inspire Mind and Govern Matter*, Vol. 5. New York: A. J. Davis.

Deaver, Michael K. (2001). *A Different Drummer: My Thirty Years with Ronald Reagan*. New York: Harper Collins.

Dembo, L. S. (1972). *The Contemporary Writer: Interviews with Sixteen Novelists and Poets*. Madison: University of Wisconsin Press.

Desmond, William. (2008). *God and the Between*. Oxford: Blackwell.

Dewey, John. (1998). *The Essential Dewey*, Vol. I. Bloomington: Indiana University Press.

Dhiravamsa, Vichitir Ratna. (1989). *The Way of Non-Attachment*. Great Britain: Crucible/Aquarian Press.

Dodds, E. R. (1973). *The Ancient Concept of Progress and Other Essays on Greek Literature and Belief*. New York: Oxford University Press.

Dossey, Larry. (2009). *The Power of Premonitions*. New York: Dutton.

Double, Richard. (1991). *The Non-Reality of Free Will*. New York: Oxford University Press.

Dowden, Bruce. (2007). "Time." *The Internet Encyclopedia of Philosophy*, http://www.iep.utm.edu/t/time.html, as of March 26, 2008.

Ducasse, C. J. (1951). *Nature, Mind, and Death*. LaSalle, IL: Open Court.

Dumoulin, Heinrich. (2005). *Zen Buddhism: A History, Vol. 2: Japan*. Translated by James Heisig and Paul Knitter. Bloomington, IN: World Wisdom.

Dunne, J. W. (1927). *An Experiment With Time*. London: Faber & Faber.

Dürckheim, Karlfried Graf. (1989). *Hara: The Vital Centre of Man*. London: Unwin Hyman.

Eckhart, Meister. (13th cy./1941). *Meister Eckhart: A Modern Translation*. Translated by Raymond Blakney. New York: Harper & Row.

Eddy, Mary Baker. (1906). *Science and Health*. Boston: A. V. Stewart.

Einstein, Albert. (1954). *Ideas and Opinions*. New York: Crown.

Einstein, Albert. (1961). *Relativity*. New York: Random House.

Eliade, Mircea. (1955). *The Myth of Eternal Return*. Princeton: Princeton University Press.

Eliade, Mircea. (1969). *Yoga: Immortality and Freedom*. Princeton: Princeton University Press.

Eliade, Mircea. (1989a). *Journal II, 1957–1969*. Chicago: University of Chicago Press.

Eliade, Mircea. (1989b). *Journal III, 1970–1978*. Chicago: University of Chicago Press.

Eliade, Mircea. (2010). *The Portugal Journal*. Albany: State University of New York Press.

Emerson, Ralph Waldo. (1903–04). *The Complete Works of Ralph Waldo Emerson*, Vol. I, II, VIII. Boston and New York: Houghton Mifflin.

Evans, Richard I. (1976). *Jung on Elementary Psychology*. New York: E. P. Dutton.

Feinstein, Howard M. (1986). *Becoming William James*. Ithaca: Cornell University Press.

Ferguson, Robert. (1989). *Esp For Everyone*. New York: St. Martin's Press.

Feuerstein, Georg. (1989). *Yoga: The Technology of Ecstasy*. Los Angeles: Jeremy Tarcher.

Feuerstein, Georg. (1996). *The Philosophy of Classical Yoga*. Rochester, VT.

Feynman, Richard. (2013). *The Feynman Lectures on Physics*. New York: Basic Books.

Field, Richard. (1981). "William James and the Epochal Theory of Time," *Process Studies, 13*(4), 260–274.

Fields, Rick. (1981). *How the Swans Came to the Lake: A Narrative History of Buddhism in America*. Boston: Shambhala.

Fink, Eugen. (2003). *Nietzsche's Philosophy*. London: Continuum.

Fischer-Schreiber, Ingrid, Ehrhard, Franz-Karl, Friedrichs, Kurt, & Diener, Michael S. (1994). *An Encyclopedia of Eastern Philosophy and Religion*. Boston: Shambhala.

Flournoy, Theodore. (1917). *The Philosophy of William James*. Translated by Henry Holt and Willam James Jr. New York: Henry Holt.

Floyd, Keith. (1974). "Of Time and Mind: From Paradox to Paradigm." In White, John, (Ed.), *Frontiers of Consciousness: The Meeting Ground Between Inner and Outer Reality*. New York: Julian Press.

Folger, Tim, & Weiner, Jonathan. (2005). *The Best American Science and Nature Writing*. New York: Houghton Mifflin.

Fontinell, Eugene. (1986). *Self, God, and Immortality*. Philadelphia: Temple University Press.

Forbes, Winslow. (1866). *Obscure Diseases of the Mind*. Philadelphia: Henry C. Lea.

Forman, Robert K. C. (1997). *The Innate Capacity: Mysticism, Psychology, and Philosophy*. New York: Oxford University Press.

Fort, Andrew. (1984). "The Concept of Saksin in Advaita Vedanta," *Journal of Indian Philosophy, 12*, 277–290.

Fraassen, Bas C. van. (1962). "Capek on Eternal Recurrence." *Journal of Philosophy* 59 (14), 371–375.

Freeman, Anthony. (2003). *Consciousness: A Guide to the Debates*. Oxford: ABC-CLIO.

Freud, Sigmund. (1916/1977). *Introductory Lectures on Psychoanalysis*. New York: W. W. Norton.

Freud, Sigmund. (1964). *The Standard Edition of the Complete Psychological Works of Sigmund Freud, XXIII*. London: Hogarth Press.

Gale, Richard. (2005). *The Philosophy of William James: An Introduction*. Cambridge: Cambridge University Press.

Garbe, Richard. (1897). *The Philosophy of Ancient India*. Chicago: Open Court.

Gardner, Martin. (2004). *Are Universes Thicker Than Blackberries?: Discourses on Godel, Magic Hexagrams, Little Red Riding Hood, and Other Mathematical and Pseudoscientific Topics*. New York: W. W. Norton.

Gefter, Amanda. (2008). "Is Time an Illusion?" *New Scientist, 2639* (January).

Gellman, Yehuda I. (2009). http://www.myjewishlearning.com/beliefs/Theology/Free_Will/Responses/Medieval/Hasidism.shtml; as of Spring 2009.

Gemes, Ken, & Richardson, John. *The Oxford Handbook of Nietzsche*. New York: Oxford University Press, 2013.

Giles, James. (1993). "The No-Self Theory: Hume, Buddhism, and Personal Identity," *Philosophy East and West*, 43(2) (April), 195–200.

Gillman, Susan Kay. (1989). *Dark Twins: Imposture and Identity in Mark Twain's America*. Chicago: University of Chicago Press.

Glieck, James. (1988). *Chaos*. New York: Penguin.

Goldberg, Bruce. (1982). *Past Lives, Future Lives*. New York: Ballantine Books.

Goldstein, Joseph. (2002). *One Dharma: The Emerging Western Buddhism*. New York: Harper Collins.

Goldstein, Julius. (1902). "The Keynote to the Work of Nietzsche," *Mind*, 42(11), 216–226.

Golomb, Jacob, Santaniello, Weaver, Lehrer, Ronald L. (1999). *Nietzsche and Depth Psychology*. Albany: State University of New York Press.

Greene, Liz. (1989). *The Astrology of Fate*. York Beach, ME: Samuel Weiser.

Gregory, Richard L., (Ed.). (1987). *The Oxford Companion to the Mind*. New York: Oxford University Press.

Gribbin, John. (2002). *The Scientists: A History of Science Told Through the Lives of Its Greatest Inventors*. New York: Random House.

Griffin, David Ray. (1997). *Parapsychology, Philosophy, and Spirituality*. Albany: State University of New York Press.

Grinberg-Zylerbaum, J. & Ramos, J. (1987). *International Journal of Neuroscience, 36*, 41.

Grof, Stanislav. (1990). *The Holotropic Mind*. San Francisco: Harper.

Grof, Stanislav. (1992). *The Psychology of the Future*. San Francisco: Harper.

Grof, Stanislav. (1998). *The Cosmic Game: Explorations of the Frontiers of Human Consciousness*. Albany: State University of New York Press.

Guénon, René. (1991). *The Great Triad*. Translated by Peter Kingsley. Cambridge: Quinta Essentia.

Guezlo, Allen. (1999). *Abraham Lincoln: Redeemer President*. Grand Rapids: Eerdmans.

Guiley, Rosemary. (1991). *Harper Encyclopedia of Mystical and Paranornal Experience*. San Francisco: Harper's.

Gupta, Bina. (1998). *The Disinterested Witness: A Fragment of Advaita Vedanta Phenomenology*. Evanston: Northwestern University Press.

Gusnard, Debra, Akbudak, Erbil, Shulman, Gordon, & Raichle, Marcus. (2001). "Medial Prefrontal Cortex and Self-Referential Mental Activity: Relation to a Default Mode of Brain Function," *Proceedings of the National Academy of Sciences USA*, 98(7), 4259–4264.

Guthrie, W. K. C. (1979). *The Earlier Pre-Socratics and the Pythagoreans*. Cambridge: Cambridge University Press.

Gutmann, James. (1954). "The 'Tremendous Moment' of Nietzsche's Vision," *The Journal of Philosophy, 51*(25), 837–842.

Haisch, Bernard. (2006). *The God Theory*. San Francisco: Weiser Books.

Halevy, Daniel. (1911). *The Life of Nietzsche*. Translated by J. M. Hone. London: T. Fisher Unwin.

Halevy, Daniel. (1944). *Nietzsche*. Paris: Grasset.

Hameroff, Stuart, & Penrose, Roger. (1996). "Conscious Events as Orchestrated Space-Time Selections," *Journal of Consciousness Studies*, 3(1), 36–53. Cited from Hameroff's Web site athttp://www.u.arizona.edu/~hameroff/hardfina.html.

Hanegraaff, Wouter J. (1998). *New Age Religion and Western Culture: Esotericism in the Mirror of Secular Thought*. Albany: State University of New York Press.

Harada-Roshi, Shodo. (1999). *One Drop Zendo Newsletter*, 47 (August).

Hartocollis, Peter. (1983). *Time and Timelessness*. New York: International Universities Press.

Hawking, Stephen. (1993). *Black Holes and Baby Universes and Other Essays*. New York: Bantam Books.

Hayes, Charles. (2000). *Tripping*. New York: Penguin.

Heidegger, Martin. (1961). *Nietzsche, Volume One and Two*. New York: Harper Collins.

Heil, John. (1978). "Traces of Things Past." *Philosophy of Science, 45*(1), 60–72.

Herrigel, Eugen. (1971). *Zen in the Art of Archery*. New York: Vintage/Random House.

Heschel, Abraham Joshua. (1996). *Prophetic Inspiration of the Prophets*. Hoboken: Ktav.

Hewitt, Frederic William. (1901). *Anaesthetics and Their Administration*. New York: Macmillan.

Hiley, Basil. (1983). "Quantum Physics Passes the Test." *New Scientist, 1339* (January).

Hinze, Oscar Marcel. (1979). *Tantra Vidya*. Delhi: Motilal Banarsidass Publishers.

Hodgson, Shadworth. (1865). *Time and Space: A Metaphysical Essay*. London: Longmans, Green.

Hodgson, Shadworth. (1878). *The Philosophy of Reflection*, Vol. I. London: Longmans, Green.

Hodgson, Shadworth. (1898). *The Metaphysic of Experience*, Vols. I–IV. London: Longmans, Green.

Hoffman, Andrew. (1997). *Inventing Mark Twain: The Lives of Samuel Langhorne Clemens*. New York: William Morris.

Hoffman, Banesh. (1973). "Relativity," in Weiner, Phillip, Ed., *Dictionary of the History of Ideas*. New York: Scribners.

Hoffman, Edward, & Schacter-Shalom, Zalman M. (2006). *The Way of Splendor: Jewish Mysticism and Modern Psychology*. New York: Rowman & Littlefield.

Horn, Jason Gary. (1996). *Mark Twain and William James: Crafting a Free Self*. Missouri: University of Missouri Press.

Horwitz, L. P., Arshansky, R. I., & Elizur, A. C. (1988). "On the Two Aspects of Time: The Distinction and Its Implications," *Foundations of Physics, 18*, 1159–1193.

Huang Po. (9th cy. AD/1958). *The Zen Teaching of Huang Po: On The Transmission of Mind.* Translated by John Blofeld. New York: Grove Weidenfeld.

Hubris, Joe. http://joehubris.com/node/77; as of Summer 2012.

Hudson, William Henry. (1893). *Idle Days in Patagonia.* New York: D. Appleton.

Hume, David. (1826). *The Philosophical Works of David Hume.* Edinburgh: Black & Tait.

Hunt, Harry T. (1995). *On the Nature of Consciousness: Cognitive, Phenomenological, and Transpersonal Perspectives.* New Haven: Yale University Press.

Hunter, Michael. (2001). "The Discovery of Second Sight in Late 17th-Century," *History Today, 51*(6).

Idel, Moshe. (1988). *Studies in Ecstatic Kabbalah.* Albany: State University of New York Press.

Inwood, Brad. (2001). *The Poem of Empedocles: A Text and Translation with an Introduction.* Toronto: University of Toronto.

Isaacson, Walter. (2004). *Einstein: His Life and Universe.* New York: Simon & Schuster.

Jahn, Robert G., & Dunne, Brenda J. (1987). *Margins of Reality: The Role of Consciousness in the Physical World.* San Diego: Harcourt Brace Jovanovich.

James Sr., Henry. (1857/2006). "Emerson: 1904," *Atlantic Monthly, 298*(5).

James Sr., Henry. (1885). *The Literary Remains of the Late Henry James.* Boston: James R. Osgood.

James, William. (1890a). *The Principles of Psychology,* Vols. I–II. New York: Henry Holt.

James, William. (1890b/1984). "The Hidden Self." In *Essays in Psychology.* Cambridge: Harvard University Press.

James, William. (1892/1992). *Psychology: Briefer Course.* In *William James: Writings 1878–1899.* New York: Library of America.

James, William. (1894a/1992). "The Knowing of Things Together." In *William James: Writings 1878–1899.* New York: Library of America.

James, William. (1896/1986). "Address of the President before the Society for Psychical Research." In *The Works of William James: Essays in Psychical Research.* Cambridge: Harvard University Press.

James, William. (1897/1992). *The Will to Believe and Other Essays in Popular*

Philosophy. In *William James: Writings 1878–1899*. New York: Library of America.

James, William. (1898/1992). "Human Immortality." In *William James: Writings 1878–1899*. New York: Library of America.

James, William. (1899/1992). *Talks to Teachers on Psychology and to Students on Some of Life's Ideals*. In *William James: Writings 1878–1899*. New York: Library of America.

James, William. (1902/1987). *The Varieties of Religious Experience*. In *William James: Writings 1902–1910*. New York: Library of America.

James, William. (1904a/1987). "Does 'Consciousness' Exist?" In *William James: Writings 1902–1910*. New York: Library of America.

James, William. (1904b/1987). "A World of Pure Experience." In *William James: Writings 1902–1910*. New York: Library of America.

James, William. (1905a/1987). "The Experience of Activity." In *William James: Writings 1902–1910*. New York: Library of America.

James, William. (1905b/1987). "The Place of Affectional Facts in a World of Pure Experience." In *William James: Writings 1902–1910*. New York: Library of America.

James, William. (1905c/2005). "The Notion of Consciousness." Translated by Jonathan Bricklin. In *Sciousness*, 89–111. Guilford, CT: Eirini Press.

James, William. (1905d/1987). "How Two Minds Can Know One Thing." In *William James: Writings 1902–1910*. New York: Library of America.

James, William. (1907a/1986). "A Case of Clairvoyance." In *The Works of William James: Essays in Psychical Research*. Cambridge: Harvard University Press.

James, William. (1907b/1987). *Pragmatism: A New Name for Some Old Ways of Thinking*. In *William James: Writings 1902–1910*. New York: Library of America.

James, William. (1909/1978). *The Works of William James: A Pluralistic Universe*. Cambridge: Harvard University Press.

James, William. (1909a/1987). *The Meaning of Truth: A Sequel to Pragmatism*. In *William James: Writings 1902–1910*. New York: Library of America.

James, William. (1909b/1987). "The Confidences of a 'Psychical Researcher.'" In *William James: Writings 1902–1910*. New York: Library of America.

James, William. (1910a/1987). "A Suggestion about Mysticism." In *William James: Writings 1902–1910*. New York: Library of America.

James, William. (1910b/1987). "A Pluralistic Mystic." In *William James: Writings 1902–1910*. New York: Library of America.

James, William. (1911/1987). *Some Problems of Philosophy: A Beginning of an Introduction to Philosophy*. In *William James: Writings 1902–1910*. New York: Library of America.

James, William. (1912/2003). *Essays in Radical Empiricism*. Mineola, NY: Dover.

James, William. (1920). *The Letters of William James*, Vols. I-II. Boston: The Atlantic Monthly Press.

James, William. (1978). *The Works of William James: Essays in Philosophy*. Edited by Burkhardt, Frederick H., Bowers, Fredson, & Skrupskelis, Ignas K. Cambridge: Harvard University Press.

James, William. (1987). *The Works of William James: Essays, Comments, and Reviews*. Edited by Burkhardt, Frederick H., & Bowers, Fredson. Cambridge: Harvard University Press.

James, William. (1988a). *The Works of William James: Manuscripts, Essays and Notes*. Edited by Burkhardt, Frederick H., Bowers, Fredson, & Skrupskelis, Ignas K. Cambridge: Harvard University Press.

James, William. (1988b). *The Works of William James: Manuscript Lectures*. Cambridge: Harvard University Press.

James, William, & James, Henry. (1997). *Selected Letters*. Edited by Skrupskelis, Ignas, & Berkeley, Elizabeth M. Charlottesville: University of Virginia Press.

Jammer, Max. (1999). *Einstein and Religion: Physics and Theology*. Princeton: Princeton University Press.

Jaynes, Julian. (1976). *The Origin of Consciousness in the Breakdown of the Bicameral Mind*. Boston: Houghton Mifflin.

Jensen, Derrick. (1997). "The Plants Respond: An Interview with Cleve Backster," *The Sun, 259*, 4–9.

Jnaneshwar Maharaj. (13th cy./1979). *Amritanubhav*. Syda Foundation.

John, Da Free. (1980). *Scientific Proof of the Existence of God Will Soon Be Announced by the White House*. Middletown, CA: The Dawn Horse Press.

John, Da Free. (1983). *Easy Death*. Clearlake, CA: The Dawn Horse Press.

Joseph, Rhawn, (Ed.). (2002). *NeuroTheology: Brain, Science, Spirituality, Religious Experience*. San Jose: University of California Press.

Jung, C. G. (1950). *Psychology and Religion: West and East*. London: Routledge & Kegan Paul.

Jung, C. G. (1961). *Memories, Dreams, Reflections*. New York: Pantheon.

Jung, C. G. (1967). *Psychology and Religion*. New Haven: Yale University Press.

Jung, C. G. (1969). *The Structure and Dynamics of the Psyche*. Princeton: Princeton University Press.

Jung, C. G. (1973). *Synchronicity*. Princeton: Princeton University Press.

Jung, C. G. (1973b). *Psychological Reflections*. Princeton: Princeton University Press.

Jung, C. G. (1981). *Psychology and the Occult*. Princeton: Princeton University Press.

Jung, C. G. (1999). *The Essential Jung*. Princeton: Princeton University Press.

Jung, C. G. (2014). *Selected Letters of C.G. Jung, 1909–1961*. Princeton: Princeton University Press.

Kaku, Michio. (2004). *Einstein's Cosmos*. New York: W. W. Norton.

Kane, Robert, (Ed.). (2002). *The Oxford Handbook of Free Will*. New York: Oxford University Press.

Kant, Immanuel. (1787/1965). *Critique of Pure Reason*. New York: St. Martin's Press.

Kapleau, Philip. (1980). *The Three Pillars of Zen*. New York: Anchor Books.

Kaufmann, Walter. (1950). *Nietzsche: Philosopher, Psychologist, Antichrist*. Princeton: Princeton University Press.

Keane, Patrick J. (2013). "Mark Twain, Nietzsche, and Terrible Truths that Can Set Us Free," *Numero Cinq Magazine*, 4(5).

Keller, I., & Heckhausen, H. (1990). "Readiness potentials preceding spontaneous motor acts: voluntary vs. involuntary control," *Electroencephalography and Clinical Neurophysiology*, 76, 351–361.

Kelly, Edward F., Kelly, Emily Williams, Crabtree, Adam, Gauld, Alan, Grosso, Michael, & Greyson, Bruce. (2007). *Irreducible Mind*. Lanham, MD: Rowman & Littlefield.

Kennedy, J. B. (2003). *Space, Time and Einstein*. Montreal: McGill-Queen's University Press.

Kingsley, Peter. (1999). *In the Dark Places of Wisdom*. San Francisco: Golden Sufi Press.

Kingsley, Peter. (2003). *Reality*. Inverness: Golden Sufi Press.

Kirkpatrick, Sidney D. (2001). *Edgar Cayce: An American Prophet*. New York: Penguin.

Klein, Ed. (1990). "Interview with Ronald Reagan," *Parade Magazine* (August 12).

Klossowski, Pierre. (1998). *Nietzsche and the Vicious Circle*. Chicago: University of Chicago Press.

Koestler, Arthur, & Smythies, J. R., (Eds.). (1971). *Beyond Reductionism: New Perspectives in the Life Sciences*. Boston: Beacon Press.

Krichevskii, S. V. (1996). "Extraordinary Fantastic States/Dreams of the Astronauts in Near-Earth Orbit: A New Cosmic Phenomenon," *Sozn. Fiz Real, 1*(4), 66–69.

Krippner, Stanley, Bogzaran, André, & de Carvalho, Pércia. (2002). *Extraordinary Dreams and How to Work With Them*. Albany: State University of New York Press.

Krishnamurti, Jiddu. (1954). *The First and Last Freedom*. New York: Harper & Row.

Krishnamurti, Jiddu. (1979). *The Wholeness of Life*. New York: Harper & Row.

Laberge, Stephen. (2008). http://www.futurehi.net/docs/Laberge_Waking-Dreamer.html; as of January 2008.

Lamon, Ward Hill. (1911). *Recollections of Abraham Lincoln*. Cambridge: The University Press.

Lampert, Laurence. (1986). *Nietzsche's Teaching*. New Haven: Yale University Press.

Lancaster, Brian. (1991). *Mind, Brain, and Human Potential*. Rockport MA: Element Inc.

Langer, Suzanne. (1962). *Philosophical Sketches*. New York: New American Library.

Lao Tzu. (1972). *The Way of Life According to Lao Tzu*. Translated by Witter Bynner. New York: Perigee/Putnam.

Leadbeater, C. W. (1968). *Clairvoyance*. Madras, India: The Theosophical Publishing House.

Ledoux, Joseph. (2002). *Synaptic Self: How Our Brains Become Who We Are.* New York: Viking Press.

LeShan, Lawrence. (1974). *The Medium, The Mystic, and The Physicist.* New York: Arkana/Penguin.

LeShan, Lawrence. (2009). *A New Science of the Paranormal: The Promise of Psychical Research.* Wheaton, IL: Quest Books.

Lesher, J. H. (1992). *Xenophanes of Colophon.* Toronto: University of Toronto Press.

Lessing, Doris. (1965). *Landlocked.* London: MacGibbon & Kee.

Libet, Benjamin. (1983). "Time of Conscious Intention to Act in Relation to Onset of Cerebral Activity (Readiness Potential)," *Brain, 106,* 623–642.

Libet, Benjamin. (1985). "Unconscious Cerebral Initiative and the Role of Conscious Will in Voluntary Action," *The Behavioral and Brain Sciences, 8,* 529–566.

Libet, Benjamin, Freeman, Anthony, & Sutherland, Keith. (1999). *The Volitional Brain: Towards a Neuroscience of Free Will.* Exeter, UK: Imprint Academic.

Liu, X., Ramirez, S., Pang, P.T., Puryear, C.B., Govindarajan, A., Deisseroth, K., and Tonegawa, S., "Optogenetic stimulation of a hippocampal engram activates fear memory recall," *Nature,* 484 (7394), 381–385.

Lodge, Oliver. (1891/1892). *Report of the Sixty-First meeting of the British Association for the Advancement of Science, Held at Cardiff in August 1891.* London: printed by Spottewodde and Co.

Lodge, Oliver. (1900). *The Survival of Man: A Study in Unrecognized Human Faculty.* New York: George H. Doran Company.

Lommel, Pim van, et al. (2001). "Near Death Experience in Survivors of Cardiac Arrest: A Prospective Study in the Netherlands," *The Lancet, 358* (December 15), 2039–2045.

Lommel, Pim van. (2010). *Consciousness Beyond Life: The Science of the Near-Death Experience.* New York: Harper One.

Löwith Karl. (1997). *Nietzsche's Philosophy of the Eternal Recurrence of the Same.* Translated by J. Harvey Lomax. Berkeley: University of California Press.

Loy, David. (1998). *Non-duality: A Study in Comparative Philosophy.* Amherst, NY: Humanity Books.

Ludlow, Fitz Hugh. (1857). *The Hasheesh Eater: Being Passages from the Life of a Pythagorean*. New York: Harper & Brothers.

Luk, Charles. (1971). *Practical Buddhism*. London: Rider.

Lukacher, Ned. (1998). *Time Fetishes: The Secret History of Eternal Recurrence*. Durham: Duke University Press.

Luria, Alexander. (1973). *The Working Brain*. London: Penguin.

Luther, Martin. (1990). *Erasmus-Luther: Discourse on Free Will*. New York: Continuum.

Luytens, Mary. (2003). *The Life and Death of Krishnamurti*. Hampshire, UK: Krishnamurti Foundation Trust.

MacFarlane, Alan & Martin, Gerry. (2002). *Glass: A World History*. Chicago: University of Chicago Press.

Mach, Ernst. (1919). *The Science of Mechanics, a Critical and Historical Account of Its Development*. Chicago: Open Court.

MacMillan, Malcolm. (1991). *Freud Evaluated: The Completed Arc*. Amsterdam: Elsevier Science.

Maharshi, Sri Ramana. (1968). *Talks with Sri Ramana Maharshi*. Tiruvannamalai, India: T. N Venkataraman.

Mann, Richard. (1984). *The Light of Consciousness*. Albany: State University of New York Press.

Mann, Roderick. (1997). *Jung on Synchronicity and the Paranormal*. London: Routledge.

Marks, Robert W. (1953). *The Philosophic Faith of Benjamin Paul Blood: A Study of the Thought and Times of an American Mystic*. New York: New School For Social Research.

May, Rollo. (1969). *Love and Will*. New York: W. W. Norton.

Mayer, Elizabeth Lloyd. (2007). *Extraordinary Knowing*. New York: Bantam Books.

Mazur, Joseph. (2007). *The Motion Paradox: The 2,500-Year Old Puzzle Behind All the Mysteries of Time and Space*. New York: Dutton.

McTaggart, J. Ellis. (1908). "The Unreality of Time," *Mind, 17*(68) (October), 457–474.

McTaggart, Lynne. (2002). *The Field*. New York: Harper Collins.

Milarepa. (11th cy./1962). *The Hundred Thousand Songs of Milarepa, Vol. 1*. Translated by Garma C. C. Chang. Boston: Shambhala.

Mistry, Freny. (1981). *Nietzsche and Buddhism: Prolegomenon to a Comparative Study*. New York: Walter de Gruyter.

Mitchell, Edgar. (2001). "Space Flight as an Anticipatory Computing System." http://www.edmitchellapollo14.com/spaceflightasananticipatory.html; as of October, 2009.

Moller, Mark. (2008). "The Many and the One and the Problem of Two Minds Perceiving the Same Thing," *William James Studies, 3*(1). <http://williamjamesstudies.press.uiuc.edu/3.1/moller.html>.

Mossbridge, Julia, Tressoldi, Patrizio, & Utts, Jessica. (2012). "Predictive Physiological Anticipation Preceding Seemingly Unpredictable Stimuli: A Meta-Analysis," *Frontiers in Psychology, 3*.

Mourelatos, Alexander. (2008). *The Route of Parmenides*. Las Vegas: Parmenides Publishing.

Muktananda, Swami. (1978). *I am That: The Science of Hamsa from the Vijnana Bhairava*. South Fallsburg, NY: SYDA Foundation.

Müller-Laute, Wolfgang. (1971/1999). *Nietzsche: His Philosophy of Contradictions and the Contradictions of his Philosophy*. Translated by David J. Parent. Urbana: University of Illinois Press.

Myers, F. W. H. (1892). *Proceedings of the Society for Psychical Research*, Vol. 8. London: Kegan Paul, Trench, Trübner.

Myers, F. W. H. (1903a). *Human Personality and Its Survival of Bodily Death*, Vol. I. London: Longmans, Green.

Myers, F. W. H. (1903b). *Human Personality and Its Survival of Bodily Death*, Vol. II. London: Longmans, Green.

Myers, Gerald. (1986). *William James: His Life and Thought*. New Haven: Yale University Press.

Nadeau, Robert, & Kafatos, Minas C. (1999). *The Non-Local Universe: The New Physics and Matters of the Mind*. New York: Oxford University Press.

Nahin, Paul J. (1993/1999). *Time Machines*. New York: Springer-Verlag.

Nanamoli, Bhikkhu, & Bodhi, Bhikku. (1995). *The Middle Length Discourses of the Buddha: A Translation of the Majjhima Nikaya (Teachings of the Buddha)*. Somerville, MA: Wisdom Publications.

Natsoulas, Thomas. (2013). *Consciousness and Perceptual Awareness*. Cambridge: Cambridge University Press.

Needleman, Jacob. (1976). *A Sense of the Cosmos: The Encounter of Modern Science and Ancient Truth*. New York: Dutton.

Nehamas, Alexander. (1985). *Life as Literature*. Cambridge: Harvard University Press.

Newton, Isaac. (1687/2002). *Principia*. Philadelphia: Running Press.

Nicoll, Maurice. (1952/1976). *Living Time and the Integration of Life*. London: Watkins Publishing House.

Niemtschek, Franz. (1798/2006). *Mozart: The First Biography*. Translated by Helen Mautner. New York: Berghahn Books.

Nietzsche, Friedrich. (1871/2010). *The Birth of Tragedy and the Case of Wagner*. Translated and edited by Walter Kaufmann. New York: Random House.

Nietzsche, Friedrich. (1878/1996). *Human, All Too Human: A Book for Free Spirits*. Translated by R. J. Hollingdale. Cambridge: Cambridge University Press.

Nietzsche, Friedrich. (1881/1997). *Daybreak: Thoughts on the Prejudices of Morality*. Translated by R. J. Hollingdale. Cambridge: Cambridge University Press.

Nietzsche, Friedrich. (1882/2010). *The Gay Science: With a Prelude in Rhymes and an Appendix of Songs*. Translated and edited by Walter Kaufmann. New York: Random House.

Nietzsche, Friedrich. (1883/1997). *Thus Spoke Zarathustra*. Translated by Adrian del Caro. Cambridge: Cambridge University Press.

Nietzsche, Friedrich. (1886/1989). *Beyond Good & Evil: Prelude to a Philosophy of the Future*. Translated by Walter Kaufmann. New York: Random House.

Nietzsche, Friedrich. (1887/2010). *Genealogy of Morals*. In *On the Genealogy of Morals and Ecce Homo*, translated by Walter Kaufmann. New York: Random House.

Nietzsche, Friedrich. (1889/1976). *Twilight of the Idols*. In *The Portable Nietzsche*, translated by Walter Kaufmann. New York: Penguin.

Nietzsche, Friedrich. (1901/1967). *The Will to Power*. Translated by Walter Kaufmann. New York: Random House.

Nietzsche, Friedrich. (1908/2010). *Ecce Homo*. In *On the Genealogy of Morals and Ecce Homo*, translated by Walter Kaufmann. New York: Random House.

Nietzsche, Friedrich. (1969). *Selected Letters of Friedrich Nietzsche*. Edited and translated by Christopher Middleton. Chicago: University of Chicago Press.

Nietzsche. (1980). *Sämtliche Werke. Kritische Studienausgabe*, Vols. 9, 11. Berlin: Walter de Gruyter.

Nietzsche, Friedrich. (1996). *Philosophy in the Tragic Age of the Greeks*. Translated by Marianne Cowan. Washington, DC: Regnery.

Nikhilananda, Swami, & Mukerji, Dhan Gopal. (2008). *Sri Ramakrishna: The Face of Silence*. Vermont: SkyLights Paths Publishing.

Nishida, Kitaro. (1990). *An Inquiry into the Good*. New Haven: Yale University Press.

Nishitani, Keiji. (1990). *The Self-Overcoming of Nihilism*. Translated by Graham Parkes with Setsuko Aihara. Albany: State University of New York Press.

Norretranders, Tor. (1998). *The User Illusion: Cutting Consciousness Down to Size*. New York: Viking Penguin.

Nuñez, Rafael E., & Sweetser, Eve. (2006). "With the Future behind Them: Convergent Evidence from Aymara Language and Gesture in the Cross-linguistic Comparison of Spatial Construals of Time," *Cognitive Science*, 30, 1–49.

Oliver, Phil. (2000). William James's "*Springs of Delight*": *The Return to Life*. Nashville: Vanderbilt University Press.

Osborne, Arthur. (1996). *The Teachings of Ramana Maharshi*. Maine: Samuel Weiser.

Osho [aka Rajneesh, Shree Bhagwan]. (1976). *The Hidden Harmony: Discourses on the Fragments of Heraclitus*. Poona: Rajneesh Foundation.

Osho [aka Rajneesh, Shree Bhagwan]. (1983). *Philosophia Ultima: Discourses on the Mandukya Upanishad*. Oregon: Rajneesh Foundation International.

Osho [aka Rajneesh, Shree Bhagwan]. (1984). *The Book: An Introduction to the Teachings of Bhagwan Shree Rajneesh*. Oregon: Rajneesh Foundation International.

Ostrander, Sheila, & Schroeder, Lynn. (1971). *Psychic Discoveries behind The Iron Curtain*. Englewood Cliffs, NJ: Prentice-Hall.

Paine, Albert Bigelow. (1912). *Mark Twain, A Biography*, Vol. 3. New York: Harper & Brothers.

Pais, Abraham. (1991). *Niels Bohr's Times*. New York: Clarendon Press.

Panaïoti, Antoine. (2013). *Nietzsche and Buddhist Philosophy*. Cambridge: Cambridge University Press.

Pashler, Harold E. (1998). *The Psychology of Attention*. Cambridge: MIT Press.

Pauen, Michael. (2004). "Does Free Will Arise Freely?" *Scientific American, 14*(1).

Peake, Anthony. (2012). *The Labyrinth of Time: The Illusion of Past, Present, and Future*. London: Arcturus.

Peat, David. (1987). *Infinite Potential*. New York: Addison-Wesley.

Penrose, Roger. (1989). *The Emperor's New Mind*. New York: Oxford University Press.

Penrose, Roger. (2004). *The Road to Reality*. New York: Knopf.

Pepys, Samuel. (17th cy./1884). *Diary and Correspondence of Samuel Pepys, Esq.* New York: Dodd, Mead.

Perry, Ralph Barton. (1935). *The Thought and Character of William James*, Vol. I. Boston: Little, Brown.

Perry, Ralph Barton. (1935). *The Thought and Character of William James*, Vol. II. Boston: Little, Brown.

Petkov, Vesselin. (2006). "*Is There an Alternative to the Block Universe View?*" In Dieks, Dennis, (Ed.), *The Ontology of Spacetime*. Amsterdam: Elsevier.

Philip, James A. (1966). *Pythagoras and Early Pythagoreanism*. Toronto: University of Toronto Press.

Piaget, Jean. (1965). *The Child's Conception of the World*. Totowa, NJ: Littlefield, Adams.

Piaget, Jean, and Inhelder, Bärbel. (1969). *The Psychology of the Child*. New York: Basic Books.

Plato. (1871). *Theatetus*. Translated by Benjamin Jowett. Oxford: Oxford University Press.

Plotinus. (3rd cy./1991). *The Enneads*. Translated by Stephen Mackenna. New York: Penguin.

Pöppel, Ernst. (1988). *Mindworks: Time and Conscious Experience*. Boston: Harcourt Brace Jovanovich.

Popper, Karl. (1992). *The Open Universe: An Argument for Indeterminism From the Postscript to The Logic of Scientific Discovery*. London: Routledge.

Poulet, Georges. (1954). "Timelessness and Romanticism," *Journal of the History of Ideas, 15*(1), 3–22.

Poulet, Georges. (1967). *The Metamorphoses of the Circle*. Translated by Dawson, C., & Coleman, E. Baltimore: Johns Hopkins University Press.

Prescott, Michael. (2007). http://michaelprescott.typepad.com/michael_prescotts_blog/2007/08/how-martin-gard.html; as of Fall 2016.

Price, Huw. (1997). *Time's Arrow*. New York: Oxford University Press.

Price, Lucien. (1954). *Dialogues of Alfred North Whitehead: As Recorded by Lucien Price*. Boston: Little, Brown.

Radin, Dean. (1997). *The Conscious Universe: The Scientific Truth of Psychic Phenomena*. Toronto: Harper Collins.

Radin, Dean. (2006). *Entangled Minds: Extrasensory Experiences in a Quantum Reality*. New York: Paraview Pocket Books.

Radin, Dean. (2013). *Supernormal*. New York: Random House.

Raschke, Carl. (1982). "From God to Infinity, or How Science Raided Religion's Patent on Mystery," *Zygon, 17*(3), 227–242.

Rasmussen, R. Kent. (1995). *Mark Twain A–Z*. New York: Oxford University Press.

Ray, Reginald A. (2001). *Secret of the Vajra World: The Tantric Buddhism of Tibet*. Boston: Shambhala.

Rhine, J. B. (1949). *The Reach of the Mind*. London: Faber & Faber.

Rhine, Louisa E. (1955). "Precognition and Intervention," *The Journal of Parapsychology, 19*(1), 1–34.

Richardson, Robert. (2006). *William James: In the Maelstrom of American Modernism*. New York: Houghton Mifflin.

Richet, Charles. (1930). *Our Sixth Sense*. London: Rider.

Rogers, L. W. (1916). *Dreams and Premonitions*. Los Angeles: Theosophical Book Concern.

Rolland, Romain. (1960). *The Life of Ramakrishna*. Calcutta: Advaita Ashrama.

Roney-Dougal, S. M. (2013). http://www.psi-researchcentre.co.uk/documents/TibetanPsychicTradition.pdf; as of January.

Roosevelt, Theodore. (1899). *The Strenuous Life*. New York: Scribners.

Rose, Steven. (2005). *The Future of the Brain: The Promise and Perils of Tomorrow's Neuroscience*. New York: Oxford University Press.

Rosenzweig, Saul. (1992). *Freud, Jung, and Hall The King-Maker*. Kirkland, WA: Hogrefe & Huber.

Royce, Josiah. (1920). *The World and the Individual*. London: MacMillan.

Rumi. (13th cy./1995). *The Essential Rumi*. Translated by Coleman Barks. New York: Harper.

Runes, Dagobert, (Ed.). (1942). *Dictionary of Philosophy*. New York: Philosophical Library.

Russell, Bertrand. (1935). *Religion and Science*. New York: Henry Holt.

Russell, Bertrand. (1945). *A History of Western Philosophy*. New York: Simon & Schuster.

Russell, Bertrand. (1963). *Mysticism and Logic*. London: George Allen & Unwin.

Ryle, Gilbert. (1949). *The Concept of Mind*. New York: Barnes & Noble.

Sage, Michel. (1904). *Mrs. Piper & The Society for Psychical Research*. Translated and slightly abridged from the French by Noralie Robertson, with a Preface by Oliver Lodge. New York: Scott-Thaw.

Saltmarsh, Herbert Francis. (1938/2004). *The Future and Beyond: Evidence for Precognition and the Survival of Death*. Charlotesville, VA: Hampton Roads.

Sanai, Hakim. (1974). *The Walled Garden of Truth*. Translated by David Pendlebury. London: The Octagon Press.

Santayana, George. (1910). *Three Philosophical Poets: Lucretius, Dante, and Goethe*. Cambridge: Harvard University Press.

Santayana, George. (1930). *The Realm of Matter: Book Second of Realms of Being*. London: Constable.

Santayana, George. (1945). *The Philosophy of Santayana*. New York: Scribner.

Sartre, Jean-Paul. (1956). *Being and Nothingness*. New York: Philosophical Library.

Scaruffi, Piero. (2002). "The New Physics: The Ubiquitous Asymmetry." (http://www.thymos.com/tat/physics.html); as of Spring.

Schiller, F. C. S. (1891/1994). *Riddles of the Sphinx: A Study in the Philosophy of Evolution*. London: Swan Sonnenschein.

Schiller, F. C. S. (1911). "Nietzsche." In *The Encyclopedia Britannica*, 11th Ed., Volume XIX. New York: The Encyclopedia Britannica.

Schilpp, Paul Arthur. (1974). *The Philosophy of Karl Popper*. Lasalle, IL: Open Court.

Schmidt, Helmut. (1975). "A Comparison of PK Action on Two Different Random Number Generators," *The Journal of Parapsychology*, *38*, 47–55.

Schopenhauer, Arthur. (1818/1886). *The World as Will and Idea*. London: Trübner.

Schopenhauer, Arthur. (1839/1985). *On the Freedom of the Will*. Oxford: Blackwell.

Schopenhauer, Arthur. (1851/1974). *Parerga and Paralipomena*, Vol. I. Oxford: Oxford University Press.

Schrödinger, Erwin. (1954). *Nature and the Greeks*. Cambridge: Cambridge University Press.

Schrödinger, Erwin. (1958). *Mind and Matter*. Cambridge: Cambridge University Press.

Schwartz, Jeffrey. (2002). *The Mind and the Brain: Neuroplasticity and the Power of Mental Force*. New York: HarperCollins.

Schweig, Graham M. (2007). *Bhagavad Gita*. New York: HarperCollins.

Scotton, Bruce, Chinen, Allan B., & Battista, John R. (1996). *Textbook of Transpersonal Psychiatry and Psychology*. New York: Basic Books.

Sells, Michael. (1996). *Early Islamic Mysticism: Sufi, Qur'an, Mi'raj, Poetic and Theological Writings*. Mahwah, NJ: Paulist Press.

Shankara, Sri. (1982). *"That Thou Art": Chapter XVIII of The Thousand Teachings (Upadesasahasri) of Sri Shankara*. Translated by A. J. Alston. London: Shanti Sadan.

Shanon, Benny. (2001). "Altered Temporality," *Journal of Consciousness Studies*, *8*(1), 35–58.

Sheldrake, Rupert. (1988/1995). *The Presence of the Past: Morphic Resonance & The Habits of Nature*. Rochester, VT: Park Street Press.

Shrivastava, S. N. L. (1968). *Sámkara and Bradley: A Comparative and Critical Study*. Delhi: Motilal Banarsidass.

Seigfried, Charlene Haddock. (1990). *William James's Radical Reconstruction of Philosophy*. Albany: State University of New York Press.

Simon, Linda. (1999). *Genuine Reality: A Life of William James*. Chicago: University of Chicago Press.

Sinclair, Upton. (1930/2011). *Mental Radio*. Charlottesville: Hampton Roads.

Skrupskelis, I., & Berkeley, E., (Eds.). (1995). *The Correspondence of William James, Vol. 4*. Charlottesville: University of Virginia Press.

Skrupskelis, I., & Berkeley, E., (Eds.). (1995). *The Correspondence of William James, Vol. 5*. Charlottesville: University of Virginia Press.

Skrupskelis, I., & Berkeley, E., (Eds.). (1997). *The Correspondence of William James, Vol. 6*. Charlottesville: University of Virginia Press.

Skrupskelis, I., & Berkeley, Elizabeth M., (Eds.). (2000). *The Correspondence of William James, Vol. 8*. Charlottesville: University of Virginia Press.

Skrupskelis, I., & Berkeley, Elizabeth M., (Eds.). (2001). *The Correspondence of William James, Vol. 9*. Charlottesville: University of Virginia Press.

Skrupskelis, Ignas K., & Berkeley, Elizabeth M., (Eds.). (2002). *The Correspondence of William James, Vol. 10*. Charlottesville: University of Virginia Press.

Skrupskelis, Ignas K., & Berkeley, Elizabeth M., (Eds.). (2003). *The Correspondence of William James, Vol. 11*. Charlottesville, VA.: University of Virginia Press.

Skrupskelis, Ignas K. & Berkeley, Elizabeth M., (Eds.). (2004). *The Correspondence of William James, Vol. 12*. Charlottesville: University of Virginia Press.

Smith, Huston. (2001/02). *Harvard Divinity Bulletin* (Winter).

Smith, Jeffrey, MD. (1999). *Psychiatric Times, 16*(4), 1–7.

Smolin, Lee. (2013). *Time Reborn*. Boston: Houghton Mifflin Harcourt.

Sokei-an. (1940/1954). "Consider the Mind of a Child," *Zen Notes, 1*(6), 1.

Sorabji, Richard. (1983). *Time, Creation and the Continuum*. Chicago: University of Chicago Press.

Spinoza, Benedictus. (17th cy./1883). *Ethics*. Translated by William Hale White. New York: MacMillan.

Spinoza, Benedictus. (17th cy./1891). *The Chief Works of Benedict De Spinoza*. London: George Bell and Sons.

Sprigge, T. L. S. (1983). *The Vindication of Absolute Idealism*. Edinburgh: Edinburgh University Press.

Sprigge, T. L. S. (1993). *James and Bradley: American Truth and British Reality*. Chicago: Open Court.

Stack, George J. (1992). *Nietzsche and Emerson: An Elective Affinity*. Athens: Ohio University Press.

Stambaugh, Joan. (1972). *Nietzsche's Thought of Eternal Return*. Baltimore: The John Hopkins University Press.

Stambaugh, Joan. (1994). *The Other Nietzsche*. Albany: State University of New York Press.

Stcherbatsky, Theodore. (1930/1962). *Buddhist Logic*, Vol. 1. New York: Dover.

Stearn, Jess. (1963). *The Door to the Future*. Garden City, NY: Doubleday.

Stetson, Chess, Fiesta, Matthew P., & Eagleman, David M. (2007). "Does Time Really Slow Down during a Frightening Event?" *PLoS ONE*, 2(12): e1295. doi:10.1371/journal.pone.0001295.

Stewart, Jon. (2012). *Kierkegaard's Influence on Philosophy: Anglophone Philosophy*. Surrey: Ashgate.

Sumegi, Angela. (1981). *Dreamworlds of Shamanism and Tibetan Buddhism*. Albany: State University of New York Press.

Suzuki, Daisetz T. (1954). "Zen and Pragmatism—A Reply (Comment and Discussion)," *Philosophy East and West*, 4(2), 167–174.

Suzuki, Daisetz T. (1959/1973). *Zen and Japanese Culture*. Princeton: Princeton University Press.

Suzuki, Daisetz T. (1996). *Selected Writings of D. T. Suzuki*. Edited by William Barrett. New York: Doubleday.

Swedenborg, Emanuel. (1749/1910). *Arcana Coelestia*, Vol. II. Translated by Rev. John Potts. New York: The Swedenborg Printing and Publishing Society.

Talbot, Michael. (1991). *The Holographic Universe*. New York: HarperCollins.

Tanahashi, K. (1985). *Moon in a dewdrop: Writings of Zen Master Dogen*. San Francisco: North Point Press.

Tao-yüan. (1004/1969). *The Transmission of the Lamp*, selected passages translated, with an introduction, by Chung-Yuan Chang, in *Original Teachings of Ch'an Buddhism*. New York: Pantheon Books.

Targ, Russell. (1976). *Journal of Scientific Exploration*, 10(1), 77–88. http://irva.org/library/articles/targ-rvsri.html; as of Spring 2010.

Targ, Russell. (2012). *The Reality of ESP: A Physicist's Proof of Psychic Abilities*. Wheaton, IL: Quest Books.

Tart, Charles. (2009). *The End of Materialism: How Evidence of the Paranormal is Bringing Science and Spirit Together*. Oakland: New Harbinger Publications and Noetic Books.

Taylor, Eugene. (1978). "Psychology of Religion and Asian Studies: The William James Legacy," *Journal of Transpersonal Psychology*, 10(1), 67–79.

Taylor, Eugene. (1996). *William James on Consciousness beyond the Margin*. Princeton: Princeton University Press.

Taylor, Eugene, & Wozniak, Robert H. (1996). *Pure Experience, The Response to William James*. Bristol, UK: Thoemmes Press.

Taylor, Greg. (2010). "How Martin Gardner Bamboozled the Skeptics." http://www.dailygrail.com/Essays/2010/11/Skeptical-Skeptic; as of January 2013.

Taylor, Jill Bolte. (2008). http://www.ted.com/talks/jill_bolte_taylor_s_powerful_stroke_of_insight.html.

Tennyson, Hallam. (1897). *Life of Tennyson*. New York: Macmillan.

Thera, Nyanaponika. (1962/1988). *The Heart of Buddhist Meditation*. York Beach, ME: Samuel Weiser.

Thomas, Dylan. (1985). *The Collected Letters of Dylan Thomas*. London: JM Dent & Sons.

Thoreau, Henry David. (1848–1851/1990). *Journal Vol. 3*. Princeton: Princeton University Press.

Tolle, Eckhart. (1997). *The Power of Now*. Vancouver: Namaste.

Tolstoy, Leo. (1942). *War and Peace*. New York: Simon & Schuster.

Trachtenberg, Joshua. (1939/2004). *Jewish Magic and Superstition*. Philadelphia: University of Pennsylvania Press.

Trochu, Thibaud. (2008). "Investigations into the William James Collection at Harvard: An Interview with Eugene Taylor," *Streams of William James*, 3(1).

Tropp, Sandra Fehl. (1992). *Shaping Tradition: Art and Diversity in the Essay*. Fort Worth: Harcourt Brace.

Tubbs, Robert. (2008). *What Is a Number?: Mathematical Concepts and Their Origins*. Baltimore: Johns Hopkins University Press.

Twain, Mark. (1853–1866/1988), *Mark Twain's Letters*. Berkeley: University of California Press.

Twain, Mark. (1897). *Literary Essays*. New York: Harper and Brothers.

Twain, Mark. (1961). *The Autobiography of Mark Twain*. New York: Washington Square Press.

Twain, Mark. (2000). *The Complete Essays of Mark Twain*. New York: Da Capo Press.

Twain, Mark. (2011). *No. 44, The Mysterious Stranger*. Berkeley: University of California Press.

Tymn, Michael. (2013). *Resurrecting Leonora Piper: How Science Discovered the Afterlife*. Guilford, UK: White Crow Books.

Ullman, Montague, Krippner, Stanley, & Vaughn, Alan. (1973). *Dream Telepathy: Experiments in Nocturnal ESP*. New York: MacMillan.

Ustinova, Yulia. (2009). *Caves and the Ancient Greek Mind: Descending Underground in the Search for Ultimate Truth*. New York: Oxford University Press.

Utts, Jessica. (1996). "An Assessment of the Evidence for Psychic Functioning." *Journal of Scientific Exploration, 10*, (1), 3–30.

Varble, Rachel M. (1964). *Jane Clemens*. Garden City, NY: Doubleday.

Vaughan, Alan. (1973). *Patterns of Prophecy*. New York: Hawthorn Books.

Velmans, Max. (1991). "Consciousness from a First-Person Perspective," *Behavioral and Brain Sciences, 14*, 702–719.

Vivekananda, Swami. (1970–73). *The Complete Works of Swami Vivekananda, Vol. II*. Calcutta: Advaita Ashrama.

Vivekananda, Swami. (1970–73). *The Complete Works of Swami Vivekananda, Vol. III*. Calcutta: Advaita Ashrama.

Vivekananda, Swami. (1970–73). *The Complete Works of Swami Vivekananda, Vol. V*. Calcutta: Advaita Ashrama.

Vorenkamp, Dirck. (1995). "B-Series Temporal Order in Dōgen's Theory of Time," *Philosophy East and West, 45*(3) (July), 387–408.

W., Bill. (2005). *My First 40 Years: An Autobiography by the Co-founder of AA*. Center City, Minnesota.

Wallace, B. Alan. (2011). *Minding Closely: The Four Applications of Mindfulness*. Ithaca, NY: Snow Lion.

Walls, Laura Dassow. (2003). *Emerson's Life in Science*. Ithaca: Cornell University Press.

Walsh, R. N., & Vaughan, F. (1992). "Lucid Dreaming: Some Transpersonal Implications," *Journal of Transpersonal Psychology, 24*(2), 193–200.

Watts, Alan. (1957). *The Way of Zen*. New York: Vintage/Random House.

Watts, Alan. (1962). *The Joyous Cosmology*. New York: Vintage/Random House.

Watts, Alan. (1973). *In My Own Way: An Autobiography*. New York: Vintage/Random House.

Webster, Samuel Charles. (1946). *Mark Twain, Business Man*. Boston: Little Brown.

Wegner, Daniel M. (2002). *The Illusion of Conscious Will*. Cambridge: MIT Press.

Weiner, Herbert. (1969/1992). *9 ½ Mystics: The Kabbalah Today*. New York: Touchstone.

Weyl, Hermann. (1963). *Philosophy and Mathematics and Natural Science*. New York: Atheneum.

Whitehead, Alfred North. (1925). *Science and the Modern World*. New York: MacMillan.

Whitman, Walt. (1882). *Leaves of Grass*. Philadelphia: Rees Welsh.

Whitman, Walt. (1882a/2001). *Leaves of Grass: "The Death-Bed Edition."* New York: Random House.

Wiener, Philip P., (Ed.). (1973). *Dictionary of the History of Ideas, Volume IV*. New York: Charles Scribner's Sons.

Wilber, Ken. (1985). *The Holographic Paradigm And Other Paradoxes*. Boston: Shambhala.

Wolf, Fred Alan. (1995). *The Dreaming Universe*. New York: Simon & Schuster.

Wolfram, Stephen. (2002). *A New Kind of Science*. Champaign, IL: Wolfram Media.

Wolinsky, Stephen. (1993). *Quantum Consciousness*. Connecticut: Bramble Books.

Yeshe, Tsogyal, Kunsang et al. (2004). *Lotus-Born: The Life Story of Padmasambhava*. Translated by Erik Pema Kunsang. Nepal: Rangjung Yeshe Publications.

Yourgrau, Palle. (2006). *A World Without Time: The Forgotten Legacy of Gödel and Einstein*. New York: Basic Books.

Zaleski, Philip, & Lopez, Barry. (2005). *The Best Spiritual Writing 2005*. New York: Houghton Mifflin.

Zohar, Danah. (1983). *Through the Time Barrier: A Study in Precognition and Modern Physics*. London: Granada.

INDEX